Cosmic Consciousness Revisited

Cosmic Consciousness Revisited

The Modern Origins and Development
of a Western Spiritual Psychology

Robert M. May

ELEMENT

Rockport, Massachusetts ● Shaftesbury, Dorset
Brisbane, Queensland

© 1991 Robert M. May

Published in the U.S.A. in 1993 by
Element, Inc.
42 Broadway, Rockport, MA 01966

Published in Great Britain in 1993 by
Element Books Limited
Longmead, Shaftesbury, Dorset

Published in Australia in 1993 by
Element Books Limited for
Jacaranda Wiley Limited
33 Park Road, Milton, Brisbane 4064

Designed by Roger Lightfoot
Cover designed by Max Fairbrother
Typeset by Footnote Graphics, Warminster, Wiltshire
Printed and bound in the United States of America by
Edwards Brothers

British Library Cataloguing in Publication Data

May, Robert M.
    Cosmic consciousness revisited: the modern origins
    and development of a western spiritual psychology
    I. Title
    200.19
ISBN 1–85230–280–1

Library of Congress Cataloging in Publication Data

May, Robert M.
    Cosmic consciousness revisited: the modern origins and
    development of a western spiritual psychology / Robert M. May.
        Includes bibliographical references and index.
        ISBN 1–85230–280–1
        1. Psychology, Religious.   2. Spirituality.   3. Consciousness.
    I. Title.
    BL53.M42   1991
    291'.01'9—dc20   91–26159

CONTENTS

There was a Door
to which I found no Key:
There was a Veil past
which I could not see:
Some little Talk awhile
of ME and THEE.
There seemed—and then
no more of THEE and ME.

From the *Rubáiyát*
Omar Khayám

This book is dedicated to:

Margaret Todaro Williams

with whom I shared an experience
of Cosmic Consciousness in the summer of
1962 and LOVE EVERLASTING

PREFACE

In the summer of 1962, at the age of twenty, I had an experience at a small lake in upstate New York which changed my life for all the years thereafter. It was not an alone experience either, but one I shared with the woman I loved. Her name was Margaret. She and I were holding hands, as we walked by the lakefront, very much in love. Apparently, this was all that was needed to "open the doors" to the Kingdom. We rapidly ascended through all states of consciousness, and within a couple of seconds, we were both in communion with the Supreme. At the time, between my junior and senior years in college, I was philosophically an atheist. My road to faith in God took many years since that revelation. It is apparent that religious belief, or the lack of it, is not prerequisite for mystical experience. Margaret, by the way, was a believing Catholic, but the experience was not anything that she had learned to expect either. Our joy was such that I can never describe it in the words of our language. In this illumined consciousness, we walked together into the nearby woods where we felt in unity with the All. We knew, almost immediately, that there is no death; what is our true Self is immortal. We saw the universe as One Living Being animated by the force of Love. We felt "the love that moves the sun and other stars," as Dante Allighieri put it so eloquently in his *Divine Comedy*'s *Paradiso*.

That experience at the age of twenty launched me on a search that has not ended to this very day. It was followed, as the night follows the day, by its opposite: the encounter with the Satanic* and Unholy. The distinguished psychologist, Dr. Henry A. Murray, in his 1962 address to Division 8, the Division of Personality and Social Psychology of the American Psychological Association asked whether the "spirit of Satan" was operating in "modern psychology?" The following is an excerpt from his talk:

> . . . we might reasonably surmise that the Devil's target in the case of
> . . . the majority of men and women in the West consists of whatever

ix

dispositions and powers may reside in them to create conceptions of this nature: say, the conception of a better world composed of better societies of better persons and to strive to actualize it by self-transformations and social reconstructions. In other words, according to one tenable view, the Satanic aim is to prevent all developments in this direction by shattering man's faith in the existence of the necessary potentialities within himself and reducing him to cynicism and despair until the demoralization and abasement of his personality has reached a state beyond recovery and in one disgraceful debacle of genocidal fury he terminates the long, long history of his species.

And here is where our psychology comes in with the bulk of its theories, its prevailing views of human personality, its images of man, obviously in league with the objectives of the nihilistic Satanic spirit. Man is a computer, an animal, an infant. His destiny is completely determined by genes, instincts, accidents, early conditionings and reinforcements, cultural and social forces. Love is a secondary drive based on hunger and oral sensations or a reaction formation to an innate underlying hate. In the majority of our personological formulations there are no provisions for creativity, no admitted margins of freedom for voluntary decisions, no fitting recognition of the power of ideals, no bases for selfless actions, no ground at all for any hope that the human race can save itself from the fatality that now confronts it. If we psychologists were all the time, consciously or unconsciously, intending out of malice to reduce the concept of human nature to its lowest common denominator . . . then we might have to admit that to this extent the Satanic spirit was alive within us.

> Henry A. Murray – Reprinted in the *Journal of Social Issues*, 1962, No. 28, pp. 36–54

I was not grounded at the time in the Spirit, as Jesus of Nazareth was, so strongly, in his encounter with the Ancient Foe. My treasure was snatched from me. I experienced what the Medieval Christian mystics called "the Fisher Wound." These opposites inspired my Quest for the Holy Grail. Not knowing where to look, I pursued academic psychology and philosophy for about ten years. The Grail is not found there. Gautama Buddha also had his studies with the philosophers before the True Journey. My Inner Journey was ten years in length and involved studies with spiritual masters in many religious traditions, Taoists, Buddhists, Yogis, Sufis, Kabbalists, Christian teachers, and others. I wrote a book inspired by the years of my *personal search* called *Physicians of the Soul*. It is on the sacred psychologies implicit in the World Religions.

Finally, I felt it was time to "revisit" my original experience of Cosmic Consciousness. I discovered a marvelous book by the late nineteenth century Canadian psychiatrist, Richard Bucke, M.D., called *Cosmic Consciousness*. It is about this core experience of all religions. The late nineteenth century American philosopher and psychologist, William James, wrote a similar book, entitled, *The Varieties of Religious Experience*. These two books are, to this day, the classics in the psychology of religion. What happened in the psychological study of religion and religious experience in the early to mid twentieth century? To my dismay, I found that the attitude of psychology and psychiatry had turned violently anti-religious in that era of scientific materialism, beginning with the American behaviorist, John B. Watson (and his Russian counterpart, Ivan Pavlov), and the Viennese psychoanalyst, Sigmund Freud. Watson dismissed religion and religious experience as "superstition" and "voodoo," to use two of Watson's terms of ridicule. Mind itself was regarded as "transcendental fiction." Freud looked at religion in a series of four books and, nevertheless, concluded that religion was "illusion" at best, the projection of the "father complex," and religious experience was a state of "regression" to the oceanic womb. These two views which dominated both academic psychology and psychiatry for more than a half century were most strongly contradicted by my own overwhelming mystical experience of *awakening* – which Bucke's work showed to be common to mystics of all cultures, religions, and eras of humankind. I decided to research and write a *scholarly book* on the past one hundred years of psychology vis à vis religion and religious experience from the enlightened time of Bucke and James –through the dark ages of behaviorism and psychoanalysis – and to the gradual rediscovery of religious and mystical experience in the psychological work and writings of such luminaries as Jung, Gurdjieff, Maslow, Houston, and others, to the present day. I present briefer sections on such thinkers as Adler, Erikson, Assagioli, Frankl, Sanford, etc., on the subject of psychology and religion.

I found it helpful to go deeply into the biographical and historical details of the major figures – in approaching their theories as best I could through *their own eyes*. I then proceed to look at them *through the eyes* of the core-religious or mystical experience. It is a two-way study. I try to see what is the place for the universal religious experience, well-documented not only by Bucke and James, but by the religious and mystical literature of all humankind's culture and history, in each of these major psychologies of the previous one hundred years, up to and including works published in the 1990s – the present. Watson had "banished" consciousness itself to non-existence. I work through the rediscovery of what Bucke called *simple consciousness* in the next chapter. Freud certainly believed in consciousness and the unconscious, but religious experience was illusion for him. His god was scientism. In the next chapters, we rediscover *Self-consciousness* in Jung and Gurdjieff. Maslow, the founder of both humanistic and transpersonal psychology, made a major effort to "naturalize" (i.e. deny the supernatural source of) religious experience which he renamed "peak experiences." We look at this move critically. In the next chapter, I look at what is coming to be called "sacred psychology." We begin with the pioneering LSD work of Houston and Masters, followed by the Near-Death Experience as discussed by Ring, and finally, some new reports of spontaneous religious or mystical experience, much like that reported by Bucke and James, in a research book recently published by Coxhead. I look, then, briefly at two ancient sacred psychologies, Kabbala and Yoga, which preceded "modern" sacred psychology by several millenia. The last chapter looks at ten contemporary persons who wrote about their own religious or mystical experiences; in them we rediscover *Cosmic Consciousness*. One can compare these with a selection of ten historical cases of Bucke's in the first chapter. Finally, in the epilogue, I compare the ideas of the late nineteenth century psychiatrist–mystic, Bucke, with those of the twentieth century paleontologist–priest, Teilhard de Chardin. Are Bucke's Cosmic Consciousness and Teilhard's Christ–Omega one and the same truth? In this light, I examine some passages of Biblical prophecy, and consider whether these support Bucke's and Teilhard's view that humankind is evolving from Self to Cosmic Consciousness. Here and there, there have already been *awakenings*: the mystics of all religions, cultures, and eras of the human race. Are these "illumined ones" the forerunners of a future stage of human evolution?

1

Richard Maurice Bucke, M.D.: Physician and Mystic – His Life

Richard Maurice Bucke was a man of "marked personality."

> His individuality impressed itself on all who came in contact with him.
> Of striking presence, great native ability, wide and varied experience
> of the world and of human nature, he distinguished himself in more
> than one line of thought and action.[1]

To the Reverend Horatio Walpole Bucke and his wife, Clarissa,
were born seven sons and three daughters in the village of Meth-
wold in Suffolk, England. Their seventh child, born on March 18,
1837 was Richard Maurice Bucke. His father, the Reverend
Bucke, was the great grandson of the Prime Minister of England,
Sir Robert Walpole, and a grandnephew of Horace Walpole, a
distinguished man of letters. On his father's side, too, was his
great uncle, Charles Bucke, author of *Beauties of Nature* and *Ruins
of Ancient Cities*. Literature was a part of Bucke's inheritance.[2]

In 1838, the Reverend Bucke, his wife, and seven surviving
children, emigrated to Upper Canada, and settled down to the life
of a pioneer farmer. He brought with him his huge library of
several thousand volumes in several languages. These were to
form the basis of his sons' education at their homestead, Creek
Farm, in the province of Ontario, Canada. The Reverend Bucke
was a learned man who read in seven languages. He was the sole
teacher to his boys, including Richard Maurice. They were all avid
students born with the "desire to know."[3]

Maurice, as he was called, learned Latin from his father, and
read from among the thousands of books in their home library.
This was a superb foundation for his future education as a doctor
and literary man. Bucke never went to school in the ordinary

sense; there were none. He was self-educated in the highest sense of the word. In Bucke's own words, in third person singular, as he was wont to write about himself:

> He was born of good middle class English stock and grew up . . . on what was then a backwoods Canadian farm. As a child he assisted in such labor as lay within his power: tended cattle, horses, sheep, pigs; brought in firewood, worked in the hay field, drove oxen and horses, ran errands. His pleasures were as simple as his labors. An occasional visit to a neighboring small town, a game of ball, bathing in the creek that ran through his father's farm, the making and sailing of mimic ships, the search for birds' eggs and flowers in the spring, and for wild fruits in the summer and fall, afforded him, with his skates and hand-sled in the winter, his homely, much loved recreation. While still a young boy he read with keen appreciation Marryat's novels, Scott's poems and novels, and other similar books dealing with outdoor nature and human life. He never, even as a child, accepted the doctrines of the Christian church; but, as soon as old enough to dwell at all on such themes, conceived that Jesus was a man – great and good no doubt – but a man. That no one would be condemned to everlasting pain. That if a conscious God existed he was the supreme master and meant well in the end to all; but that, this visible life here being ended, it was doubtful, or more than doubtful, whether conscious identity would be preserved. The boy (even the child) dwelt on these and similar topics far more than anyone would suppose. . . He was subject at times to a sort of ecstasy of curiosity and hope. As on one special occasion when about ten years old he earnestly longed to die that the secrets of the beyond, if there was any beyond, might be revealed to him. . . The boy's mother died when he was only a few years old, and his father shortly afterwards. The outward circumstances of his life in some respects became more unhappy than can readily be told.[4]

At the age of sixteen, as Bucke describes it, ". . . the boy left home to live or die as might happen."[5] For the next five years Bucke wandered over North America from the Great Lakes to the Gulf of Mexico to the Upper Ohio to California. His adventures were remarkable for a man of any age; this was how Bucke spent his adolescence to young adulthood.

One June day of 1853, Bucke crossed Lake Erie. He lived for the next three years in the Ohio and Mississippi valleys, working at any employment he could find. He was a gardener, railroad worker, farmhand, etc. During the winter of 1854–55, Bucke made it to the cypress swamps of Louisiana. He found work as a fireman and deckhand of a Mississippi steamboat.[6]

At the age of twenty, this vigorous young man, Bucke, was

determined to cross the great plains and make it to the Pacific Ocean. He hired on with the manager of a train of freight wagons and travelled the perilous trail west. His wagon train went through Indian territory, the lands of the Pawnee and the Sioux, passing the immense herds of bison. They finally reached the Rocky Mountains, and their wondrous beauty was a revelation to the young man, Bucke.[7]

From the Rocky Mountains (of present day Colorado), Bucke and his party crossed the great American desert where they took up gold mining at Gold Canyon through which the Carson River flowed in winter (in summer it was bone dry). Bucke worked for a year as a gold miner. Contrary to our modern views of the "Wild West," based mostly on motion pictures and television, Bucke reports that:

> The social state of this small community was genuinely Arcadian in its simplicity. No civil, military, or ecclesiastical organization existed among us. There were no laws, no courts, and no churches of any denominations.[8]

Despite this lack of external authority, Bucke says:

> ... there was no theft, no violence, and hardly drunkenness or a quarrel.[9]

Leaving Gold Canyon in search of further adventure, Richard Bucke, and his friend, Allen Grosh, decided to cross the Sierra Nevadas to try to make it to the Pacific Ocean. They crossed the eastern summit, 9,000 feet high, and then came down into Lake Tahoe and Squaw Valley. They were trapped in the Sierras for a week of continuous snow in the late fall of 1857. They suffered four days of total starvation and severe frostbite. They eventually crawled upon hands and knees, wet, cold, and hungry, all the way to the "Last Chance" Mining Camp. His friend Grosh died, but Maurice's powerful physique stood him in good stead, and he survived. But, not without the loss of one of his feet, and part of the other, for a surgeon, sent for by the miners, had found it necessary to amputate. After Bucke had recovered from his injuries in the care of the "Last Chance" miners, they gave him enough gold nuggets to travel by stage coach to San Francisco. Bucke said: "I was born again."[10]

Crippled in body, but whole in soul, Bucke returned to Canada, a man of twenty-one. He was maimed, but the store of life experiences he had acquired was already far greater than that of most mature men. Bucke used his inheritance left to him by his mother to go to college. He entered medical school in the year 1858, graduating four years later, at twenty-five. He won that year's medical class prize for his doctoral thesis entitled: "The Correlation of the Vital and Physical Forces."★ Through his tremendous *will power*, and his desire to become what he could become, Bucke overcame his physical handicaps, although he suffered pain for the rest of his life. Bucke went back to Europe for post-graduate work, both University College in London, and the Hospital of the Colleges des Medicins in Paris. Returning to Canada in 1864, Bucke settled down to the practice of medicine, but then took a year off to do some mining business in California. He returned considerably richer in 1865. He married Jessie Maria Gurd that year. It was a happy marriage which produced eight children, six surviving into adulthood. [11]

Bucke met with extraordinary success in his chosen profession of medicine. The premier of Canada was his first patient! His medical career went on to psychiatry or medico-psychology as it was then called, and he was appointed superintendent of the Asylum for the Insane in Hamilton, Ontario in 1876, and the superintendent of the Asylum for the Insane in London, Ontario in 1887, a post he held till his death in 1902. [13]

Bucke wrote many papers and gave many addresses to medical and psychological societies of his time. He was among the foremost in his profession. In his work, he was the first psychiatrist to discontinue the use of restraints and seclusion in the treatment of the insane. He abandoned the strait-jacket and the locked padded cell, and treated his patients as the human beings they were. He found that the laws of love were as effective with the so-called insane as they were with the rest of humanity. [14]

In addition to his innovative work in psychiatry, Bucke was to become a friend and biographer of Walt Whitman, the "good gray poet." This is what Whitman said about the character of Dr. Bucke as a psychiatrist in Whitman's visit to the London Asylum where he observed his doctor friend at work:

★ Bucke takes a "scientific-materialist" position in this M.D. thesis: "Are these forces [the physical and vital] distinct and separate the one from the other, or are the forces which we see manifested by organized beings, another and modified form of the forces existing in the inorganic world. . .? It is the object of this paper to show that, abstractly considered, no such line can be drawn; that in fact there is no difference between these two groups of forces except in their mode of manifestation, and that this is due to the difference in the material substratum through which they in each case manifest themselves." [12]

His method is peaceful, uncoercive, quiet, though always firm – rather persuasive than anything else. Bucke is without brag or bluster. It is beautiful to watch him at his work – to see how he can handle difficult people with such an easy manner.[15]

Dr. Bucke, whose name is almost unknown in psychiatry or psychology today, perhaps because he was an avowed mystic, was president of both the Canadian and the American Medico-Psychological Associations of his day. Yet, today, one never even finds his name in the indexes of books in these fields. So extreme, it seems, is the prejudice against mystical and religious experience, that its great expositors were totally "excised" from history! One will search in vain in "modern" psychology textbooks for any references to "mystical," "religious," or "cosmic consciousness." The "psychological sciences" omit completely *the spiritual*, for which there exists more than ample evidence in the history of all cultures of humankind. Bucke was to eventually become the greatest psychologist of spiritual experience. The poet, Walt Whitman, was to become part of this development, as well. It is to this story that we will now turn.

Soon after he had settled down to the career of medicine as a family doctor in a small town, Bucke wrote this in his diary of March, 1866:

My life also now that I am married and settled down to work is so monotonous that what I said of it one day answers for every other day.[16]

It was during this period of his life, one of a state of what we would call "anomie," that Bucke first discovered Walt Whitman, who was later to have a profound effect upon him. On reading the *Leaves of Grass*, Bucke wrote the following to his close friend, Harry Buxton Forman:

You will have seen the collection of Walt Whitman's poems that have been edited by Rossetti & published by John Camden Hotten, Son, 1868. You will have got a copy and taken it home and looked at it, but have you *soaked* through the crust into the heart of it? Have you seen that here is the modern poet? Especially the American poet, and the only one so far, the founder of American literature as Goethe was of German literature? that here at last in the doings of man is something consummate with the broadcast of day and night? that here in fact is a master mind in literature – A mind too great to be confined to poems and usages . . . A mind & heart on a large scale in which there is no littleness, no humbug, no pretense, no make believe . . . In fact if I am not mistaken we have here correct revelation – For this is a *man* who reveals *himself*.[17]

In a later letter of that spring, in April, 1869, Bucke wrote again to his friend, Forman, about Whitman:

The secret of the man is the secret of success in all things – literature and everything else – Truth – Sincerity . . . here is a man who receives images of spiritual and material things from without and transmits them again without the least thought of what the world will say of this idea and how will the world like this form of expression, or into what form did such a great poet cast his thought. He speaks from his own soul with the most perfect candor, sincerity and truth. There is nothing in modern literature like it. . .[18]

His friend, Forman, was not as totally enthralled with Whitman as Bucke was, and wrote this reply in July, 1869:

Sincerity is stamped in every page – doubtless, but bad taste according to our notions is stamped on the surface of many pages, and paradoxes abound.[19]

On a visit to England in the spring of 1872, where he was vacationing for reasons of health (the harsh winter of Ontario and overwork had made him ill), Bucke had the seminal experience of his life. It was a pleasant evening of early spring, and Bucke had spent the evening reading poetry with his friends. They read to each other from the works of Wordsworth, Shelley, Keats, Browning, and Whitman, and went on like that till midnight. Bucke took his leave and drove home alone in a hansom under the influence of the inspiring ideas, emotions, and images of the evening. He felt peaceful and calm in the quiet of the night. Then, as he describes it himself in the third person:

All at once, without warning of any kind, he found himself wrapped around as it were by a flame-coloured cloud. For an instant he thought of fire, some sudden conflagration in the great city, the next he knew that the light was within himself. Directly afterwards came upon him a sense of exultation, of immense joyousness, accompanied or immediately followed by an intellectual illumination quite impossible to describe. Into his brain streamed one momentary lightning-flash of Brahmic Splendor which has ever lightened his life; upon his heart fell one drop of Brahmic Bliss, leaving thenceforward for always an after taste of heaven.[20]

Bucke goes on to say:

Among other things he did not come to believe, he saw and knew that the Cosmos is not dead matter, but a living Presence, that the soul of man is immortal, that the universe is also built and ordered, that without any peradventure all things work together for the good of each and all, that the foundation principle of the world is what we call love, and that the happiness of every one is in the long run absolutely certain. He claims that he learned more within the few seconds during which the illumination lasted than in previous months or even years of study, and that he learned much that no study could ever have taught. [21]

Bucke's experience of what he calls "Cosmic Consciousness" resembles that of the great mystics throughout history and in every culture; Hindu, Buddhist, Christian, Jewish, or no religion at all, the mystical experience is very much one and the same, although it is interpreted afterward differently through the filters of one's cultural and religious schemata. Bucke's experience of the living universe, the immortality of the soul, and the ultimate foundation of love, is universal to the mystics of all times and places. Two books flowed from this experience of Bucke's: *Man's Moral Nature* and *Cosmic Consciousness*. It took several years, however, before Bucke could render his experience in any literary form. In a February, 1875 letter to his friend, Forman, Bucke writes:

> No prospect of my book going ahead just at present, though I have as much faith in its central idea and the light thrown by it on many things in life and literature, yet I see great difficulty in carrying it out logically to its ultimate conclusion. Still I hope some day to get at least a skeleton of it set down in black & white. I have been thinking of putting a sketch of it in a series of magazine articles. But I do not know what I shall do. I am a good deal in the dumps lately. [22]

Bucke wrote articles that were precursors to *Man's Moral Nature* in the psychiatry journals of his time. He related the moral nature to the functioning of the autonomic nervous system. To Bucke, the moral nature had much more to do with feeling than thinking.

Without a doubt, the next great experience for Bucke was his meeting with the poet, Walt Whitman, which he called the turning point in his life. Its effect upon him was as strong, in its way, as his earlier experience of illumination. Bucke wrote Whitman a short letter immediately prior to his uninvited visit to the poet's home in the autumn of 1877. He wrote Whitman that he had read his books and thought very highly of them, and that he wished to meet the author, and proposed to call on him. Whitman sent no reply. Bucke went ahead and visited Whitman *sans invitation*. He describes the meeting in a letter to his wife of October, 1877:

To Jessie Bucke

My darling,
   I have had bad luck getting letters from you. I got one at New York
& one at Boston and I made sure I should find one here on my
arrival last night. Nary letter.

   I expect I shall leave here some time tomorrow though it is just
possible I may leave tonight – This will depend on how I get on
with the hospitals – I called this morning upon Walt Whitman and
we were old friends at once. He is the most delightful man I ever
saw –

   I stayed over an hour at his house and then we crossed the river to
Phil° together [!] He made a kind of half promise that he would
come and see us some time at London and spend some days – I
would give anything that he would – his health has been very poor
for years but it is now slowly mending.

   He has an invitation present to go to California on a trip but he has
not quite made up his mind whether or not to accept it–

   I think I shall certainly be home on Saturday.

   I am always my sweet darling your loving husband.

                                                              R M Bucke[23]

   Bucke wrote a letter to his friend, Harry Buxton Forman, on
the same subject of his meeting with Walt Whitman. It is a bit
more expressive of his true feelings on the occasion.

                                                        Oct. 24, –77

. . . I crossed the Delaware River to Camden, N.J. and went to see
Walt Whitman. We were old friends in less than two minutes and I
spent a good part of the forenoon with him . . . I hardly know how to
tell you about W. W. If I tried to say how he impressed me you would
probably put it down to exaggeration – I have never seen any man to
compare with him . . . he seems more than a man and yet in all his
looks and ways entirely commonplace (Do I contradict myself?). He is
an average man magnified to the dimensions of a god. . .[24]

   This is how Bucke describes his meeting with Whitman years
later in his biography of the poet:

He called on Whitman and spent an hour at his home in Camden, in
the autumn of 1877. He had never seen the poet before, but he had
been profoundly reading his words for some years. He said that Walt
Whitman only spoke to him about a hundred words altogether, and

these quite ordinary and comonplace; that he did not notice anything peculiar while with him, but shortly after leaving a state of mental exaltation set in, which he could only describe by comparing to the slight intoxication by champagne, or to falling in love! And this exaltation, he said, lasted at least six weeks in a clearly marked degree, so that, for at least that length of time, he was plainly different from his ordinary self. Neither, he said, did it then, or since pass away. Though it ceased to be felt as something new and strange, but became a permanent element in his life, a strong and living force. . .[25]

Clearly Bucke had discovered his spiritual teacher, his "guru." There is a discipleship here that is akin to that between Jesus and Peter, the Buddha and Ananda, or Krishna and Arjuna. Walt Whitman was forever to have a crucial effect upon Bucke's life and work.

During the period from his first meeting with Walt Whitman in 1877 to the latter's visit to Bucke's home in Canada in 1880, there are several letters exchanged between Bucke and Whitman. Bucke became a proselytizer for Whitman's poetry during these years. It was during this period that Bucke wrote a book called *Man's Moral Nature* which he dedicated to Walt Whitman. It was published in New York in 1879. So, we see that his meeting with the bard was the crucial element that enabled Bucke to crystallize his own ideas in literary fashion.

Man's Moral Nature borrows from the physiology, philosophy, theology, and psychology of the time, and combines these with facts of history and Bucke's own personal observations on life. The book, however, is a dry and pedantic treatise on the evolution of man's moral nature. Bucke, in this work, is no poet, like his mentor Whitman, and it is frankly a rather unwieldy work which Whitman himself apparently never commented directly upon. Whitman did make an indirect comment on it by refusing to allow Bucke to include passages from it in his biography on the poet: *Walt Whitman: A Contemporary Study* (1883). When Bucke did, Whitman deleted these passages! The intellectual scientist Bucke lacked the *living force* in his writing which he so admired in the poet-sage Whitman. It was to take twenty more years of discipleship before Bucke could begin to express himself in a manner fitting of his illumination, in his later work, *Cosmic Consciousness*, which combines both intellectual and poetic inspiration.

The principal point of *Man's Moral Nature* is that man has three natures (or at least three that Bucke had discovered): the active nature, the intellectual nature, and the moral nature. In Bucke's conception in this book, the moral nature has two sides: positive and negative. The positive side is love and faith. The negative side is hate and fear. Bucke relates the intellectual nature to the cerebrospinal nervous system, and the moral nature to the autonomic nervous system* in a somewhat crypto-scientific explanatory system. The main point of the book is that human beings are evolving from the negative side, fear and hate, to the positive side, love and faith. Whereas the intellectual nature gives rise to philosophy and science, the moral nature generates religions and works of art. The religions of humankind are expressions of faith, whereas art is the expression of love. In religion, the intellectual nature is a means of expressing doctrines which are merely tools for expressing faith. In poetry, Bucke says, those who emphasize reason are second rate. True art and true religion come from feeling. Whereas Bucke has hit upon some truth in seeing the import of the feeling components of religion and art, no doubt, his views on this are rather simplistic. Especially unconvincing is his "locating" of love and faith in the autonomic nervous system. The element of truth in this is that the autonomic nervous system mediates tension vs. relaxation, the fight or flight response vs. calmness, etc., as is admirably pointed out in Herbert Benson's book, *The Relaxation Response* (1975). But I think there is more to *love* and *faith* than the relaxation response! Jesus' commandment to "love ye one another," or "love thy neighbor as thyself," and his parables of faith, such as the "mustard seed parable," surely come from a *higher place* than that which we share with the lower animals. It is curiously consistent with the dominant materialism of his late nineteenth century era that Bucke *reduces* the bases for religion and art to a primitive anatomical feature of the nervous system. Darwin and Marx and other materialist philosophies were very much "in the air" at the time, and Bucke, although a true mystic was also a man of his historical era. It was the time when physicists thought of atoms in terms of billiard balls bouncing around. There has been a revolution in physics since that time wherein leading physicists of our era see *consciousness* as a basic ingredient, if not the underlying foundation, of nature. These views have hardly penetrated down to the biological and psychological sciences to any great extent, and the attempt to reduce the psychical or the spiritual to the readily identifiable physical brain is

* The autonomic nervous system has two branches, sympathetic and parasympathetic, which regulate involuntary action, glandular and smooth musculature, mediating tension and relaxation, respectively.

as common today as it was in Bucke's time. Oddly enough, physics may lead in a revolution against this materialism, as we shall see later. Bucke in *Man's Moral Nature* mixes good psychological and spiritual insights with a dubious materialistic reductionism.

In the concluding sections of his book, Bucke wishes *to prove* that love and faith are justified in a benevolent universe. Whitman showed the same thing in his poetry without proofs. Bucke set out to prove what he *knew* from his illumination in laborious and sometimes incredible ways. We will compare the scientist and the poet in the following quotations.

To quote from Dr. Bucke's *Man's Moral Nature*:

> I need not insist upon the fact that, speaking generally, all the religions which have originated subsequently to Buddhism . . . such as the various forms of Christianity, and Mahometanism, all differ from Buddhism and Zoroastrianism in these two essential particulars – first, that they declare the good power or principle in the government of the universe to be stronger than the evil power; and, secondly, that they represent the state beyond the grave to be, for the good man, more to be desired than feared. The meaning of this, of course, is that . . . in the last two thousand years, the scale has turned, and faith is now in the human mind in the excess of fear and consequently the ideas projected into the unknown world by man's moral nature, are on the whole, a plus quantity instead of being . . . a minus quantity or simply equal to zero.[26]

Bucke's view here, extending from an earlier discussion of animistic and polytheistic religions, is that the history of man's religions shows an *evolutionary development* from a time when fear and hate was predominant (we can imagine prehistoric man in a continual state of fear and hate, feeling surrounded by hostile forces, as it were) to a time when the highest religious impulse was the assertion that "God is love," as was expressed by St. John the Divine, a disciple of Jesus. Buddhism, historically earlier, perhaps saw a "zero state" as the best that could be attained, and Zoroastrianism saw the universe as the ground of a battle between the forces of good and evil, each being identified with a god. If there is this evolutionary development, we surely have not come very far from the time of Jesus and John, but have, it would seem, regressed rather badly, making very real the basis for fear and hate in the twentieth century with Auschwitz and Hiroshima, and a 45 year long "cold war" (now ending) which threatened us with a nuclear holocaust. Today's ecological crisis of *global warming* – due to CO_2 emissions and deforestation is surpassing nuclear war as a clear and imminent danger! Whether Bucke's "always upward and onward" optimistic evolutionism is actually true is a question to be asked. On the other hand, there is no doubt that religions showed a development from an emphasis on fear to an emphasis on love.

The poet, Whitman, expresses his truths quite a bit more directly. Perhaps this is the contrast between the thinking and the feeling functions. To quote Walt Whitman on the human soul, the following is Whitman's personal expression of his own *supreme confidence*:

> Was somebody asking to see the soul?
> See, your own shape and countenance, persons, substances, beasts, the trees, the running rivers, the rocks and sands.
> All hold spiritual joys and afterwards loosen them;
> How can the real body ever die and be buried?
> Of your real body and any man's or woman's real body,
> Item for item it will elude the hands of the corpse-cleaners and pass to fitting spheres,
> Carrying what has accrued to it from the moment of birth to the moment of death.
> Not the types set up by the printer return their impression, the meaning, the main concern,
> Any more than a man's substance and life return in the body and the soul,
> Indifferently before death and after death,
> Behold, the body includes and is the meaning, the main concern, and includes and is the soul;
> Whoever you are, how superb and how divine is your body, or any part of it?[27]

Perhaps influenced by Whitman's poetical feeling expression, more than by the materialistic sciences of his time, Bucke concludes *Man's Moral Nature* with a splendid moral injunction.

> This, then is the end, the conclusion of the whole matter. Love all things – not because it is your duty to do so, but because all things are worthy of your love. Hate no thing. Fear nothing. Have absolute faith. Whoso will do this is wise; he is more than wise – he is happy.[28]

Walt Whitman is, for Richard Bucke, the *living proof* of his evolutionary hypothesis. Bucke dedicated the book "to the man who of all men past and present that I have known has the most exalted moral nature – WALT WHITMAN."[29]

In the summer of 1880, Whitman finally paid Bucke the visit he had long hoped for. Bucke accompanied the poet from Camden,

New Jersey to London, Ontario. Bucke found himself in the exhilarating situation of living on a day to day basis for the next four months with the "god man," Walt Whitman. It was during these months that Bucke began to gather the information he needed for his biography of Whitman. He also visited Whitman's ancestral home in Long Island, and corresponded with poets and writers from all over the world who knew the American master poet. Bucke occasionally wrote to Whitman asking him to reveal his "interior life." These requests from the scientist to the poet were never answered. Whitman's response was no response. Here is one example of such a letter from Bucke to Whitman:

To Walt Whitman

[London] Jan 19th 1880

My dear Walt,

   I am going to ask a great favor of you – I want you to write a sketch of your interior life – especially in relation to the conception & elaboration of "Leaves of Grass." The germancy & growth of such a product as "Leaves of Grass" is a psychological expression almost unique in the history of the race and some record of it ought to remain if possible – I need not explain any further what I want from you for you will understand at once what I mean and you must surely have often thought of putting it upon record.

   I hope you will take this matter into serious and favorable consideration.

       And I am

Faithfully yours,
R. M. Bucke[30]

   The poet, Whitman, never revealed his "inner life" to the scientist, Bucke, except to continue writing his poetry. His poetry is at once inner and outer. It is a direct expression. The poet does not dissect reality into inner and outer like the scientist. There is no "inner thought" which expresses itself in the "outer poem." There is just the poem! It is the inner and the outer. Whitman had nothing to report to Bucke on this except to write poems.

   Whitman was never to visit Bucke's house again because Bucke's wife began to resent her husband's extreme attachment to the poet, and she refused to allow him into their home. Bucke respected his wife's wishes in this, but told her that she would never succeed in ending his friendship with Walt Whitman. He said that if the rest of the universe were on one side and Walt Whitman were on the other, he would go with Whitman! Speak of loyalty. Bucke completed his biography of Whitman in 1883.

Underlying Bucke's letters to Whitman of the rest of the 1880s is the fact that the poet is slowly dying. Bucke is greatly concerned with Whitman's health and comfort. He appointed a full-time doctor to look over him. The following is a representative letter from Bucke to Whitman during this period. The replies of Whitman, if there were any, are lost.

Dec. 17, 1888

Dear Walt,

You have had a hard fight and a long fight, but we may say of you to-day that you have won the battle. If you have fallen at the end (though I trust even yet you may still have before you some good days), but even if you are to fall now, your fame is safe beyond all peradventure. Your work is well done; and here or elsewhere (I do not know that it matters which – except for those you leave a little while behind you), you will always live and be honored always. Yes, and loved always.

R. M. Bucke[31]

The warmth and love expressed between these two late nineteenth century men is quite extraordinary, and reflects, I believe, a far more humane age than our own. The following is a poem sent by Walt Whitman to Dr. Bucke:

17 July 1891

The College Welcome to Dr. Bucke

> Comrade – stranger, glad we greet you.
> One and all are pleased to meet you;
> Cordial friendship here shall heat you,
>   whilst with us you stay
> Friend of Walt! Be that the token,
> That enough our hearts be open,
> Though no other word be spoken
>   Friends are we alway
>
> Friendship let us treasure
>   Love to greatest measure,
> Comrades true our journey through
>   Life's thus made a pleasure.
>
> Hail! to Whitman, Lover's poet!
> Here his portrait. All we know it
> To the world we gladly show it
>   Proud his friends to be.

Doctor Bucke, Walt's brave defender,
Thanks to you we gladly tender
Noble service did you render
    To our hero's fame.

You, his chosen "explicator,"
"Leaves of Grass's" indicator
You, his life's great vindicator
Honoured be your name.

Health to Walt's glory!
Long live the poet hoary!
Noble life through
    Peace and strife
Immortal be his story!

Let us cherish his example,
Kind, heroic, broad and ample
Be our lives of his a sample
Worthy friends prove we.[32]

Walt Whitman concluded the letter with the statement: "I'm a flickering well-burnt candle, soon to be all out." The "good gray poet" died March 26, 1892. Bucke was an honorary pall bearer at Whitman's funeral, and he delivered a short oration at the grave site:

In your own right you took the rank here below as a supreme creative workman; in your own right to-day you rank among the supreme creative gods.[33]

Indicative of Bucke's almost religious veneration for Whitman is the following letter to his friends J. W. Wallace and John Johnston:

10 April 1892

Dear Wallace and Johnston,
    Many thanks for your good kind letter. I can not write to you yet – my heart is heavy as lead. But it will pass off and please God we will work for dear Walt harder than ever. Over & over again I keep saying to myself: The Christ is dead! And this time there seems to be an end of everything. But I *know* he is not dead and I *know* that this pain will pass. Give my love to all the dear College fellows – *Now* we are really brothers. God bless you all.

R. M. Bucke[34]

Some have suggested that Bucke regarded Whitman as a kind of "messiah figure." There is some truth in that.★ In the Jungian view, he *projected* the archetype of the Self onto his hero, Walt Whitman. Some beings, who are very highly evolved, somehow *attract* this projection, without doing anything consciously about it. The best teachers will not encourage it, and we cannot see anything that Whitman did to encourage this projection on the part of Bucke. Usually he did this by *not* responding to what he considered inappropriate questions or statements. To Bucke this made Whitman seem all the greater. This is the most difficult juncture in the teacher/pupil relationship: the *withdrawing of projections*. In the case of Jesus, his followers could not withdraw their veneration from him, so he withdrew from them, and said that it would be better this way. He will send *another*: the Holy Spirit. After this happened, in the Christian story of Crucifixion/Resurrection/Ascension/and Pentacost, the disciples found new strength. We could say they awakened to their own true Selves. They would call this the *Christ*. Similarly with Bucke, his own spiritual teacher-mentor, the poet Walt Whitman, had to withdraw from him. He died. Bucke actually went on to do his very best work after Whitman's death, his magnum opus, *Cosmic Consciousness*.

Bucke's chief project of the 1890s was the examination of the faculty which he called "Cosmic Consciousness" based upon his examination of fifty instances. His sources of inspiration for this work were twofold: his own mystical illumination in 1872 and his long friendship with the poet-sage, Walt Whitman, whom Bucke considered the "greatest instance" of this emergent gift. In May, 1894, Bucke spoke on "Cosmic Consciousness" to the American Medico-Psychological Association. He completed his book, *Cosmic Consciousness* in 1898, but it did not find a publisher immediately. It was finally published in 1901, one year before Bucke's death in 1902. Only five hundred copies of this book were printed and sold during Bucke's remaining year of life. Yet, today, ninety years later, it continues to exist in several paperback forms, and is in the home library of nearly every person with an interest in mysticism and spiritual psychology.

★ Bucke compares Whitman's *Leaves of Grass* with the holy scriptures of other civilizations in his biography of the poet: "What the Vedas were to Brahmanism, the Law and the Prophets to Judaism, the Avesto and Zend to Zorastrianism, the Kings to Confucianism and Taoism, the Pitakas to Buddhism, the Gospels and Pauline writings to Christianity, the Quràn to Mohammedanism, will *Leaves of Grass* be to the future American civilization. Those were all Gospels. . ."[35]

The author, Bucke, finds the state of Cosmic Consciousness in such diverse persons as the Buddha, Jesus of Nazareth, St. Paul, Plotinus, Dante, St. John of the Cross, Francis Bacon, Jacob Boehme, and, of course, Walt Whitman. His instances cover the greats of religion, mysticism, poetry, and science. It is a truly unique book which looks at mystical experience from the point of view of psychology. Bucke created his own psychology to cover what he saw as *all* the states of consciousness that are possible from the perceptual consciousness of lower animals to the illumined cosmic consciousness of the religious sage or mystic. He did not live to see this book's success, and it has still not yet made its impact on psychology or psychiatry, Bucke's disciplines, because of the extreme materialistic turn of these two subjects in the twentieth century. Psychology and its sister, psychiatry, have hardly begun to assimilate the archetypal psychology of Carl Gustav Jung, let alone the spiritual psychology of Richard Maurice Bucke. Bucke's psychology is a whole domain of consciousness deeper than Jung's (although it skips over many facts that Jung brought out), and leaves Freud far behind, even though Bucke lived and died before the time of Freud or Jung. Dr. Bucke was a century ahead of his time.

Death came to Richard Maurice Bucke quite suddenly on February 19, 1902. After dinner with friends on an intensely cold Canadian night, Bucke returned home. He went outside on the veranda to take what was to be his last look at the stars. He slipped on a patch of ice, being after all a man with only one foot, and struck his head violently against a pillar. He died instantly.[36] Bucke was sixty-five years of age, still vigorous of mind and body. The world lost one of its truly great and many-sided men. He died at the beginning of our twentieth century.

BUCKE'S EVOLUTIONARY THEORY OF
COSMIC CONSCIOUSNESS

Cosmic Consciousness is a difficult book to classify. It has nothing to do with formal religion or with the conscious preparation of traditional mysticism. Bucke was first and foremost a psychologist, a student of the human mind. He treated illumination from the standpoint of psychology, as a very rare and extraordinary state of mind which is recognizable and well-authenticated in the religious and mystical literature of every culture of humankind.

Bucke takes no position for or against one religion or another, but rather penetrates to the common core of all religions, the state of cosmic consciousness. Bucke's view is that the human race is, very slowly and sporadically, in the process of developing a new consciousness so far above the ordinary human consciousness that we shall prove true the Biblical prophesy: "I have said, Ye *are* gods, and all of you *are* children of the most High."[37]

Bucke deals first with three distinct stages of consciousness which precede cosmic consciousness which are observable in living creatures: the perceptual mind of the lowest animals on the phylogenetic scale, the receptual mind of higher animals, and the conceptual mind of human beings. Bucke also calls receptual mind (which includes perceptual mind) "simple consciousness," and conceptual mind, he refers to as "self consciousness." Bucke was not the first to recognize that self-consciousness is distinctly human, in fact, the sine qua non of the human race.

By virtue of self-consciousness, we humans are not only conscious of our external environments, our bodies and movements, but are conscious of ourselves as distinct entities, apart, as it were, from the rest of the universe: individual selves. Bucke says that there is no other animal who can do this, ask the question, "Who am I?"

> The animal is, as it were, immersed in his own consciousness, as a fish in the sea; he cannot, even in his imagination, get outside of it for one moment so as to realize it.[38]

How do we know that humans are self-conscious, Bucke asks? We know because he/she can speak to us, because he/she possesses language. "Language is the objective of which self-consciousness is the subjective."[39] Self-consciousness and language are two halves of the same coin. No animal has conceptual language; no animal possesses self-consciousness, according to Bucke. Signal systems, which occur in many animal species, do not imply concepts. The possession of self-consciousness and language in the human creates an enormous gap between us and our nearest neighbors in the animal world.★ It is "Adam," or man/woman, to whom God,

---

★ The sciences of language, animal communication, linguistics, and psycholinguistics, present strong evidence that language is uniquely human and species specific. It is associated with fairly recent evolutionary developments of the brain: language capacity tends to be localized in the left cerebral hemisphere – Broca's and Wernicke's areas. However, studies of chimps and apes have proven they possess rudimentary language learning capacities, not vocal, but utilizing sign

according to the Bible, gave the ability to name things. It is, therefore, he/she who has dominion (or stewardship) over the created world. Bucke points out that conceptual mind and linguistic communication are an enormous power making possible human social life, manners, customs, institutions, industries of all kinds, arts useful and fine, all of human history, culture, and development. From the dances and hunts of paleolithic man to the space explorations of contemporary man it is the gift of self-consciousness and conceptual mind, including language.

Yet, there is a new stage of consciousness so far beyond self-consciousness that it enables the man or woman who experiences it to directly *see* the oneness of the universe, the immortality of the soul, and the divine love behind it all. Beyond perceptual mind, receptual mind, and conceptual mind, is intuitional or Cosmic Conscious mind, as Bucke calls it. In almost prophetic language, Bucke predicts that Cosmic Consciousness will appear more and more often until it becomes the everyday consciousness of humanity.

Professor William James, the great American philosopher and psychologist, read *Cosmic Consciousness* soon after it appeared and wrote a letter to Richard Bucke, its author, saying:

> I believe that you have brought this kind of consciousness "home" to the attention of students of human nature in a way so definite and unescapable that it will be impossible henceforward to overlook or ignore it . . . But my total reaction on your book, my dear Sir, is that it is an addition of first rate importance, and that you are a benefactor of us all.[40]

Despite these warm and felicitous words by William James, the professions of psychology and psychiatry were to very soon "close the door," as it were, on religious and spiritual experience for more than a half century. The behaviorists, Watson in America, and Pavlov in Russia, to name two of its chief exponents, were to "banish consciousness" itself from psychology's ken. Freud, and the psychoanalytic tradition, was, in its way, as hostile to the religious experience. Nonetheless, we will go back to these earlier and more propitious days of psychology's path to look at the

---

learning or tokens, and studies of our large-brained sea mammal relatives, the dolphins, are in their infancy. Yet the best scientists of language, especially since Noam Chomsky's revolutionary work in transformational grammar, do conclude that this kind of rule learning, necessary to acquire human language, syntax and semantics, is biologically specific to *Homo sapiens*.

Figure 1.1   From Bucke's Table on the Psychogenesis of Man:

Name of Faculty	Approximate Age of Appearance in Man	How Frequent?	When is the Faculty lost in Man?
Simple Consciousness	Few days after birth	Universal	Only lost in deep sleep and coma; present in dreams
Self Consciousness	Three years	Nearly Universal; absent in 1 in a 1,000	Lost in coma, delirium, and mania
Cosmic Consciousness	Thirty-five years	One in many millions	Only present for a few seconds to a few hours in any case; then passes away of itself

work of a truly great mind, Richard Bucke, who synthesized an all-embracing theory of the stages and evolution of human consciousness.

"Cosmic consciousness," according to Bucke, is a higher form of consciousness than that possessed by ordinary men and women. This last is called self-consciousness and is the faculty upon which rests all human life as we know it, both subjective and objective. Before we look at Bucke's theory of the unfolding of cosmic consciousness from self-consciousness, we will go back to the evolution of self-consciousness from sentient life.

Beginning with simple consciousness which is possessed by the animal kingdom, it is by means of this faculty that a dog or a horse, for instance, is conscious of things about him, and is also conscious of his own limbs and body as part of himself. Simple consciousness is a miracle in itself having arisen from non-conscious sentient life. This is how Bucke puts it:

> Later in the history of creation comes the beginning of Simple Consciousness. Certain individuals in some one leading species in the slowly unfolding life of the planet, some day – for the first time – become conscious; know that there exists a world, a something without

them. Less dwelt upon, as it has been, this step from the unconscious to the conscious might well impress us as being as immense, as miraculous and as divine as that from the inorganic to the organic. [41]

In this powerful book, Bucke has a way of making us awaken to the *mystery* of much of what we simply take for granted: life, consciousness, self-awareness, etc. Simple consciousness, no less than self or cosmic consciousness, is nothing to be merely assumed as "the way things are." Bucke leads us to think about this mystery of consciousness.

This simple consciousness that has arisen in the animal kingdom, perhaps first among invertebrates and simple fishes, is composed of two constituents: perceptual mind and receptual mind in Bucke's view. What is perceptual mind? It occurs in evolution when the primary quality of excitability or sensitivity is established in living organisms. At this point began the acquisition and registration of sense impressions, that is, of percepts. A percept is a sound heard, an object seen, a pressure felt, and so on. If we could go far back enough in the evolution of the human species, we could find creatures whose whole "mind" was made up simply of these percepts. Many of the species of planet earth are at this stage now: hydra, jellyfish, earthworms, protozoa. They can sense and respond, and that is about all. They truly follow the classic "Stimulus – Response" formula of the behaviorists! We, indeed, carry much of this early evolutionary machinery in us, as well, in our elementary reflexes. In infants, these would include the plantar response, the knee jerk reflex, the crying response, the sucking reflex, the visual tracking response, and so on. The infant is mostly taking in vast inputs through its sensory apparatus into its nervous system, and responding to some of these in simple ways. The registering and response to sense impressions, or perceptual mind, is our elementary beginning, both phylogenetically and ontogenetically.

What are recepts? From generation to generation, our perceptual creatures accumulated countless millions of percepts and the constant repetition of these led in the struggle for existence to an accumulation in the central nervous system of groupings of these percepts throughout the nerve ganglia into what we may call "recepts." [42] A recept is a group percept. Similar percepts, say of a tree, are registered one over the other, until they are generalized; this is a recept. It seems to involve memory and a form of "stimulus generalization" and also "response generalization." Hence trees are grouped, as are rocks, certain species of animals, etc. Behavior becomes more efficient that way. One can learn to avoid certain enemies, such as snakes, or seek out and find certain prey, or edible substances. One does not have to respond to each case individually anymore. Percepts and recepts make up what Bucke calls "simple consciousness." It involves perception and memory, and moreover, concrete classifications, such that one exists in a world of relatively stable objects over time. With receptual mind, consciousness of the "out there" comes into existence. With merely perceptual mind, there is barely the faintest glimmer of consciousness, if we can call immediate sensation consciousness at all. It is proto-consciousness at best. In our infant, there is now recognition of a certain recurring pattern of stimuli as the "mothering one," and another as the "breast from which one sucks nourishment," etc. There are no linguistic concepts or names whatsoever at this point, merely the consciousness of certain objects quite concretely cognized. If you can "enter into this" scenario, you can experience what this receptual mind of the baby of about age six months to a year, or of the higher animal, is like. You once experienced the world in this way yourself! Species of all kinds from the dinosaurs to the woolly mammoths of ages past, to the leopards and kangaroos and sheep and elephants and rhinosoruses and racoons of today are creatures of simple consciousness. Obviously, there is a continuum of intelligence within the world of simple consciousness with levels of problem-solving ability. Yet in all these creatures, there is not the slightest glimmer of conceptual mind or self-consciousness. If there was, we would know it, animal communications experiments notwithstanding, it has not been shown, to this date anyway, that there is an animal species who is *self-conscious* and *conceptual* besides the human race. As stated earlier, sign language learning capacities of primates and dolphins *suggest* a proto-self-conscious stage between simple and self-consciousness in these large-brained mammals. Self consciousness is our peculiar burden. It involves a suffering that animals do not know, as is symbolized in the myth of Adam and Eve who eat of the "tree of knowledge of good and evil" – and become self-conscious human beings! They are forced to leave the Edenic paradise of simple consciousness forever.

What is self-consciousness? A recept is a composite image of hundreds or thousands of percepts. It is an image abstracted from many images. But a concept is that same recept *named* for some abstract quality that it possesses.[43] For example, when members of a class of furry creatures who run on all fours, and bark sometimes, and lick your hand other times, are recognized as "doggies," that is the beginning of concept formation. There is a similar but somewhat different class of furry creatures which "meow" rather than bark, and they behave somewhat more shyly and less gregariously, and these we recognize as "kitties." This is what it's like for a recept to become a concept. The revolution by which concepts are substituted for recepts is a gigantic increase in the efficiency of the brain. It made possible language formation, tool invention and use, and simple mores and customs in humanity's early history. Likewise, the child with concepts and language begins to communicate with others, use simple implements, and not so simple (like the computer), and, in general, become a socialized member of his/her human subculture. The young human individual, who is in possession of concepts, hence language, inevitably comes to self-consciousness. The being with language can ask itself: "Who am I?" This is not just a philosophical speculation, but a real fact of early childhood development. It is curious that the great child psychologist, Jean Piaget (1896–1980) who raised all kinds of questions about childhood conceptual or from the concept of number to the concept of time to the concept of physical causality etc., deals very little with the origin of the child's concept of self, or the dawning of self-consciousness.* This is a question which Bucke, his nineteenth century predecessor in the history of ideas looked at very much. The study of consciousness per sé seems to be almost as "taboo" among the cognitivists as it was among the behaviorists.

In the individual development of the human child, the transition from simple to self-consciousness begins between two and three years old and corresponds closely to the development of language. This is a question which the psycholinguists, even the Chomskians, with their emphasis on innate structures, have looked at virtually not at all. I have looked in vain among the psycholinguistics texts for some reference to this subject. I think that the impact of behaviorism on psychology has been far more devastating than is commonly acknowledged. To look at the question of consciousness, and its development, one does well to look back to the great psychologists of the late nineteenth century, such as William James and Richard Bucke.

The present author had a psycholinguistic period in his psychology study and looked a bit into the question of language and

---

* Among the many works of Piaget, one finds some reference to self-consciousness, or specifically *its absence* in the following quote from *The Moral Judgement of the Child* (1965): "Every observer has noted that the younger the child, the less sense he has of his own ego. From the intellectual point of view he does not distinguish between external and internal, subjective and objective."[44]

self-consciousness. One can observe that children of about two already have the beginnings of language, certainly words used meaningfully and simple sentences. There is a peculiarity in the usage of two-year-old children in that they tend to refer to themselves objectively rather than subjectively. For example, "Benjy want ice cream!" At about three years old, the personal pronoun "I" comes into the vocabulary, as for example, "I want ice cream, Mommy!" Does the use of "I" imply the dawning of self-consciousness? I certainly believe so. You may recall vaguely that this was the time that you first began to become conscious of yourself as a separate being: *I am.* "*I*" comes into existence signifying self-consciousness. Bucke points out that what took the human race several hundred thousand years to develop is the possession of every human child of today by about three years old.

> For some hundreds of thousands of years, upon the general plane of Self-Consciousness, an ascent, to the human eye gradual, but from the point of view of cosmic evolution, rapid, has been made. In a race, large brained, walking erect, gregarious, brutal, but king of all other brutes, man in appearance but not in fact, the so-called alalus homo, was, from the highest Simple Consciousness born the basic human faculty Self Consciousness and its twin, language. [45]

In each case, there is an enormous hiatus that is jumped, from sentient life to simple consciousness, and from simple consciousness to self-consciousness. Bucke does not speculate too much about what was the "mechanism" which "jumped the gap," whether chance factors and natural selection, as Darwinians would have it, or some purposive intelligence manifesting itself in nature, as creative evolutionists would claim, as for example, Teilhard de Chardin. Needless to say, Bucke points out *the mystery* with wonderment and awe.

Once there exists conceptual mind and self-consciousness, there is an immense and complex development both in the history of the human race, and correspondingly, in the development of the human individual from infancy to adulthood. Bucke treats of this development in his chapter called "On the Plane of Self-Consciousness." Simple consciousness, Bucke estimates, appeared many millions of years ago; self-consciousness, he judges, is perhaps three hundred thousand years old. This is a long development on the plane of self-consciousness! Just as simple consciousness phylogenetically evolved from the simplest vertebrates to the nearly human higher primates, and perhaps dolphins, self-consciousness, historically and anthropologically speaking, evolved from the simplest food-gatherer in the forests to the philosophers and playwrights of the Greek city-states ... whether we have evolved much from Plato and Sophocles, I am not sure!

Bucke first treats of the development of intellect and language, the inner and outer sides of the same thing – conceptual mind. He tends to look mostly at historical and racial developments; I will supplement this with a look at the development of the human individual which was the subject of much of my graduate school studies. Bucke looks at the work of the linguist, Max Mueller, who estimated that the Indo-European ancestral language may be reduced to one hundred and twenty-one root concepts.[46] From these came the millions of words in the various descendant Indo-European languages of today. Bucke goes further and says that these over one hundred roots words of Indo-European probably were derivatives of about one half dozen words. After all, human language had to begin somewhere; it did not appear in full-blown form suddenly out of nowhere! We can imagine our cave-dwelling ancestors coining a very few basic words: hungry, eat, danger, love, and so on. You get the idea.

In quite exact parallel to this, the human child begins his language developmental history with a very few words. Some possibilities are: "mama," "dada," "doggie," "see," "want," and "no." These kinds of records exist in psycholinguistic developmental studies. From these single words, simple two-word sentences are formed, such as, "see doggie," or "see dada," or "want doggie," and so on. Of course, vocabulary is continually and rapidly enriched from the few words of age two to the, perhaps, five hundred words of the five-year-old child of kindergarten age. Not that development stops here by any means. By age thirty, our child may have become an author of several books, and a "linguistic athlete" with a vocabulary of hundreds of thousands of words and the capacity to forge these into totally novel sentences, paragraphs, chapters, and whole books!

Bucke speculates that the entire intellectual development of the human race could have evolved from *a single initial concept.*[47] I wonder what that was? I suppose that nobody will ever know. Parallel to this is the possibility that individual mental development begins with a single concept. This would be very difficult, if not impossible, to ascertain. Bucke's analogy is the development of the whole complex human (or animal) organism from a single cell. Whether this analogy between the development of the organism from a single cell and the development of the mind from a single idea is accurate or not, I do not know. It is interesting to speculate on the analogues between biological and conceptual evolution as Bucke did, and likewise Piaget, with their biological science backgrounds.*

After his discussion of the development of language and intellect, "on the plane of self-consciousness," Bucke looks at other developments, such as the evolution of the color sense. Based upon the study of ancient documents, it can be fairly well demonstrated that our ancestors recognized fewer colors than we do. Even Aristotle spoke of a "tricolored rainbow!"[48] We see the rainbow as seven colors: red, orange, yellow, green, blue, indigo, and violet. Obviously the Greeks of Aristotle's era made fewer distinctions among the colors. The Rig Veda, Bucke points out, also mentions only three colors. The Bible never mentions the color blue! It takes sky and sea for granted, apparently. The earliest human documents of the ancient civilizations of the fertile crescent utilize only two color names: red and black. I do not think it is logically possible for there to be only one color! Then, everything is the same. Children, as is well known, have to learn to use color names and concepts.

Anticipating by more than fifty years the "moral development" specialists in child psychology such as Kohlberg, Bucke looks at the development of man's moral nature, his conscience, his sense of right and wrong, his sense of duty and responsibility, and his love of his fellow men, as another, and crucial aspect of development in the obviously very complex "plane of self-consciousness." Bucke, based upon his own study of history, asserts that human moral nature is not more than ten or twelve thousand years old.[49] Of course, Bucke, as any scholar, is limited to the study of the historical period, in the nature of the case, as "prehistory" is beyond the range of investigation! We do not know what the morality or lack of it of our neolithic or paleolithic ancestors was like. However, we had on our own continent, a neolithic culture, that of the Native American, and they surely had a moral code of highest level stressing honor, honesty, duty to one's fellow man, etc. Our concept of democracy comes from the Indian tribes of the Northeast. Who knows that paleolithic, or old stone age man, did not have a moral code? Bucke, here, as elsewhere, often claims more than he can know. He does, however, suggest the study of

* Bucke was trained as a physician with an M.D., and Piaget was a Ph.D. in biology.

the written historical documents of the early Romans, Hellenes, Hebrews, Egyptians, Assyrians, Babylonians, and so on, to ascertain whether there is a moral development. I would suspect that there is. Whether it is "always upward" is another question. One of Gautama Buddha's ten commandments was "kill no sentient being." This was his teaching of 2,500 years ago. Jesus of Nazareth, the Jewish rabbi and central figure of Christianity of two thousand years ago, taught that even anger, or hate of one's fellow human being, was the moral equivalent of murder. Yet in our twentieth century, amoral monsters such as Adolf Hitler and Joseph Stalin ruled over millions of people in "civilized countries" and set their own standards of violence and murder. We are just emerging (since late 1991) from a 45 year "cold war" during which time we lived under a nuclear "sword of Damocles" which threatened us with human extinction. There may be major regressions as well as progressions in moral evolution! As to the moral development of the child from infancy to adolescence, it is commonly believed that there is a progression.

I attended the William James lecture at Harvard Divinity School given by the psychiatrist, Dr. Robert Coles. He talked about the case of a little black girl named Ruby, who caused him to throw all "theories of moral development" out the window. She was about six years old, and would be in the "pre-operational stage" of Piaget, hence, presumably was "incapable" of true moral reasoning. In any event, Ruby was one of the early cases of school integration in the deep South. While Ruby was jeered at and threatened by violent redneck types, Dr. Coles observed that she muttered something to herself. He asked her what she was doing. She replied that she was praying. He said, "For whom?" She said, "For those men who are shouting at me." Dr. Coles in disbelief, asked her, "Why, Ruby, why?" Ruby replied that it was because they needed prayer, and besides, "Jesus told us to love our enemies." I think that this makes the point without further comment. Strangely, Bucke states that moral development in the child is very late, and usually does not appear until mid-adolescence! I think the doctor errs here. But he is correct in looking at moral development as one of the chief features on "the plane of self-consciousness."

Bucke concludes this chapter by looking at some other self-conscious faculties such as musical sense. It is clear that self-consciousness is a vast subject and it is amazing how many complexities of human psychology and culture are developments thereof.

It will be interesting to compare the four-stage developmental theory of Richard Bucke with the likewise four-stage developmental theory of Jean Piaget, the well-known child psychologist and genetic epistemologist of our time, before we go "beyond self consciousness" to Bucke's discussion of the emergence of cosmic consciousness. Bucke anticipates Piaget's theory in certain ways, and also goes a giant step beyond it.

Piaget's Stages of Moral Development[50]
Sensori-Motor: The sensori-motor stage spans roughly the age range that most psychologists call infancy from birth to age two. According to Piaget, the salient feature of this first stage is that internalized thinking processes are absent. In other words, infants cannot carry out many activities "inside their heads." Infants, at least according to Piaget, are capable only of those processes that can be manifest in overt behavior. Examples would be sucking, grasping, crying, and overall motor processes.

Preoperational: This stage covers ages approximately two to seven. Piaget believes that children in this stage acquire internalized thought processes that they lacked as infants. These processes are said to originate in the child's internalization of overt action schemas that dominated the sensori-motor stage. So, the early precursors of thought are the internal representations of overt actions. This is very primitive thinking by adult standards. The preoperational is the stage of Piaget's well-known "conservation" experiments. The child of this stage lacks the abstract concept of the conservation of substance despite transformations.

Concrete Operational: The third or concrete operational stage is said to begin about age seven and end at age eleven. Children can now "figure things out." They can reason. However concrete operational cognitive processes produce logical thinking only when applied to concrete informational inputs. The child at this stage lacks the abstract thinking capacity of the adolescent or adult. He is able to "solve," however, the "conservation" experiments mentioned above.

Formal Operational: This stage begins at about eleven years old and goes on indefinitely, according to Piaget, into adulthood. The thinking processes are capable of reaching full abstraction at this stage. Thinking processes are no longer dependent upon concrete observed data. Thought operations can be carried out on hypothetical information making possible higher mathematics, experimental science, and philosophical reasoning.

Piaget believed that intelligence has arrived at its ultimate equilibrium by the formal operational stage, and no further qualitative structural improvements can or will occur. By fifteen the child is capable of mathematics and science, and abstract reasoning of a philosophical character. Further adult developments are simply elaborations upon this in Piaget's view. Of course, there are enormous individual differences in intelligence and capacity for abstract reasoning from the checkout clerk's figuring your bill at the supermarket to the nuclear physicist's complex equations of quantum theory. These are just variations within the formal operational scheme according to Piaget. This is man's "highest attainment." This is a peculiarly narrow academic view of things! It does not take into account that achievements in certain fields, such as literature and poetry, can take place in midlife and later. It certainly does not include within its range of possibilities the experiences of the mystics and sages, nor their teachings, some of which are considered holy scriptures, e.g., the *Bible, Upanishads*, etc. Piaget, as admired as he is by the new and trendy "cognitive psychology," simply falls far short of including the "possible human," to use Jean Houston's expression, within its range of sight. The cognitivists, and Piaget was one of the best in that school, raise the human vision from "S – R" to the "formal operational schemata," but there is an enormous jump beyond this in human possibilities, and Piaget and the cognitivists do not make this jump. Interestingly enough, Bucke, of the previous century, *did*, somewhat negating his own optimistic theory of continual "upward development."

Comparing Piaget's stages with Bucke's, we see considerable overlaps. The sensori-motor stage of Piaget compares very well with the perceptual mind stage of Bucke. However, from what I know of early child development, I would say that the infant by age six months to a year has certainly begun to form recepts from its initial percepts, and is therefore a being of receptual mind, or simple consciousness. So, simple consciousness is the term that corresponds most completely with the sensori-motor stage. The infant, even of a year, does not possess self-consciousness in any way yet and is comparable (if not behind) in cognitive capabilities to a chimpanzee of the same age. It differs only in that it has *the potential* for self-consciousness and conceptual mind (it has this potential in its genes even as a fertilized ovum!).

By age two, rudimentary concepts and language have begun in most human beings. This is the beginning of Piaget's preoperational stage. The thinking process at this stage is extremely concretistic, and moreover, lacks the "reversibility" of later thought. In the famous "conservation experiment," the young child of between two and seven is shown a ball of clay. He can look at it or touch it. Then, the adult experimenter stretches out the clay ball into an elongated tubular shape, for example. He asks the child, "Is it the same amount of clay or is it more?" The child will inevitably say, "It's more clay." This experiment can be done with water too. The experimenter first shows the child water in a short fat glass. He can look at or feel the water. Then, the water is poured by the adult into a tall thin glass. Again, when queried as to whether there is the same amount of water, or more, the child will respond, "There's more water." In both cases the child will be a bit puzzled about the "mystery" about how clay or water came from "nowhere." The child's mind at this stage lacks reversible operations, even at the very concrete level. Try it with your four or five year old, and you will see that it "works." There is no way to teach the preoperational child about concrete operations either. His internal schemata have not gotten to that stage. It would be like trying to teach calculus to a chimpanzee. By seven, on the average, based upon much experience of concrete things, the child's mind will make the "jump" to concrete operations, and hence, Piaget calls this the "concrete operational stage." Yet no child of seven or eight will be capable of abstract mathematical or scientific reasoning. This is the achievement of the stage of formal operations which is reached by about eleven or twelve (with the onset of puberty approximately – although it may have no relation of sex hormones).

This pioneering work of Piaget's is of vast importance to educational theory and practice, along with his concepts of "schemata, assimilation, accommodation, and equilibrium." Schemata have to do with inner mental structures, assimilation with taking in information via these structures, accommodation with modifying these structures based upon experience, and equilibrium with a "fit" between inner structures and the external world. All of this complex development from the preoperational to the formal operational stage of mental development corresponds with Bucke's stage of "conceptual mind." You recall that Bucke dealt with the complex developments of this period, for instance, concepts and language evolving from the very few and simple to the very many and complex. There is something of the idea of the epi-genetic interaction between organism and environment in Bucke, as with Piaget. Organisms move from percepts to recepts because percepts alone become too inefficient in dealing with the world. Recepts are a jump in efficiency. The jump from recepts to concepts, a monumental one, is also spurred by interactions between the brain and the outer world which force an accommodation to a new and higher synthesis. Within the conceptual stage, movement is from simple to complex. Piaget delineates the substages of the conceptual stage, perhaps more elaborately than Bucke does. Piaget's great insights were within the area of the development of conceptual thought. We see the adumbrations of Piagetian "genetic epistemology," i.e. the development of knowing, in Bucke's question about the development of the "concept of science" from early childhood to mid-adulthood. Piaget wrote an entire book on the child's concept of causality, and how it evolves. So, preoperational, concrete operational, and formal operational are sub-stages of what Bucke would call "conceptual mind" which he recognized had a long and complex development.

Whereas Piaget thinks that formal reasoning goes on forever, Bucke asks the question whether there is a limit to the growth and complexification of concepts just as there was a limit to the growth and complexification of percepts and recepts.[51] He says that anyone who seriously considers the question will see that there must be a limit. No such processes could go on into infinity. To be illustrative, if you study the history of philosophy from Plato to Wittgenstein, you will see endless complexification of concepts, often going around in circles within circles. The philosophers seem to be "trapped" in conceptual thought. In the play, *Godspell*, there is a scene in the beginning in which philosophers from every period of history and culture are all spouting their philosophies simultaneously. The result is babble! On the scene comes John the Baptist who announces the "coming of the Lord!" This is a *breakthrough* which symbolizes the coming to a new and higher level. To quote Bucke on this subject:

> We have seen that the expansion of the perceptual mind had a necessary limit . . . led . . . up to and into the receptual mind. That the receptual mind by its own growth was inevitably led up to and into the conceptual mind. A priori considerations make it certain that a corresponding outlet will be found for the conceptual mind.[52]

Bucke, the psychiatrist-mystic who had experienced cosmic consciousness some years earlier, probably did not get to this hypothesis via "a priori considerations," but through his own spontaneous experience of illumination. It is clear that Piaget never came to any such thing, and seems to have had no idea that such a thing could exist as "cosmic consciousness." Contrary to this, Bucke says that we do not have to depend upon abstract reasoning to demonstrate the necessary existence of the supraconceptual mind, since it exists and can be studied with no more difficulty than other natural phenomena.

It was the genius of Bucke to not only recognize the existence of cosmic consciousness, or supraconceptual mind, but to dare to say that this was a natural phenomenon, ergo, it is potentially researchable by science. Others who would recognize the truth of scriptures, for example, would relegate this to the "untouchable realm" of religious faith. I am not sure I agree entirely with Bucke's naturalism which sometimes involves a kind of reductionism. The supernatural may be as real an aspect of reality as the natural, and moreover, the two may in no way be in contradiction. In simpler language, if God created the world, He is in no way "alien" to it. In the mystical view of the Kabbalists (Jewish mystics), for instance, God pervades the world. In a later chapter, I will argue that Cosmic Consciousness may be a breakthrough of ego or Self to God. The mention of "God" to many in our secular-materialist world, especially to scientists of the biological, or behavioral, or social science variety, seems to bring immediate grimaces of extreme discomfort and irritation. Their immediate response is "It's not scientific!" I would be more concerned with "Is it *true*?" There may be much in the universe, both inner and outer, which is beyond the range of what we currently call science (it is overly narrowly defined). Bucke, who was himself an instance of Cosmic Consciousness, could not in truth to his experience "rule it out of existence." Nor can I. Further, it is not just a rare and anomalous experience, it is the central experience of all religions! Bucke had the boldness and the courage to open the doors of a much broader conception of science to this *reality*. Some of today's physicists, e.g. David Bohm with his concept of the "implicate order," are opening doors, as well. We will look at that later.

Bucke says, writing back in the 1890s, that the existence of supraconceptual mind is an established fact. He says that the elements of supraconceptual mind are intuitions rather than concepts. Beyond the self-conscious mind, Bucke is dealing here with the cosmic conscious mind. In this, he goes as far beyond Piaget and the cognitive school as the Buddha and Jesus went beyond the philosophers of their time.

Let us review Bucke's theory of the four levels of consciousness:

Bucke's Stages of Consciousness[53]

(1) Perceptual Mind – In a mind made up wholly of percepts, there is only the barest glimmer of consciousness as we understand it. For example, is the starfish conscious?

(2) Receptual Mind – When receptal mind comes into existence, simple consciousness is born. This means that animals are conscious of the things they see, hear, smell, and feel around them. The animal is conscious of the objects which he sees, but he does not *know* that he is conscious of it. He is not conscious of his consciousness; neither is the animal conscious of itself as a distinct and separate entity, or personality. Surely the zebra running in its herd is conscious of sights, sounds, and smells, etc., but it is hardly conscious of its consciousness or identity. Nor does it possess the capacity for concepts or language.

(3) Conceptual Mind – When a creature has reached self-consciousness, it is not only conscious of what it sees and hears and feels, but it knows that it is conscious of it. It is conscious of itself as a separate entity and personality. It can stand apart and contemplate itself. It can observe and judge the contents of its own mind, as it can observe and judge external objects. This creature is a human being! Only human beings are self-conscious. Self-consciousness entails the existence of concepts and language.

(4) Intuitional or Cosmic Conscious Mind – Finally, the basic fact of Cosmic Consciousness, implied by its name, is the consciousness of the cosmos as a living presence. It involves the immediate perception of the immortality of one's soul. It is what the Hindus of the East call the "Brahmic Splendor." The beings who are cosmic conscious are human beings who have attained to enlightenment or illumination.

Most of twentieth century psychology and psychiatry are about levels of consciousness one, two, and three. From Freud to Piaget, and from Skinner to Chomsky, they *have ignored consciousness of the fourth level*. Whether even the brilliant innovator, Jung, deals with this is a question we will look at in one chapter. A priori, then, all of these "modern psychologists" have ignored or denied the reality of religious or spiritual experience. They either deny its existence, or reduce it to something else, perhaps "delusion," or "regression to the womb," etc. We will look into more of this in later chapters. Bucke did not ignore or reduce the irreducible and inescapable reality of Cosmic Consciousness. He could not because *he had sampled, he had seen.* Others, less enlightened, and less illumined, chose to totally ignore him! We ignore him today at our peril because we live in an age of "conceptual mind" gone nearly mad in our world of potential nuclear annihilation and environmental suicide, not to mention the depersonalization and anomie of late twentieth century life. Bucke would say that the answer to this problem is not endless conferences and studies by self-conscious men and women, but the heeding of the *holy truths* of the enlightened beings who have been on this planet from time to time and left high religions in their wake. He emphasized the value of contact whether directly or through readings or religious forms with the persons of Cosmic Consciousness. An example was Bucke's long association with Walt Whitman. Bucke very much believed that Cosmic Consciousness was the key to bringing in a *new age.*

What does Cosmic Consciousness reveal about the world? Bucke says that:

> . . . this consciousness shows the cosmos to consist not of dead matter governed by unconscious, rigid, and unintending law; it shows it on the contrary as entirely immaterial, entirely spiritual and entirely alive; it shows that death is an absurdity, that everyone and everything has eternal life; it shows that the universe is God and that God is the universe. . .[54]

Mystics have experienced this consciousness for moments, and have been changed for life by the experience. Enlightened ones like Jesus and the Buddha *lived* in this consciousness: the *Kingdom of God* or *Nirvana.* We are the beneficiaries of these supraconscious human beings. Bucke would also claim that they represent the future of the human race. In saying this, Bucke is in agreement with the prophesies of a Messianic Age found in many, if not most, of the high religions. Bucke sees this in "naturalistic" as opposed to "supernaturalistic" terms. I am not sure that this is a real distinction at all, but rather two different ways of seeing one and the same reality: the way of science vs. the way of revelation. These seemed in opposition for the past several centuries during which time science declared its independence from religion, but now in the late twentieth century, at the dawn of a new millenium, there is the very real beginning of a convergence between science and religion, which was predicted by no less a mind than Teilhard de Chardin, himself a scientist and a mystic. Bucke makes a wonderful statement along these lines when he says:

If it has taken the race several hundred thousand years to learn a smattering of the science of humanity since its acquisition of self-consciousness, so it may take it millions of years to acquire a smattering of the science of God after its acquisition of cosmic consciousness.[55]

Bucke says that it is upon self-consciousness that our human world is based, as we see it, with all its works and ways. Upon self-consciousness are based capitalist and communist economic and political systems, philosophical materialism and idealism, business, science, literature, art, laws, customs, folkways, and ethics. All are the products of self-conscious minds. Human culture is the self-conscious world, whereas the animal kingdom is the simple conscious world. In this world of self-consciousness walked from time to time a man or woman of cosmic consciousness. It is the cosmic conscious world that is revealed in the holy scriptures of the higher religions. It has been dealt with by no twentieth century psychologist whom I know of as it was by Richard Maurice Bucke, M.D., the late nineteenth century Canadian psychiatrist-mystic. Dr. Bucke knew it firsthand. Bucke gives the following speculative account of the birth of Cosmic Consciousness from self-consciousness:

> The philosophy of the birth of cosmic consciousness in the individual is very similar to that of the birth of self consciousness. The mind becomes overcrowded, as it were, with concepts and these are constantly becoming larger, more numerous and more complex; some day (the conditions being all favorable) the fusion or what might be called the chemical union of several of them and of certain moral elements takes place; the result is an intuition and the establishment of intuitional mind, or, in other words, cosmic consciousness.[56]

Where Bucke is theorizing about the evolution of Cosmic Consciousness from self-consciousness, he is a self-conscious scientist like any other, and his theory is no better or worse than that of any other self-conscious scientist, except for the fact that he knew and experienced Cosmic Consciousness, however briefly. This is a "naturalistic theory" of Cosmic Consciousness in which the higher emerges from the lower by some form of synthesis. This viewpoint has been criticized by others of more metaphysical inclination, such as, P. D. Ouspensky, and we shall look at his views in a later chapter. We must observe that Bucke lived during the heyday of the Darwinian theory and was surely influenced by it. He was also influenced by Spencer's social evolutionism. We can detect in his enthusiasm for socialism that he was also influenced by Marx's dialectical theory. Bucke was, after all, a man of his time. His theories have to be understood in this historical context. But, *his experience* of Cosmic Consciousness cannot be so understood. That experience is essentially the same whether it is that of a late nineteenth century Canadian psychiatrist named Bucke, or that of a thirteenth century Persian poet named Rumi, or a first century Pharisee called Saul of Tarsus. Theory is one thing, direct experience is another. Cosmic Consciousness comes to atheists as well as believers. Bucke's theory of Cosmic Consciousness bears considerable resemblance to theories of "emergent evolution," such as that of Henri Bergson, and to "purposive evolutionary" theories, such as that of Pierre Teilhard de Chardin. These connections were pointed out in a doctoral thesis by James Robert Horne called "Cosmic Consciousness: Then and Now" which was done at the Religion Department of Columbia University in 1964. Horne views Bucke in terms of his social context. As a scientist and theorist, Bucke was influenced by his times, but as a mystic, he was a man of all times. Mystical experience is universal and not much influenced by culture, except in the *interpretation of it.*

There is a certain basis in truth to Bucke's theory that conceptual mind becomes "overloaded" leading to a new level of synthesis: "intuitional mind." This idea resembles the practice of Rinzai Zen which involves meditating upon a Koan. The student is given an unsolvable riddle, such as, "What was your Original Face before your parents were born?" One can see that since this is a "logical" and "scientific" impossibility that it would tend to "overload" the circuits of the conceptual mind. The student wrestles incessantly with this Koan for days, weeks, or months until it becomes "too much" for his existing mental machinery. Here, he may experience a *breakthrough*, as it were, to a higher form of consciousness, known as "satori" in Zen Buddhism. This is the realm of pure intuition. Now, the Zen student can answer the question satisfactorily to the Zen master. He speaks from enlightened consciousness. Prior to this he spoke from ego consciousness, and, in some Zen schools that would involve getting a whack on the head by the Zen master! Bucke is speaking about the evolutionary process to higher forms of consciousness over the millenia, however, the individual process of the spiritual aspirant may involve a similar mechanism.

However, the question is whether Cosmic Consciousness *is created* by a synthesis of elements from the lower forms of consciousness, as hydrogen and oxygen give rise to water in chemical union, or whether the cosmic consciousness pre-exists in some potential form awaiting realization. This may be a philosophical rather than a scientific question, bringing to mind the nominalist-realist debates. What I have in mind here is whether God, the Supreme Consciousness, conveys Cosmic Consciousness when "the time is right," or whether Cosmic Consciousness is an "emergent" from the elements of self-consciousness, and that from simple consciousness, and that from elementary percepts, and that from sentient life, and that from organic molecules, and so on. Bucke, in his theory, in keeping with the Darwinism of his time (which is only being questioned in very recent times in biology) seems to favor evolution "from below." Yet, he does sometimes talk about God and a "science of God," which appears contradictory. I suppose that Bucke was not overly concerned with "the hobgoblin of consistency" which Ralph Waldo Emerson said was the characteristic of lesser minds! It is quite possible, probably certain, that there is a higher synthesis between emergent evolution and the idea that God is the Creator of all. Emergent evolution may be the "way" He does it! In this sense, then, Cosmic Consciousness was "awaiting" sentient beings from the time of unicellular life in *potentia*. You will notice my Platonic bias. Be this as it may, Bucke was the first psychologist of the modern era who treated these issues of the emergence of self and Cosmic Consciousness (and perhaps, he was the best). Speaking of the great drama of the evolution of life and consciousness, Bucke waxes poetic when he says:

> As life arose in a world without life; as simple consciousness came into existence where before was mere vitality without perception; as self-consciousness leaping wide winged from simple consciousness soared over land and sea, so shall the race of man which has been thus established, continuing its beginningless and endless ascent, make other steps . . . and attain to yet higher life than any heretofore experienced or even conceived. [57]

Bucke makes me think of such "New Age" philosophers of today as David Spangler, who writes eloquently of the coming of a "transformation" in such recent books as *EMERGENCE: The Rebirth of the Sacred* (1984). Pierre Teilhard de Chardin also spoke of these things, in Christian terms, as the convergence upon the Omega-Point, or Christ, in such books as *CHRISTIANITY And EVOLUTION* (1969). Based upon my own brief experience of

Cosmic Consciousness, similar to Bucke's in some ways, I can say that were we to enter collectively into this illumined state, we would know what "rebirth" is. We would know what Jesus meant by the "Kingdom," and the Buddha by "Nirvana." We would know the prophesied age of peace of which all prophets spoke. It will come, however, not as self-conscious utopians of various stripes *plan*. The *enlightened ones* of our planet earth's history seem rather more to respect the human race's gradual process of development, nature's slow, and sometimes rapid ways, and God's transcendence over all. Even Jesus said that only "the Father" knows the day of "Christ's second coming." Bucke considered "the Christ" to be Cosmic Consciousness, as we shall see in his interpretation of St. Paul. The "second coming" would be the day when we all have "the mind which was in Christ Jesus," as the Apostle put it. Can you imagine a race of Christs and Buddhas on this planet? Richard Maurice Bucke, M.D. was creative genius enough to imagine such a possibility. In fact, he considered it to be not a possibility but a *certainty*. In the last forty centuries of human history, there have existed such men and women on planet earth and this is what Bucke says about them:

> The trait that distinguishes these people from other men is this: Their spiritual eyes have been opened and they have seen. The better known members of this group who, were they collected together, could be accommodated all at one time in a modern drawing-room, have created all great modern religions, beginning with Taoism and Buddhism, and speaking generally, have created, through religion and literature, modern civilization. [58]

Bucke gives in his book the most complete list of criteria of the Cosmic Conscious experience that has been given by any modern writer on the subject. Any case of Cosmic Consciousness has at least several of these characteristics. It forms an excellent basis for looking at the exemplars of the next section.

Bucke's Criteria of Cosmic Consciousness [59]
a. The subjective light: "The person, suddenly, without warning, has a sense of being immersed in a flame, or rose-coloured cloud. . ."
b. The moral elevation: "At the same time he is, as it were, bathed in an emotion of joy, assurance, triumph, 'salvation.'"
c. The intellectual illumination: ". . . there comes to the person an intellectual illumination quite impossible to describe. Like a flash there is a presented to his consciousness a clear concep-

tion (a vision) in outline of the meaning and drift of the universe."

d. The sense of immortality: "This is not an intellectual conviction, such as comes with the solution of a problem, nor is it an experience such as learning something unknown before. It is far more simple and elementary, and could better be compared to that certainty of distinct individuality, possessed by each one, which comes with and belongs to self-consciousness."

e. The loss of the fear of death: "With illumination the fear of death which haunts so many men and women at times all their lives falls off like an old cloak – not, however, as a result of reasoning – it simply vanishes."

f. The loss of the sense of sin: "The same may be said of sin. It is not that the person escapes from sin; but he no longer sees that there is any sin in the world from which to escape."

g. The suddenness, instantaneousness, of the awakening: "The instantaneousness of the illumination is one of its most striking features. It can be compared to a dazzling flash of lightning in a dark night, bringing the landscape which had been hidden into clear view."

h. The previous character of the man – intellectual, moral, and physical: "The previous character of the man who enters the new life is an important element in the case."

i. The age of illumination: "So is the age at which illumination occurs. Should we hear of a case of cosmic consciousness occurring at twenty, for instance, we should at first doubt the truth of the account, and if forced to believe it we should expect the man (if he lived) to be a veritable spiritual giant."

j. The added charm to the personality: "The added charm to the personality is always, it is believed, a feature in the case."

k. The transfiguration of the subject: "There seems to the writer to be sufficient evidence that, with cosmic consciousness, while it is actually present, and lasting (gradually passing away) a short time thereafer, a change takes place in the appearance of the subject of illumination. This change is similar to that caused in a person's appearance by great joy, but at times (that is, in pronounced cases) it seems to be much more marked than that. In these great cases in which illumination is intense the change in question is also intense and may amount to a veritable 'transfiguration.' "

BUCKE'S EXEMPLARS OF COSMIC CONSCIOUSNESS –
TEN CASES

(1) Gautama the Buddha

Siddhartha Gautama was born of immensely wealthy parents in India of the sixth century B.C. He grew up a prince, and he married at the age of nineteen. Ten years later, his only son was born. Shortly afterward, having seen the "three woes" of sickness, old age, and death, Gautama left home to devote himself to the quest for enlightenment, and the solution to the mystery of suffering. He studied first with the philosophers of his time, and then he practiced self mortification with the ascetics. Neither course worked for him. Then, he sat for forty days under a Bodhi tree, resisting the temptations of Mara, the Evil One, meditating until the "doors of enlightenment" swung open to him. Gautama entered Nirvana, or illumination. He became the Buddha, or "Enlightened One." Among the Buddha's first words after he had attained enlightenment were:

> As the rays of the sun drown the darkness of the world, so he who perseveres in his search will find the truth and the truth will enlighten him. [60]

Gautama sounds remarkably like Jesus who said "You shall know the truth and the truth shall set you free." Gautama the Buddha said that all the enlightened ones speak the *same truth*. Following his enlightenment, the Buddha expounded upon the "four noble truths": (1) the existence of suffering, (2) the cause of suffering, (3) the cessation of suffering, (4) the eightfold noble path that leads to the cessation of suffering. [61]

Basically, what is the Buddha saying? He sees suffering as inherent in the nature of the ego or self (i.e. individual existence apart from the rest of reality), and its cause to be *desire*, among other things, desire for the continuation of the ego or self. He sees that suffering can cease through the abnegation of desires and the "way to do this" is the eightfold noble path culminating in meditation which leads to Nirvana. Dr. Bucke would see all of this as the road from self to Cosmic Consciousness. Suffering seems to be inherent in the transition from the simple consciousness of the animal to the self-consciousness of the human being, as symbolized so beautifully in the Western tradition in the Garden of Eden myth. To "eat from the fruit of the Tree of Knowledge" is to form an ego. This entails the tremendous suffering of the expulsion from Eden! The only salvation from this suffering is Cosmic Consciousness. Dr. Bucke's predecessor in the history of ideas by about 2,500 years was Gautama the Buddha, who said:

> There is self and there is truth. Where self is, truth is not. Where truth is, self is not. Self is the fleeting error of samsara; it is individual separateness and that egotism which begets envy and hatred. Self is the yearning for pleasure and the lust after vanity. Truth is the correct comprehension of things; it is the permanent and everlasting, the real in existence, the bliss of righteousness . . . Perfect peace can dwell only where all vanity has disappeared. [62]

The following passages come from the Dhammapada, the oldest and most sacred scriptures of Buddhism:

Words of the Buddha

Earnestness is the path of immortality (Nirvana), thoughtlessness the path of death. Those who are in earnest do not die, those who are thoughtless are as if dead already. These wise people, meditative, steady, always possessed of strong powers, attain to Nirvana, the highest happiness. A Bhikshu (mendicant) who delights in reflection, who looks with fear on thoughtlessness, cannot fall away (from his perfect state) – he is close upon Nirvana. One is the road that leads to wealth, another the road that leads to Nirvana; if the Bhikshu, the disciple of the Buddha, has learnt this, he will not yearn for honor, he will strive after separation from the world.

Men who have no riches, who live on recognized food, who have perceived void and unconditioned freedom (Nirvana), their path is difficult to understand, like that of birds in the air. Some people are born

Bucke's Interpretations

It has been many times pointed out in this volume that earnestness of mind is a sine qua non to the attainment of cosmic consciousness. This verse here quoted brings out strongly this point.

After Confucius had seen Lao Tzu he said to his disciples: "I know birds can fly, fish swim and animals run, but the runner may be snared, the swimmer hooked and the flyer shot with the arrow. But there is the again; evil-doers go to hell; righteous people go to heaven; those who are free from all worldly desires attain Nirvana. If, like a shattered metal plate (gong), thou utter not, then thou hast reached Nirvana; contention is not known to thee. The Awakened call patience the highest penance, long-suffering the highest Nirvana; for he is not an anchorite (pravagita) who strikes others, he is not an ascetic (stramana) who insults others.

Hunger is the worst of diseases, the body the greatest of pains; if one knows this truly, that is Nirvana, the highest happiness. Health is the greatest of gifts; contentedness the best riches; trust is the best of relationships; Nirvana the highest happiness. He in whom a desire for the Ineffable (Nirvana) has sprung up, who is satisfied in his mind, and whose thoughts are not bewildered by love, he is called urdhvamsrotas (carried upward by the stream). The sages who injure nobody, and who always control their body, they will go to the unchangeable place (Nirvana), where, if they have gone, they will suffer no more. Those who are ever watchful, who study day and night, and who strive after Nirvana, their passions will come to an end. Cut out the love of self like an autumn lotus, with thy hand! Cherish the road of peace. Nirvana has been shown by Sugata (Buddha).

dragon; I cannot tell how he mounts on the wind through the clouds and rises to heaven. Today I have seen Lao Tzu and can only compare him to a dragon." We might say the same in our own way of nearly any of the persons mentioned in this book as having attained the cosmic sense.

The true place of the body and of the appetites in life can only be perceived by one having cosmic consciousness.[63]

Bucke concludes that Siddhartha Gautama was a true case of Cosmic Consciousness, and that Nirvana was the doctrine of the Cosmic Sense. As Bucke sees it, the whole of Buddhism is simply: "There is a mental state so happy, so glorious, that all the rest of life is worthless compared to it, a pearl of great price to buy which a wise man willingly sells all that he has; this state can be achieved."

(2) Jesus the Christ

Jesus was born a Jew nearly two thousand years ago in the time of King Herod when Israel was a Roman protectorate. His father was a carpenter, and his mother, a young Jewess. The circumstances of his birth in a stable in Bethlehem are well known. Jesus, except for unusual intelligence and precociousness, grew up as any other Jewish youth. He was trained in the synagogue in the Jewish scriptures and tradition, and by his father in the trade of carpentry. It was at age thirty, or so the scriptures have it, that Jesus was to undergo a profound transformation that began his career as a preacher and miracle worker. In the Biblical account, Jesus went down to the Jordan River to receive Baptism from John the Baptist and it was here that the "heavens opened":

> And straightway coming out of the water, he saw the heavens rent asunder, and the Spirit as a dove descending upon him: and a voice came out of the heavens saying thou art my beloved Son, in thee I am well pleased.[64]

Bucke interprets this passage as a description of the coming of the Cosmic Sense, which is spontaneous, sudden, and as if "a veil" were being torn from the mind's eye, letting vision come through. St. John of the Cross said: ". . . it is as if God drew back some of the many veils and coverings that are before it, so that it might see what he is."[65]

It is interesting that Jesus interprets this new state of being in the personal language of his Jewish culture as the "Kingdom of God," as contrasted with Gautama's non-personal view of this radically new consciousness as "Nirvana." Bucke would claim that Jesus and Gautama experienced one and the same thing: Cosmic Consciousness. These men of the Cosmic Sense stand spiritually at the summit of the human race and are considered the "founders" of new world religions: Buddhism and Christianity. Bucke looks at some passages of the Gospels in terms of his theory, as he looked at some lines of the Dhammapada. The following are words reported to have been spoken by Jesus of Nazareth:

Words of Jesus

Blessed are the poor in spirit for theirs is the kingdom of heaven.

Bucke's Interpretation

A proud man is hardly likely to acquire the Cosmic Sense.

But seek ye first his kingdom (the kingdom of God) and his righteousness, and all these things shall be added unto you.

Let a man have the Cosmic Sense and he will not be likely to worry about worldly goods. He will probably have all he wants, be his possessions ever so little.

Verily I say unto you, among them that are born of women there hath not arisen greater than John the Baptist; yet he that is but little in the kingdom of heaven is greater than he.

Among the merely self-conscious (among "those who are born of women" distinguishing between those who are not and those who are "born anew") there are none greater than John. But the least of those who have the Cosmic Sense is greater than he.

Unto you is given to know the mysteries of the kingdom of heaven, but to them it is not given.

Through their personal intimacy with Jesus they saw and realized the preterhuman loftiness of his mind. They saw, in him, the kingdom of heaven – the higher life.

The kingdom of heaven is likened unto a man who sowed good seed in his field; but while men slept his enemy came and sowed tares also among the wheat, and went away. The kingdom of heaven is like unto a mustard seed which a man took and sowed in his field; which indeed is less than all seeds; but when it is grown, it is greater than the herbs, and becometh a tree, so that the birds of the heaven come and lodge in the branches thereof.

The antagonism between the Cosmic Sense and the merely self-conscious mind and the final subjection of the latter to the former. A perfect image of the initial apparent insignificancy of the Cosmic Sense as it exists in one of a few obscure individuals, and of its ultimate overwhelming preponderance in view both of the universal influence of the teaching of these (say Gautama, Jesus, Paul and Mohammed), and more especially in view of the inevitable universality of the Cosmic Sense in the future.

The kingdom of heaven is like unto leaven, which a woman took and hid in three measures of meal, till it was all leavened.

If possible a still more exact simile – the Cosmic Sense leavens the individual, and is today leavening the world.

The kingdom of heaven is like unto a treasure hidden in the field; which a man found and hid; and in his joy he goeth and selleth all that he hath and buyeth that field.

Men who have the Cosmic Sense give up everything for it – this whole volume is proof of it.

The kingdom of heaven is like unto a man that is a merchant seeking goodly pearls; and having found one pearl of great price he went and sold all he had and bought it.

The same statement in other language.

I will give unto thee the keys of the kingdom of heaven; and whatsoever thou shalt bind on earth shall be bound in heaven and whatsoever thou shalt loose on earth shall be loosed in heaven.

The Cosmic Sense is the final arbiter of good and ill. Jesus seems to have looked forward to the establishment of a school or sect the members of which should possess the Cosmic Sense.

It is easier for a camel to go through a needle's eye than for a rich man to enter the kingdom of God.

The writer has found no instance of a man absorbed in money-making entering into Cosmic Consciousness. The whole spirit of the former is antagonistic to the latter.

The kingdom of heaven is like unto a man that is a householder, which went out early in the morning to hire laborers into his vineyard. And when he had agreed with the laborers for a penny a day he sent them into his vineyard. And he went out about the third hour and saw others standing in the market-place idle; and to them he said: Go ye also into the vineyard and whatsoever is right I will give you. And they went their way.

The Cosmic Sense is not given for work done or according to merit, as this can be estimated by the self-conscious mind. Why should Jesus, Yepes, and Behmen be chosen, and Goethe, Newton and Aristotle left?

And again he went out about the sixth and the ninth hour and did likewise. And about the eleventh hour he went out and found others standing: And he saith unto them: Why stand ye here all the day idle? They say unto him: Because no man hath hired us.

He sayeth unto them: Go ye also into the vineyard. And when even was come the lord of the vineyard saith unto his steward: Call the laborers and give them their hire, beginning from the last unto the first. And when they came that were hired about the eleventh hour, they received every man a penny.

And when the first came, they supposed they would receive more; and they likewise received every man a penny. And when they received it, they murmured against the householder, saying: These first have spent but one hour, and thou hast made them equal unto us, which have borne the burden of the day and the scorching heat. But he answered and said to one of them: Friend, I do thee no wrong: didst thou not agree with me for a penny? Take up that which is thine, and go thy way: it is my will to give unto this last even as unto thee. Is it not lawful for me to do what I will with mine own? or is thine eye evil, because I am good? So the last shall be first and the first last.

And being asked by the Pharisees when the kingdom of God cometh he answered them and It is not outside but inside. It is a part (a faculty) of the mind itself.[66]

said: the kingdom of God cometh
not with observation; neither
shall they say, Lo here! or there,
for lo, the kingdom of God is
within you.

Bucke concludes, as if we needed proof, that Jesus like Gautama
before him, was a man who had attained the Cosmic Sense. His
teachings come from the Cosmic Sense and they lead men toward
Cosmic Consciousness, or as Jesus would call it, the Kingdom of
God.

(3) Paul

Paul, or Saul of Tarsus, as he was known before his conversion
experience, was an Orthodox Jew born in a Greek land of the
Roman Empire. The date of his birth was approximately A.D. 10
or 12. He never met Jesus of Nazareth during the latter's lifetime, and, in fact, he was among the chief of the persecutors of the
early Jewish Christian sect. He says: "I persecuted this way unto
the death, binding and delivering into prison both men and
women." As regards Paul's illumination experience, we are told
that:

> As I journeyed it came to pass that he drew nigh unto Damascus: and
> suddenly there shown round him a light out of heaven; and he fell
> upon the earth and heard a voice saying unto him, Saul, Saul, why
> persecutest thou me? And he said, Who art thou Lord? And he said, I
> am Jesus whom thou persecutest: but rise and enter into the city, and it
> shall be told thee what thou must do. And the men that journeyed
> with him stood speechless, hearing the voice, but beholding no man.
> And Saul arose from the earth; and when his eyes were opened, he saw
> nothing; and they led him by the hand into Damascus. And he was
> three days without sight, and did neither eat nor drink. [67]

This illumination experience was indeed the turning point in
Paul's life (the name-change from Saul to Paul indicates, as do
other name changes in the Bible, e.g. Abram to Abraham or Jacob
to Israel, a transformation of consciousness and being), and the
chief persecutor of the fledgling Christian sect becomes its most
outspoken exponent, and, moreover, the apostle to the Gentiles.
The following are words of Paul beginning with his account of his
own illumination fourteen years later.

Words of Paul

I must needs glory, though it is not expedient; but I will come to visions and revelations of the Lord. I know a man in Christ, fourteen years ago (whether in the body I know not or whether out of the body I know not; God knoweth) such a one caught up even to the third heaven. And I know such a man (whether in the body or apart from the body I know not: God knoweth) how that he was caught up into a paradise and heard *unspeakable words*, which it is not lawful for a man to utter. On behalf of such a one will I glory; but on mine own behalf I will not glory, save in my weaknesses. For if I should desire to glory I shall not be foolish; for I shall speak the truth; but I forbear, lest any man should account of me above that which he seeth me to be or heareth from me. And by reason of the exceeding greatness of the revelations – wherefore that I should not be exalted overmuch there was given me a thorn in the flesh, a messenger of Satan to buffet me.

For this we may unto you by the word of the Lord, that we are alive, that are left unto the coming of the Lord, shall in no wise precede them that are fallen asleep. For the Lord himself shall descend from heaven, with a shout, with the voice of the archangel, and with the trump of God, and the dead in Christ shall rise first: Then we that are alive, that are left, shall together

Bucke's Interpretation

"Christ" is Paul's name for Cosmic Consciousness.

Unspeakable words, to Whitman: "When I undertake to tell the best I find I cannot, my tongue is ineffectual on its pivots; my breath will not be obedient to its organs; I become a dumb man."

The usual assurances of immortality that belong to Cosmic Consciousness.

with them be caught up in the clouds, to meet the Lord in the air; and so shall we ever be with the Lord. Wherefore comfort one another with these words.

For I make known to you, brethren, as touching the gospel which was preached by me, that it is not after man. For neither did I receive it from man. For neither did I receive it from man, nor was I taught it, but it came to me through the revelation of Jesus Christ.

As regards his "Gospel," Paul was instructed by the Cosmic Sense only.

But when it was the good pleasure of God, who separated me, even from my mother's womb, and called me through His grace to reveal His Son in me, that I might preach him among the gentiles; immediately I conferred not with flesh and blood; neither went I up to Jerusalem to them which were apostles before me; but I went away into Arabia; and again I returned unto Damascus.

He knew, however, enough about Jesus and his teachings to be able to recognize (when it came to him) that the teachings of the Cosmic Sense were practically identical with the teachings of Jesus.

For as in Adam all die, so also in Christ shall all be made alive. But each in his own order, Christ the first fruits; then they that are Christ's, at his coming. Then cometh the end when he shall deliver up the kingdom to God, even the Father; when he shall have abolished all rule and all authority and power.

A comparison between the self-conscious and the Cosmic Conscious states. Self-consciousness, he says, the Adamic state, is a condition of death. With "Christ" begins true life which shall spread and become universal . . .

If any man is in Christ he is a new creature; the old things are passed away; behold they are become new.

No expression could be more clear cut, more perfect. The man who enters Cosmic Consciousness is really a new creature, and all his surroundings "become new" – take on a new face and meaning.

There is therefore now no con-
demnation to them that are in
Christ Jesus. For the law of the
Spirit of life in Christ Jesus
made me free from the law of
sin and death. For what the law
could not do, in that it was weak
through the flesh, God, sending
His own Son in the likeness of
sinful flesh and as an offering for
sin, condemned sin in the flesh;
that the ordinance of the law
might be fulfilled in us, who
walk not after the flesh but after
the Spirit. For they that are after
the flesh do mind the things of
the flesh; but they that are after
the Spirit the things of the Spirit.
For the mind of the flesh is
death; but the mind of the Spirit
is life and peace . . .

In Cosmic Consciousness there
is no sense of sin nor of death,
the person feels that this last is
an incident in continuous life.
The merely self-conscious man
cannot, by the keeping of the
"law" or in any other way, destroy sin or the sense of sin, but,
"Christ" – i.e. the Cosmic Sense,
can and does accomplish both.

And we know that to them
that love God all things work
together for good . . .

An expression of the optimism which belongs to Cosmic
Consciousness. . .[68]

In the case of Paul, there are many of the characteristics of the
coming to Cosmic Consciousness, including the suddenness of its
onset, the subjective light, in this case, very strongly manifested,
the intellectual illumination, moral exultation, and the absolute
conviction of immortality, and the extinction of the sense of sin
and the fear of death. The Christ, or Cosmic Sense, must have
been with him, for Paul literally put Christianity on the map of the
Roman world.

(4) Moses

Bucke, curiously enough, places Moses, the literal key figure of
the Old Testament and the Jewish religion, in the category of
"imperfect and doubtful instances of Cosmic Consciousness." His
explanation of this is the fact that he is a figure of four millenia
ago, and we have no certainty of his actual existence. We do have
with absolute certainty the account given in the *Book of Exodus* of
the story of Moses the liberator and lawgiver, who was saved

from premature death by the ingeniousness of his mother who put him in a basket and floated him upon the Nile to avert the evil decree of Pharaoh that all male newborn Hebrews be put to death. He was found by Pharaoh's daughter, who took him to be an answer to prayer, and was raised in Pharaoh's court as a prince. You know the story of how Moses slays the Egyptian, and escapes into the Sinai desert. There he becomes a shepherd and has a mystical experience at a "burning bush" which was to transform his life, and to change the course of the history of his people, the Israelites, and all human history, for that matter. Doubtful case indeed! The following is a direct quotation from scripture of Moses' encounter with God, whom he knew as YHWH, on Mt. Horeb from the burning bush. It comes from Exodus, chapter three, of the Hebrew Bible:

> Now Moses was keeping the flock of Jethro his father-in-law, the priest of Midian; and he led the flock to the farthest end of the wilderness, and came to the mountain of God, unto Horeb. And the angel of the LORD appeared to him in a flame of fire out of the midst of a bush, and said: "Moses, Moses," And he said: "Here am I." And He said "Draw not nigh hither; put off thy shoes from off thy feet, for the place whereon thou standest is holy ground."[69]

God tells Moses that He is the God of Moses' ancestors, the God of Abraham, the God of Isaac, and the God of Jacob. He tells Moses that He will deliver the children of Israel (the descendants of Jacob, renamed Israel: "He who wrestles with God") from their affliction in Egypt into a land flowing with milk and honey (Canaan). Moses requests that this voice speaking out of the burning bush reveal its name to him.

> And Moses said unto God: "Behold, when I come unto the children of Israel, and shall say unto them: The God of your fathers hath sent me unto you; and they shall say to me: What is His name? What shall I say unto them"? And God said unto Moses: "I AM THAT I AM"; and He said: "Thus shalt thou say unto the children of Israel: I AM hath sent me unto you."[70]

Although Bucke does not make his usual commentaries on the "imperfect and doubtful instances" of Cosmic Consciousness, this can obviously be viewed as a dialogue between Self and Cosmic Consciousness taking place within Moses. It has all the marks of the Cosmic Conscious experience: the suddenness of appearance, the subjective light, in this case exteriorized in projection, the intellectual elevation, the moral exultation, and so on. Without a doubt Moses *was* one of the greatest instances of Cosmic Consciousness in human history. The Jewish tradition regards Moses as the greatest prophet, the only man who "viewed God face to face." On a second trip to the "top of the mountain," Moses came down with the Ten Commandments, the later-to-be moral code of both Judaism and its offspring, Christianity. It was to Moses that the Most High Name of God was given: I AM. This connotes that God is the Very Being and Essence of the Universe. He is the I AM in every being including the *I am* that we are. This means, if it is true, that we live in a universe in which consciousness-in-itself precedes what we call "matter," and will outlive it. In fact, it means that consciousness created matter. A *mind* such as ours, except on an infinitely greater plane, willed the space-time-matter-energy universe into being and becoming, from a single point of light which contained all the energy that was, and is, and will be to the "grand explosion" into the universe as we know it in all its beauty and complexity. This is the account given in the Kabbala, the mystical teaching of Judaism, and it agrees remarkably with the modern "big bang" theory of the origin of the universe. In "the mind" of Ain Soph (Without Limit), the Godhead, the *intention to create* shattered the prevailing nothingness with the awesome glory of creation. This creation has culminated in the appearance on a small planet of a being who can envision his Creator. That's us.

Moses envisioned his Creator as I AM THAT I AM. YHWH, "He causes to be" is given slightly later. These sacred names are considered "too awesome" in the Jewish tradition, and are replaced by "Adonai" or "Lord," or "Adoshem" or "The Name" in prayerbooks. The Christian "God the Father" is even further removed from the original revelation. Removing God from "His" original meaning as "I AM" tends to project "Him" into the literal sky for the simple minded and into the metaphysical sky for the complex minded. But for the shepherd-mystic-prophet, Moses, God was "I AM" who "spoke" in the solitude of Mt. Horeb. He was Being-Itself. Consider that the patriarchs, Abraham, Isaac, and Jacob, knew God as "El Shaddai," or "Mountain God," and you will realize what a quantum leap in theological and mystical insight was made by Moses that day he encountered: I AM THAT I AM. His predecessors located God spatially on a mountain as an "El," or "Power" of that mountain. Moses knew God as Existence Absolute, as much in your heart as on a mountain top or a distant galaxy. The Hasids say "There is no place empty of Him."

Moses, as was true of Jesus, "heard" a "subjective voice." This is characteristic of the religious history of the Middle Eastern monotheistic faiths. The Far East gave rise to more monistic conceptions. There are two ways of relating to Cosmic Consciousness: impersonal and personal.

(5) Dante

Dante Allighieri was born in 1265 and died in 1321. Not much is known about Dante's life, but a contemporary of his said that even as a young man in Florence, he was:

> Taken by the sweetness of knowing the truth of the things concealed in heaven, and finding no other pleasure dearer to him in life, he left all other worldly care and gave himself to this alone, and, that no part of philosophy might remain unseen by him, he plunged with acute intellect into the deepest recesses of theology, and so far succeeded in his design that, caring nothing for heat or cold, or watchings, or fastings, or any other bodily discomforts, by assiduous study he came to know of the divine essence and of the other separate intelligences all that the human intellect can comprehend. [71]

Bucke comments that this kind of thoughtful, studious, and earnest nature that led to a life of poetic genius was typical of the kind of men who came to Cosmic Consciousness. Dante's magnum opus, which he wrote in exile from Florence, was the *Divine Comedy*. It is an account of his own inner journey, in concrete metaphor, through hell, purgatory, and paradise. Hell is the place of utter hopelessness. Purgatory is the place where the imperfect human soul is purified until it is worthy to ascend to heaven. Paradise is, at least in Bucke's conception, Dante's word for the Cosmic Sense. It has been called the Kingdom of Heaven, Nirvana, Brahman, and so on in various religious traditions of the world. In his journey through hell and purgatory, Dante is led by his guide, Virgil. But it is Beatrice, the divine feminine, who leads Dante on his final ascent into paradise. The following quotation from *Paradisio* is accompanied by Bucke's interpretation.

Dante's Words	*Bucke's Interpretation*
A lady appeared to me robed with the color of living flame. I turned me to the left with confidence with which the little	The Cosmic Sense robed with the subjective light. At the threshold of the new sense, Virgil (the type here of human

child runs to his mother when he is frightened, or when he is troubled, to Virgil: "Less than a drachm of blood remains in me that does not tremble, I recognize the signals of the ancient flame." But Virgil had left us deprived of himself.

And as my face stretched upward my eyes saw Beatrice. Beneath her veil and beyond the stream she seemed to me more to surpass her ancient self than she surpassed the others here when she was here.

faculty short of it) leaves Dante. Not that simple and self-consciousness leave us when we enter Cosmic Consciousness, *but they do cease to guide us* – "the eyesight has another eyesight, the hearing another hearing, and the voice another voice."[72]

Bucke completed his book, *Cosmic Consciousness*, when Carl Jung, the great Swiss psychiatrist, was only twenty-three years old and still a medical student in Zurich. If Bucke had lived in a somewhat later time, he surely would have availed himself of the vast writings and researches of Jung. He would have realized that Dante, in encountering Beatrice was not yet experiencing Cosmic Consciousness, or even the Self in the Jungian sense, but the *anima*, or the mysterious inner feminine in the male who is a guide to the deeper unconscious. Virgil, who had taken Dante through hell and purgatory, was a *wise man* figure who must indeed "bow out" and transfer one to the deeper entity within one, or the *numinous anima*. This is how Jung speaks about the anima:

> Whenever she appears, in dreams, visions, and fantasies she takes on pesonalized form, thus demonstrating the factor she embodies possesses all the outstanding characteristics of a feminine being. She is not an invention of the conscious mind, but a spontaneous production of the unconscious. Nor is she a substitute for the mother. On the contrary, there is every likelihood that the numinous qualities which make the mother imago so dangerously powerful stem from the collective archetype of the Anima, which is incarnated anew in every male child.[73]

Beatrice is an anima figure, as Virgil is a wise man figure in the deep unconscious of Dante. Here, as in other places, there are serious gaps in Bucke's psychology which skips from conscious self, or ego, to the illumined state of Cosmic Consciousness. Being a pre-Freudian, he largely ignores the personal unconscious, the repressed early history of the individual, and being a pre-Jungian, he omits the collective unconscious and its great archetypes, and skips all the way to the "beyond Jungian" state of Cosmic Consciousness. Great gaps need to be filled in that bridge of the "immense distance" between conscious self, or ego, and Cosmic Consciousness, *even though* this gap seems to be almost instantly jumped in the spontaneous illumination experience whenever and wherever it occurs. As one who has had both the Cosmic Conscious experience, and one who has suffered the long ordeals of the inward journey (hell and purgatory), I can report to you that the "distance" bridged between ego self and Cosmic Consciousness is *immense*. By Grace, it occurs in a fraction of a second, but by inner work, it is many years! Bucke is speaking more to the spontaneous experience of "illumination" than to the incredibly slow process of the inner journey. Dante, who knew both, recognizes both the fantastically slow process of the journey through hell and purgatory (within oneself) and the marvelous spontaneity and instantaneousness of the transport into *paradise*. Bucke rejoins Dante, who is now truly ascended into paradise, Beatrice, the divine feminine, having led the way.

Dante's Words	*Bucke's Interpretation*
The glory of Him who moves everything penetrates through the universe and shines in one part more, in another less. In the heaven that receives most of its light I have been, and have seen things which he who descends from there above neither knows how nor is able to recount.	St. Paul heard "unspeakable words," and Whitman when he "tried to tell the best" of that which he had seen became dumb.[74]

Finally, Dante ascends to the highest heaven, having come all the way from the "dark wood" to the "heavenly rose." The book was twenty-one years in the writing from 1300 to 1321, and Bucke surmises that the poet wrote it *after* his illumination. It is, perhaps, possible that Dante wrote the *Divine Comedy* parallel with his inner journey, or at least, that it came from his personal journals of these years. Dante Allighieri was surely a case of Cosmic Consciousness, and his poetic epic is one of the truest tellings of the story of the soul's journey.

(6) John Yepes (St. John of the Cross)

John Yepes was born in 1542 and died in 1591. He was born in

Spain. His father died when he was a child and his mother was left very poor. John studied with the Jesuits, and at twenty-one he took religious orders among the Carmelite Friars in Medina. He became a priest at twenty-five. In his early thirties, he passed through what he called "dark nights of the soul," periods of profound despair and inner troubles. At one point, "he seemed to see hell open, ready to swallow him up." He knew well from personal experience, the Inferno and Purgatorio of Dante Allighieri. This first "dark night" was followed by a period of illumination:

> After some time certain rays of light, comfort and divine sweetness scattered these mists and translated the soul of the servant of God into a paradise of interior delights and heavenly sweetness. [75]

This was followed by another "dark night of the soul." The first dark night, he called the "dark night of the senses"; the second, even more terrible, he called the "dark night of the spirit." Following this, John Yepes experienced a still more perfect illumination and happiness, which Bucke would say is characteristic of the Cosmic Conscious state.

> A certain brightness darted from his countenance on many occasions – especially when he came from the altar or from prayer. It is said that a heavenly light at times shone from his countenance. [76]

For originating or adhering to certain monastic forms, he was imprisoned for several months, and it was during this imprisonment that John entered into Cosmic Consciousness. This is how one of his biographers describes it:

> His cell became filled with light seen by the bodily eye. One night the friar who kept him went as usual to see that his prisoner was safe, and witnessed the heavenly light with which the cell was flooded. He did not stop to consider it, but hurried to the prior, thinking that someone in the house had keys to open the doors of the prison. The prior, with two religious went at once to the prison, but on his entering the room through which the prison was approached, the light vanished. The prior, however, entered the cell, and, finding it dark, opened the lantern with which he had provided himself, and asked the prisoner who had given him light. St. John answered him, and said that no one in the house had done so, that no one could do it and that there was neither candle nor lamp in the cell. The prior made no reply and went away, thinking that the gaoler had made a mistake.

> St. John, at a later time, told one of his brethren that the heavenly light which God so mercifully sent him, lasted the night through, and that it

filled his soul with joy and made the night pass as if it were but a moment. When his imprisonment was drawing to a close he heard our Lord say to him, as it were out of the soft light that was around him, "John I am here; be not afraid; I will set thee free."

A few moments later, while making his escape from the prison of the monastery, it is said that he had a repetition of the experience as follows:

He saw a wonderful light, out of which came a voice saying, "follow me." He followed, and the light moved before him towards the wall which was on the bank, and then, he knew not how, he found himself on the summit of it without effort or fatigue. He descended into the street, and then the light vanished. So brilliant was it, that for two or three days afterwards, so he confessed at a later time, his eyes were weak, as if he had been looking at the sun in its strength.[77]

After his illumination, Yepes wrote several books to try to convey to others the *new life* that had come to him. The following passages are some examples from his writings with commentaries from Bucke in terms of the theory of Cosmic Consciousness:

Yepes' Words

It is clearly necessary for the soul, aiming at its own supernatural transformation, to be in darkness and far removed from all that relates to its natural condition, the sensual and rational parts. The supernatural is that which transcends nature, and, therefore, that which is natural remains below. Inasmuch as this union and transformation are not cognizable by sense or human power, the soul must be completely and voluntarily empty of all that can enter into it, of every affection and inclination, so far as it concerns itself.

The more the soul strives to become blind and annihilated as to all interior and exterior things, the more it will be filled with faith and love and hope. But this love at times is neither comprehended nor felt, because it does not establish itself in the senses

Bucke's Interpretations

This is the doctrine of the suppression and effacement of thought, and the subjection of desire taught by Hindu illuminati from the time of the Buddha until today – a doctrine undoubtedly resting upon actual experience.

So Balzac says that self-consciousness while glorious for what it has done, is at the same time baneful, because it precludes man from entering the Cosmic Conscious life, which leads to the infinite – which can alone explain God.

with tenderness, but in the soul with fortitude, with greater courage and resolution than before; though it sometimes overflows into the senses, and shows itself tender and gentle. In order, then, to attain to this love, joy and delight which visions effect, it is necessary that the soul should have fortitude and be fortified, so as to abide willingly in emptiness and darkness, and to lay the foundation of its love and delight on what it neither sees nor feels, on what it cannot see nor feel – namely, on God incomprehensible and supreme. Our way to Him is therefore, of necessity, in self-denial.

Though it be true, as I have said, that God is always in every soul, bestowing upon it and preserving to it, by His presence, its natural being, yet for all this He does not always communicate the supernatural life. For this is given only by love and grace, to which all souls do not attain, and those who do, do not in the same degree, for some rise to higher degrees of love than others. That soul, therefore, has greater communion with God which is most advanced in love – that is, whose will is most conformable to the will of God. And that soul which has reached perfect conformity and resemblance is perfectly united with, and supernaturally transformed in God. For which cause, therefore, as I have already explained, the more the soul cleaves to created things, relying on its own

The distinction between self-conscious life even at its best and the life of Cosmic Consciousness. [78]

strength, by habit and inclination, the less is it disposed for
this union, because it does not
completely resign itself into the
hands of God, that He may
transform it supernaturally.

Yepes' thought is that God is always existent within the human
soul but in a passive or unconscious state. What Yepes calls the
waking of God within the soul is what Bucke terms "Cosmic
Consciousness."

(7) Jacob Boehme

Jacob Boehme was born in Germany in the year 1575 and died in
1624. His only education was in a town school. He later appren-
ticed as a shoemaker. In 1599, he settled in Gorlitz, a master
shoemaker, and married Katharina, the daughter of the town
butcher.

The humble shoemaker, Boehme, had two distinct illuminations. The first was in 1600 at the age of twenty-five, and his
biographer describes it as follows:

Sitting one day in his room his eyes fell upon a burnished pewter dish,
which reflected the sunshine with such marvelous splendor that he fell
into an inward ecstasy, and it seemed to him as if he could now look
into the principles and deepest foundation of things. He believed that it
was only a fancy, and in order to banish it from his mind he went out
upon the green. But here he remarked that he gazed into the very heart
of things, the very herbs and grass, and that actual nature harmonized
with what he had inwardly seen. He said nothing of this to anyone,
but praised and thanked God in silence. He continued in the honest
practice of his craft, was attentive to his domestic affairs, and was on
terms of good-will with all men.[79]

In Bucke's view the first illumination was not complete, and
Boehme did not really attain to true cosmic consciousness on that
day; "he passed into the dawn but not into the perfect day." Ten
years later, at the age of thirty-five, Boehme entered into the
Cosmic Conscious state. In his own words:

The gate was opened to me that in one quarter of an hour I saw and
knew more than if I had been many years together at a university, at
which I exceedingly admired and thereupon turned my praise to God

for it. For I saw and knew the being of all beings, the byss and abyss and the eternal generation of the Holy Trinity, the descent and the original of the world and of all creatures through the divine wisdom: I knew and saw in myself all the three worlds, namely, (1) the divine (angelical and paradisical) (2) and the dark (the original nature of the fire) and (3) then the external and visible world (being a procreation or external birth from both the internal and spiritual worlds). And I saw and knew the whole working essence, in the evil and the good, and the original and the existence of each of them; and likewise how the fruitful-bearing-womb of eternity brought forth. So that I did not only greatly wonder at it but did also exceedingly rejoice. [80]

Bucke says that "As utterances of the Cosmic Sense all the writings of Boehme are well-nigh totally unintelligible to the merely self-conscious mind." Nonetheless, like those of Paul, Dante, Balzac, Whitman, and others of the Cosmic Sense, they are a veritable gold mine of wisdom and insight. The following passages are quoted from the writings of Boehme with Bucke's comments:

Boehme's Words

If you will behold your own self and the outer world, and what is taking place therein, you will find that you, with regard to your external being, are that external world.

Not I, the I that I am, know these things: But God knows them in me.

He alone, therefore, in whom Christ exists and lives, is a Christian, a man in whom Christ has been raised out of the wasted flesh of Adam.

If thou climbest up this ladder on which I climb up into the deep of God, as I have done, then thou climbest well: I am not come to this meaning, or to this work and knowledge

Bucke's Interpretations

"Strange and hard that paradox true I give, objects gross and the unseen soul are one," and Gautama, Plotinus and Carpenter are all equally definite upon the same point.

"The other I am." "'Tis thee (myself) that for myself I praise. The recognition of the duplex individuality of the Cosmic Conscious person – i.e. the self-conscious self and the Cosmic Conscious self.

"Christ" here was used as Paul uses the word, as a name – that is, of Cosmic Consciousness.

None of those who have attained Cosmic Consciousness "sought" for it; they could not, for they did not know there was such a thing. But it would seem that all the pronounced cases through my own reason, or through my own will and purpose; neither have I sought this knowledge, nor so much as know anything concerning it. I sought only for the heart of God, therein to hide myself from the tempestuous storms of the devil.

were men who earnestly sought for the "heart of God" – i.e., for the highest and best life.[81]

If this author may introduce a personal note at this point, the statements of Jacob Boehme and Richard Bucke concerning the spontaneity and unplanned nature of the experience of Cosmic Consciousness were totally true in my own case which is described in the preface. I did not "seek for" Cosmic Consciousness because I had no way in the world to know that there was such a thing. And even if I had read the accounts of the mystics, I would not have understood them in the least, because the language of the self-conscious mind or intellect can never truly express the experience of Cosmic Consciousness. As Boehme said that his "own reason, . . . will and purpose" could not bring him to this, I fully concur. As a youth, however, I did seek for *something*, I knew not just what, that gave meaning and purpose to existence, and had read very widely in philosophy, for example, from Bertrand Russell to Alfred North Whitehead, and from Ludwig Wittgenstein to Henri Bergson. However, no philosophy that has ever been or will ever be, in the nature of the case, will raise the human soul "up the ladder," as Bucke puts it, from self to Cosmic Consciousness. Even the much touted "cognitive psychologists" of today, whether of Piagetian, of Chomskian, or other variety, have not the slightest inkling, based upon their writings, of a state of consciousness as far beyond the rational mind or intellect as waking consciousness surpasses sleep in terms of awareness. The philosophers and cognitivists, as highly as they think of themselves, are beings who inhabit the cave of shadows in Plato's metaphor as far as Cosmic Consciousness is concerned. Plato himself was master as well as philosopher, that is, a likely candidate for the status of Cosmic Consciousness. If he did not walk in that realm, he had a definite glimmer of it. I will end this section with a passage from a dialogue between a scholar and a master from Boehme's writings:

Scholar. – What shall be after this world, when all things perish?

Master. – The material substance only ceaseth – viz., the four elements, the sun, moon, and stars, and then the inward world will be wholly visible and manifest. But whatsoever hath been wrought by the spirit in this time, whether evil or good, I say, every work shall separate itself there in a spiritual manner, either into the eternal light, or into the eternal darkness; for that which is born from each will penetrateth again into that which is like itself. [82]

(8) William Blake

William Blake, the poet–artist–mystic, was born in 1757 and died in 1827. W. M. Rossetti in his admirable biographical sketch helps us to answer the question: Was Blake a case of Cosmic Consciousness?

The difficulty of Blake's biographers, subsequent to 1863, the date of Mr. Gilchrist's book, is of a different kind altogether. It is the difficulty of stating sufficiently high the extraordinary claims of Blake to admiration and reverence, without slurring over those other considerations which need to be plainly and fully set forth if we would obtain any real idea of the man as he was – of his total unlikeness to his contemporaries, of his amazing genius and noble performances in two arts, of the height by which he transcended other men, and the incapacity which he always evinced for performing at all what others accomplish easily. He could do vastly more than they, but he could seldom do the like. By some unknown process he had soared to the top of a cloud-capped Alp, while they were crouching in the valley: But to reach a middle station on the mountain was what they could readily manage step by step, while Blake found that ordinary achievement impracticable. He could not and he would not do it; the want of will, or rather the utter alienation of will, the resolve to soar (which was natural to him), and not to walk (which was unnatural and repulsive), constituted or counted instead of an actual want of power.

Rapt in a passionate yearning, he realized, even on this earth and in his mortal body, a species of Nirvana: his whole faculty, his whole personality, the very essence of his mind and mould, attained to absorption into his ideal ultimate, into that which Dante's profound phrase designates "il Ben dell' intelletto."

In the preface to "The Jerusalem" Blake speaks of that composition as having been "dictated" to him, and other expressions of his prove that he regarded it rather as a revelation of which he was the scribe than as the product of his own inventing and fashioning brain. Blake considered it "the grandest poem that this world contains;" adding, "I may praise it, since I dare not pretend to be any other than the secretary – the authors are in eternity." In an earlier letter (April 25th, 1803) he said: "I have written this poem from immediate dictation, twelve or sometimes twenty or thirty lines at a time, without premeditation, and even against my will."

Blake had a mental intuition, inspiration, or revelation – call it what we will; it was as real to his spiritual eye as a material object could be to his bodily eye; and no doubt his bodily eye, the eye of a designer or painter with a great gift of invention and composition, was far more than normally ready at following the dictate of the spiritual eye, and seeing, with an almost instantaneously creative and fashioning act, the visual semblance of a visionary essence.

His unworldliness, extreme as it was, did not degenerate into ineptitude. He apprehended the requirements of practical life, was prepared to meet them in a resolute and diligent spirit from day to day, and could on occasions display a full share of sagacity. He was of lofty and independent spirit, not caring to refute any odd stories that were current regarding his conduct or demeanor, neither parading nor concealing his poverty, and seldom accepting any sort of aid for which he could not and did not supply a full equivalent.[83]

In other words, Blake was clearly a man who had come to Cosmic Consciousness which gave him Divine vision and inspiration in his poetry and art. He called Cosmic Consciousness the "imaginative vision." Quoting Blake's own words, with Bucke's comments:

Blake's Words	*Bucke's Interpretations*
The world of imagination is the world of eternity. It is the divine bosom into which we shall all go after the death of the vegetated body. This world of imagination is infinite and eternal, whereas the world of generation, of vegetation, is finite and temporal. There exist in that eternal world the permanent realities of everything which we see reflected in this vegetable glass of nature.	Blake's name for Cosmic Consciousness. With this paragraph compare Whitman's "I swear I think now that everything without exception has an eternal soul! The trees rooted in the ground! The weeds of the sea have! The animals."
We are in a world of generation and death, and this world we must cast off if we would be artists such as Raphael, Michel –	The world of self-consciousness. Balzac says: (Self-conscious) "Man judges all things by abstractions – good, evil,

Angelo and the ancient sculp-
tors. If we do not cast off this
world we shall be only Venetian
painters, who will be cast off
and lost from art.

virtue, crime. His formulas of
right are his scales, and his justice is blind; the justice of God
(i.e. of the Cosmic Sense) sees –
in that is everything." [84]

In the following passage from Blake, Bucke inserts his own terms
as explanatory (in [] brackets):

Beneath the figures of Adam and Eve (descending the generative
stream from there) is the seat of the harlog, named mystery [self-con-
scious life], in the Revelations. She (*mystery*) is seized by two beings
[life and death], each with three heads; they represent vegetative existence. As it is written in Revelations, they strip her naked and burn her
with fire [i.e. death strips her naked, and the passions of self-conscious
life burn it as with fire]. It represents the eternal consumptions of
vegetable life and death [the life and death of the merely self-conscious]
with its lusts. The wreathed torches in their hands [in the hands of life
and death] represent eternal fire, which is the fire of generation or
vegetation; it is an eternal consummation. Those who are blessed with
imaginative vision [Cosmic Consciousness] see this eternal female
[mystery – the self-conscious life] and tremble at what others fear not;
while they despise and laugh at what others fear. [85]

The master poet and artist, although also family man who ran a
practical printing shop for a living, said that:

I am not ashamed, afraid or averse to tell you what ought to be told –
that I am under the directions of messengers from heaven, daily and
nightly. But the nature of such things is not, as some suppose, without
trouble or care. [86]

Bucke concludes that Blake seems to have had the Cosmic Conscious experience at about thirty years of age. Of his exact experience, nothing is known. He clearly is a case of great intellectual
illumination and moral elevation, and had a clear sense of immortality which belongs to the Cosmic Conscious. Blake ranks with
the greats.

(9) Henry David Thoreau

Henry David Thoreau, born in America, July 12, 1817, and died at
the rather early age of forty-five on May 6, 1862, shares with
Moses, Lao Tzu, Isaiah, and other luminaries, the designation
"imperfect and doubtful instances." The base of Bucke's distinc-

tions in these cases is very unclear indeed for surely the greatest Hebrew prophet, the founder of Taoism, and the prophet who prophesied the Messiah, were persons of the Cosmic Sense. Bucke thinks they *may be*, although he has no more direct access to the minds of others, such as Paul, Plotinus, and Dante, whom he feels *definitely are*. Be this as it may, Henry Thoreau, who spent two years as a mystic recluse at Walden Pond near Concord, Massachusetts, is as clearly to me a case of Cosmic Consciousness as Blake is, or Dante is, etc. Thoreau says of himself:

> I hearing get who had but ears,
> And sight who had but eyes before,
> I moments live who lived but years,
> And truth discern who knew but learn-
>   ings lore.
>
> I hear beyond the range of sound,
> I see beyond the range of sight,
> New earths, and skies and seas around,
> And in my day the sun doth pale his
>   light. [87]

Bucke says that if Thoreau experienced illumination the evidence should be found in *Walden* which was written between 1845 and 1854 when the author was twenty-eight to thirty-seven years of age. Bucke finds passages in *Walden* which do suggest to him, the presence of Cosmic Consciousness:

> Sometimes, when I compare myself with other men, it seems as if I were more favored by the gods than they, beyond any deserts that I am conscious of; as if I had a warrant and surety at their hands which my fellows have not, and were especially guided and guarded. I do not flatter myself, but if it be possible they flatter me. I have never felt lonesome, or in the least oppressed by a sense of solitude, but once, and that was a few weeks after I came to the woods, when, for an hour, I doubted if the near neighborhood of man was not essential to a serene and healthy life. To be alone was something unpleasant. But I was at the same time conscious of a slight insanity in my mood and seemed to foresee my recovery. In the midst of the gentle rain, while these thoughts prevailed, I was suddenly sensible of such sweet and beneficent society in Nature, in the very patterning of the drops, and in every sound and sight around my house, an infinite and unaccountable friendliness all at once, like an atmosphere, sustaining me, as made the fancied advantages of human neighborhood insignificant, and I have never thought of them since. Every little pine needle expanded and swelled with sympathy and befriended me. I was so

distinctly made aware of the presence of something kindred to me, even in the scenes which we are accustomed to call wild and dreary, and also that the nearest blood to me and humanest was not a person nor a villager, that I thought no place could ever be strange to me again. [88]

What Thoreau has said in the preceding paragraph gives one a sense of his pantheism; a sense of God's presence in everything. Much of *Walden* gives one this sense.

I have a great deal of company in my house; especially in the morning, when nobody calls. Let me suggest a few comparisons, that someone may convey an idea of my situation. I am no more lonely than the loon in the pond that laughs so loud, or than Walden Pond itself. What company has that lonely lake, I pray? And yet it has not the blue devils, but the blue angels in it, in the azure tint of its waters. The sun is alone, except in thick weather, when there sometimes appears to be two, but one is a mock sun. God is alone, but the devil, he is far from being alone; he sees a great deal of company; he is legion. I am no more lonely than a single mullein or dandelion in a pasture, or a bean leaf, or sorrel, or a horse-fly, or a bumblebee. I am no more lonely than the Mill Brook, or a weathercock, or the north star, or the south wind, or an April shower, or a January thaw, or the first spider in a new house. [89]

Thoreau does not often speak of God per se, but He is there nonetheless with the sage of Walden Pond. Bucke does not find a specific description of an illumination experience in *Walden*, but that is perhaps because the author *already writes from an illumined perspective.* Bucke did not have Thoreau's journals available to him at the time, but in the year 1851, at age thirty-four, Thoreau wrote:

Methinks my present experience is nothing; my past experience is all in all. I think that no experience which I have today comes up to, or is comparable with, the experiences of my boyhood. And not only this is true, but as far back as I can remember I have unconsciously referred to the experiences of a previous state of existence. "For life is a forgetting," etc. Formerly, methought, nature developed as I developed, and grew up with me. My life was ecstasy. In youth, before I lost any of my senses, I can remember that I was all alive, and inhabited my body with inexpressible satisfaction; both of its weariness and refreshment were sweet to me. This earth was the most glorious musical instrument, and I was audience to its strains. To have such sweet impressions made on us, such ecstacies begotten of the breezes! I can remember how I was astonished. I said to myself, I said to others, "There comes into my mind such an indescribable, infinite, all-absorbing, divine, heavenly pleasure, a sense of elevation and expansion, and [I] have had nought to do with it. I perceive that I am dealt with by superior powers. This is a pleasure, a joy, an existence which I have not procured myself. I speak as a witness on the stand, and tell what I perceived." The morning and the evening were sweet to me, and I led a life aloof from society of men. I wondered if a mortal had ever known what I knew. I looked in books for some recognition of a kindred experience, but, strange to say, I found none. Indeed, I was slow to discover that other men had had this experience, for it had been possible to read books and to associate with men on other grounds. The maker of me was improving me. When I detected this interference I was profoundly moved. For years I marched as to a music in comparison with which the military music of the streets is noise and discord. I was daily intoxicated, and yet no man could call me intemperate. With all your science can you tell me how it is, and when it is, that light comes into my soul?[90]

Without a doubt Henry David Thoreau was a man of the Cosmic Sense.

(10) Walt Whitman

In Walt Whitman, whom we have discussed already, we find the man whom Bucke (and probably Bucke alone) regards as the "highest instance of Cosmic Consciousness." This judgment of Bucke's seems a bit exaggerated and out of balance, considering that he is comparing Whitman with such figures as Jesus the Christ, and Gautama the Buddha, who founded world religions that have survived 2,000 and 2,500 years respectively, and have given spiritual comfort and blessing to peoples of both Western and Eastern cultures for millenia. Gautama overcame samsara or ignorance, and Jesus proved himself master of sin and death itself. Both holy masters stood their ground and moreover bested the Evil One, call him Satan or Mara. Buddha showed the way out of suffering, and Christ transcended death itself! To say that the admittedly illumined poet, Walt Whitman, was greater than Christ or Buddha, is in the Californian lingo, a very "far out" claim. On the other hand, Bucke knew Whitman personally, and Whitman may have had a stronger effect upon him than anyone else. Therefore, the preeminence of Whitman is a rather subjective judgment on Bucke's part. He does state that Whitman, unlike all the others, values equally self and Cosmic Consciousness, and does not put one down at the expense of the other. No doubt Whitman was a very great man and a poet inspired by the Cosmic Sense.

Walt Whitman, the American poet, was born in 1819 and died in 1892. He lived through the American Civil War and worked as a nurse in that bloody conflict. However, his greatest love and devotion was for his book of poems he called *Leaves of Grass* which though sometimes derided in his time, went on to become *the* classic of American poetry of the nineteenth century.

What was Whitman like? The following description is Bucke's own based upon his visit with him when the poet was sixty-one years of age:

> At first sight he looks much older, so that he is often supposed to be seventy or eighty. He is six feet in height, and quite straight. He weighs nearly two hundred pounds. His body and limbs are full-sized and well proportioned. His head is large and rounded in every direction ... Though his face and head gave the appearance of being plentifully supplied with hair, the crown is moderately bald; on the side and back the hair is long, very fine, and nearly snow white. The eyebrows are highly arched, so that it is a long distance from the eye to the centre of the eyebrow ... The eyes themselves are light blue ...[91]

Bucke goes on to say:

> His face has no lines expressive of care, or weariness, or age – it is the white hair and beard, and his feebleness in walking (due to paralysis) that make him appear old. The habitual expression of his face is repose, but there is a well-marked firmness and decision.[92]

Bucke describes Whitman as a man of extraordinary physical attractiveness, what we would call "charisma." He has a magnetism about him which is a very rare thing. Bucke said that Whitman dressed very plainly, but neatly, and he was, in a word, *ordinary*, but this is *the ordinary* of the Zen masters. Bucke says that Whitman had a very calm and self-contained manner, and he never saw him lose his temper, or become mean or bad-spirited. His favorite occupation was strolling or sauntering about outdoors looking at the grass, the trees, and the flowers, and listening to the birds and crickets. He was very fond of children. "Wandering amazed," Whitman said, "at my own lightness and glee." Bucke believes that *Leaves of Grass* gives all the evidence that one needs of the fact of Cosmic Consciousness in Whitman. Speaking of his soul, Whitman says:

I believe in you my soul . . . the other I am must not abase itself to you,
And you must not be abased to the other.
Loaf with me on the grass . . . loose the stop from your throat,
Not words, nor music or rhyme I want,
   custom or lecture, not even the best,
Only the lull I like, the hum of your valved voice.
I mind how we lay in June, such a transparent summer morning;
You settled your head athwart my hips and gently turned me over
   upon me,
And parted the shirt from my bosom-bone, and plunged your tongue
   to my bare-stript heart.
And reached till you felt my beard, and reached till you held my feet.
Swiftly arose and spread around me the peace and joy and knowledge
   that pass all the art and argument of the earth;
And I know that the hand of God is the elder hand of my own,
And I know that the spirit of God is the eldest brother of my own,
And that all the men ever born are also my brothers,
   . . . and the women my sisters and lovers,
And that a kelson of creation is love. [93]

Here, Bucke notes that Whitman has come to the experience of
deep self, even Cosmic Consciousness, but he points out that the
old self must not be abased to it, or overridden by it. Henceforth,
Whitman says that his life is inspired by the newcomer, the new
self. Whitman sums up the poem by expressing a direct sense of
God as his "eldest brother." This is an intimacy with the Divine
that the Cosmic Conscious have. Jesus spoke of God as Abba, or
"Papa."

Bucke states that the following lines make a clear case for
Whitman as an instance of Cosmic Consciousness:

> As in a swoon, one instant,
> Another sun, ineffable full – dazzles me,
> And all the orbs I knew, and brighter, unknown orbs;
> One instant of the future land, Heaven's land. [94]

Bucke states that all men (or women) before Whitman, who
experienced Cosmic Consciousness were carried away by it, and
subjugated to it. Even St. Paul and Gautama seemed to despise the
"old self," or the "fleshly self." But, Whitman, according to
Bucke, who knew him personally:

> . . . saw, what neither Gautama nor Paul saw, what Jesus saw, though
> not so clearly as he, that though this faculty is truly Godlike, yet it is
> no more supernatural or preternatural than sight, hearing, taste, feel-
> ing, or any other, and he consequently refused to give it unlimited

sway, and would not allow it to tyrannize over the rest. He believes in it, but he says the other self, the old self, must not abase itself to the new; neither must the new be encroached upon or limited by the old; he will see that they live as friendly co-workers together.[95]

This reminds me of Jung who called it a "disaster" if the ego is "swallowed up" by the Self. Jung saw the ideal as a healthy relationship between ego and Self. I am assuming here that there is a precise analogy between Bucke's distinction between self and Cosmic Consciousness and Jung's ego/Self relationship. I am not sure that the parallel is exact. Self-consciousness in Bucke's theory means ego consciousness in Jung's. There is no higher Self in Bucke's theory, but an immediate jump from ego-self into Cosmic Consciousness. Jung, on the other hand, never really reaches true Cosmic Consciousness in his theory (as we shall see). Nor is there any evidence in his writings that he experienced such himself, as Bucke did. If we take Bucke and Jung together, we have a fuller picture which includes ego, higher Self, and Cosmic Consciousness, and the physical body, of course. These are distinguished in the great metaphysical systems of the past, such as Kabbala, as separate and distinct, and not reducible to each other. Bucke's insight about Whitman is significant.

2

William James on "The Varieties of Religious Experience"

In *A Pluralistic Universe*, William James declares that "a philosophy is the expression of a man's *intimate character*, and all definitions of the universe are but the deliberately adapted reactions of human characters upon it."[1] William James, as we shall see, was the last of the great religious psychologists for many years to come, and he was a man of deep and sensitive character, this character being expressed in such epic works as his book: *The Varieties of Religious Experience.*

The first and deepest influence upon William James was his father, Henry James, Sr., to distinguish him from his illustrious son, Henry James, Jr., the novelist. The patriarch of this noble family was the elder William James, who was both a self-made multi-millionaire merchant and trader, and a pious Presbyterian and Calvinist. Henry James, Sr., rebelled against his father's puritanical theology and his materialism. His rebellion was made easier by the considerable inheritance he received from his father's estate which made him independently wealthy. Henry James, Sr., devoted himself to writing books on liberal theology, inverting Calvin. James declared that all men are *born innocent* and subsequently subverted by society's influence. He reversed his father's puritanical belief in "original sin," one interpretation of the Eden story, and the need for severe discipline to check man's "evil impulses." Quite the opposite for Henry James, Sr.: man needs to return to his original goodness and innocence before he is corrupted by society! This is the classic liberal versus conservative position. Henry James was a disciple of Charles Fourier, the French socialist, and Emmanuel Swedenborg, the Swedish mystic.

He was also a close friend and correspondent of Ralph Waldo Emerson, the American transcendentalist.

William James, the American philosopher and psychologist-to-be, was born in 1842 in New York City. He received a novel education as a result of his father's *philosophy of freedom*. Henry James, Sr., said: "I desire my child to become an upright man, in whom goodness shall be induced not by mercenary motives as brute goodness is induced, but by love for it or a sympathetic delight in it. And inasmuch as I know that this character or disposition cannot be forcibly imposed upon him, but must be freely assumed, I surround him as far as possible with an atmosphere of freedom."[2]

William James attended private schools, had a succession of tutors, and studied in various places in Europe including France and Switzerland. His father did not want him to specialize or choose a profession "too soon," so subsequently his son, William, was very late in choosing a profession at all! He studied painting for a year, and gave that up for Harvard Science School where he studied chemistry, zoology, and anatomy. William went on to Harvard Medical School, but took two long interruptions, one to accompany the naturalist, Louis Agassiz, on a zoological expedition to Brazil, and the other to study physiology at the University of Berlin, where he was exposed to the psychophysics and experimental psychology of Helmholtz and Fechner. He finally returned to Cambridge, Massachusetts where he completed his medical degree in 1869. But, William James was never to become a practising doctor, a profession for which he was temperamentally ill-suited. He fell into severe depressions in 1869 and 1870; he was paralyzed with neurasthenia and moral impotence. From his diary of February 1, 1870, James wrote: "Today I about touched bottom and perceive plainly that I must face the choice with open eyes. . ."[3]

By spring of that year, James discovered the philosopher, Renouvier, who championed the freedom of the will. James wrote in his diary: "My first act of free will shall be to believe in free will."[4] This philosophic insight was the beginning of his recovery. It was later to have an influence on his philosophy of pragmatism which argued that an idea's meaning and, indeed, its truth value, depend upon its *practical consequences*. If the non-belief in free will results in illness, and the belief in it in health and psychological recovery, then it is an idea with real meaning, and positive truth value.

In the year 1873, William James was appointed instructor of anatomy and physiology at Harvard College. He was to hold his professorship at Harvard for the rest of his life; teaching and writing were to be his career. He began in the biological sciences, and twelve years later gave a course on psychology based upon what he had learned of the *psychophysik* of the Germans. In 1876, James established an experimental psychology laboratory; this was three years before Wundt opened his Institute at Leipzig, which is the date given in psychology texts for the beginning of "scientific psychology." In 1878, James gave a lecture at Johns Hopkins University and at Lowell Institute in Boston on "The Brain and the Mind" which traced the development of scientific theories on the brain and the nervous system.[5] He pointed out that no one had yet been able to explain *consciousness* (nor have they to this day!). James said in that lecture:

> . . . I, for one, as a scientific man and a practical man alike, deny utterly that science compels me to believe that my conscience is an *ignis fatuus* or outcast, and I trust that you too . . . will go away strengthened in the natural faith that your delights and sorrows, your loves and hates, your aspirations and efforts are real combatants in life's arena, and not impotent, paralytic spectators of the game.[6]

In other words, James was claiming that consciousness was real, and its effects were real, in fact, the very real stuff of life. This was later to be denied by the behaviorists, as we shall see. James was a champion, not a denier, of man's spirit.

In his classic books on psychology, *The Principles of Psychology* and *Psychology: Briefer Course*, James speaks of consciousness as a *flowing river*. The "stream of consciousness" is a term that began with William James' psychology, and had an influence on literature as well (Marcel Proust and James Joyce). James says this about the stream of consciousness:

> Consciousness, then, does not appear to itself chopped up in bits. Such words as 'chain' or 'train' do not describe it fitly as it presents itself in the first instance. It is nothing jointed; it flows. A 'river' or a 'stream' are two metaphors by which it is most naturally described.[7]

James, the master of phenomenological psychology, or introspection (seeing within), saw consciousness as a "flowing river." Watson and the later behaviorists tried to reduce this "stream of consciousness" to "sub-vocal chains of stimuli and responses." James already denied that "chain" or "train" would do to describe

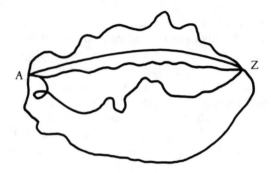

Figure 2.1   William James' Model of the Stream of Consciousness

consciousness. James, unlike his behaviorist successors in American (and Russian) psychology, defined psychology as: "the description and explanation of states of consciousness as such."[8] It should be noted that James was also an opponent of the traditional associationistic psychology of such philosophers as John Locke and David Hume who treated consciousness as the "association of atomistic sensations." James observed no such thing! What he did see was the "free waters of consciousness" which he said psychologists "resolutely overlook."[9] "Elementary sensations" are high abstractions never actually observed in the holistic flow of total consciousness, which contains *whole entities* (gestalten) in complex interrelationship with one another, and a periphery or background which shades off into the "subconsciousness," which was a term already used by James, who was a contemporary of Freud's, although fourteen years older, and died many years earlier – the two met at the latter's legendary lectures at Clark University in Worcester, Massachusetts in 1909.

James' theory of emotions was somewhat behavioristic and physiological in that it stated that what we call our emotions such as fear, rage, love, etc., are actually the after-effects of bodily changes in response to external situations. We feel fear because we have certain physiological changes, we freeze in terror, or run. We feel love because we have quite different physiological changes, and we approach the loved object. And so on through the emotions. Careful self-observation, not only of consciousness but of our own behavior, reveals that this is so: ". . . we feel sorry because we cry, angry because we strike, afraid because we tremble, and not that we cry, strike, or tremble, because we are sorry, angry, or fearful."[10]

Although James had a behaviorist sounding theory of emotions, he refused to reduce consciousness to an epiphenomenon of the brain. He conceived mind to be teleological, "a fighter for ends."[11] Although he was already very well aware of the objections of the early behaviorists to introspection, its "inaccuracy," its "fallibility," its "difficulties," James said that these same difficulties of observation accrue to all observations of any kind whatsoever from physics to history. Physics, as we know today, has its profound difficulties in determining the nature and behavior of the elusive sub-atomic particles that make up the atom. They are altered by our mere observation of them according to quantum theory. Certainly, history has its deep difficulties too, such as ascertaining the historicity of Biblical figures, for example. Does this mean that we give up physics or history? Certainly not. Nor would James, like his successors, the behaviorists, give up psychology's subject: *human consciousness and mental life.*

Regarding states of consciousness, James states certain universal characteristics:

(1) Every "state" tends to be part of a personal consciousness.
(2) Within each personal consciousness states are always changing.
(3) Each personal consciousness is sensibly continuous.
(4) It is interested in some parts of its objects to the exclusion of others, and welcomes or rejects – *chooses* from among them, in a word – all the time.[12]

James points out that when we speak of "states of consciousness," we are always dealing with "personal consciousness": minds, selves, "I's," "you's." James makes the observation:

> Each of these minds keeps its thoughts to itself. There is no giving or bartering between them. No thought comes into direct *sight* of a thought of another personal consciousness *than its own.*[13]

The later behaviorists, such as Watson, whom we will discuss in the next chapter, seem positively unable to comprehend the personal nature of consciousness, and therefore they deny its existence! This would be akin to physicists denying the existence of electrons because they are difficult to observe. In fact, consciousness is far easier to observe than electrons are. Truly, we are observing it all the time: *within ourselves.* However, despite the usual privacy of consciousness, we sometimes communicate directly mind to mind, as in extrasensory perception. James himself was an early supporter of psychical research. Be that as it may, the privacy rather than the communicability of states of consciousness is the far more general fact. We have our thoughts, ideas, and feelings, and unless we *speak them*, they are known to us alone. Who is this "us?" What is this "me?" James deals with this question, and says that "No psychology, at any rate, can question the existence of personal selves."[14] James distinguishes several aspects of the personal self:

> *The Material Me*: The body is the innermost part of the material me in each of us . . . The clothes come next. Next our immediate family is part of ourselves. Our father and mother, our wife and babes, are bone of our bone and flesh of our flesh. When they die, part of our very selves is gone . . . Our home comes next. Its scenes are part of our life . . . An equally instinctive impulse drives us to collect property and the collections thus made become, with different degrees of intimacy, parts of our empirical selves.[15]

> *The Social Me*: A man's social me is the recognition which he gets from his mates. We are not only gregarious animals, liking to be in sight of our fellows, but we have an innate propensity to get ourselves noticed, and noticed favorably by our kind. No more fiendish punishment could be devised . . . than that one should be turned loose in society and remain absolutely unnoticed by all the members thereof. . . Properly speaking, *a man has as many social selves as there are individuals who recognize him* and carry an image of him in their minds. To wound any one of these images is to wound him . . . He generally shows a different side of himself to each of these . . . We do not show ourselves to our children as to our club companions, to our customers as to the laborers we employ . . . From this there results what practically is a division of man into several selves; and this may be a discordant splitting, as where one is afraid to let one set of his acquaintances know him as he is elsewhere; or it may be a perfectly harmonious division of labor, as where one tender to his children is stern to soldiers . . . under his command. The most peculiar social self which one is apt to have is in the mind of the person one is in love with. The good or bad fortunes of this self cause the most intense elation or dejection. . .[16]

> *The Spiritual Me*: The very core and nucleus of our self, as we know it, the very sanctuary of our life . . . This sense of activity is often held to be a direct revelation of the living substance of our soul.[17]

In these observations, James anticipates much of twentieth century personality theory, social psychology, and even psychoanalysis.

James goes on to speak of the "rivalry and conflict" of the different "me's" in much the same way that Freud spoke of the tripartite psychodynamics of ego, id, and superego, several decades later. The goal, James says, is to seek "the truest, strongest, deepest self . . . the one on which to base . . . salvation."[18] Here, James anticipates the self-actualization psychologists, such as Maslow and Assagioli, of the mid-twentieth century.

James goes on to discuss not the self which is known, the "me," but the self which knows, the "I".

> *The Self as Knower*: The I, or "pure ego," is a much more difficult subject of inquiry than the Me. It is that which at any given moment *is* conscious, whereas the Me is only one of the things which it is conscious *of*. In other words, it is the *thinker*; and the question immediately comes up *what* is the thinker? Is it passing states of consciousness itself, or is it something deeper and less mutable? The passing state we have seen to be the very embodiment of change, yet each of us spontaneously considers that by "I" he means something always the same. This has led most philosophers to postulate behind the passing state of consciousness a permanent substance or Agent . . . This Agent is the thinker . . . "soul," "transcendent Ego," "Spirit," are so many names. . .[19]

Here James reminds one of the discussions of the sages of the *Upanishads*:

> The Self is one. Unmoving, it moves faster than the mind. The senses lag, but Self runs ahead. Unmoving, it outruns pursuit. Out of Self comes the breath that is the life of all things.[20]

The Upanishadic sages argue for the eternal Atman or transcendental Self. Gautama Buddha, also from India, argues for the reverse position, that the Self is an illusion composed only of its parts, i.e., changing states of consciousness. James comes to a rather Buddhistic conclusion when he speaks of the

> *Sameness in the Self as Knower*: Successive thinkers, numerically distinct, but all aware of the same past in the same way, form an adequate vehicle for all the experiences of personal unity and sameness which we actually have. And just such a train of successive thinkers is the stream of mental states . . . which psychology treated as natural science has to assume.[21]

Which is the truth to you? This author, like Bucke perhaps, would go with the Upanishadic sages who argue for the reality of the Self. This is also the Western, or Judeo-Christian tradition, whose esotericism as expressed in the *Kabbala,* or "revealed knowledge," sees the Self as the central archetype of the Tree of Life: "*Tifereth.*"

James approaches religion not as a theologian or a metaphysician, but as an empirical and phenomenological psychologist who looks at religious experience as an important and mysterious *content of consciousness.* After James' classic work, *The Varieties of Religious Experience* (subtitled "A Study in Human Nature"), no serious student of religion can ever again deal only with abstract theological concepts, ignoring their pragmatic meaning, or absence of it, in real human experience. Mystics, of course, have always sought for God in the depths of their souls (not in "outer space" somewhere).

James defined religion in the following highly individualistic way, somewhat ignoring its sociological and historical sides, as well as its theological aspects:

> . . . the feelings, acts and experiences of individual men in their solitude, so far as they apprehend themselves to stand in relation to whatever they may consider divine. [22]

James believed in the *ultimacy* of individual experience in religious history. As we have already seen in looking at some of the great exemplars that Bucke described, when the individuals are religious geniuses, their experiences sometimes become the foundations of new religions! James would hold that all conceptions of the divine from the most primitive to the most sophisticated and highly developed creeds, theologies and metaphysical systems, are secondary products; they are at best interpretations of religious experience (and often they are not even that). Theologies reflect the peculiar intellectual habits and biases of individuals in various cultures which produce them. We all know about the disputes on every matter of doctrine from the resurrection to the eucharist in Christianity. The hundreds of varieties of Christianity are a reflection of this; not of the original experiences of Jesus and Paul, but of the interpretations of them by less enlightened men, albeit "scholars" and "theologians." They never come to any agreement! Mystics, i.e., those who have religious experiences, tend to be in far more agreement even across religions, let alone within various varieties of one religion, e.g., Christianity. James did not bother to make an intensive study of theologies, but an intensive study of individual religious experiences. In this respect, he resembled Bucke considerably. However, James had no religious experiences of his own, as he understood it, no commerce with the divine. In this respect, he differed from Bucke, who had the classical mystical experience or "cosmic consciousness." So, James, the philosophical psychologist, was no mystic, but he nonetheless must have had enough of a "germ" of mysticism in him to make him as responsive as he was to the religious experiences of others, and, furthermore, to appreciate as he did, their importance for a total view of our universe.

The Varieties of Religious Experience was based upon the Gifford Lectures that James delivered at Edinburgh in 1901–1902. James felt himself greatly honored as an American to be speaking to this learned European audience, and he made mention of that. James' reputation as a psychologist and philosopher was already established during his lifetime. James, unlike Bucke, was an international man. Commenting on crude materialistic reductionism which would deny God and the soul *a priori*, James said that:

> Medical materialism finishes up Saint Paul by calling his vision on the road to Damascus a discharging legion of the occipital cortex . . . It snuffs out Saint Theresa as an hysteric. Saint Francis of Assisi as an hereditary degenerate.[23]

These statements of James are not as extreme as they sound. It is difficult to pick up a Freudian psychoanalytic journal, even today, without finding some equally fantastic reduction of religion or religious figures. The last time I looked at such a journal, they had an article about Jesus as an "obviously extreme example of the male Oedipal complex." The behaviorists, very early in their program, denigrate religion as akin to "black magic." Neuroscientists do not tend to engage in this kind of thing anymore, as their science has its own very immense challenges without taking pot shots at religion! In fact, some neuroscientists, as we will see later, have a definitely religious point of view, e.g., Sir John Eccles, the Nobel Laureate neurophysiologist. The radical empiricist, William James, was radical enough not to exclude any human phenomena or experience from the realm of actuality *a priori* because it did not "fit" some preconceived narrow view of science. James excludes nothing from a universe so great and varied that he called it a "pluralistic universe."

James makes philosophical mincemeat of the proposition that because mind-states depend upon brain-states (if they do – this is a debate); that therefore the real significance of religious experiences is thereby undermined. Atheism, James points out, as well as religious experience, has an "underlying physiological brain correllate;" does this rule it out as well as its opposite: theism? The organic causation of a mental state, or lack of it, has no bearing whatsoever on the truth value of that mental state. There may be a physiology of religious experience, just as there is a physiology of sexual experience. This does not invalidate the reality of the religious experience any more than it would do so of the sexual experience! As we know, too, sexual experiences usually have "aims," i.e. a sexual object or partner. Likewise, it is quite entirely possible, indeed very likely, that religious experiences have an aim, i.e., God. One's conception of God, whether monotheistic or polytheistic, infinite or finite, etc., is another matter.

In characterizing the religious life in the broadest possible way, James states:

> . . . one might say that it consists of the belief that there is an unseen order and that our supreme good lies in harmoniously adjusting ourselves thereto. This belief and this adjustment are the religious attitude in the soul. [24]

Perhaps, religion is the *belief* in the unseen order; mysticism is the *direct experience* thereof. James says that probably most religious persons have the recollection of a particular crisis or crises in which a direct intuition of the living God's existence overwhelmed the languor of the more ordinary belief. To quote a letter to James from a friend, James Russell Lowell:

> I had a revelation last Friday evening. I was at Mary's, and happening to say something of the presence of spirits (of whom I was dimly aware). Mr. Putnam entered into an argument with me on spiritual matters. As I was speaking, the whole system rose up before me like a vague destiny looming from the Abyss. I never before so clearly felt the Spirit of God in me and around me. The whole room seemed full of God. The air seemed to waver to and fro with the presence of Something. I knew not what. I spoke with the calmness and clearness of a prophet. I cannot tell you what this revelation was. I have not yet studied it enough. But I shall perfect it one day, and then you shall hear of it and acknowledge its grandeur. [25]

This is a religious experience, surely. Is it a case of cosmic consciousness in Bucke's sense? We do not have a complete enough account of it to determine if it had the various characteristics that Bucke gave (see chapter one) as criteria. However, it does resemble some of Bucke's instances of which he, too, was unsure, and labelled "lesser, imperfect and doubtful instances." Here is such an instance from Bucke's *Cosmic Consciousness*; it is a woman whose initials, C.Y.E., are given:

> On the afternoon of Wednesday I went to see a friend, a farmer's wife, and we drove over the harvest fields to take some refreshment to her husband who was working with his men. When I was going away she gave me two very beautiful Marechal Niel roses. I had always had a passionate love of flowers, but the scent of these and their exquisite form and color appealed to me with quite exceptional force and vividness. I left my friend and was walking slowly homeward, enjoying the calm beauty of the evening, when I became aware of an unutterable stillness, and simultaneously every object about me became bathed in a soft light, clearer and more ethereal than I had ever before seen. Then a voice whispered in my soul: "God is all. He is not far away in the heaven; He is here. This grass under your feet is He; this bountiful harvest, that blue sky, those roses in your hand – you yourself are all one with Him. All is well for ever and ever, for there is no place or time where God is not."[26]

Bucke's instance seems more dramatic than James', but perhaps C. Y. E. was a more gifted writer than James' Russell Lowell. In any event, both of these individuals definitely had experiences of what seemed to them to be the presence of God. I note that the non-believer tends to scoff at these experiences as "mere belief." It is possible that a strong preexisting belief in God may "set one up" for a religious experience of this kind. However, many devout believers never have any such experience of the "unseen order." And some atheists at the time, myself included, have had cosmic conscious experiences that transcended anything they ever believed in or conceived of.

Regarding these religious experiences, James says that "One may indeed be entirely without them. ... but if you do have them, and have them at all strongly, the probability is that you cannot help regarding them as genuine perceptions of truth, as revelations of a kind of reality which no adverse argument, be it ever unanswerable by you in words, can expel from your belief."[27]

The opinion in philosophy that is in principle opposed to mystical experience, James speaks of as "rationalism." It holds that beliefs are only warranted on the basis of sensory observation or logical deduction. "Vague impressions of something indefinable have no place in the rationalist system. . ."[28] James counters this incredibly narrow academic philosophy of rationalism with the argument that:

... if we look on man's whole mental life as it exists ... we have to confess that the part of it which rationalism can give an account of is relatively superficial. It is the part that has *prestige* undoubtedly, for it has the loquacity, it can challenge you for proofs, and chop logic, and put you down with words ... But it will fail to convince or convert you all the same. [29]

Surely, the great intuitions and inspirations that gave birth to great religions, and moral values, poetry, and art, and even *true science*, come from a deeper level of human nature than logic chopping rationalists can even conceive of. Einstein himself came to his relativity theory based upon intuitions and visions of an almost mystical nature, such as seeing himself riding a light beam into infinity. He did not operate merely upon sense impression and logical deduction. Science, not to mention religion and poetry, would have died out long before Plato and Aristotle if people were constrained by the narrow rules of knowledge of rationalistic systems of philosophy. James points out that rationalistic "proofs" of God's existence are as boring and dreary as are "proofs" of his nonexistence. Blaise Pascal, the mathematician and philosopher, and probable rationalist before this, wrote this about an experience of God he had in 1654 on a piece of parchment he carried with him at all times in an amulet:

The year of grace 1654, Monday 23 November, day of St. Clement, Pope and Martyr. From about half-past ten in the evening until about half-past twelve, midnight, FIRE. God of Abraham, God of Isaac, God of Jacob, not of the philosophers nor of the Wise. Assurance, joy, assurance, feeling, joy, peace. GOD OF JESUS CHRIST, my God and thy God. Thy God shall be my God. Forgotten of the world and of all except GOD. He is only found in the ways taught in the Gospel. THE SUBLIMITY OF THE HUMAN SOUL. Just Father, the world has not known thee but I have known thee. Joy, joy, joy, tears of joy. I do not separate myself from thee. They left me behind, me a fountain of living water. My God, do not leave me. Let me not be separated from thee eternally. This is eternal life that they should know thee the only true God and him whom thou hast sent. JESUS CHRIST-JESUS CHRIST. I have separated myself from him; I have fled, renounced, crucified him. Let me not be forever separated from him. One is saved only by the teaching of the Gospel. RECONCILIATION TOTAL AND SWEET. Total submission to JESUS CHRIST and to my DIRECTOR. Continual joy for the days of my life on earth. I shall not forget what you have taught me. Amen. [30]

I would guess that if you are a believer that this would strengthen your belief, and if you are a non-believer, your non-belief would remain unchanged, and you would, furthermore, "explain away" Pascal's experience in some fashion. Most psychologists choose to explain everything in terms of their own system. I am sure that many psychiatrists would see a "case of temporary insanity" here. But to Pascal, and C.Y.E., and James Russell Lowell, and millions of others throughout human history, and in all cultures of humankind, there is *no doubt whatsoever* about the overwhelming reality of their experience of the "unseen order." James claimed no religious experiences of his own, but he was the true scientist enough to grant the importance and reality of these experiences in others. He did not "explain them away," either. Nor, however, did they lead him to an orthodox theism. His point of view was unsystematic on these things, and untheoretical; he tended to take reality and experience as they were given in an empirical and pluralistic way. He did not know whether there was a One behind the Many; he had not experienced it. He knew that others had and he never mocked them as later psychologists (so-called) tended to do with what lay outside of their narrow ken. We will see more of this later.

James next takes up the topic of the religion of "healthy-mindedness" versus the "sick soul." In many persons, James noted, happiness is almost congenital. They are enthusiastic and optimistic even despite adverse circumstances of life. These people, James calls the "once born." These people seemingly have not suffered, do not know what depression is, have a continuous positive outlook. I have known such persons myself and they never cease to amaze me. They are temperamentally weighted heavily on the side of cheer. "Positive thinking" philosophies of life seem to arise out of this type of character; Norman Vincent Peale and Robert Schuller to name two contemporary examples who come to mind. James says that the sanguine and healthy minded live habitually on the "sunny side of life." Their motto might be: "*God is well, and so are you. You must awaken to the knowledge of your real being.*"[31]

By no means do all the successful and famous persons of this earth live in this optimistic frame of mind. The immensely successful (in several vocations) Johann Wolfgang von Goethe said

I will say nothing against the course of my existence. But at bottom it has been nothing but pain and burden, and I can affirm that during the whole of my 75 years, I have not had four weeks of genuine well being.[32]

Martin Luther, the great reformer of Christianity, who certainly had considerable success in his enterprises, and a wife and several children, said:

> I am utterly weary of life; I pray the Lord will come forthwith and carry me hence, let him come. . .[33]

In the Bible, it says:

> What profit hath a man of all his labor which he taketh under the sun? I looked on all the works that my hands had wrought, and behold, all was vanity and vexation of spirit. [34]

The fact is that life has both a sunny side, and a dark side. Just like in the Tai Chi symbol of the Taoists, darkness and light make up the whole, but there are those in life who seem to live perpetually in the one side (the light) or the other (darkness). Probably, as the Jungians imply, the truly whole person embraces both sides: lightness and darkness. But, in his chapter, "The Sick Soul," James discusses in detail those persons who know more of the darkness than the light. James himself knew this side well from his own long periods of severe depression and neurasthenia. James quotes from a letter of a depressed patient from a French hospital to give his readers an idea (if they have none of their own) of the depths of despair into which the soul can fall:

> I suffer too much – Besides the burnings and the sleeplessness . . . fear, atrocious fear presses me down, holds me without respite, never lets go. Where is the justice in it all? What have I done to deserve this excess of severity? . . . All I have known so far has been the devil. After all, I am afraid of God as much as of the devil, so I drift along, thinking nothing but suicide, but with neither the courage nor means to execute the act . . . O God! What a misfortune to be born![35]

Depression and suicide are a widespread plague of our late twentieth century civilization. The majority of complaints that people bring to psychiatrists in this era are those of depression and the loss of meaning in life. I think that many readers can identify with the plight of this patient whose letter James quoted.

The great Russian novelist, Leo Tolstoy, went through a prolonged and severe period of melancholy which he overcame through a spiritual rebirth and reawakening. In Tolstoy's case, the sense that life had meaning had been totally withdrawn, even though he was at the height of literary success and moved in elite social circles. "I felt," said Tolstoy "that something had broken within me on which my life had always rested, that I had nothing left to hold on to, and that morally my life had stopped. An invincible force impelled me to get rid of my existence, in one way or another. It cannot be said that I *wished* to kill myself, for the force which drew me away from life was fuller, more powerful, more general than any desire. It was a force like my old aspiration to live, only it impelled me in the opposite direction. It was an aspiration of my whole being to get out of life."[36]

Tolstoy had some very definitely suicidal thoughts: "Behold me, a man happy and in good health, hiding the rope in order not to hang myself to the rafters of the room where every night I went to sleep alone; behold me no longer going shooting, lest I should yield to the too easy temptation of putting an end to myself with my gun."[37] During the course of this year, when Tolstoy was unceasingly asking himself how to end it all, he said that his heart kept languishing with another principal emotion which he called none other than "a thirst for God."[38]

James states that when disillusionment has gone as far as it had for Tolstoy, there is seldom a *restitutio ad integrum*, for one has already eaten of the bitter fruit of the tree of knowledge of good and evil. The original happiness of Eden never will come again. What one can hope for is not a reversion to original innocence, but a *redemption by some factor of grace*. The happiness that does come is not a simple ignorance of ill, but something vastly more complex which includes the awareness of evil as one of its elements, but finding this evil no more a stumbling block, or terror, because it has been encompassed by *a greater good*, or *wholeness*, if you will. The religion of the once born is a "one-storied affair," says James; for the twice born, the world is a "double-storied mystery."[39]

However this be that man is reborn, Tolstoy, pursuing his unending questions of life, came to insight after insight. He came to *the intuition* that his conclusion that his life was meaningless took only his small finite life into account, and meaning is not found in the addition of finites. Reason cannot discover the infinite, but *faith can*. Tolstoy concluded that belief in the infinite is what makes life content for the simple peasants he observed, and it was what he needed to make his life possible again. To quote Tolstoy:

> Since mankind has existed, wherever life has been there also has been the faith that gave the possibility of living. Faith is the sense of life, that sense by virtue of which man does not destroy himself but continues to live on. It is the force whereby we live. If Man did not believe that he must live for something, he would not live at all. The idea of an

infinite God, of the divinity of the soul, of the union of men's actions with God – these are ideas elaborated in the infinite secret depths of human thought. They are ideas without which there would be no life, without which I myself would not exist. I began to see that I had no right to rely on my individual reasoning and neglect these answers given by faith, for they are the only answers to the question. [40]

This conviction of faith was the beginning of Tolstoy's recovery from his years of despair: "to believe in God, therein lay happiness again." [41] Tolstoy describes a sense of God's presence which came to him in a forest alone in early spring:

I remember one day in early spring, I was alone in the forest, lending my ear to its mysterious noises. I listened, and my thought went back to what, for these three years, it always was busy with – the quest for God. But the idea of him, I said, how did I ever come by the idea? And again there arose in me, with this thought, glad aspirations toward life. Everything in me awoke and received a meaning . . . Why do I look farther? a voice within me asked. He is there: he without whom one cannot live. To acknowledge God and to live are one and the same thing. God is what life is. Well, then! Live, seek God, and there will be no life without him. . . [42]

Tolstoy goes on to describe his complete sense of cure of his melancholy and suicidal depression in his realization of God:

After this, things cleared up within me and about me better than ever, and the light has never wholly died away. I was saved from suicide. Just how or when the change took place I cannot tell. But as insensibly and gradually as the force of life had been annulled within me, and I had reached my moral death-bed, just as gradually and imperceptibly did the energy of life come back. And what was strange was that this energy that came back was nothing new. It was my ancient juvenile force of faith. . . [43]

Was this a case of Cosmic Consciousness in Bucke's sense? Yes and no. It was nothing sudden; it was *very gradual*, as Tolstoy himself describes it. Was there a "subjective light?" Well, there was nothing dramatic, as in the "blinding light" that St. Paul experienced. Yet Tolstoy does say, "the light has never wholly died away." Was there moral elevation? Yes, surely. Intellectual illumination? There was that too. A sense of immortality? I would say so. The loss of the fear of death? I would say that, too. The loss of the sense of sin? Surely. The suddenness or instantaneousness of the awakening? No, Tolstoy's conversion was definitely not sudden or instantaneous. The previous character of the man?

Tolstoy was a literary giant, and a questor after truth. The age of his illumination? Tolstoy was middle-aged at the time of his gradual spiritual rebirth. Added charm to the personality? Absolutely, for Tolstoy had regained his will to live, his life force. Transfiguration? Probably not in the sense of Moses or Jesus, but quite likely so "new light" came into his eyes and his presence.

James does us a great service in discussing these cases of gradual spiritual rebirth and reawakening. These are probably far more common than cases of sudden or instantaneous rebirth, or "Cosmic Consciousness." Yet they contain many of the same features, only that the *new life* is attained very gradually, and almost "imperceptibly" to use Tolstoy's word.

James also discusses the spiritual autobiography of the English author, John Bunyan who wrote *Pilgrim's Progress*. Bunyan, like Tolstoy, went through years of profound melancholy and despair. James says that he was beset by self-doubts, fears, and incessant despondent thoughts. In Bunyan's own words:

> Nay, thought I, now I grow worse and worse; now I am farther from conversion than ever I was before. If now I should have burned at the stake, I could not believe that Christ had love for me; alas, I could neither hear him, nor see him, nor feel him, nor savor any of his things . . . But my original and inward pollution, that was my plague and my affliction. By reason of that, I was more loathsome in my own eyes than was a toad; and I thought I was so in God's eyes too. Sin and corruption, I said, would as naturally bubble out of my heart as water would bubble out of a fountain. I could have changed heart with anybody. I thought none but the Devil himself could equal me for inward wickedness and pollution of mind. Sure, thought I, I am forsaken of God; and thus I continued a long while, even for some years together. [44]

Bunyan's recovery was even slower and more gradual than Tolstoy's was. His peace came intermittently with disturbance as he describes it:

> My peace would be in and out twenty times a day; comfort now and trouble presently; peace now and before I could go a furlong, as full of guilt and fear as ever heart could hold. [45]

But gradually Bunyan's healthy periods accumulated:

> And now remained only the hinder part of the tempest, for the thunder was gone beyond me, only some drops would still remain . . . and at last: Now did my chains fall off my legs indeed; I was loosed from

my afflictions and irons; my temptations also fled away ... now I
went home rejoicing, for the grace and love of God.[46]

James concludes that neither Tolstoy nor Bunyan could be considered "healthy-minded" even after their recovery beause "they
had drunk too deeply of the cup of bitterness ever to forget its
taste. . ."[47] However, now both of them lived in what James
called the "two-storied universe," and they both realized a Greater
Good which broke the edge of their sadness. Tolstoy calls this
"that by which men live."[48]

James makes an interesting observation when he says that the
real core of the religious problem is: "Help! Help!"[49] He says that
no prophet can claim to have a true message unless he says things
that answer the questions of those in such despair as we have seen.
Jesus and the Buddha were certainly such, and Buddhism and
Christianity certainly deal with the problem of human suffering.
The Buddha called suffering the "first noble truth." Jesus addressed
himself to the "poor in spirit," "they that mourn," "the meek,"
"they which do hunger and thirst after righteousness," ... and he
addressed those who were "reviled" and "persecuted" and about
whom "all manner of evil" was spoken. The Buddha promised
those in suffering, Nirvana; Jesus promised all of us in exile, the
Kingdom of Heaven.

Conversion is a central topic of Christianity, and religion in
general. In James' words:

> To be converted, to be regenerated, to receive grace, to experience
> religion, to gain an assurance, are so many words which denote the
> process, gradual or sudden, by which a self hitherto divided, and
> consciously wrong, inferior and unhappy, becomes unified and con-
> sciously right, superior and happy, in consequence of its firmer hold
> upon religious realities.[50]

James' student, Starbuck, makes the important observation that to
to continue to exercise the personal will (ego) is "still to live in the
region where the imperfect self is the thing most emphasized."[51]
What must a person do to be converted (i.e. saved)? Well, Dr.
Starbuck says, he must give up trying "to do it himself." He
"must relax." This sounds peculiarly modern with the best seller,
The Relaxation Response still on the market. It is also rather Taoist.
Those who have read the *Tao Te Ching* (The Way of Life) know
that Lao Tzu says: "By non-action everything can be done."[52]

To relax, or give up the ego's self-will and control is to give
"one's self over to the new life, making it the centre of a new

personality, and living from within. . ."[53] This can be viewed in several ways: physiologically, psychologically, and theologically. Physiologically, "letting go" is to relax the state of perennial tension that makes one sick, and let the nervous system take over its own self-healing process. Psychologically, James states it nicely: "When the new centre of personal energy has been subconsciously incubated so long as to be just ready to open into flower, 'hands off' is the only word for us, it must burst forth unaided!"[54] Theologically, none has stated it better than Martin Luther who considered redemption a *free gift of grace*, and not something which we can accomplish by our own efforts. Thus, physiology, psychology, and theology are in perfect harmony on this point. However, physiology calls this the "nervous system," psychology, the "subconscious," and theology, "God."

James replies to supposed objections by orthodox Christians who would see a contradiction between these things: the nervous system, the subconscious, and God:

> But if you, being orthodox Christians, ask me as a psychologist whether the reference of a phenomenon to a subliminal self does not exclude the notion of the direct presence of the Deity altogether, I have to say frankly that as a psychologist I do not see why it necessarily should. The lower manifestations of the Subliminal, indeed, fall within the resources of the personal subject: his ordinary sense-material, inattentively taken in and subconsciously remembered and combined, will account for all his usual automatisms. But just as our primary wide-awake consciousness throws open our senses to the touch of things material, so it is logically conceivable that *if there be* higher spiritual agencies that can directly touch us, the psychological condition of their doing so *might be* our possession of a subconscious region which alone should yield access to them. The hubbub of waking life might close a door which in the dreamy Subliminal might remain ajar or open.[55]

In the marvelous genius, then, of James, the subconscious mind (or the unconscious) is viewed as a possible *doorway* to the spiritual reality. In this insight, he far surpasses Freud who would reduce religious experience to an illusion created by the projective features of the unconscious mind as we shall see in chapter five.

Another important religious psychologist of James' time was his colleague, Professor Leuba, who spoke about the faith-state thusly:

> When the sense of estrangement fencing man about in a narrowly limited ego breaks down, the individual finds himself 'at one with all

creation.' He lives in the universal life; he and man, he and nature, he and God, are one. That state of confidence, trust, union with all things, following upon the achievement of moral unity, is the *Faith-state*. Various dogmatic beliefs suddenly, on the advent of the faith-state, acquire a character of certainty, assume a new reality, become an object of faith. . .[56]

Can you imagine a psychologist of our secular-materialistic era speaking of the discovery of oneness with God and the *faith-state* spoken of by Leuba? By and large, psychology of the twentieth century has either totally ignored this vital dimension of ordinary human life, faith in God, or put it down as "primitive supersti-tion" or "illusion" in the words of the behaviorists or Freudians, asserting their own self-proclaimed "superiority" over the ordinary man and woman of this world for whom the life of prayer and faith is an everyday reality.

James finally turns to the subject of mysticism. He, unlike Bucke whom we have discussed at length, had no special access to the mystic state and he candidly says:

Whether my treatment of mystical states will shed more light or darkness, I do not know, for my own constitution shuts me out from their enjoyment almost entirely, and I can speak of them only at second hand.[57]

Nonetheless, James says that he will look at the mystical experi-ence as objectively and receptively as he can, and he thinks he will convince the reader of its importance and validity. James sees four characteristics that for him describe the mystical experience (you recall that Bucke listed eleven characteristics of the true experience of Cosmic Consciousness).

James' Four Criteria of Mystical Experience[58]
(1) *Ineffability* – The handiest of the marks by which I classify a state of mind as mystical is negative. The subject of it immedi-ately says that it defies expression, that no adequate report of its contents can be given in words. It follows from this that its quality must be directly experienced; it cannot be imparted or transferred to others.
(2) *Noetic quality* – Although so similar to states of feeling, mysti-cal states seem to those who experience them to be also states of knowledge. They are states of insight into the depths of truth unplumbed by the discursive intellect. They are illumi-nations, revelations, full of significance and importance . . .

and as a rule they carry with them a curious sense of authority for after-time.

(3) *Transiency* – Mystical states cannot be sustained for long. Except in rare instances, half an hour, or at most an hour or two, seems to be the limit beyond which they fade into the light of common day.

(4) *Passivity* – Although the oncoming of mystical states may be facilitated by preliminary voluntary operations, as by fixing the attention, or going through certain bodily performances, or in other ways which manuals of mysticism prescribe; yet when the characteristic sort of consciousness once has set in, the mystic feels as if his own will were in abeyance, and indeed sometimes grasped by a superior power.

I can verify, as a mystic myself (I have known the mystical experience), that these four criteria are accurate. They add some new insights to Bucke's list of criteria, and overlap with them in certain respects, too. "Ineffability" and "noetic quality" are excellent words chosen by James to describe the mystical state of consciousness. But, I can say: *even much more than that.* One thing that James leaves out is the sense of Oneness of all Creation; and the experience of the *One* behind the *Many* known to the mystics themselves. On the mystical experience, James speaks as a highly sensitive outsider who emphasizes its "ineffability," whereas Bucke had spoken as a true insider who could speak very specifically of such things as "the subjective light," "the moral elevation," "the intellectual illumination," "the sense of immortality," and so on.

James makes a statement which is now a classic one on the possibilities for higher states of consciousness beyond the ordinary:

> . . . our normal waking consciousness, rational consciousness as we call it, is but one special type of consciousness, whilst all about it, parted from it by the flimsiest of screens, there lie potential forms of consciousness entirely different. [59]

In illustration of this, James gives an account from the memoirs of the German idealist, Malwida von Meysenburg:

> I was alone upon the seashore as all these thoughts flowed over me, liberating and reconciling; and now again, as once before in distant days in the Alps of Dauphine, I was impelled to kneel down, this time before the illimitable ocean, symbol of the infinite. I felt that I prayed

as I had never prayed before, and knew now what prayer really is: to return from the solitude of individuation into the consciousness of unity with all that is, to kneel down as one that passes away, and to rise up as one imperishable. Earth, heaven, sea resounded as in one vast world-encircling harmony. It was as if the chorus of all the great who had ever lived were about me. I felt myself one with them, and it appeared as if I heard their greeting: "Thou too belongest to the company of those who overcome."[60]

James looks at some of the great mystical traditions, Hindu, Buddhist, Mohammedan, and Christian. In the Christian tradition, he quotes St. Teresa of Avila on the "orison of union:"

In the orison of union the soul is fully awake as regards God, but wholly asleep as regards the things of this world and in respect of herself. During the short time the union lasts, she is as it were deprived of every feeling, and even if she would, she could not think of any single thing. Thus she needs to employ no artifice in order to arrest the use of her understanding: it remains so stricken with inactivity that she neither knows, nor in what manner she loves, nor what she wills. In short, she is utterly dead to the things of the world and lives solely in God.[61]

James the non-mystic makes some important observations about the mystic state:

This incommunicableness of the transport is the keynote of all mysticism. Mystical truth exists for the individual who has the transport, but for no one else.[62]

And:

This overcoming of all the usual barriers between the individual and the Absolute is the great mystic achievement. In mystic states we both become one with the Absolute and we become aware of our oneness. This is the everlasting and triumphant mystical tradition, hardly altered by differences of clime or creed.[63]

Finally:

Yet, I repeat once more, the existence of mystical states absolutely overthrows the pretensions of non-mystical states to be the sole and ultimate dictators of what we may believe.[64]

The great philosopher and psychologist, William James, finally resigned his position at Harvard in 1907, wrote his last book, *A Pluralistic Universe*, and died at his country home in rural New Hampshire in 1910.

A NOTE ON THE LOWELL LECTURES

Eugene Taylor, who lectures at the Harvard Medical School, wrote an interesting book on the never-before-published 1896 Lowell Lectures of William James in his *William James on Exceptional Mental States* (1982, 1983). Taylor states that:

> William James advocated a balance between science and religion in an age when religious themes had been plowed under and the scientific outlook had just begun its meteoric rise within American culture. He spoke out against the Social Darwinists by supporting the supremacy of individual choice in mental, as opposed to strictly biological, evolution; he attacked medical materialism by emphasizing the healing power of personal religious experience; and he argued against the supremacy of the intellect by stressing the primacy of emotions, the importance of our sentiments and the efficacy of our beliefs in his total view of human personality.[65]

By the 1890s, James, who was one of the founders of "scientific psychology," had already become disenchanted with the narrowness of its positivistic view of the human mind. James gave a series of lectures in Boston, in 1896, called "the Lowell Lectures," in which he discussed various topics of interest to him. These lectures indicate the very broad scope of James' thought in an increasingly narrow world of "scientific psychology" (which narrows down to "stimulus-response" in behaviorism). Here is a summary of the Lowell Lectures:

> Each lecture introduces a major idea. James' first talk, on "Dreams and Hypnotism," focuses on the hypnagogic state, or the twilight region between waking and sleeping common natural sleep and hypnotism. Hypnotism then becomes a means for experimentally inducing at will an otherwise inaccessible experience. His second lecture, on "Automatism," introduces the reality of subliminal consciousness – that each of us has within himself two simultaneously operating systems of intelligent consciousness, one above the threshold of awareness and one below, with its separate characteristics. The third lecture, on "Hysteria," demonstrates the power of the buried idea. Split off from consciousness because of traumatic shock, the buried idea operates parasitically in the subconscious according to laws of its own. The fourth lecture, on "Multiple Personality," argues for the existence of a growth-oriented dimension within each personality. Although psychic fragments can often develop into seemingly independent personalities, what may emerge are permanently superior dimensions not normally accessible to waking awareness.

In the fifth lecture, on "Demoniacal Possession," James demonstrates the phenomenon of hysterical mass contagion within large populations – imitative neuropathic hysteria on a grand scale, he called it. The sixth, on "Witchcraft," clearly shows that the accusers and the judges were really insane, while many of the victims of the Inquisition and the Salem epidemic were clearly hysterics. The seventh lecture, on "Degeneration," hints at the great potential inherent in our understanding of psychosis if we would but apply the methods of the new experimental psychology of the subconscious. And in the final lecture, James shows that true geniuses are not morbid types but are, rather, the solitary heroes of humanity.[66]

Taylor points out that some of the contents of the Lowell Lectures of 1896 contributed their contents to major sections of several chapters of *The Varieties of Religious Experience* which was published in 1902. It was truly tragic (as we shall see in the following chapter) that psychology in the ensuing twentieth century failed to follow James' own lead in studying altered states of consciousness, inner phenomena, and religious experience, and opted instead for a simplistic imitation of nineteenth century physical science.

3

John B. Watson's Behaviorism and the "Banishment of Consciousness" from Psychology's Curriculum

John Broadhus Watson was born in 1878 in the rural town of Greenville, South Carolina. It was a very religious place. His mother, Emma, was a Baptist and a fundamentalist believer. Watson was the son of a poor farmer named Pickens Watson. His mother, Emma, employed a black nurse to care for John who used to tell him that the Devil lurked in the dark and that if he went walking during the night, the Evil One might well snatch him. To be terrified of the Devil was only wise and prudent. All of this left Watson with a lifelong phobia of the dark of which he was never able to rid himself.[1] These early experiences may explain, in part, Watson's later contemptuous attitude toward religion, and anything that "smacked of" religion such as God and the soul. His fear of the dark may have related to his fear and distrust of the inward and mysterious, i.e., mind and consciousness, and his preference for the outer and tangible realities. The adult Watson was evangelical only in his crusade against soul, mind, and consciousness.

The Reedy River Church to which Emma Watson took John believed in strict Christian discipline. Even smoking, drinking and dancing were forbidden. But all of Emma's attempts to mold John into a religious person failed. He did everything he could to escape from his mother's religious fundamentalism. John preferred his father, Pickens, who taught him a whole variety of practical and manual skills. Father and son got along well. Pickens was a hillbilly character who was given to drinking and womanizing. He left his wife and son when the latter was thirteen years old. John felt that his father had betrayed him, and he was devastated by this rejection. Years later when Pickens was in New York

95

City to get in touch with his then famous son, John refused to see him, though he was well over eighty.[2] He rejected the father who had rejected him. However, some of his father's bad habits had rubbed off on him. John Watson drank and swore a lot, and he had affairs with women even after he was married. One of these was to have a disastrous effect upon his academic career.

John was a rather wild, rough-and-ready boy who mocked his teachers and fought a lot. He also engaged in that Southern pastime of "nigger fighting." On the way home from school, he set upon blacks with his friends.[3] Manual work became Watson's consolation after his father left him and his mother. Watson would later define true happiness as forgetting one's self; when one was really happy, one did not think.[4] Watson and his mother became very close when his father left; Emma had a considerable hold over him that did not pass until her death. Because of this, Watson was tremendously afraid of homosexuality.[5]

Watson's life took a radical turn when he was fifteen years old. He got himself admitted to Furman University in his hometown despite his poor school record.[6] At Furman, Watson took courses in algebra, history, Latin, Greek, and science. He studied, also, the philosophy and psychology of the time (1895) which consisted largely of the study of consciousness.[7] There were introspective exercises – no searching of your soul – but watching something like three dots on a screen and reporting on what went on in your mind. This was introspective psychology on the undergraduate level in the 1890s. His psychology teacher taught him of Wundt, the German psychologist who founded the first psychology laboratory in Leipzig in 1879. Wundt believed that the "elements of consciousness" could be dissected out by introspection in much the manner that chemists analyzed substances into their basic chemical constituents. Early introspectionism was not a holistic but an atomistic science; later behaviorism was to have this in common with its predecessor, at least in the forms practiced by Wundt in Europe and Titchener in America. James' psychology resembled more closely the Gestaltists in that it dealt with the wholes of experience as the basic facts.

Watson left Greenville in 1900 for the University of Chicago. He never set foot in church again. He rejected religion completely and turned to the "behavioristic creed."[8] He took the train from Greenville to Chicago with fifty dollars at the age of twenty-two. Eight years later he left Chicago with a national reputation as an animal psychologist at Johns Hopkins University at the age of twenty-nine. He first studied philosophy at the University of Chicago – the Greek philosophers, Kant, etc. – but he got nothing out of them. He did like Hume who taught that the belief that the sun will rise is just an "associative habit."[9] Watson said that Hume "freed him intellectually,"[10] and there is surely a real connection between the British associationist philosophers, Hume and Locke, and the behaviorist psychologists of America and Russia. However, Watson, the atheist, regarding philosophy said: "God knows, I took enough philosophy . . . but it wouldn't take hold . . . the spark was not there."[11]

At the University of Chicago, Watson came under the influence of the psychologist, James Angell, who was an introspectionist who said that the main task of the psychologist was to analyze the stream of consciousness, habits, the will, the self, and the soul. Angell was obviously a disciple of William James. Via Angell, Watson always had a soft spot in his heart for James even as an archbehaviorist. At the University, Watson worked on the learning ability of white laboratory rats. His Ph.D. thesis was called: "Animal Education." It was in the work with the rats that Watson had his first glimpses of behaviorism. Wrote Watson: "If you could understand rats without the convolutions of introspection, could you not understand people in the same way?"[12]

A contemporary of Watson, the American psychiatrist Dr. Louis Berman wrote a book called *The Religion Called Behaviorism* (1927). In it he said:

> Now while the human being is the subject par excellence of human psychology, he cannot be that of behaviorism, for it is not feasible to carry out many behavioristic experiments upon human beings.[13]

Hence, instead of the human being, another animal had to be substituted. Curiously, that animal turned out to be not any of the higher primates, but the standard white or albino rat. That rodent with the soft yielding body, that could easily be grasped in one hand, had been appointed by the fates to be the instrumentality through which the behaviorists deemed fit to penetrate the profound secrets of the human heart. Never until the twentieth century, did the auspicious moment arrive that a lowly mammal, the rodent, was set before us as the great exemplar for the elucidation of the true laws of human nature! Berman, in speculating on the meaning of behaviorism in the wider context, states that we live in an age of anti-feeling, anti-soul, anti-human values, an age of materialism and mechanism. The inner life is derided and denied.

He says that behaviorism is the product of this age. No matter that behaviorism's simplistic stimulus–response formula, says Berman, is totally inadequate to the most elementary facts of human actions and insight. [14]

Returning to the young graduate student, Watson, he said that he personally hated to serve as a subject in introspection experiments almost as much as he hated church! Watson said, "with animals I was at home." [15] Watson had a nervous break-down before he graduated from the University of Chicago, and he took a three-month vacation with friends in Michigan to recover. [16]

While still at the University of Chicago, Watson taught psychology. Until 1909, he used Titchener's manual on introspection. But, when he abandoned introspectionism, he turned to animal psychology. He said that there was no point in the study of animal behavior, in the inferring of "states of consciousness." [17] Their behavior itself was all that was worth studying. Watson would eventually make the same claim about human behavior.

On February 23, 1913, Watson gave his first lectures on be-havioristic psychology at Columbia University in New York City. In his lecture, "Psychology as the Behaviorist views it," he said:

> Psychology as the behaviorist views it is a purely objective experimen-tal branch of natural science. Its theoretical goal is the prediction and control of behavior. Introspection forms no essential part of its methods, nor is the scientific value of its data dependent upon the readiness with which they lend themselves to interpretations in terms of consciousness. The behaviorist, in his efforts to get a unitary scheme of animal response, recognizes no dividing line between man and brute. [18]

We have here in Watson's proclamation the diametric opposite of James who defined psychology as "the description and explana-tion of states of consciousness as such." [19] Watson's "behavioristic revolution" was the death knell of the science of mind (in America at least) for a half century. Why his views, so obviously counter-intuitive, have been so influential is a question for future intellec-tual historians. I myself attended undergraduate college during the last years of the "behaviorist dynasty" and my questions about mind and soul were not answered or even dealt with in the context of the academic psychology of the time (early 1960s). I eventually left academia to pursue the spiritual path and study the *sacred psychologies* in the various religious traditions of humankind as I describe in my book, *Physicians of the Soul*.

Watson was so adamant and radical in his denunciation of psychology as the "science of consciousness" that he went on to say in the same lecture:

> I believe we can write a psychology . . . and never go back upon our definition, never use the terms consciousness, mental states, mind . . . It can be done in terms of stimulus and response, in terms of habit formation, habit integration and the like. [20]

Watson went on to make this self-contradictory statement:

> Our minds have been so warped by the fifty odd years that have been devoted to the study of the states of consciousness that we can envisage these problems only in one way. [21]

Rather than dealing with the profound mysteries of consciousness, denial of its existence was Watson's strategy.

We saw in Richard Bucke, M.D. the beginnings of a science of consciousness with the elaboration of four levels of mind from the perceptual to the cosmic conscious. In his theory, Bucke encompassed everything from the simple consciousness of lower animals to the illumined consciousness of saints and mystics. In John B. Watson, Ph.D., we see this work eliminated in one fell swoop, and we are told that all creatures from protozoa to Gautama the Buddha are reflex organisms based upon response to stimulation! If psychology had lost its soul in the seventeenth through nineteenth centuries, it *truly lost its mind* with the behaviorism of Watson.

What were the reactions of some of the other leading psychologists of Watson's time?

E. B. Titchener, the famous introspectionist psychologist said that Watson's program was to found a "technology," not a psychology. Titchener reaffirmed that psychology was about the mind. [22]

James Angell, the functionalist disciple of William James, wrote to E. B. Titchener: "I am wholly impatient of his position on this issue which seems to me scientifically unsound and philosophically essentially illiterate." [23]

Other psychologists, McDougall, Munsterberg, Cattell, Woodsworth, and Thorndike, attacked Watson's extreme position which "ruled out mind." [24] Still others pointed out that Watson's behaviorism related to the positivistic philosophy of

Compte and the materialistic physics of La Mettrie, both late nineteenth century figures. Finally, it was pointed out by other critics that behaviorism was not based on new discoveries at all, but merely upon a new paradigm. Watson discovered nothing. He offered a new method: Study behavior – ignore consciousness.

Watson's "vision" hardly swept away all other psychologies. Psychoanalysis and its various offshoots flourished in Europe, as did Gestalt psychology, and phenomenology. It did do profound damage to the progress of the science of mind, or soul, in America. (We will look at his counterpart, Pavlov, in Russia, later.) Watson had attacked introspection and consciousness; it is strange that he went on to try to diminish the importance of the brain and central nervous system as well! He identified consciousness with the cortex and attempted to show that psychologists "revere the cortex" because they were trying to "smuggle in the mind,"[25] or even – heaven forbid – "the soul." Therefore Watson proclaimed ex cathedra:

> There are no centrally initiated processes. In itself, the brain can conjure up nothing. It is utterly dependent on stimulation from the periphery.[26]

We will see in the next chapter, both in the work of the great neuropsychologist, Karl Lashley, and in the work of the Nobel Laureate neurophysiologist, Sir John Eccles, that Watson spoke a profoundly unscientific untruth when he made that statement. Watson in his fanaticism to "wipe out" the study of consciousness (as earlier philosophers, Hume and Locke, had denied the immortal soul) even extended his attack upon the physical brain itself, the central nervous system!

In Watson's presidential address to the American Psychological Association in 1915 called "The Conditioned Reflex and Its Place in Psychology," he gave an account of the work of the Russian physiologists, Pavlov and Bechterev. He suggested that the ideas of the Russians could have wide application in psychology.[27] But Watson used the physiological term "reflex" so broadly that it applied both to salivation or a muscle twitch and to complex human behavior such as drawing a revolver and shooting someone, or painting a picture, or giving a speech to the members of the American Pyschological Association! This may be called stretching a simple idea so broadly that it loses all meaning and all sense.

Watson had studied Freud over several years, and he felt that what Freud said was true, but not in the way that Freud put it.

Having "swept consciousness out of psychology," the behaviorist, Watson, was hardly about to accept "the unconscious mind" as a reality. Watson translated Freud in this way:

> The central truth that I think Freud has given us is that youthful, outgrown ... habit and instinctive systems of reaction can and possibly always do influence the functioning of our adult systems of reactions and influence, to a certain extent, even the possibility of our forming new habit systems which we must reasonably be expected to form . . .[28]

Watson argued that many of the so-called "mental diseases" were conditioned reflexes of which the conditioning was essentially inappropriate.[29] Whereas there is truth to the idea that emotions are, in part, conditionable, and neuroses may be based upon early traumatic experiences, few psychiatrists, even those of the biological school, would agree with Watson's denial of the existence and importance of mind, both conscious and unconscious. Nevertheless, there is no doubt that Watson laid down the basis for what is now called "behavior therapy."

Watson published his magnum opus, *Behaviorism*, in 1924, and it has gone through a number of revisions since then. It is his classical expression of behavioristic psychology. It will be instructive to look at it in the light of the two previous psychologies we have looked at, that of Bucke and that of James. It is, essentially, the denial of all that Bucke and James so brilliantly elucidated about the nature of consciousness from the most ordinary to the most illumined. The light of consciousness *goes out* with John Broadhus Watson. Let us look at this work of Watson's. His book begins by associating the soul with religion, which he then proceeds to denigrate as "prescientific," "superstitious," and worse. To quote Watson:

> Behaviorism claims that consciousness is neither a definite nor a usable concept. The behaviorist . . . holds further, that belief in the existence of consciousness goes back to the ancient days of superstition and magic.[30]

Watson goes on to say that:

> One example of such a religious concept is that every individual has a *soul* which is separate and distinct from the *body*. This soul is really part of a supreme being. This ancient view led to the philosophical platform called 'dualism.' This dogma has been present in human psychology from earliest antiquity. No one has ever touched a soul, or seen

one in a test tube, or has in any way come into relationship with it as he has with other objects of his daily experience. Nevertheless, to doubt its existence is to become a heretic . . .[31]

Watson is correct that the soul is a religious concept. It is also a concept of every culture of humankind from time immemorial. Why on earth did people of all cultures form the concept of the soul if it had no reality or referred to no definite experience? Were all our ancestors, including the great saints, sages, and prophets (whom Bucke looked at courageously and scientifically), merely "bewitched" by magic and superstition as Watson claims? Is it possible that Watson overgeneralized from his own rather punitive experiences with the religious fundamentalism of his Southern rural subculture, including that of his mother, as well as his black governess who frightened him with the idea that "the Devil lurked in the dark?" Quite the contrary from Watson's assertion that the soul refers to nothing experienced, the soul refers to the deepest and most immediate reality within each of us. It is obvious that Watson lost contact with his own soul, and generalizes this to the idea that *there is no soul.* One true statement of Watson's is that "the soul is really part of a supreme being." The Hindus believe that the soul, or Atman, is really part of the supreme soul, or Brahman. The American Indians believed that the individual soul, or manitou, is part of the supreme soul, or Great Manitou. Christian mystics have expressed this view, as well, from Meister Eckhart to Jacob Boehme to St. John of the Cross. However, Watson's purpose in stating this was different than that of the mystics. Since, in Watson's day, atheism and materialism were the "obvious positions" of so-called intellectuals and scholars, the association of the soul with the "supreme being" was one way to denigrate this concept. Guilt by association! Watson's defamation of religion goes on in the earliest pages of his book:

The great mass of the people even today has not yet progressed very far away from savagery . . it wants to believe in magic. The savage believes that incantations can bring rain, good crops, good hunting, that an unfriendly voodoo doctor can bring disaster to a person or a whole tribe; that an enemy who has obtained a nail paring or a lock of your hair can cast a harmful spell over you and control your actions . . . Almost every era has its new magic, black or white, and its new magician. Moses had his magic; he smote the rock and water gushed out. Christ had his magic: he turned water into wine and raised the dead to life . . . Mrs. Eddy had a similar one.[32]

Glory be! John Watson, the founder of "scientific behaviorism" refers to both Moses and Christ. But rather than study their profound teachings as theologians do, or speculate as to their consciousness as Bucke and James did, Watson mentions the founders of Judaism and Christianity to associate them with the terms "savagery," "voodoo doctor," and "magician." In terms of Watson's own conditioning theory, we are evidently meant to "learn by association" to react in similar ways to the terms "soul" and "consciousness," and the names "Moses" and "Jesus" as we already do to the words "savagery," "voodoo doctor," and "magician." By this facile verbal game, Watson dismisses the history of religion and mysticism, including the experiences of the religious mystics, as so much "hogwash" or "balderdash." Going on in this anti-religious vein, Watson says that:

> Magic lives forever. As time goes on, all of these critically undigested, innumerably told tales get woven into the folklore of the people. Folklore in turn gets organized into religions – Religions get caught up into the political and economic network of the country. Then they are used as tools. The public is forced to accept all of the old wives' tales, and passes them on as gospel to its children's children. [33]

Hence, for Watson, the religions begin in "old wives' tales." He gives no credence whatsoever to the existence of religious and mystical experience. This is curiously as dogmatic and unscientific as the bishops at the time of Galileo who refused to look through the telescope lest they see the craters of the moon, the rings of Saturn, and the moons of Jupiter! What Watson has done from the start of his book is to mock religion, and then associate the soul with religion, and hence discredit the soul. He associates this with "science," the rejection of religion, and thereby religious experience. In the next chapter we shall see that the greatest scientists of our time believe in all that Watson denies: consciousness, soul, and even God. Watson came out of a peculiar era of science which felt itself in violent opposition to religion and all that has ever been associated with religion, even the human soul. Watson himself had his even more extreme personal battle with religion.

Watson claims that psychology and its ancestor, philosophy, found it difficult to "escape the language of the church." [34] He feels that "we have the church to blame" for the fact that psychologists down to the late nineteenth century considered soul and consciousness to be their subject of inquiry. Watson felt that Wundt, the founder of experimental psychology, could not see his way clear to "scientific behaviorism," so he substituted the term "consciousness" for the older theological term, the "soul." Watson says that consciousness is not quite as unobservable as soul, as we sometimes glimpse the former by "peeking in and catching it unawares as it were."[35] This method is called introspection. Watson does not have too high a respect for this method as a basis for a scientific psychology. Watson also speaks of William James, the American philosopher-psychologist of the late nineteenth century whom we looked at in the previous chapter. He does not have much use for his "subjectivist" concepts such as "sensations," "images," "feelings," and the like. Watson does not even deem fit to mention James' book, *The Varieties of Religious Experience* (which we have discussed in detail). If Watson can make the outrageous claim that even sensations do not exist, then how much less credence would he give to reports of mystical experience and cosmic consciousness? Watson said that the behaviorist begins by "sweeping away all medieval conceptions. . ." dropping from his "scientific vocabulary" all "subjective terms," such as "sensation," "perception," "image," "desire," "purpose," and "even thinking and emotion as they were subjectively defined."[36] We must sacrifice very much before the behaviorist's altar of scientism! With Watson, psychology makes a "new beginning" by dropping its subject matter: the *human psyche*. In terms of Bucke's evolutionary theory of consciousness, Watson returns to preconscious sentience as the standard for all organismic behavior. To quote Watson:

> The rule, or measuring rod, which the behaviorist puts in front of him always is: Can I describe this bit of behavior in terms of "stimulus and response?" By stimulus we mean any object in the general environment or any change in the tissues themselves due to the physiological condition of the animal. . . By response we mean anything the animal does – such as turning toward or away from a light, jumping at a sound, and more organized activities such as building a skyscraper, drawing plans, having babies, writing books, and the like.[37]

It is Watson's and other behaviorists' claim, then, that "the behavior" of writing books or designing skyscrapers, to take two of his examples, is "explainable" in terms of the same "general principles" as simple reflexes such as turning toward or away from a light, or jumping at a sound! In Watson's view, as we shall see, complex behavior is no more than the "concatenation" of elementary S-R reflexes. In the next chapter, we shall discover that this claim is profoundly unscientific and untrue as shown by the work of such scientists as Karl Lashley, the neuropsychologist, Sir John Eccles, the neurophysiologist, and David Bohm, the physicist. When we speak a sentence, for example, we begin with a conscious or semiconscious *whole idea* which in turn breaks down into a grammatical and semantical sentence which is composed of word phrases, which is composed of single word concepts, which is expressed by a group of phonemes, each of which is an incredibly complex act of neuromuscular integration. Watson would assert that the sentence is simply a chain of muscular stimuli and responses at the laryngeal level. As if Shakespeare's tongue and larynx wrote his plays and not his very great and illumined brain and mind. The absurdity of the behaviorists' claims are only exceeded by the arrogance with which they state them.

Watson was an "innovator" in bringing the newborn human being into his behaviorist experimental laboratory. He asks:

> What is the baby doing now? What is the stimulus that makes him behave this way?[38]

Watson made an investigation of the "fear response" in newborns. He is hesitant to use any term so subjective as "fear" and says that to be objective we might call it reaction X! He does make the finding that such "stimuli" as snakes, fish, darkness, fire, etc., will not bring out a "fear response," and that only two things will, namely, a loud sound and the loss of support. This is one of Watson's few actual empirical findings.

J. B. Watson wondered how it is that in real life, outside the laboratory, hundreds of stimuli will call out fear. In order to study this Watson suggested and carried out the following experiment on an infant. Its questionable morality will occur to any thoughtful reader. Watson suggests to take a snake, mouse, dog, fur hat, or whatever, and allow the child to play with it. He says you will see no fear reaction. Then he suggests picking up a steel bar and striking it loudly behind the infant's head while he is playing with the object in question. He says that you will see a very strong fear reaction. Now, the next time you show him the animal or object he was playing with you will find that it produces the same response as the loud sound originally did. Watson is applying Pavlovian conditioning in this "experiment." Pavlov conditioned dogs to salivate to the sound of a bell by essentially the same method. These are Watson's notes about his "experiment" with conditioning a fear response in an eleven-month-old infant, baby Albert:

Eleven months, 3 days—. (1) White rat which he had played with for weeks was suddenly taken from the basket (the usual routine) and presented to Albert. He began to reach for rat with left hand. Just as his hand touched the animal the bar was struck immediately behind his head. The infant jumped violently and fell forward, burying his face in the mattress. He did not cry, however. (2) Just as his right hand touched the rat the bar was again struck. Again the infant jumped violently, fell forward and began to whimper.[39]

Watson noted that "On account of his disturbed condition no further tests were made for a week."[40] Seven days later, Watson notes "objectively":

Eleven months, ten days – Watson presents the rat with and without the violent sound for eight more trials – on the seventh trial: (7) Combined stimulation. Startled violently and cried, but did not fall over. On the eighth (8) Rat alone. The instant the rat was shown the baby began to cry. Almost instantly he turned sharply to the left, fell over, raised himself on all fours and began to crawl away so rapidly that he was caught with difficulty before he reached the edge of the mattress.[41]

With total unconcern for the possibly grievous emotional harm that he has done to a very young child, Watson proudly proclaimed: "Surely this proof of the conditioned *origins* of a fear response puts us on a natural science ground in our study of emotional behavior."[42]

Watson had no opportunity, he said, to "uncondition" Albert's "experimental phobia" of white rats, which had generalized to all furry objects, such as dogs, cats, furry hats, a fur coat, a person's hair, and even a Santa Claus mask! Since this experiment was done in the 1920s, we wonder whether somewhere there is a man in his seventies who still has nightmares about rats, dogs, cats, and furry objects? Such a consequence would weigh little for Watson whose reverence seemed reserved for the "Great God Science."

In an incredibly shocking statement on page 185 of his classic book, *Behaviorism,* Watson shows us the behaviorist "morality" when he states:

The question as to whether the hopelessly insane should be etherized has of course been raised time and time again. There can be no reason against it except exaggerated sentiment and medieval religious mandates.[43]

I might point out that this is exactly what Adolf Hitler *did do*. He exterminated the mentally ill using gas to do so. They were the first to suffer mass death at the hands of the Nazis before their attentions turned to the Jews. It is most interesting that the *same consequences* flow from both the behaviorist creed of Watson and the Nazi creed of Hitler. You recall in the previous chapter the brief discussion of William James' philosophy of pragmatism. It has to do with the *practical consequences* of ideas or theories. If behaviorism and, for that matter, Nazism, were merely intellectual theories of use only in the philosophy classroom, we would not be too much concerned with them; they would be of little import to practical life. We do not much care about the semantic hair-splitting of philosophers. But, quite to the contrary, both behaviorism and Nazism lead to very drastic actual consequences. Both philosophies seem to lead to the conclusion that the "less fit" or "inferior," as defined by "those in charge," should surely be eliminated forthwith from our midst. This monstrous "philosophy" is the diametric opposite of the Judeo-Christian moral tradition encapsulated by Moses in the Ten Commandments and by Jesus in the Golden Rule. Watson would dismiss these as "medieval religious mandates."

Watson scoffs at the Christian Mass, a holy ritual that has sustained countless millions of believers for the past two millenia:

> Bread is something to be eaten when hungry. Wine is something to be drunk with meals or on festive occasions. But these simple, commonplace, unemotional objects call out kneeling, prayer, bowing of the head, closing the eyes, and a whole mass of other verbal and bodily responses, when fed to individuals at church under the guise of communion. [44]

Contrast this with the profound depth of Jung's psychological study of the Mass which we will examine in chapter six. I am a Jewish-Christian, and I find Watson's remarks to be beneath contempt. If there is any doubt that behaviorism is a fundamentally atheistic and anti-Judeo-Christian philosophy, the above quote from Watson's own book should settle that matter once and for all. Later behaviorists of the more "purely scientific" vein do not speak much about these aspects of their founding father, John Watson, his anti-moral and his anti-religious views. They are not peripheral, but central to his conception.

What were Watson's socio-economic and political views? He expresses them neatly in the following statement:

> Naturally, no human being – criminal or otherwise – should be deprived of air, sunshine, food, exercise, and other physiological fac-

tors necessary to optimum living conditions. On the other hand, strenuous work twelve hours per day will hurt no one. Individuals put aside thus for additional training should of course be kept in the hands of the behaviorists.[45]

When Watson spoke of "prediction and control of behavior," he was not merely talking "scientific method." He had in mind "control by the behaviorists." Is this not totalitarianism of the order of Hitler or Stalin? I think so. Watson's successor to the behavioristic throne, B. F. Skinner, tries to express the behavioristic social and ethical credo in more mellifluous terms in his book *Walden Two* which is about a "utopian community" which bases itself upon behavioristic principles.

Watson makes it plain that the behaviorist is not just a disinterested observer or even experimenter in the realm of behavior. He goes beyond scientific explanation and prediction to *control* when he says:

> The interest of the behaviorist in man's doings is more than the interest of the spectator – he wants to control man's reactions as physical scientists want to control and manipulate other natural phenomena. It is the business of behavioristic psychology to be able to predict and control human activity.[46]

Behaviorism would seem to be an ideal ally of authoritarian and totalitarian states, Fascist and Communist, in its obsession with both predicting and controlling human behavior. It is hardly an ally of democracy and freedom. The free man and woman have no place in behavioristic philosophy.

Yet, despite these consequences for religion, morality, and social behavior, behaviorism is an extremely simple-minded doctrine. This is how Watson characterizes it:

> We can throw all of our psychological problems and their solutions into terms of stimulus and response. Let us use the abbreviation S for *stimulus* . . . and R for *response*.[47]

This is the schema of the behaviorists: "S-R." How can such a simple-minded notion do any harm you might wonder? It is not really what behaviorism affirms (almost nothing of any significance) but what it denies (all that is significant) that causes the problem. It denies that *there is anything going on* between the stimulus and the response! I am sitting here at my typewriter writing about behaviorism critically. According to the behaviorists, there is no "me" who is doing the writing; there is no self.

There is only my immediate environment, and past environmental history, and the responses that it elicits or evokes: writing this chapter on behaviorism. It is the universal tendency of bigots and racists to deny the humanity of their victims or scapegoats, whether it be the black, or the Jew, or the Armenian, and so on. The behaviorist would victimize us all by denying our essential humanity, that we are living souls with minds and hearts. In his introduction to *Behaviorism*, Watson says that he makes no distinction between a human being and "an ox being led to the slaughter."[48] A strange and revealing metaphor indeed!

Characteristically human are the functions of language and thinking. Most thinkers of the past and present consider these to be the unique possessions of the *Homo sapiens*. This is what Watson, the original behaviorist, does with language and thinking. To the question, "what is language?":

> Language as we ordinarily understand it, in spite of its complexities, is really a manipulative habit.[49]

Words, for Watson, are "conditioned verbal responses" to "environmental stimuli." He says that after word responses have become established, phrase and sentence habits form. It is all "stimulus – response." This is a profound falsehood about the nature of human language at every level from the phoneme to meaningful discourse as Noam Chomsky, the linguist, has shown in his critique of Watson's successor B. F. Skinner's *Verbal Behavior* (1957). Let me simply say here that language is hierarchical, recursive, holistic, and creative to a degree beyond the capacity of any linguist to fully characterize it, or any computer to simulate it. Language, it can be said, is infinitely creative. The human child learns his native language in a remarkably rapid way based upon extremely limited data on the basis of, Chomsky believes, innate mental structures, and a prodigious ability to hypothesize, check hypotheses, and form complex theories, i.e., "grammars." Watson's and Skinner's theories of verbal chaining fail completely in explanatory power in accounting for language acquisition and use.

To the next question, "What is thinking?":

> The behaviorist advances the view that what the psychologists have hitherto called thought is in short nothing but talking to ourselves.[50]

If language consists of "S-R" chains for the behaviorists, thinking is the recitation of the same subvocally. Thought for the behaviorist

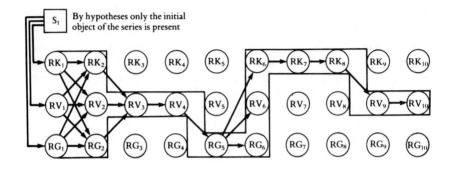

Figure 3.1   This diagram shows the behaviorist's theory of thinking. Sometimes we think by using manual, verbal and visceral organizations simultaneously. Sometimes only the verbal, sometimes only the visceral and at other times only the manual. In the diagram the organization taking part in the whole thinking process is enclosed between the two continuous solid lines.

is internal speech. Does this explain problem solving, novelty, creativity, insight, or intuition? Watson is even reluctant to admit that *the brain* has a part in thinking, having already "banished" the mind. To quote Watson:

> The alternative sometimes advanced to this theory is that so-called central processes may take place in the brain . . .[51]

No neuroscientist of today worth his salt, not even those who would not touch the soul-idea with a hundred-foot pole, would deny that the brain is the organ of thought!

We have covered the behaviorist "theory" of language and thought. What about the self, or personality, the "I" and the "me" which James so brilliantly described? In his chapter on personality in *Behaviorism*, Watson makes these statements:

> Let us try to think of man as an assembled organic machine ready to run.[52]

Watson goes on to say:

> Personality is the sum of activities that can be discovered by actual observation of behavior over a long enough time to give reliable information. In other words, personality is but the end product of our habit systems.[53]

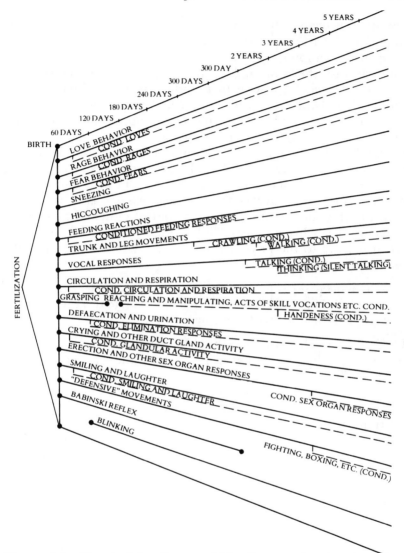

Figure 3.2 The Activity Stream. This diagram showing increasing complexity of certain human action systems. The black solid line shows the unlearned beginning of each system. The dotted line shows how each system is made complex by conditioning.

Some of the systems apparently are not modified. They exist in the stream throughout life without increasing in complexity.

The chart is neither complete nor accurate. Until more thorough genetic work has been done, a chart of this kind cannot be used as a measuring rod of what to expect of infants at different ages.

Freudian psychoanalysis, with its conscious and unconscious mind, and later the ego, the id, and the superego, is dismissed by Watson as "demonology." That name stuck, and behaviorists ever since dismiss the profound contributions of the psychoanalytic school of psychology with that epithet. Watson criticizes Freud for his view that consciousness or the unconscious is a "real force" which can do something, initiate something, inhibit something, or check something that is going on. Watson is saying that what we think of as our minds is a fiction; it does not exist! He equates this view with "science." We will see in the next chapter that the greatest scientists of our century, e.g., in neurophysiology, physics, and even psychology, see *consciousness* as a basic constituent of reality from the atom to the human brain/mind. Watson reveals his simplistic "billiard ball" view of the universe when he says to the physician who deals with the behavior, the psychiatrist:

> ... face the physical fact that the only way you can get a billiard ball on the table in front of you to start moving ... is to strike it with a cue or get another ball already moving to strike it ...[54]

Unless the psychiatrist faces these "materialistic facts," according to Watson, they "will never get a scientific viewpoint about behavior."[55]

Since Watson's time, the "billiard ball" theory of the universe and matter has gone out the window with the advent of the relativity theory and quantum physics. We will look at the views of the modern physicists on consciousness, soul, and even God, in the next chapter. Yet despite this total revolution in physics, current behaviorists still cleave to the same century-old outmoded physicalism which Watson cleaved to as strongly as the believer to the Almighty. Having discarded God and religion, Watson needed a substitute: materialism. Materialism applied to human behavior is behaviorism.

Finally, Watson sees his behaviorism as the basis for a "brave new world" (as does Skinner):

> I am trying to dangle a stimulus in front of you, a verbal stimulus which if acted upon will gradually change this universe. For the universe will change if you bring up your children, not in the freedom of the libertine, but in behavioristic freedom.[56]

Watson ends his book with a contradiction in terms: "behavioristic freedom." Watson's own career in psychology ended in some contradiction. Perhaps, he acted upon "behavioristic freedom." He had a love affair with a nineteen-year-old graduate student, Rosalie Raynor, breaking up his marriage of many years to Mary Watson and losing his academic position at Johns Hopkins University, as well.[57] Watson never obtained another academic position. Watson showed remarkable adaptability by obtaining a job with the New York City advertising firm of J. Walter Thompson, and going on to apply his behaviorism to the promotion and sale of commercial products. It was Watson who invented "market research."[58] Watson's behaviorism was to have a major influence upon the Madison Avenue advertising industry which has not diminished even to this day. When we have come to "associate" cigarette smoking with sexiness or talcum powder with purity, and so on, we have John Broadhus Watson, Ph.D. to thank for this. Watson also wrote articles and books on child care and he warned in these against "excessive parental affection," saying that "Mother love is a dangerous instrument."[59] Watson's son, Billy Watson, curiously enough, went on to become a Freudian psychoanalyst, much to his father's dismay.

Watson did become a very wealthy man through his advertising and market research endeavors. He retired to Westport, Connecticut in 1947 at the age of sixty-nine. His name surfaced again in psychology in 1957 when the American Psychological Association awarded him a citation and gold medal for his contributions to the field. In true "behavioristic freedom," Watson refused to attend this convention. His psychoanalyst son, Dr. William Watson, accepted the gold medal for his father.[60]

FURTHER NOTES ON IVAN PAVLOV AND B. F. SKINNER

Ivan Pavlov, the Russian Nobel Laureate physiologist, was the contemporary of John Broadhus Watson, the American behavioral psychologist. Unlike his American counterpart, Watson, Pavlov was greatly interested in the structure and function of the brain, particularly the cerebral hemispheres. Three hundred years ago, Descartes had evolved the idea of the "reflex," considering the animal essentially a biological machine who responds to external stimulation via the medium of the nervous system. Descartes reserved the "soul" for man alone, speculating that the place of connection between the soul and brain was the pineal gland. The nineteenth-century Russian physiologist, I. M. Sechenov, attempted to relate Descartes' idea of the reflex to the activities of the cerebral hemispheres in a paper entitled "Reflexes of the Brain" published in 1863.[61] He regarded both human thought and emotion as basically reflex activity; thought he regarded as affector path inhibited reflexes and emotion as exaggerated reflexes with wide irradiation of excitation.[62] Pavlov discusses the work of the American experimental psychologist, Thorndike, the author of *The Animal Intelligence* (1898) in terms of reflexology. Pavlov said that he discovered the so-called "psychic reflex" accidentally while investigating the physiology of digestion in dogs. He found that various "extraneous stimuli" would elicit the salivation response just as well as food powder. In his classic book, *Conditioned Reflexes* (1927), Pavlov says:

> It became clear that the only satisfactory solution of the problem lay in an experimental investigation by strictly objective methods.[63]

Pavlov, like his American contemporary, Watson, claims to have come to the conviction of the futility of subjective methods of inquiry. If the psychology of a people is an expression of the soul of that people, it is clear that both Russian and American psychology was the assertion of the soul's non-existence, and consciousness's insignificance! Although they differ in other respects, both the capitalist and the communist world views are essentially *materialistic*, and we see that the psychological expressions of both cultures, at least in the early twentieth century, *were behavioristic*. Pavlov himself states:

> Work on the lines of purely objective investigation into the highest nervous activities has been conducted in the main in the laboratories under my control, and over a hundred collaborators have taken part. Work on somewhat similar lines to ours has been done by the American psychologists.[64]

Pavlov points out an essential difference between the work of the American behaviorists and the Russian behaviorists is that the Americans were essentially psychologists who were interested merely in the external stimuli and responses, whereas the Russians were physiologists who were deeply interested in the brain activities taking place between the "stimulus" and the "response." Pavlov sums up this "physiological viewpoint" of the Russian behaviorists:

> ... An external or internal stimulus falls on some one or other nervous receptor and gives rise to a nervous impulse; this nervous impulse is transmitted along nerve fibres to the central nervous system, here on

account of existing nervous connections, it gives rise to a fresh impulse which passes along outgoing nerve fibres to the active organ, and here it excites a special activity of the cellular structures: Thus a stimulus appears to be connected of necessity with a definite response, as cause and effect. [65]

This sounds very "scientific," but it is a gross simplification of the way the brain works as we shall see in the following chapter in which we will look at the views of such modern neurophysiologists as Lashley, Sherrington, Penfield, and Eccles. Pavlov's account is that of a philosophical materialist and determinist. His ultimate "thinking mentor" was, after all, Karl Marx, the dialectical materialist. We wonder why the American, Watson, reared in the American supposed philosophy of freedom came to essentially the same behavioristic psychology. Our founding fathers, such as Jefferson, Franklin, and Paine, were men reared in the value of human freedom. But our socio-economic system of capitalism, like the counterpart socio-economic system of communism, is materialistic. Adam Smith's law of "supply and demand" is as deterministic as Karl Marx's laws of "dialectics" and "class struggle." Both Pavlov and Watson were reared in materialistic thought milieus.

Pavlov, the utter determinist, finds that he has to postulate a "freedom reflex" (reminds one of Watson's talk of "behavioristic freedom"):

In the course of the researches which I shall presently explain, we were completely at a loss on one occasion to find any cause of the peculiar behavior of an animal. It was evidently a very tractable dog, which soon became very friendly with us. We started off with a very simple experiment. The dog was placed in a stand with loose loops round its legs, but so as to be quite comfortable and free to move a pace or two. Nothing was done except to present the animal repeatedly with food at intervals of some minutes. It stood quietly enough at first, and ate quite rapidly, but as time went on it became excited and struggled to get out of the stand, scratching at the floor, gnawing the supports, and so on. This ceaseless muscular exertion was accompanied by breathlessness and continuous salivation, which persisted at every experiment during several weeks, the animal getting worse and worse until it was no longer fitted for our researches. For a long time we remained puzzled over the unusual behavior of this animal. We tried out experimentally numerous possible interpretations, but though we had long experience with a great number of dogs in our laboratories we could not work out a satisfactory solution of this strange behavior, until it occurred to us at last that it might be the expression of a special *freedom reflex*. [66]

Pavlov even has to reduce an organism's struggle to be free to the machine-like "reflex" concept! Can you imagine the puzzlement of Pavlovian theoreticians at the great uprisings of prisoners, even in the most "comfortable camps," throughout history from the revolts of Spartacus, the gladiator, to the uprising of the Warsaw Ghetto? Alexander Solzhenitsyn describes what went on in *the mind* of one inmate during one day in a Soviet gulag. That prisoner was himself! Even in the subhuman dog, there is *an instinct to be free.* Is freedom a "reflex"? Is it explainable neurologically? Is it a "response" to "stimulation"? Assuredly not. It is the inborn desire *to determine one's own behavior.* It implies *a self,* not merely a neurological network of organismic machinery! Freedom is a value that can be understood by no behaviorist. Their "psychology" is more the handmaiden of totalitarianism than democracy.

B. F. Skinner, the successor to J. B. Watson in American behaviorism, wrote a book called *Beyond Freedom and Dignity* (1971). In it, he decries the traditional view of human behavior which holds that *a person* is responsible for his or her behavior in some moral sense of freely choosing between good and evil. Skinner says:

> A scientific analysis of behavior disposes of autonomous man and turns the control he has been said to exert over to the environment.[67]

Why is this "scientific"? Are materialism and determinism "scientific"? Modern physics, on the level of sub-atomic particles, the "building blocks of matter," no longer regards materialism or determinism as true. How much less are they true of human behavior where *self-consciousness,* as Bucke puts it, enters in? This is the "autonomous man" which Skinner would dispose of. What about the Cosmic Conscious being? The teachings of Christ and Buddha imply *a far greater freedom* to those who have been "born again," or "enlightened." Richard Maurice Bucke, M.D., the late nineteenth-century Canadian psychiatrist, mystic, man-of-letters, looked at these facts squarely and analyzed them deeply. Behaviorists never mention these truths except in derision and scorn. The following quotation from Skinner is his version of Watson's mockery of religion, in this case, Greek religion, which is distant enough not to take offense!

> As late as 1965 Karl Popper could put the question this way: "What we want is to understand how such non-physical things as *purposes, deliberations, plans, decisions, theories, tensions,* and *values* can play a part in bringing about physical changes in the physical world. And of course we want to know where these non-physical things come from."[68]

Skinner responds to Popper thusly:

> To that question the Greeks had a simple answer: from the gods. As Dobbs has pointed out, the Greeks believed that if a man behaved foolishly, it was because a hostile god had implanted infatuation in his breast. A friendly god might give a warrior an extra amount of courage with the help of which he would fight brilliantly. Aristotle thought there was something divine in thought, and Zeno held that the intellect was God.[69]

Skinner imperiously says: "We cannot take that line today."[70] Skinner has thus smugly "disposed of religion" (in his narrow view). The fact was, as Jung and the Jungians have so brilliantly discovered, these ancient Greeks were very close to the truth! The gods or archetypes are quite real indeed, and these "visitors" in our nightly dreams and daytime visions surely do give us our infatuations and our courage, as anyone who is at all sensitive to the inner life will soon discover. Regarding the divinity of thought and the intellect, no less than the prophets and sages of our Judeo–Christian tradition said the human being was (is) created in the *divine image*. Are we to believe the inspired writers of the *Bible*, as well as the other holy scriptures of humankind, e.g., the *Koran*, the *Tao Te Ching*, the *Upanishads*, and so on, or are we to believe the Skinners and Pavlovs who worship at the throne of the new "god," scientism? The choice is yours, dear reader.★

What were the contributions of Pavlov and Skinner? Pavlov found that when he paired tones (conditioned stimuli) with food powder (unconditioned stimuli), he could "condition" strapped-in dogs to salivate (unconditioned responses now become conditioned responses) to aforesaid auditory stimuli. This is called "classical" or "respondent conditioning." It involves the involuntary glands and smooth muscles of the viscera, and their neurological correlates in the autonomic nervous system. It has to do with our emotions, our likes and dislikes, our fears and hates, over which we usually have little conscious control. This was anticipated by Richard Bucke in his concept of man's "moral nature" which he related to the sympathetic nervous system. Gurdjieff, as we shall see, says that we must gain conscious control over our

★ Has anti-religion disappeared from contemporary behaviorism? In *BEHAVIOR SCIENCE* (1986), the authors, Reese and Parrott, state that "The major obstacle to the development of a natural science of psychology was the theologically inspired conceptualization of man as a composite of soul and flesh. This conceptualization, although having no basis in observation, served . . . religious purposes."[71]

emotions if we are to be free. Recent work in biofeedback indicates that this may indeed be quite possible. Yogis have been doing this for millenia in their exercise of control over "involuntary functions." These ancient traditions believed in "mind over matter." This old view was, at first, completely rejected by early twentieth century psychology, but it is now rapidly becoming the dominant viewpoint as we approach the dawning of the new millenium as books on meditation, and even faith, are flowing from the pens, or word processors of Harvard Medical School professors, e.g., Dr. Herbert Benson's *The Relaxation Response*, and now, *Beyond the Relaxation Response* – on the "faith factor."

Skinner discovered that rats and pigeons in "Skinner boxes" learn to press levers when these "responses" are followed by the "reinforcing consequences" of food pellets. He discovered that the "contingencies of reinforcement" govern the organism's behavior in fairly regular ways, at least in the rat and pigeon. Reward strengthens behavior, punishment suppresses behavior, and non-reinforcement (or nothing at all) "extinguishes" a given pattern of responding. Skinner called all of this "operant conditioning" subsuming it to a rather simple-minded reflexology. He generalizes widely, and inappropriately, from the lower organisms to human behavior, such as language (verbal behavior), personality (behavior repertoires), and even complex social and political conduct (interpersonal operant behavior). The basic truth is that we can allow ourselves to be controlled by our environments, or we *can choose* the more difficult *path of freedom*.

4

A Scientific and Philosophical Refutation of Behaviorism: The Recovery of Consciousness

In spite of our century's wealth of scientific research on the brain and behavior, very few serious efforts have been directed by science toward the exploration of human mind and consciousness. The behaviorist credo combined with the positivist philosophy of science known as "operationalism" to cut off the "stream of consciousness" from the area of "legitimate scientific study" for more than a half century since John B. Watson's 1913 speech at Columbia University ushered in the behaviorist era. Its damage to the psychology of religious experience was so thoroughgoing that no such course has been taught in the psychology department* at Harvard University since the time the illustrious philosopher-psychologist, William James, gave his lectures based upon *The Varieties of Religious Experience*. Countless thousands of rats have been "run" in mazes and Skinner boxes, and more lately, many hundreds of human "subjects" have been "run" in all manner of computerized "cognitive experiments," but the *human soul* and its *real experience* have long since been forgotten. In order to find true teachers of the soul, one must look elsewhere (as I did in my ten-year-long spiritual search). Nevertheless, even beginning in Watson's time, there was the beginning of a counterbehavioristic movement in the form of two who were originally behaviorists: E. C. Tolman and Karl S. Lashley. We will now look at

TWO BEHAVIORISTS WHO CHANGED THEIR MINDS

E. C. Tolman was a contemporary of J. B. Watson's in American

* Harvard Divinity School, as is true of many religious seminaries, has offered courses in the psychology of religion.

psychology of the 1920s which was already practically "officially behavioristic." It would be difficult indeed for any but a behaviorist to secure employment in academic psychology of that time (until the 1950s or 1960s, at least). Tolman taught at the University of California at Berkeley which was a little adventurous even in those days, and he distinguished his "molar behaviorism" from the "molecular behaviorism" or "muscle-twitch" psychology of J. B. Watson of Johns Hopkins University. Nonetheless, true to the behaviorist credo of denying consciousness, Tolman, in 1926, said this:

> The orthodox psychologist, whom I shall oppose and whom we shall call for convenience the "mentalist," conceives ideas as lying in, or as bits of a unique type of conscious stuff. Ideas are described by him in their character as states or processes in this stuff. Overt behavior intrigues him only in so far as he believes he can infer conscious stuff happening from it.[1]

Tolman, somewhat in the manner of Watson, "pokes fun" at the mentalists for believing in anything so unscientific as "consciousness" which he parodies as "conscious stuff." Tolman goes on:

> Turn now to the behaviorists. We behaviorists, whatever else our divergences, are agreed in viewing overt behavior as the primi datum for psychology. It is from a study of such overt behavior and its environmental settings that we believe we will obtain our causal understanding both of the grosser activities of the lower animals, and of the higher conscious activities of human beings.[2]

Tolman, the then behaviorist, admits that there are "higher conscious activities" in human beings, having in mind, no doubt, thinking and problem-solving, and the like. But he believes that a real "causal understanding" is only possible through the study of environment-behavior relations rather than through introspection about one's own states of consciousness. Displaying some genuine humor, which is altogether lacking in Watson (as well as in Pavlov and Skinner), Tolman says this about his own private consciousness:

> I may have private mental contents, but if I have, only God and myself will know them.[3]

Tolman does not seem the archbehaviorist that Watson was, at war, as it were, with the soul and God! Tolman merely seems restrained by the then prevailing positivist philosophy of science and the predominant ethos of behaviorism in psychology. He even separates out the "private realm," which may even include the personal soul and God, from the "public realm" of science qua science. Scientists of a later generation than Tolman's, namely the best scientists of our era, no longer seem satisfied with this philosophy of bifurcation of the universe into the private realm where religion and art are possible, and the public realm of empirical science. Any such division exists only in the mind of the divider, not in nature! Mind is no more, or less, "unknowable" than electrons are; as for scientific theory, and as for everyday every minute phenomenological reality, *we all know* that consciousness is the *pervasive fact*. We are never *not* observing consciousness! When science and common sense reality are so far apart as they were in the days of positivism's reign in philosophy and behaviorism's domination of psychology, then something is very wrong indeed. We have what appears to be a "scholarly neurosis" of the worst order in the days of behaviorism-positivism. It had little to do with real science as open-minded inquiry or search for truth.

Tolman's mind seemed to open up about six years later in his book *Purposive Behavior in Animals and Men* (1932) when he begins to distance himself from orthodox behaviorism based upon his years of ingenious maze-learning experiments with rats. It is Tolman who began to bring psychology back to "its mind." He distinguishes in this book between "S-R behaviorism" of muscle twitches and glandular secretions and his own "purposive behaviorism" which treats of *acts*.

> An act *qua* 'behavior' has distinctive properties of its own . . . A rat running a maze, a cat getting out of a puzzle box, a man driving home for dinner, a child hiding from a stranger . . . my friend and I telling each other our thoughts and feelings . . . [4]

Tolman goes on to say:

> Behavior as behavior, that is, as molar *is* purposive, *is* cognitive. These purposes and cognitions are of its immediate descriptive warp and woof . . . behavior as behavior reeks of purpose and cognition. [5]

Although he still strives to call himself a "purposive behaviorist" at this point, it was with this book that Tolman literally inaugurated American cognitive psychology, which is, perhaps, the dominant movement in academic psychology in the last decade, or so. Tolman was quite sympathetic to the work of the European Gestaltists, and he introduced his American audience to some of their work, e.g., Wolfgang Köhler's *The Mentality of Apes* (1925).

In Köhler's most well-known experiment, he found that chimpanzees could solve the now famous problem of reaching food beyond their arm's reach, while in a cage, by fitting together two hollow bamboo sticks to make a longer stick, and then raking in the food. This was a genuine *insight*. It was not a previously learned "response" to a "stimulus." It was a "flashing" in the mind of the chimp of a new "figural gestalt" necessary to solve the problem in question. Köhler sees this as the emergence of a sudden new configuration, something rather passive based upon his Gestalt principles. Tolman sees it in somewhat more active terms as inventive ideation resulting in the formation of new "sign-gestalten."

When does consciousness appear for Tolman? Precisely at times of new learning, or at the formation of a sign-gestalt. For Tolman, Pavlov's "conditioned reflexes" were no such thing, but rather the acquisition of new sign-gestalten to the effect that waiting in the presence of a tone or color, etc., the "sign-gestalt" will lead to a "significate," in this case, food. The tone becomes a "sign" for the food. A "sign" is a cognitive content, whereas a "conditioned stimulus" is merely a sound or light wave energy in the physical environment. What do Skinner's rats or pigeons learn? They learn sign-gestalt relations, e.g., pushing a bar in a given environment (such as a Skinner box) leads to a goal object, namely the food. Learning is not about the "stamping in" of S-R connections, but of the building up of sign-gestalt expectations. This implies consciousness or mind. In an article in *Psychological Review* (1948) entitled "Cognitive Maps in Rats and Men," Tolman distinguishes between two current schools of psychology:

> First, there is the school of animal psychologists which believes that the maze behavior of rats is a matter of mere stimulus-response connections. Learning according to them, consists in strengthening some of these connections and weakening of others. According to this "stimulus-response" school the rat in progressing down the maze is helplessly responsive to a succession of external stimuli – sights, sounds, smells, pressures, etc., impinging upon his external sense organs – plus internal stimuli coming from the viscera and from the skeletal muscles. These external and internal stimuli call out the walkings, runnings, turnings, retracings, smellings, rearings, and the like which appear. The rat's central nervous system according to this view, may be likened to a complex telephone switchboard. There are incoming calls from the sense organs and there are the outgoing messages to the muscles . . . *Learning* according to this view, consists in the respective strengthening and weakening of various of these connections . . . [6]

Tolman describes precisely the simple-minded connectionism of Watson and Pavlov which can be called S-R psychology.

> Let us turn now to the second main school. This group (and I belong to them) may be called the field theorists. We believe that in the course of learning something like a field map of the environment gets established in the rat's brain. Secondly we assert that the central office itself is far more like a map control room than it is like an old-fashioned telephone exchange.[7]

Tolman has clearly here separated himself out from any form of behaviorism or S-R psychology, and placed himself in the "field theory" position of such psychologists as Köhler, Goldstein, and others. Tolman presents a series of novel rat maze learning experiments which strongly support the field theoretical position as against any S-R behaviorist one. These involve experiments in latent learning in which the rats are shown to learn mazes by mere observation and not "stamped in" responses to stimuli. In another group of experiments, the rats are shown to quite spontaneously form hypotheses, and test them, such as the hypothesis "to always turn right," or "to choose the darker of two doors," or "choose the door with the circle rather than the square pattern," etc. Experiments in spatial orientation indicate that rats do indeed form broad "cognitive maps" and can go directly to food goal objects along paths they have never before tread based upon correct cognitive inferences on the angle of relation between starting position and goal. They had previously learned highly indirect paths involving going in the *opposite direction*, and turning toward the goal in several steps; these were the "overt responses" practised. But the rats, when given the opportunity, did not repeat the former "responses to stimuli," but rather took the logically straight path.

This would not seem "remarkable" to anyone who was not totally brainwashed in S-R behaviorist psychology. We assume that animals, and even rats, "think" to some extent. It took Tolman to prove that they do! This is, of course, prelinguistic quasi-conceptual behavior, somewhat along the lines, in Bucke's language of receptual, or "simple consciousness." This is mental and not just behavioral as Tolman discovers again and again in his experiments which provide complex choices for his rats. Skinner's rats could not do anything but press bars or not press them, and Pavlov's strapped-in dogs had little choice but to salivate or not salivate. The experimenters contrived these behaviors in highly limited environments to look like "S-R." They imposed artificial limitations on the scope of the animal's possible behavior. Such is not the case for rats or dogs in nature. How far less for human beings? Amazingly, it was Tolman's rats who brought mind back into American psychology laboratories! Tolman, however, did not conceive of mind or consciousness as an independent reality in its own right, but as an emergent property of the complex brains of animals and human beings. He, however, like most others of the cognitivist school, ultimately "reduces" (in principle anyway) mind or consciousness to the physico-chemical activities of the brain to be explained by "future science." Regardless of his ultimate philosophical position on the mind/brain problem, with Tolman we regain access to the *mental world* which was closed off for a time by the behaviorists.

Karl Lashley was originally a colleague and collaborator of John Watson's in animal behavioral research. They published several papers together. Lashley was originally a behaviorist who believed in the reflex concept. He later turned to work on the animal cerebral cortex "in search of the engram," that is, the physiological "memory trace" which he assumed was "laid down" in the brain in somewhat the S-R fashion that both Pavlov and Watson postulated. Lashley found no such thing. Rather, he found that with rats, for example, who are trained in simple habits, such as turning left in a two-way maze, or choosing the darker of two doors, etc., no specific brain lesions whatsoever, no matter how extensive, up to the point of crippling or killing the animal, would abolish the habit. The severely brain-injured rat, for example, would still crawl to the goal object along the path that was learned. One would suspect, if learning consisted of the establishment of specific S-R connections, in some literal way, that these connections could be severed surgically. Such is not the case.

Lashley did his research over many years, with both rats and monkeys, employing many kinds of learning. It was impossible to physically "abolish" a piece of learned behavior by tampering with the brain of the animal. This put into serious question the simplistic reflex ideas of Pavlov and Watson, i.e., that learning consists in the formation of "S-R connections" between environmental stimuli impinging upon the sense organs and muscular or glandular responses, connected, it was thought, by "telephone wire-like" connections in the central nervous system's one-way neurons interacting via synapses. Rather, Lashley concluded that learning must be a function of the cerebral cortex as a whole. Lashley's ideas were those of *equipotentiality* and *mass action*. This was the neurophysiological side of Tolman's cognitive field theory. As Tolman had severed the "S-R bond" from without via his ingenious experiments, Lashley severed the "S-R bond" from within surgically, and found it equally irrelevant. It just is not the way that the brain and mind work, as "scientific" as it may sound. Lashley began his critique of reflex theory as early as 1929, in his presidential address to the American Psychological Association during S-R behaviorism's heyday. By 1937, he said:

> We have to consider that there are fields of force operating in the brain. [8]

In 1930, Lashley wrote his now classic paper, "In Search of the Engram," in which he came to the following conclusion, in refutation of the S-R reflexology of his old colleague, Watson:

> The mass of evidence . . . shows conclusively that it is the pattern and not the localization of energy . . . that determines its functional effect. [9]

To Watson's idea (if behaviorists have "ideas") that the brain merely passively responds to environmental stimuli, in quite mechanistic fashion, Lashley says:

> . . . all cells of the brain are constantly active and are participating, by a sort of algebraic summation in every activity. There are no special cells reserved for special memories. [10]

Speaking to the American Society of Naturalists in 1947, Lashley said:

> The evolution of mind . . . consists in increasing the capacity of the organism to discover relations, to form novel integrations, to effect new neural patterns. [11]

The old behaviorist, Lashley, is speaking about the evolution of mind, but to be sure, he reduces mind to "new neural patterns." Yet surely, we feel we have come a long way from the S-R behaviorism of Watson and Pavlov who "turned out the light of consciousness" for American and Russian psychology, respectively.

Reminiscent of James' treatment of consciousness, Lashley compares the brain to the surface of a lake in the following poetical description of what might be happening in the living brain of a person:

> The prevailing breeze carries in all ripples in its direction, the basic polarity of the system. Varying gusts set up crossing systems of

waves, which do not destroy the first ripples, but modify their form, a second level in the system of space coordinates. A tossing log with its own period of submersion sends out periodic bursts of ripples, a temporal rhythm, the low wave of a speeding boat momentarily sweeps over the surface, seems to obliterate the smaller waves yet leaves them unchanged, in passing, the transient effect of a strong stimulus. . .[12]

Lashley evidently sees the brain in "field theory" terms as picturing the events of the external world impinging upon it via the sense organs in a somewhat "isomorphic" fashion similar to the theory of the Gestaltist Köhler, and interfacing nicely with the views of the experimental psychologist, Tolman. We wonder how *consciousness* arises even in a "sea of electrochemical activity." Lashley has no direct answer for this question, but he is aware of it, as when he says in the following address to colleagues:

> Today I shall discuss a subject which, like our Oedipus complexes, has probably troubled many of us but has been *suppressed*, especially at scientific meetings. Suppression is a sign of conflict . . . and I hope that I may be able to contribute something to lessen the tension. I refer to the problem of how the brain knows that it knows. What characteristics of neural activity constitutes mind?[13]

Mind, for psychologists since Watson, had become a "naughty word." Both Watson and Skinner actually proposed "language reforms" to eliminate "mentalistic vocabulary" from human language! Such is the extent to which crypto-totalitarians will go to save their theories, despite the facts to the contrary! It is to the great credit of Tolman and Lashley that they recovered mind, simple consciousness at least, as a "scientific fact," as if we need the imprimatur of science to believe in what we have always intimately known – that we are *conscious*. Neither Tolman, nor Lashley, however, nor any other academic psychologists whom I know of are willing to consider that *mind may be a reality in its own right*. Lashley notes that there was an increasing interest in the problem of mind among leading neurophysiologists in his time, and that three leaders in this field – Sherrington, Penfield, and Eccles (all three of them Nobel Laureates) – have actually been so bold as to assert that *mind cannot be explained by the activities of the brain*. Lashley says that Eccles even evolves a theory as to how mind could act upon matter appealing to the facts of telepathy, and also quantum physics. This sounds too close to the concept of the "soul" for Lashley who says "I am not ready to accept these doctrines of scientific despair and Christian hope."[14] We Christians hope for much more than this – but Lashley's comments aroused my interest to look at

THREE NOBEL LAUREATE NEUROPHYSIOLOGISTS WHO BELIEVE IN MIND

Sir Charles Sherrington won the Nobel Prize for his classical studies of reflexes and the integrating action of the nervous system. In his book, *Man – On His Nature* (1940), he states that:

> The sun's energy is part of the closed energy cycle. What leverage can it have on the mind? Yet through my retina and brain it seems to be able to act on my mind, the theoretically impossible happens . . . I assert that it does act on my mind. Conversely my thinking "self" thinks that it can bend my arm. Physics tells me that my arm cannot be bent without disturbing the sun. My mind then does bend my arm. Or the theoretically impossible happens. Let me prefer to believe that the theoretically impossible does happen. [15]

Sherrington, the greatest neurophysiologist of our century, concludes:

> We have to regard the relation of mind to brain as still not merely unsolved, but still devoid of a basis from the very beginning. [16]

Wilder Penfield, M.D., a student of Sherrington's, won his Nobel Prize in medical research in epilepsy. He later went on to write a book about the mind-brain problem based upon his very practical research findings called *The Mystery of the Mind* (1975). Penfield notes the work of Karl Lashley who spent thirty years "in search of the engram" in the animal brain without apparent success. Penfield, as neurologist and surgeon, was in a position to study the brain-mind relation on the human level. He states that it was Hippocrates, the Greek physician of the fifth century B.C., who discovered that it was the brain and not the heart which was the "organ of thought." To quote Hippocrates:

> Some people say that the heart is the organ with which we think . . . But it is not so. Men ought to know that from the brain and from the brain only arises our pleasures, joys, laughter, and tears. Through it . . . we think, see, hear and distinguish the ugly from the beautiful, the bad from the good, the pleasant from the unpleasant. . . [17]

Penfield says that Hippocrates' treatise was the finest work on the brain and mind until the discovery of electricity! Penfield acknowledges from the start that the brain and mind are ostensibly two different realities. As defined by *The Merriam Webster Dictionary*:

Mind: "the part of an individual that feels, perceives, thinks, wills, and especially reasons."[18]

Brain: "the part of the vertebrate nervous system that is the organ of thought and nervous coordination, is made up of nerve cells and their fibers, and is enclosed in the skull."[19]

The brain, as anyone with an elementary course in biology knows, is composed of neurons, which are elongated cells capable of carrying an electric charge. They have two branches, the dendrite and the axon, which carry the electric charge in that direction. Between two neurons is what physiologists call a "synapse," which is a gap which the nervous impulse has to jump to move from one neuron to the next. Neurons are thought to comprise "modules" in the brain of about ten thousand cells each, and each of these interrelate to other modules in vastly complex ways to form the larger structures; for example, the cerebellum, the medulla oblongata, the thalamus, the hypothalamus, the reticular formation, and the cerebral cortex. With supporting cells, the brain comprises about 100 billion cells, equal to the number of stars in the Milky Way Galaxy of which our sun is one member! Perhaps there is something to the old saying: "As above, so below." In any event, the cerebral cortex of this brain, comprising approximately 10 billion neurons, consists of two hemispheres, joined by the corpus callosum. Each hemisphere is a vast convoluted sheet of neurons with cosmic numbers of interconnections within, as well as connections between the hemispheres via the corpus callosum. The cortex is an enormous living neural network in the relatively small space of our skulls. It is almost infinitely more complex than any existing electronic computer. It acts in total fashion, as a whole, never in sequential linear fashion, as is the case with digital computers. The only similarity, perhaps, is that neurons follow the "all or nothing principle," they either fire or they do not, and the same thing is true of the circuits of digital computers which are also binary: on or off. It should be remembered that it was the human brain and mind which invented the computer and so some similarity is not surprising! However, whereas the mathematics of the digital computer is understandable according to the principles of Turing, we have in our heads an organic *living computer* whose logical and mathematical principles have exceeded the understanding of any neuroscientists to date, except in the simplest functions.

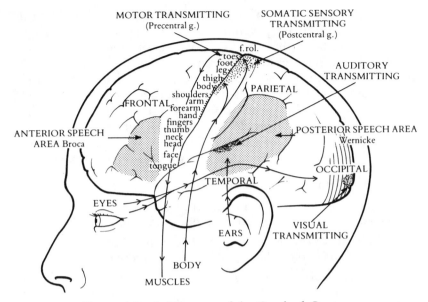

Figure 4.1   A Diagram of the Cerebral Cortex.

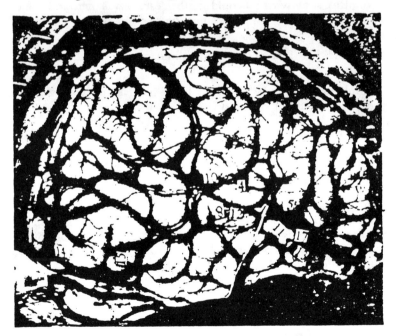

Figure 4.2   Cerebral Cortex of Penfield's Patient.

Penfield's researches at the Montreal Neurological Institute could be called neuropsychological. He operated on epileptic patients to remove the irritating portions of their brains to cure their epileptic seizures. He secured their permission to stimulate their brains with a mild electric current, while they were fully awake under only local anaesthesia during the operation, and made discoveries that surprised him. He found that he could elicit long forgotten memories depending upon where he placed his electrodes in the patient's brain. These are some examples from Penfield's records of a twenty-six-year-old woman patient:

I heard something, I do not know what it was. [20]

Yes, sir, I think I heard a mother calling her little boy somewhere. Seemed to be something that happened years ago. [21]

Yes. I heard voices down along the river somewhere. A man's voice and a woman's voice calling . . . I think I saw a river. [22]

(A needle, insulated except at the tip, was inserted to the superior surface of the temporal lobe, deep in the fissure of Sylvius, and the current was switched on.) 'I had the same very, very familiar memory, in an office somewhere. I could see the desks. I was there and someone was calling to me, a man leaning on a desk, with a pencil in his hand.' [23]

(I warned her I was going to stimulate, but I did not do so.) 'Nothing.' [24]

(Stimulation without warning.) I had a little memory – a scene in a play – they were talking and I could see it. [25]

Penfield said, "I was more astonished each time my electrode brought forth such a response. How could it be? This had to do with mind!" [26] Penfield asks the further question and gives it a tentative answer:

Can reflex action in the end account for . . . the action of mind? After years of studying the emerging mechanisms within the human brain, my own answer is no. Mind comes into action and goes out of action with the highest brain mechanism, it is true. But the mind has energy. The form of that energy is different from that of neuronal potentials that travel the axone pathway. There I must leave it . . . [27]

Such depth psychologists as Freud, Jung, Reich, and others have speculated about the "psychic energy" which none of them entirely identified with the physical energy of the brain. Freud and Jung called it "libido" (with differing meanings), and Reich called it "orgone energy." The philosopher, Henri Bergson, called this the "élan vital," and the ancient spiritual writers called this "ruach," "prana," "ch'i," etc., depending upon the culture. I think they are all talking about the *same mystery*. Commenting on William James, Penfield says that James' material was psychological, whereas his was neurophysiological. But, it is James' "stream of consciousness" that Penfield refers to when he says:

> The contents of the stream . . . are recorded in the brain, including everything to which the man . . . paid attention, but none of the things that he ignored. [28]

It is the *conscious mind* that watches and directs. Penfield points out that in the electrode stimulation experiment, there is a "double level of awareness," both of the event recalled, and of everything going on in the operating room. There is also reported the sense of a self which observes and distinguishes between both. Can brain tissue make these distinctions between past and present experience, while keeping them separate, and provide us with a sense of self-identity, or is this a function of mind? Penfield, the Nobel Laureate neurophysiologist, would opt for the latter. It is strange that the psychologists whom we have looked at (and most others in psychology) would reduce mind to brain. It is possible that the psychologists, who know the brain less well, feel content in their ignorance to reduce mind events to brain events, while the neurophysiologists who know the brain far more deeply, know that they cannot in justice to *the facts* reduce mind and consciousness to neurophysiology. To quote Penfield once more:

> It is what we have learned to call the mind that seems to focus attention. The mind is aware of what is going on. The mind reasons and makes new decisions. It understands. It acts as though endowed with an energy of its own. It can make decisions and put them into effect by calling upon various brain mechanisms. It does this by activating neurone mechanisms. This, it seems, could only be brought about by expenditure of energy. [29]

What is the relationship between mind and brain? Do neuroscientists have light to throw on this ancient philosophical conundrum?

This is how the Nobel Prize Laureate neurophysiologist, Sir John Eccles, coauthor with the philosopher, Karl Popper, of *The Self and Its Brain* (1977), views the mind-brain relationship:

> Briefly, the hypothesis that the self-conscious mind is an independent entity that is actively engaged in reading out from the multitudes of

active centres in the modules of the liaison areas of the dominant cerebral hemisphere. The self-conscious mind selects from these centres in accord with its attention and its interests and integrates its selection to give the unity of conscious experience from moment to moment. It also acts back on the neural centres. Thus it is proposed that self-conscious mind exercises a superior interpretive and controlling role upon the neural events by virtue of a two-way interaction across the interface of world 1 and world 2. It is proposed that the unity of conscious experience comes not from an ultimate synthesis in the neural machinery but in the integrating action of the self-conscious mind on what is read out from the immense diversity of neural activities in the liaison brain.[30]

Eccles argues that the operative features of the cerebral cortex are of such subtlety that they could be acted upon by the "weak actions" exerted by the self-conscious mind across the interface. To make this less mysterious, two examples of this which are constantly taking place during our waking hours are voluntary movement and the recall of memories upon demand. Mind-body interaction is not the exception, such as in "extra-sensory perception," but the everyday reality, e.g., raising your hand in a class, or typing a letter, or recalling happy events of last summer. Eccles deals with this everyday reality of conscious functioning.

Eccles also states that the treatment of the self-conscious mind as an independent reality in relationship to the physical brain gives a real opportunity for interpreting the phenomena of sleep, dreams, and altered states of consciousness, up to and including "near death" experiences in an unbiased and direct way. Eccles, in a personal aside, alludes to a "sudden overwhelming experience" which he had at age eighteen. One strongly suspects that this was a mystical experience, perhaps one such as Bucke reported. In our materialistic age, however, people, especially Nobel Laureate scientists, are rather reluctant to report religious or mystical experiences in any detail lest they be considered "crazy." This is due to the unfortunate anti-religious bias of psychiatry in our century, in part due to Freud's atheism. We will look at this more in the next chapter.

Returning to the more scientific speculations of Eccles, he reports the remarkable investigations of Roger Sperry and his associates on commissurotomy patients whose corpus callosums have been surgically severed as a treatment for certain brain disorders. In these patients, truly the left brain does not know what the right brain is doing! This work indicates that self-consciousness is associated principally with the left hemisphere where the language centers are located. Bucke theorized about the connection between self-consciousness and language. We have now seen Bucke's speculations on self-consciousness confirmed by neuroscience. However, more recent work on right-left brain function indicates that the left brain deals with linguistic and logical information, e.g., science and philosophy, whereas the right brain deals with the intuitive and the aesthetic, e.g., art and music. We are a left-brained culture in the West. There are Eastern cultures which are predominantly right-brained. I would suspect that mystical experience is far more frequent in these; for instance, India. So I would question Eccles' strong preference for the left hemisphere as the "seat of consciousness" (his own perhaps?).

In general, there are two theories about human beings and animals. Eccles summarizes them as follows:

> Firstly, there is the explanation inherent in monistic materialism . . . in current neurological theory the diverse inputs into the brain interact on the basis of all the structural and functional connectivities to give some integrated output of motor performance. The aim of the neural sciences is to provide a more and more coherent and complete account of the manner in which the total performance of an animal and of a human being is explainable on those terms. Without making too dogmatic a claim, it can be stated that the goal of the neurosciences is to formulate a theory that can in principle provide a complete explanation of all behavior of animals and men, including man's verbal behavior.[31]

Even though the above would delight both behaviorists and cognitivists as well, Eccles states that the reductionist strategy will fail to account for the higher levels of conscious performance of the human brain.

> Secondly, there is the dualist-interactionist explanation which has been specially developed for the self-conscious mind and human brains. Its role for animals and for the minor hemisphere is debatable. It is proposed that superimposed upon the neural machinery in all its performance . . . there are at certain sites of the cerebral hemisphere (the liaison areas) effective interactions with the self-conscious mind, both in receiving and giving.[32]

Eccles points out that there is a *unitary character* about the experiences of the self-conscious mind (so did William James in his discussion of the "I" and the "me"). He assumes that the experiences of the self-conscious mind have a relationship, but not an

MODES OF INTERACTION BETWEEN HEMISPHERES

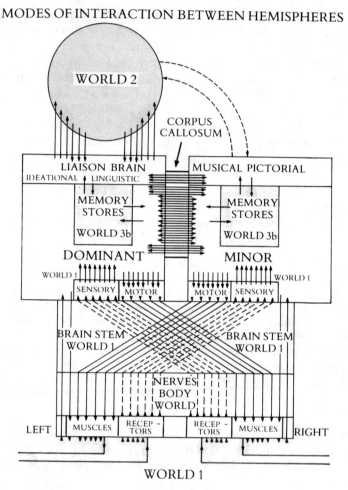

Figure 4.3   Eccles' Dualistic-Interactionist Model

identity, with the neural events of the "liaison brain." Although dualist–interactionism is the minority view in neuroscience of some of the greatest neuroscientists of our century, including Nobel Laureates such as Sherrington, Penfield, and Eccles, and the psychoneural identity theory is the prevalent view, Eccles states that:

No scientific evidence is presented for this identity.[33]

It is certainly true that psychoneural identity is the normative view not for reasons of empirical evidence, but for reasons of meta-physical bias in favor of a materialistic worldview. Eccles presents considerable *scientific evidence* against psychoneural identity and in favor of the dualist-interactionist hypothesis. For example, the experiments of Libet show that there can be a temporal discrepancy between neural events and the experiences of the self-conscious mind in such phenomena as backward masking and antedating. To explain, subjects report an experience as occurring *before* the neurological events have taken place, such as, in the perception of a visual or auditory stimulus. This is based upon the known speeds of neural transmissions, and actual measurements of brain cell responses to stimulation. People experience events as taking place more in correspondence to the external events than in corres-pondence to the neural consequences of these events in the brain.

Eccles reports on interesting experiments on the temporal events in the brain in conjunction with voluntary movement. There is a "readiness potential" that seems to have to build up over a certain duration of time between the "willing of an act" and its initiation into motor cell activity leading to actual movement.

> The self-conscious mind does not effect a direct action on these motor pyramidal cells. Instead, the self-conscious mind works remotely and slowly over a wide range of the cortex so that there is a time delay for the surprisingly long duration of 0.8 sec. . . . The readiness potential indicates the sequential activity of many hundreds of neurones is involved in the incubation time of the self-conscious mind in eventually evoking discharges from the motor pyramidal cells.[34]

This slowness of the readiness potential in voluntary movement can be appreciated when you realize that the speed of neural transmission along a single neuron is something on the order of one millisecond. What Eccles is indicating is that when you will a movement, such as picking up a pencil, or opening a door, and so on, you initiate an exceedingly complex and time-consuming activity in the cerebral cortex which precedes the motor perform-ance. This neural activity has been measured by neuroscientists. It is independent of external stimulation; it is entirely dependent upon the *mental act of willing*. We all know from the simplest introspection that *we choose*, and we can initiate actions with our voluntary choices. Will is no mystery to ordinary human living. How this could be denied by behaviorism and materialistic psychologies is fantastic. For a psychologist to deny the existence of conscious volition is akin to a physicist denying the existence of electricity!

Eccles goes on to report on neurophysiological research on short- and long-term memory. Short-term memory has to do with such things as remembering a phone number for a few seconds after it has been repeated to you by the telephone operator. Such memories last a short time and then disappear. Some short-term memories are transferred to long-term memory storage, and this seems to require some *conscious attention*. It is generally agreed that short-term memory depends upon short-term reverberating neural electrical circuits in the brain. It can easily be disrupted, as when someone interrupts you when you are trying to remember something. Long-term memory, however, has never been adequately understood. Various theories about it are: increased synaptic conductivity due to experience, changes in RNA molecules, and even holographic patterns in the brain, as in Karl Pribram's research.★ The first theory seems to have been ruled out by Lashley's work, the second theory is still current, although it seems implausible that RNA molecules can take as many different forms as there are mental experiences to recall, and the third is in its early stages of research. One biologist, Rupert Sheldrake, in his book, *A New Science of Life* (1981), argues that memories may not be stored in the physical brain at all, but may exist as non-physical "morphogenetic fields." He actually presents some impressive evidence in support of this theory. For example, when a group of rats is trained in a particular maze problem, successive generations of these rats learn the same problem more and more easily. This has Lamarckian as opposed to Darwinian implications. A more impressive test would be to see whether training a group of rats on a particular maze problem in one place enhances the performance of similar rats elsewhere. At a symposium at Harvard Science Center, Sheldrake reported that this has been done recently with positive results. Sheldrake is in the process of repeating these findings on the human level. This is the most innovative theory in biology since Darwin, and it provides a basis to explain widespread human cultural, social, and religious phenomena. This author spoke with Sheldrake about the idea that the power of the Holy Communion sacrament in Christianity could be viewed, at least in part, as the continuing existence of a very powerful morphogenetic field originally initiated by Jesus at the Last Supper, and continually reinforced for twenty centuries after-

★ Pribram has provided evidence backing up the theory that memories are recorded *all over the brain* in a non-localized fashion. This storage resembles a hologram in its function.

ward all over the world. Many puzzling phenomena begin to "make sense" in terms of what Sheldrake calls "morphogenetic fields" and "morphic resonance." Ilya Prigogine, the Nobel Laureate chemist, has a theory of "dissipative structures," i.e. the appearance of spontaneous order that is counter-entropic, which bears a definite relation to the non-local fields described by Sheldrake. When we speak of non-physical fields, we need to turn to physics, and we will look at the work of one of the greatest living physicists, who has had dialogues with the biologist, Sheldrake, on the connection between their theories.

DAVID BOHM: AN ENLIGHTENED PHYSICIST

As a boy in Wilkes-Barre, Pennsylvania, David Bohm climbed the rolling hills surrounding his hometown on one late evening, and he looked at the lights below. He had an experience of light extending beyond and throughout the universe as a web of "living energy."[35] This was an apparently mystical experience. Bohm went on to become a physicist, and he was a doctoral student of Robert Oppenheimer during World War II. He went on to teach at Princeton University, and became a friend and colleague of Albert Einstein at the Institute for Advanced Study. Einstein and Bohm engaged in a continuing dialogue on the deep questions of physics. It is reported that Einstein said that if there was anyone who could unify relativity theory and quantum theory it was David Bohm. Bohm went on to write a now classic text in quantum physics published in 1951. In it, he says that "Quantum concepts imply that the world acts more like a single indivisible unit in which the intrinsic nature of each part (wave or particle) depends upon its relation to the sum."[36]

In Bohm's studies of the collective nature of astronomical numbers of electrons in metals, the "electron plasma," he remarked that he often had the distinct impression that the electron sea was alive. Traditional physicists would quake at this admission – shades of vitalism! In a second book, Bohm took up the question of causality. He considered the traditional view to be limited. He espouses the idea that the cause of everything is: everything else. Bohm is the obvious predecessor of the "holistic movement." In a book on special relativity, Bohm stresses the role of consciousness in science, and he states that scientific theories are "maps that guide how and what things are seen."[37] Bohm warns not to confuse the map with the reality (Korzybski's "general semantics" makes the same point). Bohm opposes the premise, since Aristotle, that nature can be divided into parts, analyzed, or fragmented. He calls nature, instead, an undivided whole, and speaks elsewhere of the *Holomovement*. This is Lao Tzu's *Tao* in modern terms!

In his extraordinary book, *Wholeness and the Implicate Order* (1980), Bohm traces the development in physics from the old "Mechanistic Order," which started with Democritus and reached its culmination with Newton, as the view that the world is composed of atomistic entities which are "outside of each other," the machine being the typical illustration, to relativity theory, which makes the concept of an independently existing particle untenable, rather reality is constituted of fields which obey relativistic principles, to quantum theory which challenges the old "Mechanistic Order" to its very foundations in the following ways:

1. Movement is in general *discontinuous*, in the sense that action is constituted of *indivisible quanta* (implying that an electron, for example, can go from one state to another without passing through any states in between).
2. Entities, such as electrons, can show different properties (e.g. particle-like, *wave*-like, or something in between) depending on the environmental context with which they exist and are subject to observation.
3. Two entities, such as electrons, which initially combine to form a molecule and then separate, show a peculiar non-local relationship, which can best be described as a non-causal connection of elements that are far apart.
4. . . .The laws of quantum mechanics are statistical and do not determine individual future events uniquely and precisely. This is, of course, different from classical laws, which do in principle determine events. This last is not a key feature – There are probabilistic events in the classical order too, such as, dice, pinball machines, etc.[38]

The first three features of quantum theory do, however, clearly and strongly show the inadequacy of all mechanistic notions. Thus, if all actions are in the form of discrete quanta, the interactions between different entities constitute a single structure of indivisible links so that the entire universe has to be thought of as an *unbroken whole*. This kind of a universe has more in common with a living organism than with a mechanism according to Bohm, and other quantum physicists. Bohm presents the "hologram" as a model, an albeit static rather than dynamic analogue. In the hologram, the whole is contained within every part, unlike a photographic image, which is just a collection of parts. In the Universe, or *Holomovement*, the whole is *implicated* in each of the parts. This is much the same vision as inspired William Blake who spoke of seeing "the world in a grain of sand" and "eternity in an hour." Bohm writes:

> We propose that a new notion of order is involved here which we called the *implicate order* . . . In terms of the implicate order one may say that everything is enfolded into everything. This contrasts with the *explicate order* now dominant in physics in which things are unfolded in the sense that each thing lies only in its own particular region of space (and time) and outside the regions belonging to other things.[39]

Bohm's distinction between the implicate and explicate orders has truly revolutionary implications for the understanding of both matter and mind, and the relationship between them. For our context in looking at brain and consciousness, it is obvious that what most psychologists and neuroscientists mean by the "brain" is a relatively stable "entity" in the explicate order. Most see it as based on rather mechanistic physico-chemical processes and laws. It is most difficult to see how "mind events," such as thinking, or feeling, or will, could be related to "brain events" such as electro-chemical impulses of various complex patterns. One can, without understanding, rhyme or reason, just assert that they are "identical," as most biological and behavioral scientists do, mind, therefore, being reduced to matter. The best philosophers, from Plato to Popper, have shown that this is logically absurd. The "sensation of redness" or the "smell of a rose" or a "mental image," etc., are just not the same realm of reality as "a pattern of electro-chemical activity in the cerebral cortex." They may be related, but they are not "the same." Such considerations gave rise to the psychophysical dualism of Eccles and Penfield, whom we have looked at, who postulate an independent self-conscious mind. They do not explain where it came from, or what it is; they just postulate it. Something is inadequate about this move, although it, at least, respects the facts as they are. It by no means makes sense of them. The physics of the implicate and explicate orders of Bohm have some greater promise for a deeper understanding of mind and brain. To quote the physicist, Bohm:

> To obtain an understanding of the relationship of matter and consciousness has, however, thus far proven extremely difficult, and this

difficulty has its root in the very great difference in their basic qualities as they present themselves in our experience. This difference has been expressed with particularly great clarity by Descartes, who described matter as 'extended substance' and consciousness as 'thinking substance.' Evidently by 'extended substance' Descartes meant something like distinct forms existing in space, in an order of extension and separation basically similar to the one we have been calling explicate. By using the term 'thinking substance' . . . he was clearly implying that the various distinct forms apparent in thought do not have their existence in such an order of extension and separation . . . but rather in a different order, in which extension and separation have no fundamental significance. The implicate order has just this latter quality . . . [40]

Bohm states that when we start, as Descartes did, with extension and separation in space as primary for matter, i.e., the explicate order, then he sees no possibility of comprehending the relationship between matter, i.e., brain and consciousness whose orders are so different. Is thinking of an old friend with tender sentiment "reducible" to complex "physico-chemical" processes of the brain? An identity theorist would have to say "yes" based upon his metaphysical assumptions. A dualist-interactionist, such as Eccles or Penfield, would say absolutely "no" based upon his ontology. Neither end of this dichotomy seems the deep truth. Bohm says this about the mind-body problem:

This connection of the mind and body has commonly been called psychosomatic (from the Greek 'psyche,' meaning 'mind' and 'soma' meaning 'body'). This word is generally used, however, in such a way as to imply that mind and body are separately existent but connected by some sort of interaction. Such a meaning is not compatible with the implicate order. In the implicate order we have to say that mind enfolds matter in general and therefore body in particular. Similarly, the body enfolds not only the mind but also in some sense the entire material universe. [41]

What Bohm is saying is that there is a higher dimensional reality, which he calls the implicate order, which *projects* the lower dimensional elements that have a non-local and non-causal relationship, and the sort of mutual enfoldment which Bohm has suggested for "mind" and "brain." Bohm states that:

Descartes clearly understood this difficulty and indeed proposed to resolve it by means of the idea that such a relationship is made possible by God, who being outside of and beyond matter and consciousness (both of which He has indeed created) . . . Since then, the idea that

God takes care of this requirement has generally been abandoned, but it has not commonly been noticed that thereby the possibility of comprehending the relationship between matter and consciousness has collapsed.[42]

Some kind of Transcendent Principle is a reality for Bohm and other quantum physicists of our era. This is indeed a revolutionary development. Bohm goes on to say:

> So we are led to propose further that the more comprehensive, deeper, and more inward actuality is neither mind nor body but rather a yet higher-dimensional actuality, which is their common ground and which is of a nature beyond both. Each of these is then only a relatively independent sub-totality and it is implied that this relative independence derives from the higher dimensional ground in which mind and body are ultimately one . . .[43]

Bohm asserts:

> In this higher-dimensional ground the implicate order prevails.[44]

What exactly does Bohm mean by the "implicate order?" He often describes it in quasi-religious terms, as "the ground of all that is," "the immeasurable," "unbroken wholeness," etc. Bohm's language resembles that of the great mystics.

Fascinated by what I had discovered in the writings of David Bohm, I looked into *Quantum Questions* (1984) edited by Ken Wilber, on: the *Mystical Writings of the World's Great Physicists*.

Werner Heisenberg (1901–1976) invented what is known as matrix quantum mechanics at the age of twenty-four. He went on to win the Nobel Prize in physics for his brilliant contributions. He wrote several books of a philosophical nature, including *Physics and Beyond* (1971), *Across the Frontiers* (1974), and *The Physicist's Conception of Nature* (1955). He said that if we want to go beyond physics, however, and begin to philosophize, then the worldview that can most easily *explain* modern physics is not that of Democritus, but of Plato. You recall that Democritus was the ancient Greek atomist and materialist. Plato was the great idealist philosopher who believed in the reality of Universal Forms or Archetypes, which underlie the more obvious material world of "things." Unfortunately, it is materialism and not idealism which is the predominant view of what we call "modern science." These scientists, especially prevalent in the biological and behavioral sciences, seem to espouse materialism as the "prolegomena" to their scientific work. Their ancestors are the ancient

Greek materialists, Leucippus and Democritus. Heisenberg writes that:

> When Plato himself took up the problems raised by Leucippus and Democritus, he adopted the idea of smallest units of matter, but he took strongest exception to the tendency of that philosophy to suppose the atoms to be the foundation of all existence, the only truly existing material objects. Plato's atoms were not strictly material, being thought of as geometrical forms . . . These bodies, in keeping with the starting point of his idealistic philosophy, were in some sense the Ideas underlying the structure of matter . . . The structure underlying the phenomena is not given by material objects like the atoms of Democritus but by the form that determines the material objects. The Ideas are more fundamental than the objects. [45]

While admitting that Democritean atomism was useful in the development of the sciences of biology and chemistry, up to a point, Heisenberg unequivocally states:

> I think that on this point modern physics has definitely decided for Plato. For the smallest units of matter are, in fact, not physical objects in the ordinary sense of the word; they are forms, structures or – in Plato's sense—Ideas. . . [46]

Erwin Schroedinger (1887–1961) discovered "wave mechanics." "Schroedinger's wave equation" became the heart of quantum mechanics. Schroedinger was awarded the Nobel Prize in physics for his seminal work in 1933. Schroedinger wrote several philosophical works, including *My View of the World* (1964), *Mind and Matter* (1958), *Science and Humanism* (1951), and *What is Life* (1947). In an essay entitled "The I That Is God," Schroedinger writes:

> For the sake of argument, let me regard this as a fact, as I believe every unbiased biologist would, if there were not the well-known unpleasant feeling about 'declaring oneself to be a pure mechanism.' For it is deemed to contradict Free Will as warranted by direct introspection.

> But immediate experiences in themselves, however various and disparate they be, are logically incapable of contradicting each other. So let us see whether we cannot draw the correct, non-contradictory conclusion from the following two premises:

> (i) My body functions as a pure mechanism according to the Laws of Nature.

> (ii) Yet I know, by incontrovertible direct experience, that I am directing its motions, of which I foresee the effects, that may be fateful and all-important, in which case I feel and take full responsibility for them.

The only possible inference from these two facts is, I think, that I—I in the widest meaning of the word, that is to say, every conscious mind that has ever said or felt 'I'—am the person, if any who controls the 'motion of atoms' according to the Laws of Nature.[47]

In this remarkable statement, Schroedinger is identifying himself, as a physicist of world rank with the perennial philosophy as it is expressed, for example, in the *Upanishads*, which recognize the mystical insight: ATMAN = BRAHMAN, which is to say that the innermost Self equals the Universal Self, or God. Schroedinger's view is quite similar to that of Bohm's, in fact.

Albert Einstein (1879–1955) is regarded by many as the greatest physicist who ever lived. His contributions include the special and general theory of relativity, Brownian movement theory, the quantum photoelectric effect, and his immortal discovery: $E = mc^2$. He was awarded the Nobel Prize for his contributions in the year 1921. Was Einstein a religious man? Not in the sense that be believed in the personal God of the Bible, but yes, in the sense that he believed in a Cosmic Divine Order. He speaks in his book *Ideas and Opinions* (1954) of the "anthropomorphic God" of the Old and New Testament. There is the level of the "religion of fear," and the next level of the "religion of morality and love," and, ". . .*there is a third stage of religious experience* which belongs to all of them, even though it is rarely found in a pure form: I shall call it cosmic religious feeling."[48]

Einstein states that this "cosmic religious feeling" is found among the scientific geniuses of humankind's history. One of Einstein's own famous statements is "God does not play dice." In this statement he implied that the order of nature is derivable from a greater order of Cosmic Being which men and women throughout history have commonly called "God." Einstein says:

> The interpretation of religion, as here advanced, implies a dependence of science on the religious attitude, a relation which, in our predominantly materialistic age, is only too easily overlooked. While it is true that scientific results are entirely independent from religious or moral considerations, those individuals to whom we owe the great creative achievements of science were all of them imbued with the truly religious conviction that this universe of ours is something perfect and susceptible to the rational striving for knowledge.[49]

Einstein's "cosmic religious feeling" comes close to, but it does not quite reach, Bucke's "Cosmic Consciousness." He was moving in that direction, if he did not attain to the definitive mystical experience of Cosmic Unity.

Max Planck (1858–1947) ushered in the quantum age. He had a stroke of genius in 1900 that nature is not continuous but comes in discrete packets or "quanta." He was awarded the Nobel Prize in 1918 for his contributions. In his book, *Where is Science Going?* (1932), Planck writes: "There can never be any real opposition between religion and science. Every serious and reflective person realizes . . . that the religious element in his nature must be recognized and cultivated."[50]

Wolfgang Pauli (1900–1958) was considered by some to be the most brilliant physicist of our century. He won the Nobel Prize in 1945 for his contributions to physics, including the "exclusion principle," and the prediction of the neutrino. He writes in *Across the Frontiers: "I consider the overcoming of opposites, including a synthesis embracing rational understanding and the mystical experience of unity to be the mythos, spoken or unspoken, of our present day and age.*"[51]

Sir James Jeans (1877–1946) was a mathematician, physicist and astronomer, who made basic contributions to the dynamic theory of gases, the mathematics of electromagnetism, and the evolution of stars and nebulae. He was knighted in 1924. The following quotation comes from Jeans' *The Mysterious Universe* (1931):

> Creations of an individual mind may reasonably be called less substantial than creations of a universal mind. A similar distinction must be made between the space we see in a dream and the space of everyday life; the latter, which is the same for us all, is the space of universal mind. It is the same for time, the time of waking life, which flows at the same rate for us all, being the time of universal mind. Again we may think of the laws to which phenomena conform in our waking hours, the laws of nature, as the laws of universal mind.[52]

Physicists, such as Jeans, have turned the tables on materialism, and behaviorism is materialism posing as science. Radical behaviorists "deny consciousness." What can we say? Can we describe seeing to the blind? Physiological behaviorists reduce psychological events to biological ones, and biological events to biochemical ones, and biochemical events to physical ones, i.e. matter and energy. Here the "bedrock" of materialism disappears. What is matter? Einstein showed that it is energy. What is energy? The great quantum physicists of our century: Heisenberg, Schroedinger, Planck, Pauli, Jeans, Bohm, etc., reveal that energy, or "quantum stuff," *implies mind.* Sir Arthur Eddington (1882–1944), the first physicist to verify Einstein's relativity theory, wrote: "The elements of consciousness are particular thoughts and feelings; the elements of the brain cell are atoms and electrons. Whilst, therefore, I contemplate a spiritual domain underlying the physical world as a whole. . ."[53] Via the physicists, the "scientists of matter," we have *recovered consciousness.*

5

Sigmund Freud's Reduction of Religious Experience

I was born on May 6, 1856, at Freiberg in Moravia, a small town in what is now Czechoslovakia. My parents were Jews, and I have remained a Jew myself.[1]

By "a Jew," Freud must have meant his ethnic Jewish identity because he was, by his student years, to have rejected the monotheistic faith of his forefathers in favor of the scientific materialism and atheism so common to the "intelligentsia" of his time, the late nineteenth century.

When Freud was a child of four, his father, Jacob, moved his family to Vienna, Austria. Freud went through the whole of his education there at the "Gymnasium." He was at the top of his class for seven years in a row.[2] Freud, the atheist, makes this paradoxical statement in his autobiography regarding the importance of the Bible to him:

Neither at that time, nor indeed in my later life, did I feel any particular predilection for the career of a physician. I was moved, rather, by a sort of curiosity, which was, however, directed more toward human concerns than toward natural objects; nor had I grasped the importance of observation as one of the best means of gratifying it. My early familiarity with the Bible (at a time almost before I had learnt the art of reading) had, as I recognized much later, an enduring effect upon the direction of my interest.[3]

The last book of Freud's life was *Moses and Monotheism* which was his attempt to essentially *rewrite* the Biblical story in terms of psychoanalytic theory. We will look more at this later in the chapter.

As much as he was interested in the Bible stories as a youth,

146

Freud, the student, was much attracted to the scientific evolutionism of his day:

> At the same time, the theories of Darwin, which were then of topical interest, strongly attracted me . . . and it was in hearing Goethe's beautiful essay on Nature read aloud at a popular lecture by Prof. Carl Brühl just before I left school that decided me to become a medical student.[4]

When Freud joined the university to study medicine, he experienced considerable anti-semitism. He says that:

> Above all, I found that I was expected to feel myself inferior and an alien because I was a Jew. I refused absolutely to do the first of these things. I have never been able to see why I should feel ashamed of my descent, as people were beginning to say, of my race.[5]

Despite the prejudicial climate of Austria toward Jews, Freud excelled as a student of medicine. He first worked at the physiological laboratory of Ernst Brücke from the years 1876 to 1881 where he studied among other things the histology of the nervous system. He was slow in completing his medical studies, but was awarded the M.D. in 1881. Due to his financial situation, which was not very strong, Freud abandoned his theoretical career as a medical scientist, despite his early promise, to become a practicing doctor. He entered the General Hospital in Vienna and worked in various departments as a resident physician. He eventually became a worker in the Institute of Cerebral Anatomy.

> . . . with an eye to material considerations, I began to study nervous diseases. There were, at that time, few specialists in that branch of medicine in Vienna. . .[6]

Freud became a neurologist. He was never formally trained in either psychiatry or psychology despite his immense future contributions to these fields. Early in his career as neurologist, he published some papers on his clinical observations of organic diseases of the nervous system. Concerning the neuroses he said:

> I understood nothing about the neuroses.[7]

In the spring of 1885, Freud was appointed Lecturer in Neuropathology based upon the excellence of his histological and clinical publications. Soon afterward, Freud was awarded a Travelling Fellowship to Paris where he was to study under Jean Charcot. He translated some of Charcot's lectures from French into German, and thereby became part of his circle at the clinic at Salpêtrière.

> What impressed me most of all while I was with Charcot were his latest investigations upon hysteria, some of which were carried out under my own eyes.[8]

Charcot had proven the genuineness of hysterical paralyses, and that they were of psychogenic, not organic origin. He could produce and remove hysterical paralyses by hypnotic suggestions. Before he left the clinic, Freud discussed with Charcot his view that hysterical paralyses conformed to popular, not anatomical, ideas of the body. Before he returned to Vienna, Freud spent some time at the Kassowitz Institute of childhood disorders in Berlin.

In 1886, Freud settled in Vienna as a physician, and married. He was a specialist in nervous diseases. When he tried to present to Viennese medical circles what he learned from Charcot, he met with a bad reception. The idea of the psychogenic origin of nervous diseases seemed "sheer nonsense" to the Viennese medical circles. Freud was excluded from the Laboratory of Cerebral Anatomy. He withdrew from academic life to become a practicing doctor of nervous diseases. He said:

> Anyone who wanted to make a living from the treatment of nervous patients must clearly be able to do something to help them. My therapeutic arsenal contained only two weapons, electro-therapy and hypnotism. . .[9]

Electro-therapy was essentially a placebo and Freud had problems with hypnosis as well. He was unable to succeed in hypnotizing every patient and he had had difficulty in putting individual patients into as deep a trance as he would have wished. Freud returned to France to study under Bernheim at his hospital in Nancy. There he says that:

> . . . I received the profoundest impression of the possibility that there could be powerful mental processes hidden from the consciousness of men.[10]

In the last chapter we had witnessed the recovery of *consciousness* by science from the "Dark Ages" of behaviorism, which had banished it into "non-existence." We will see, in Sigmund Freud, and later in Carl Jung, the discovery (or essentially, the rediscovery, as it was known to the great mystical traditions of both Eastern and Western humankind) of the *unconscious mind*.

Between 1886 and 1891, Freud said that he did little scientific work and published scarcely anything. He said that he was occupied in establishing himself as a practicing physician, and with providing the material necessities of life to his rapidly growing family. Freud said that, during this period, he used hypnosis, not only as suggestion, but as a way to question patients about the origins of their symptoms which could not be recalled in the waking state.

Freud speaks of his association with Dr. Josef Breuer and his hysterical patient, Anna O. (Bertha Pappenheim), who was a gifted young woman who had fallen ill while nursing her father in the hospital. She had hysterical paralyses, inhibitions, and mental confusion. Breuer treated her by putting her under deep hypnosis and made her say what was oppressing her mind. In this way he succeeded in alleviating her symptoms.

> It turned out that all her symptoms went back to moving events which she had experienced while nursing her father; that is to say, her symptoms had a meaning and were residues or reminiscences of these emotional situations. It turned out in most instances that there had been some thought or impulse which she had to suppress while she was by her father's sickbed, and that, in place of it, as a substitute for it, the symptom had afterward appeared . . . When the patient recalled a situation of this kind in a hallucinatory way under hypnosis and carried through to its conclusion, with free expression of emotion, the mental act which she had originally suppressed, the symptom was abolished and did not return.[11]

Freud says that he began to repeat Breuer's investigations with his own patients and he now worked at nothing else. In 1895, Breuer and Freud published the book, *Studies in Hysteria*. It introduced a "dynamic factor" by which a symptom arises by the damming up of an affect, and an "economic factor" by regarding that same symptom as the product or equivalent of a quantity of energy which would otherwise have been employed in some other way. Breuer called the method "cathartic." Freud later called this "conversion."[12] Breuer retired from this work for various reasons, and Freud was to become the sole administrator of his legacy.

Freud was very early to take the "sexual turn" in his theorizing. He says:

> I now learned from my rapidly increasing experience that it was not from *any* kind of emotional excitation that was in action behind the phenomena of neurosis but habitually one of a sexual nature.[13]

Freud's increasing dogmatism about his "sexual theory" was to lose him some of his major disciples, including Adler and Jung, and others, who recognized other factors in both the formation of neuroses, and in the normal development of the personality. Adler was to look at the "striving for power" as his chief issue, and Jung took a more inclusive view, including both sex and power, in a wider striving for self-realization. Still others, such as Rank, looked at the birth trauma as the major factor in the human psyche's health or illness.

In his practice, Freud eventually abandoned the use of hypnosis because despite even brilliant "curative results," it could all be wiped away if the personal relationship between doctor and patient became disturbed. In one such instance, a woman patient awakening from hypnotic trance threw herself into Freud's arms.

> So I abandoned hypnosis, only retaining my practice of requiring the patient to lie upon a sofa while I myself sat behind him, seeing him, but not seen myself.[14]

Freud gradually replaced the hypnotic method, in a series of steps, with the classical psychoanalytic method of "free association" in which the patient must follow the "fundamental rule" of saying whatever comes into his or her mind without censorship, no matter how offensive, or how trivial the thoughts and images might seem. Thus was psychoanalysis born as a treatment of hysterical neuroses.

Freud raised the question of how it is that mental activities become repressed or forgotten:

> How had it come about that the patients had forgotten so many of the facts of their external and internal lives but could recollect them if a particular technique was applied? Observation supplied an exhaustive answer to these questions. Everything that had been forgotten had in some ways or other been painful; it had been either alarming or disagreeable or shameful by the standard of the subject's personality.[15]

This was the essential basis of Freud's theory of "repression." It was his first understanding of the "unconscious mind." He was later to discover more "primal" or "archaic" contents of the unconscious which were never repressed because they had never been conscious in the first place. Jung was to take this further in his theory of the "collective unconscious." In any event, the theory of dynamic repression became the basis for Freud's early work in neuroses, dreams, and the psychopathology of everyday life (e.g. accidents, slips of the tongue, etc.).

Based upon his theory of repression, Freud took a new view of psychotherapy. Its aim was no longer simply "catharsis" or "abreaction," but the *uncovering* of repressions and their replacement by conscious acts of judgment, i.e., to make the unconscious conscious. It is perhaps a secular version of Jesus' statement: "You shall know the truth and the truth shall set you free."

Freud's original theory is called the "topographical approach." It divides the mind into three regions: the conscious, the preconscious, and the unconscious. The conscious region is the mind's smallest zone and it contains what one is aware of *right now*. Introspection leads to the contents of consciousness. The preconscious is a much larger domain containing everything of the mind which one can easily, if one chooses, become conscious of, ranging from events during the summer when you were three years old to the football game you attended last week. Finally, the unconscious is the greatest realm which consists of all that is mental, but which is not available to consciousness except via special methods such as hypnosis, free association, and dream interpretation. Freud sees this realm of the unconscious mind basically as one realm. Jung, as we shall later see, distinguishes between the personal unconscious of one's own life history, and the collective unconscious of humankind's history, which is just as much a part of oneself. Freud's later views are very similar, however, when he speaks about the "archaic contents" of the unconscious which we all carry within us, albeit unconsciously. He called this the "collective mind."

Following his joint publication with Breuer of *Studies in Hysteria*, Freud's next great work was *The Interpretation of Dreams* (1900) which was actually published at about the same time that Bucke published *Cosmic Consciousness* (1901) and James published *The Varieties of Religious Experience* (1902). Freud was just forty-four years old at the time of the publication of this magnum opus, whereas Bucke and James were at or near the end of their lives. This was just the beginning of Freud's incredibly creative career.

Freud's view of dreams is essentially that they are disguised wish fulfillments, in certain ways analogous to neurotic symptoms in their genesis. Dreams are compromise formations between the demands of the repressed wish impulse and the resistance of the censoring force of the ego, which although weaker during sleep, is by no means entirely inoperative.

> I have given the name of dream work to the process which, with the cooperation of censorship, converts the latent thoughts into the mani-

fest content of the dream ... Dreams *condense, displace, dramatize, elaborate,* and visually *symbolize* ... the unconscious latent wishes – as censored by the ego – into the *manifest dream.*[16]

This is Freud's view, that the manifest dream is a *disguised form* of the latent dream wishes. Jung, as we shall see, accepted the dream as it was, as a "message," as it were from the Creative Unconscious. Freud's Unconscious is not like Jung's, a source of creativity, as much as a cauldron of dark and repressed wishes, sexual, and aggressive.

Freud did characterize the dream as the "royal road to the unconscious mind." He employed the same basic methods in investigating the dreams of his patients, as he did in exploring their neurotic symptoms: basically, free association and interpretation. These methods, as a means of dream analysis, may not be so original with Freud as is commonly thought among those who elevate Freud to almost godlike "original genius" status. David Bakan, in a most interesting book, *Sigmund Freud and the Jewish Mystical Tradition* (1958) writes:

> It is clear, if we seek some explanation of Freud's psychoanalytic developments in the formal preparation and the professional work of his pre-psychoanalytic years, we find little there to give us insight. The tradition of severe materialism of Brücke, Helmholtz, and the like with which he came in contact was certainly not one which he seemed to draw upon in any essential way for psychoanalysis.[17]

Although Charcot played some part in "starting" Freud, as did Breuer, as "harbingers of psychoanalysis," from the standpoint of the history of ideas, there are shrouds of mystery about Freud's ideas and methods, unless we blindly accept the "original genius" hypothesis about Freud. There is in psychoanalysis, a theory of neurosis; a theory of healing; a theory of sexuality; an armamentarium of technical methods; a theory of personality; and even a philosophy of religion. Did this entire tapestry come solely from the mind of Freud, or did he have sources which he did not, and perhaps could not acknowledge? Bakan, in his most novel approach to Freud, says:

> The thesis of this essay is that the contributions of Freud are to be understood largely as a contemporary version of, and a contemporary contribution to, the history of Jewish mysticism.[18]

Bakan claims that Freud, consciously or unconsciously, secularized Jewish mysticism and that psychoanalysis can be intelligibly seen as such a secularization. By separating the supernatural elements of Jewish mysticism from its other contents, Freud, according to Bakan, succeeded in making major contributions to the science of psychology. Bakan indicates that Freud had most excellent reasons for not specifying this source of his ideas: anti-Semitism was a chief one. Besides, in his era of scientific materialism, any association of his ideas with mysticism would have proven fatal to their acceptance. His ideas about sexuality were controversial enough! Bakan goes on to say:

> We believe that Freud often wrote with obscurity, that was motivated, consciously or unconsciously, to hide the deeper positions of his thought, and that these deeper positions were Kabbalistic in their source and content. The Kabbalistic tradition itself has secrecy as part of its nature . . .[19]

"Kabbala" is a Hebrew word which means "revealed knowledge." Bakan points out that both of Freud's parents came from Galicia, a region whose atmosphere was saturated with Hasidism. He also points out that Breuer, like Freud, was a Jew who grew up under similar cultural-religious influences. Bakan points out that a figure of particular note in the Kabbala, following the period of the classic texts, the Sepher Yetsirah and the Sepher Zohar, dated from the second and thirteenth centuries, A.D., was Abraham Abulafia.* Among the psychological and spiritual objectives of Abulafia was to "unseal the soul, to untie the knots which bind it . . ."[20] One of Abulafia's methods was meditating upon, and combining and recombining, in spontaneous ways, the letters of the Hebrew alphabet. Another method was what he called "jumping or skipping," from one conception to another. Every "jump" opens a new sphere, and within each sphere, the mind may "freely associate." "Jumping and skipping" brings to light the hidden processes of the mind. If this is not a forerunner of Freud's method of free association, then I do not know what is!

Furthermore, Abulafia regards the relationship between the Kabbalistic teacher and the pupil as very important. Bakan sees this as a harbinger of the analyst-analysand relationship.

Israel Baal Shem Tov, the "Master of the Good Name," was the founder of Hasidism, a folk-movement stemming from the Kabbala. He saw his task as one of liberating the minds of his pupils

---

* Abraham ben Samuel Abulafia was born in Spain in 1240. He travelled in search of lost traditions in the Near East, becoming a mystic and visionary in the process of his journey.

from illusion, and bringing them to personal freedom. Freud, in his way, was a secular-scientific "liberator" of the minds of his patients from the illusions of their own unconscious minds which kept them from seeing reality as it is, and dealing with it with maturity and effectiveness.

Bakan points out that the fundamental principles of dream interpretation used by Freud are already present in the Talmud (which is exoteric and not esoteric Judaism) which contains extensive treatises on dreams and their interpretation. Even sexual symbolism in dreams is discussed in the Talmud: "I dreamt that there was a shade above me, and yet it was beneath me ... It means unnatural intercourse."[21]

The *Berakoth*, a treatise of the Talmud, laid down the fundamental principles of dream interpretation. The first is that all dreams have a meaning: "A dream which is not interpreted is like a letter which is not read."[22] The second fundamental principle formulated in *Berakoth* is that "all dreams follow the mouth" or "all dreams follow their interpretation."[23] According to this principle the interpretation of dreams has priority over the dream itself; it offers a tremendous conviction to the interpretation of dreams. Finally, *Berakoth* uses word play to plumb the hidden depth of dreams. What else is "free association" but a modern version of "word-play?"

Freud's profound concern for sexuality can be seen in the *Zohar*. One of the Kabbala's fundamental concepts is the "Shekinah," which is the *Female Presence of God* within Material Creation. The *Zohar* repeatedly refers to *the union* of God with His Shekinah. There are parallels to Freud's "libido," or universal sexual energy, in the Kabbala, as well. It is not surprising that Freud, whose family came from Orthodox Jewish sources, was familiar with the Kabbala, and drew upon it, in his way, without acknowledging it per sé in both his healing methods and his interpretation of dreams.

Following his classic *The Interpretation of Dreams*, Freud wrote books applying his psychoanalytic methods to new areas, such as, *The Psychopathology of Everyday Life, Jokes and Their Relation to the Unconscious, Three Essays on the Theory of Sexuality*, between the years 1900 and 1909. In 1909, Freud, with Jung, visited America and spoke at Clark University. He met the philosopher, William James, in his old age by then. By 1910, the unknown Freud of 1900 was now an international figure, and there was now an International Psychoanalytical Association. Between 1911 and

1913, two of his chief disciples, Adler and Jung, withdrew from his circle, each in his turn, forming movements of their own. Freud refers to his former disciples as "the two heretics," borrowing the language of Medieval Christianity. The lonely scientist in-search-of-truth has now become a formidable authoritarian leader of his own "movement," in many ways a secular religion, offering its brand of salvation through science.

Before we look at Freud's series of four books on religion, or psychology of religion, we will look at Freud's later psychodynamic theory as he presents it in *The Ego and the Id* (1923) and *An Outline of Psychoanalysis* (1940) which he calls the "structural model." We have seen the "topographical theory" with its conscious, preconscious, and unconscious; we will now look at the ego, id, and superego, another way of looking at the psyche (which does not in any way invalidate the older view).

Freud begins by describing the "psyche" or "mental life" as an "apparatus to which we ascribe the characteristics of being extended in space and being made of several portions . . ."[24]

> *The Id*: To the oldest of these mental provinces or agencies we give the name of *id*. It contains everything that is inherited, that is present at birth, that is fixed in constitution – above all, therefore, the instincts, which originate in the somatic organization and which find their mental expression in the id in forms unknown to us.[25]

> *The Ego*: Under the influence of the real external world which surrounds us, one portion of the id has undergone a special development. From what was originally a cortical layer, provided with organs for receiving stimulation, a special organization has arisen which hence-

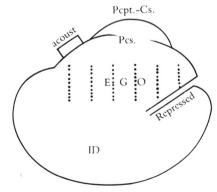

Figure 5.1   Freud's "Model of the Mind"

forward acts as an intermediary between the id and the external world. This region of the mental life has been given the name of *ego*. [26]

Superego: The long period of childhood, during which the growing human being lives in dependence upon his parents, leaves behind a precipitate, which forms within his ego a special agency in which this parental influence is prolonged. It has received the name of *superego*. In so far as the superego is differentiated from the ego or opposed to it, it constitutes a third force which the ego must take into account. [27]

This tripartite division of the psyche implies a three-way psychodynamics:

Thus, an action by the ego is as it should be if it satisfied simultaneously the demands of the id, of the superego, and of reality, that is to say, if it is able to reconcile their demands with one another. The details of the relation between the ego and the superego become completely intelligible if they are carried back to the child's attitude toward his parents. The parents' influence naturally includes not merely the personalities of the parents themselves but also the racial, national, and family traditions handed on through them as well as the demands of the immediate social *milieu* which they represent. [28]

Freud represents in his three-part psychodynamic theory the influences of biology: id, psychology: ego, and sociology: superego, all of which join together to determine behavior. One's psyche can function relatively harmoniously, and this is psychological health. Or one's psyche can be in severe inner-conflict, id versus ego, ego versus superego, and superego versus id, in the inner war of neurosis. The conditions of health or neurosis are probably the experiences of one's early childhood, particularly surrounding what Freud calls the "Oedipus complex," in the male, and the "Electra complex," in the female, which involve the love/hate relationships between the child and his/her mother and father. In the male, according to Freud, the Oedipus complex involves love for the mother, and rivalry and hate of the father, and a wish to replace him. But the small boy is overwhelmed by the father's superior force, which he views as "castration threat," and he represses his desire for his mother, and identifies with his father. This is a relatively healthy outcome. Unhealthy outcomes, according to Freud, lead to the various forms of psychoneuroses.

It is curious, however, that Freud's version of the Oedipal myth has relatively little to do with the actual story of *Oedipus Rex* by Sophocles. In the actual myth, the issue is the passage of "the sins of the father," Laius, unto his son, Oedipus. Oedipus actually kills his father, whom he does not know as his father, before he meets and marries his mother, whom he does not know as his mother. His father had committed a sin of the homosexual rape of a son of a king, which resulted in the boy's suicide. It is then prophesied that his own son will kill him. When his son is born, Laius pierces his son's ankles and hangs him on a tree to die. Oedipus is rescued from almost certain death, and raised by the King and Queen of Corinth. He is named "Oedipus," Greek for his symptom, swollen ankles. He grows up to fulfill the oracle, quite unconsciously, killing his father, Laius, whom he met as a stranger on a road over a bridge, and marrying his mother, Jocasta, whom he did not know to be his mother, after he solved the riddle of the Sphinx, and was made King of Thebes. When he found out the unconscious crimes he had committed, he took out his guilt and rage on himself by blinding himself in both eyes with the sharp pin of a brooch taken from the person of his mother, who had hung herself. This is not exactly the pattern of jealousy and rivalry in Freud's version, and it contains much deeper truths, such as the passing on of the sins of the fathers to the sons, or the mothers to the daughters which the Bible speaks about. The sufferings of Oedipus were his generational "heritage" passed on to him by his father, Laius, who had committed the sin of homosexual rape, resulting in suicide, of Chrissipus, the son of King Pelops at whose castle Laius was a guest. Laius committed a later sin of attempted murder against his own unnamed son, who was to become Oedipus Rex, and fulfill the oracle, and suffer himself horribly in the process.

The psychiatrist, Morton Schatzman, in his profound book, *Soul Murder* (1973), discusses the "Laius complex" and he makes a truly convincing case against Freud's "psychodynamic" treatment of the case of Schreber whom Freud "analyzed" as a paranoid schizophrenic. Schatzman investigated the real historical facts, and found that Schreber's father was a pre-Nazi type, who authored books on "childhood education and discipline" which would have pleased the Gestapo! He also found in the actual home of Schreber's father "disciplinary devices" that were, in fact, instruments of torture. Schreber was a case of real child abuse, not unconscious fantasy based upon his "Oedipus complex"! Other recent books, such as, Masson's *Assault on Truth* (1984), and Peck's *The People of the Lie* (1985) make the same point in different ways. The moral: go back to the *actual myths*; they may be more revealing than modern psychologists' reinterpretations of them.★

In Freud's structural theory, "the power of the id" expresses the true purpose of the individual's life, that is, the satisfaction of its innate needs, i.e., the "pleasure principle." Only the impact of the complications of "brute reality" forces the evolution of the ego out of the id, and the substitution of the "reality principle" for the "pleasure principle." Finally, the great length of human childhood dependency upon one's parents and social group causes the "superego" with its moral principles of "good" and "bad" to evolve out of the ego. Critics have pointed out that true *conscience* has nothing to do with the superego's dictates, and may even oppose them. It is likely that the conscience is a function of the *higher Self,* which has no place in Freud's tripartite psychodynamic system. For Freud, as we shall see, the superego has a lot to do with "God," particularly in the form of the "father complex."

Finally, in Freud's theoretic system, what is the relation of the conscious, preconscious, and unconscious of the older topographical approach with the ego, id, and superego of Freud's later structural model? The only organ of the personality with even the potential for consciousness is the ego, although it is predominantly preconscious, and is, in part, unconscious, as Freud found in his analysis of the dream work. The superego and the id operate chiefly from the state of unconsciousness, and can be known, only indirectly, through their effects, e.g., symptoms, dreams, personality traits, etc. In the psychology of Freud's former colleague, and then rival, Jung, one can indeed learn to recognize figures of the unconscious, particularly in dreams, in highly personified and symbolic ways. In both Freud's and Jung's psychotherapeutic psychology, becoming conscious of the unconscious is the sine qua non of psychic health and integration. Somewhere, Freud says, "Where there was id, let there be ego."

We will look now, keeping in mind his theoretical views about the human psyche and personality, at Freud's series of four books that could be called his psychology of religion. We might point out from the beginning that Freud, unlike James and Bucke, *never once* considers the possibility that God may be a reality, and that religious experience may relate to something *real*. Religion and

★ There is even more to be said about King Oedipus, who goes on in Greek mythology to become the archetype of the "wounded healer."

religious experience are real only inasmuch as they are psychological facts to be *explained away* in terms of Freud's psychoanalytic theorizing.

Freud's first book to treat the subject of religion was *Totem and Taboo* (1913). In the words of its own author it contains a theory of religion which the reader may well find fantastic. This reader was no exception.

Freud begins *Totem and Taboo* by looking at various primitive peoples' "horror of incest," which was, in fact, much more rigorously guarded against than it is in modern civilizations in which it, nevertheless, still maintains its "taboo" aspects. He also looks at the related phenomenon of the "totem" which is usually an animal that is regarded as sacred to the clan. The taboo against incest extends beyond biological relatives, parent–child, brother–sister, etc., to include all members of the common totem clan. A man may not have sexual intercourse with, or marry, a member of his own totem clan. The totem animal is regarded as the common ancestor of everybody in the clan. Among Australian aborigines, Freud found that the penalty for sexual intercourse with a woman of one's own clan was death. The woman, too, might be killed, beaten, or banished. When one violated a taboo, one became taboo.

Freud notes the "striking similarity" between the incest taboo of primitive peoples and the mental life of neurotic patients. He says that: "Psychoanalysis has taught us that a boy's earliest choice of objects for his love is incestuous and that these objects are forbidden ones – his mother and his sister."[29] Here we have the incestuous attraction and the taboo against it, which is enforced psychically, in the child's mind, conscious or unconscious, by the "threat of castration," real or imagined, by the feared and admired rival, the boy's father. This is what Freud has termed the "Oedipus complex." Its successful resolution leads to emotional health; its lack of resolution, to the various forms of psychoneurosis.

What is the relationship between these seemingly disparate facts – totemism and taboo – and the Oedipus complex in the neurotic, as well as normal, individual? In both cases there are presumably incestuous wishes, and likewise there is the perceived or real threat of punishment for the violation of these taboos. In the primitive society, the totem is a kind of "spiritual father," and the taboo against incest extends much further than it does in modern civilization. The persistence of taboos, the earliest unwritten form of law, indicates that the original desire to do the prohibited thing must still persist and hence the need for the threat resulting in the fear of doing the wished for act. Of course, there are still sometimes persons in both primitive and modern societies who violate taboos, and they are dealt with in various ways, from death or banishment to psychotherapy!

Freud goes on to review some current theories of his time about the "evolution" of views of the universe from animism to religion to science, as if this is a progression from simple-minded wrong-headedness to mature rational truth. Animism is the doctrine of souls. The American Indian peoples, for example, consider that everything has a "manitou," or "soul," from simple rocks, which have a "rock soul," to trees, which have a "tree soul," to deer, which have a "deer soul," to human beings who have a "human soul." Scientistic★ minds from Freud to the present tend to deride animism as "prescientific superstition." But, might there not be *a truth* expressed in this belief of all so-called "primitive peoples" in a soul, or life-force, indwelling every being, as opposed to sterile mechanistic rationalism?

In Freud's Darwinian mechanistic thinking, the mantle of respectability passed from animism, or the belief in souls, to religion, or the belief in supernatural spirits, many: polytheism, or one: monotheism, and then to his own late nineteenth-century version of "science," in which nature was no more alive, and souls were long since banished to unreality, and spirits, including the Supreme Spirit, were explained away as "delusions of the past." In Freud's neat little scientistic world, only art and literature remained as outlets for some free and creative spirits whose inspirations in the past gave rise to the great religions.

How does Freud *explain away* religion: the belief in a Supreme Being, in terms of what he has said about "totem and taboo" and the "Oedipus complex"? He does so in most fantastical ways, as we will see. Based upon Darwin's speculations about the original state of the human race being small groups, or "primal hordes," akin to the social arrangements of gorilla bands, Freud concocts the following story. Its truth has been disputed by every anthropologist, archaeologist, historian, prehistorian, and scholar of the origins of religion who has taken it seriously enough to look at it. Its only adherents are the most doctrinaire Freudians who have made psychoanalysis their *weltanshuuang.*

★ "Scientism" means making an idolatry out of science as a cover-up for a philosophical materialism and atheism, "Science" from the Latin *scientia*, means "knowledge".

Freud first recalls Darwin's speculation about the "primal horde":

> There is, of course, no place for the beginnings of totemism in Darwin's primal horde. All that we find there is a violent and jealous father who keeps all the females for himself and drives his sons away as they grow up. This earliest state of society has never been an object of observation.[30]

Despite the fact that this earlier "primal state" has never been, and in the nature of the case, could never be, observed, Freud goes on to speculate:

> If we recall the celebration of the totem meal to our help, we shall be able to find an answer. One day the brothers who had been driven out came together, killed and devoured their father and so made an end of the patriarchal horde. United, they had the courage to do and succeed in doing what would have been impossible for them individually. (Some cultural advance, perhaps, command over some new weapon, had given them a sense of superior strength). Cannibal savages as they were, it goes without saying that they devoured their victim as well as killing him. The violent primal father had doubtless been the feared and envied model of each one of the company of brothers: and in the act of devouring him they accomplished their identification with him, and each one of them acquired a portion of his strength. The totem meal, which is perhaps mankind's earliest festival, would thus be a repetition and a commemoration of this memorable and criminal deed, which was the beginning of so many things – of social organization, of moral restrictions and religion.[31]

How in the world did this bizarre and violent act of the primordial past give rise to what we know as religion? According to Freud, their hated father who had been such a formidable obstacle to their sexual and power cravings was now, after they had gotten rid of him, a source of remorse and guilt. The memory of the dead father became more powerful than the reality of the living one had ever been. Through some kind of strange mental transmutation, they substituted an animal figure for their dead father to take his place as the "ancestor" of the tribe. Freud points out the similarity between this and the animal phobias in young children which turn out to be displaced fears of their own fathers. Let us say, now, that the clan has chosen the bear as its "totem" or "father substitute." It will now be forbidden to kill the bear (any bear) or eat its flesh, except at an annual totem feast, which is a re-enactment, presumably, of the original crime, or "original sin." Furthermore, the women of the bear clan, representing the many wives of the primal fathers whom they had lusted after, will become taboo as sexual objects. The men will have to marry out of the clan (perhaps a woman from the wolf clan!). This totemism, in Freud's view, was the earliest religion. Later, for unknown reasons, the animal-father was transformed back into a human-father who was projected into a god with virtually unlimited power. "He" may be regarded as the tribal god among other gods, as was probably originally the case among the Hebrews who worshipped their mountain god, "El Shaddai." Eventually, in the evolution of religious thinking, some religious genius, like Moses, made him the supreme God of the universe, still based, mind you, on the projection of the "primal father." Freud points out that:

> The psychoanalysis of individual human beings, however, teaches us with quite special insistence that the god of each of them is formed in the likeness of his father in the flesh and oscillates and changes along with that relation, and that at bottom God is nothing but an exalted father. [32]

Freud calls the root of every form of religion "a longing for the father." [33] Presumably, then, both the primal father of antiquity carried in the collective mind, which Freud did in fact believe in, and one's personal father, are the unconscious bases for the "heavenly father" of religion. This is a very neat explanatory tour de force, I must admit, and there is clinical evidence of the role of the father in people's god images (at least in this culture), but it surely is not the basis of all religions. Buddhism, for example, has no concept of a "father god," but of a supreme state of consciousness called "nirvana." The deity of Taoism has no personal features at all, but is a universal uniting power which makes all things one. Hinduism has many kinds of god images, both male and female, in its polytheistic forms. In its monotheistic, or perhaps more accurately, monistic form, Hinduism's God, Brahman, is the universal ground of being, not an anthropomorphized deity. Truly speaking, Judaism's God is no anthropomorphic figure with a long white beard, either, but rather, Eternal Being who answered the prophet, Moses' query about his name, or nature, as "I AM THAT I AM." The only image of God in that story is a *divine light* from a burning bush. It does not conjure up the "father figure" to me. The God Name, YHWH, is usually translated "the Eternal" in Orthodox Jewish prayer books. This, again, does not imply a "father figure" projected into the sky! It is true that Jesus the Christ, referred to his God as "Abba," or "Father." But I would take that as a *personal way of talking* about the Divine Ground of Existence rather than any literal conception in Jesus' mind of an "exalted father figure." Indeed, the Jewish Scriptures themselves in the Decalogue (Ten Commandments) strictly *forbids idolatry* in no uncertain terms:

> I *am* the LORD thy God, which have brought thee out of the land of Egypt, out of the house of bondage.
>
> Thou shalt have no other gods before Me. Thou shalt not make unto thee a graven image, nor any manner of likeness, of any thing that is in heaven above, or that is in the earth beneath, or that is in the water under the earth; thou shalt not bow down unto them, nor serve them; for I the LORD thy God am a jealous God. . .[34]

Judaism, and Freud was a Jew (in fact his grandfather and great-grandfather were Orthodox Rabbis), strictly *forbade imagery* with regard to God. The Jewish Scriptures themselves refer to God in his highest revelation as a verb: *to be*. This is hardly anthropo-mophism or projections of the father figure into the heavens. True, in the history of Christianity, Christian art frequently *is* literal and anthropomorphic. This is strictly un-Jewish. It is pagan. Neurotic and psychotic patients in studies I have seen do draw images of God, when requested to do so, that frequently look like a father figure, even their own. Sometimes, they draw more abstract symbols, like the sun. Presumably normals would do this kind of thing too if asked to "draw God." If asked to describe him, people's statements about God sometimes are related to statements about their fathers or mothers, as was shown in a remarkable book by a woman psychoanalyst, Ana-Maria Rizzuto, M.D. entitled: *The Birth of the Living God: A Psychoana-lytic Study* (1979). For example, a woman patient in her sixties described God and her father, as follows:

God	Father
If I were to describe God accord-ing to my experiences with him, I would say that he is great because he has helped me through some hard times.	Oh! My father was kind . . . He was a lovely man. I wouldn't change my father in any way. My father was an angel.[35]

The patient drew God as a very kindly fatherly-motherly figure with hands clasped in prayer. If this seems like mere coincidence, the following are the parallel words of another patient, a twenty-seven year old physician who suffered from a schizoid personality disorder. He drew God, incidentally, as a very stern, bearded

God is praying to us and looking over us

Figure 5.2

father figure. Rizzuto makes the somewhat incredible claim that his picture represents the "primal father;" adding however, that it looks like his personal father, too, and himself.

God	Father
I have never experienced any closeness to God.	I was never close to my father.[36]

A third patient, a woman in her thirties who suffered a most traumatizing childhood, drew God not as a person but as a bright warm sun. Dr. Rizzuto interprets this strictly in terms of personal emotion; that she needs warmth and love. She does not indicate what Freud himself would claim, that it was the God-image of Atonism, or sun-worship, one of the religions of ancient Egypt. Freud makes use of this in *Moses and Monotheism*, as we will see later. Instead of the father per sé, this woman related to God in the same way she did her whole family.

God	Parents/Family
I do not pray because I feel that God will not listen to me if I don't follow his rules.	The members of my family I felt the most distant from was my whole family, because they never listened to what I felt or wanted . . .[37]

These were simply selections from many parallel statements about God and father or mother taken from the records of the patients whom Rizzuto studied through interviews and questionnaires. Her study reveals that in hospitalized mental patients, anyway, the

This is my image of God - Extremily wise - but sad at mens inhumanity to man - also patient and sensative to suffering of mankind

Figure 5.3

a bright, clean, warm feeling

Figure 5.4

God image does function as something of a "projective test" and one's experiences with one's personal parents may *influence* one's conception of God. It surely does not explain why some people become believers, and others, agnostics and atheists. I have known atheists with positive and healthy relations with their parents, and theists with very poor ones. This subject is much deeper than one study of a limited population of mental patients would reveal. This kind of thing is decidedly *not* the God conception of the mystics. For them God is *being, nothingness*, the *mystery of existence, limitless light*, to name a few terms that come to mind. In the teachings of the mystics and saints, the deepest truth about God is simply: *He is*. Whatever else one might say about Him is in danger of idolatry. The I AM revelation of the Book of Exodus in the Bible is the highest revelation of Western religion. It has nothing whatever to do with "a bearded old man with a gold crown sitting on a throne in the sky." It is strange that Freud's projection theory relates to the most concretistic, literalistic, and childish conception of God. Freud's "disbelief" was based upon this primitive conception, arrested at the Piagetian concrete operational stage.

Freud's next book that relates to his psychology of religion is *The Future of an Illusion* (1927). He begins with the discussion of his idea that all civilizations are built up on renunciation of instinct (lust and aggression) via coercion. This is a rather conservative and pessimistic view of man and society. It sees man as running wild, raping, and killing, or acting out his "id impulses," were it not for the very strong "superego checks" of society via parents, teachers, police, courts, and judges, etc. It does not see in man much capacity for love and cooperation. The humanistic psychologists, such as Maslow, and Rogers, etc., will see things from a characteristically opposite liberal optimistic point of view.

Freud sees religion as perhaps the most important item in the psychical inventory of civilizations. Religions are one of the cultural manifestations of the superego, in other words, is what Freud is saying, with its priests and pastors, churches and synagogues, creeds and moral teachings, etc. Next Freud goes on to look at religion as playing a parental role to human beings who are childlike in response to the really big questions of life.

> For once before one has found oneself in a similar state of helplessness; as a small child, in relation to one's parents. One had reason to fear them, and especially one's father; and yet one was sure of his protection against the dangers one knew.[38]

In analogy, then, to parent-child, Freud sees the human being's sense of primal helplessness in the face of nature and fate.

> . . . man's helplessness remains and along with it his longing for his father and the gods. The gods retain their threefold task: they must exorcize the power of nature, they must reconcile men to the cruelty of fate, particularly as it is shown in death, and they must compensate them for the sufferings and privations which a civilized life in common has imposed on them.[39]

Freud uses the pronouns "they" and "them" with regard to "helpless man," never "I" or "we." Presumably, he has been emancipated from any feeling of weakness or vulnerability via his god, which he said was "reason." He says that in the position of "protector," although it is first the mother, the father soon takes her place for the rest of childhood.

> But the child's attitude to its father is coloured by a peculiar ambivalence. The father himself constitutes a danger for the child . . . Thus it fears him no less than it longs for him and admires him. The indications of this ambivalence to the father are deeply imprinted in every religion . . .[40]

When the growing individual finds that with regard to the overarching questions of sickness and health, life and death, his or her destiny, and the meaning of it all, he is destined to remain a child forever,

> . . . he lends those powers the features belonging to the figure of his father; he creates for himself the gods whom he dreads, whom he seeks to propitiate, and whom he nevertheless entrusts with his own protection.[41]

Freud turns to the question of the psychical origins of religious ideas, and he says:

> It will be found if we return our attention to the psychical origins of religious ideas, these which are given out as teachings are not precipitates of experience or end-results of thinking: they are illusions, fulfillment of the oldest and most urgent wishes of mankind. The secret of their strength lies in the strength of those wishes.[42]

This is Freud's famous wish-fulfillment theory of the origin of religion. It is *the wish* that this universe be a friendly and positive place rather than a place of arbitrary cruelty and ultimate death. There is no doubt that we human beings have religious wishes, just as we have wishes for food when we are hungry, and for water when we are thirsty, and sexual partners when we are motivated by sexual desire. Does the attribution of a wishful origin of religion deny the existence of the object of that wish, namely God? It is not the case for hunger, thirst, and sex – here desires are matched by objects of desire, although we must learn how to obtain these goal objects. The German theologian, Hans Kung, in his book, *Does God Exist?* (1978) takes up this question:

> Of course, religious belief would be in a bad way if there were no genuine grounds for it or no grounds remained after a psychoanalytic treatment of the subject: however devout its appearance, such a faith would be immature, infantile, perhaps even neurotic. But is a faith bad and its truth dubious simply because – like psychoanalysis itself – it also involves all possible instinctual motivations, lustful inclinations, psychodynamic mechanisms, conscious and unconscious wishes? Why should I not be allowed to wish that the sweat, blood and tears, all the sufferings of millenia, may not have been in vain, that definitive human happiness may finally be possible for all human beings – especially the despised and downtrodden? And why should I not, on the other hand, feel an aversion to being required to be satisfied with rare moments of happiness and – for the rest – to come to terms with "normal unhappiness"? May I not feel an aversion also in regard to the idea that the life of the individual and of mankind is governed by the pitiless laws of nature, by the play of chance and by the survival of the fittest, and that all dying is a dying into nothingness?
>
> It does not follow – as some theologians have mistakenly concluded – from man's profound desire for God and eternal life, that God exists and that eternal life and happiness are real. But some atheists too, are mistaken in thinking that what follows is the non-existence of God and the unreality of eternal life. It is true that the wish alone does not contain its own fulfillment. It *may* be that nothing corresponds to the oldest, strongest and most urgent wishes of mankind and that mankind has actually been cherishing illusions for millenia. Just like a child that, in its solitude, forsakeness, distress, need for happiness, wishes wholeheartedly, longs, imagines, and fantasizes that it might have a father in some distant Russian camp, cherishes illusions, gives way to self-deception, pursues wish images, unless, unless . . .? Unless the father, long assumed to be dead, whom the child knows from hearsay, had by some chance remained alive and – although no one believed it any longer – was still existing. Then – then indeed – the child would actually be right against the many who did not believe in the father's existence. Then there would in fact be a reality corresponding to the child's wishful thinking and one day perhaps might be seen face to face . . .
>
> *Perhaps* this being of our longings and dreams does *actually* exist. Perhaps this being who promises us eternal bliss does exist.[43]

For the hungry, there is food, for the thirsty, water, and for the lustful, a sexual partner. There is even fulfillment of the wish for *true love*. May it not be that the deepest wish of all, the wish for God, or Ultimate Reality, our Source, Sustainer, and Redeemer, has a basis in truth? This is the report of all mystics, saints, sages, and prophets of humankind, of every time, place, and culture. The literature of the spiritual quest is vast and deep. Any thorough reading of Freud will indicate that he was almost totally ignorant of the literature of mysticism and the spiritual quest – he avoided it completely. Early in Freud's adolescence, he chose his god: *science*; furthermore, the materialistic science of the late nineteenth century:

> The riddles of the universe reveal themselves only slowly to our investigations; there are many questions which science to-day can give no answer. But scientific work is the only road which can lead us to a knowledge of reality outside ourselves. [44]

Is *science* the "only road" to reality? Religion has traditionally regarded *revelation* as a valid path to *the real*. Mystic experiences such as we have looked at in the chapter on Bucke and James, and will look again in chapters to come, are forms of revelation. Regarding the claim of revelation, Freud dismisses it out of hand when he sets up "reason" as the highest court of appeal to knowledge claims:

> There is no appeal to a court above that of reason. If the truth of religious doctrines is dependent on an inner experience which bears witness to that truth, what is one to do about the many people who do not have this rare experience? [45]

This is the closest Freud comes, except in a brief discussion of the "oceanic feeling" in *Civilization and Its Discontents*, to alluding to mystical or religious experience. He seems to rule it out because of its "rarity" to dubious reports of some distant past, such as "Moses at the burning bush" or "Jesus at the River Jordan," etc., that could not possibly be of interest to "scientific thinkers" of today! The fact is that Freud's *atheism* was not based upon his empirical science of psychoanalysis at all, but was something of which he was convinced long before he made his psychological discoveries into the psychic mechanisms of hysteria and psycho-neuroses.* His atheism is a *dogmatic claim* that the only path to

---

* Hans Kung has pointed out that the German philosopher, Ludwig Feuerbach (1804–1872) was Freud's intellectual predecessor in the psychological reduction of religious belief to wishful thinking and imaginative projections. [46]

knowledge is materialistic-mechanistic science, as he knew it in the late nineteenth century: sense-observation of "externals" and experimental testing of hypotheses submitting to positivist epistemology. Freud's *a priori epistemology* (theory of knowing) simply would not admit mystical or spiritual experiences into the domain of "valid knowledge." They did not submit to the high court of "reason and sense experience."

However, even in Freud's time, there were already two classic works by two contemporary psychologists which offered over-whelming evidence of both the reality and the widespread occur-rence of mystical and religious experience, William James' *The Varieties of Religious Experience* (1902) and Richard Bucke's *Cosmic Consciousness* (1901). James and Bucke were still living when Freud published his first great work, *The Interpretation of Dreams* (1900), although James and Bucke were old men, and Freud was in the prime of his middle age. Freud actually met the old man, William James, in 1909 at the former's visit to and lectures at Clark University in Worcester, Massachusetts, and they talked with one another. Yet, the younger Freud never saw fit to quote James' work on religious experience one single time, much less intelli-gently discuss its contents and ideas, even in his (Freud's) later books on religion. It is conceivable that Freud never heard of Bucke's book which was printed in Canada in small numbers, but it is not possible that Freud had not heard of James' book. Not only does Freud, then, ignore the best works on psychology of religion, he totally abstains from even looking at the vast literature of the religious mystics of all religions and cultures as seemingly unworthy of his serious study!

Freud's atheism, and his rejection of religious and mystical ex-perience is not empiricism at all, but *materialistic prejudice* based upon an incredibly narrow selection of evidence, the protocols of some neurotic patients, and shamefully narrow-minded thinking for a man of such great genius in his *own areas of competency*, such as the psychoneuroses, and the early childhood roots of adult personality. Nevertheless, despite his refusal to look at the vast evidence of mysticism and religious experience, and despite his *a priori* materialist metaphysics and positivist epistemology, which would rule out any serious consideration of the reports of the mystics and saints, Freud does not hesitate to attack all realms of religion with his limited repertoire of psychoanalysis, as violently as Alexander the Great attacked all neighboring countries with his Macedonian army, with the apparent goal of the conquest and annihilation of religion!

In *Civilization and Its Discontents* (1930) Freud speaks of a friend to whom he sent a copy of *The Future of an Illusion* who replied that Freud had not properly appreciated the true source of religious sentiments which he had dismissed as wish fulfillments. His friend said:

> This . . . consists in a peculiar feeling, which he himself is never without, which he finds confirmed in many others, and which he may suppose is present in millions of people. It is a feeling which he would like to call a sensation of "eternity," a feeling as of something limitless, unbounded – as it were, oceanic! This feeling, he adds, is a purely subjective fact, not an article of faith; it brings with it no assurance of personal immortality, but it is the source of religious energy . . . One may, he thinks, rightly call oneself religious on the ground of this oceanic feeling alone, even if one rejects every belief and every illusion. [47]

Based upon Freud's reactions to this friend, it would seem that this is the closest to a "borderline mystical experience" in someone else that he ever came. One must add, however, that the "oceanic feeling" of Freud's friend is far from the true mystical experience reported by both Bucke and James. The latter is *overwhelming*, and it leaves *no doubt* as to immortality. A sense of immortality clearly and directly perceived was one of the criteria listed by Bucke of the "Cosmic Conscious" state. His friend describes his experience as "purely subjective"; the mystics report their experience as a direct revelation of *the real*. In this author's experience, what the mystical experience reveals is far *more objective* than what we call "objective reality." In fact, the latter seems *an illusion* by comparison. This is the report of all mystics if you read their testimony. Freud did not. In any event, this is how Freud reacted to the quasi-mystical experience of his friend:

> The views expressed by the friend whom I so much honor . . . caused me no small difficulty. I cannot discover this 'oceanic' feeling in myself . . . If I understood my friend rightly, he means the same thing by it as the consolation offered by an original and somewhat eccentric dramatist to his hero who is facing a self-inflicted death. 'We cannot fall out of this world.' That is to say, it is a feeling of an indissoluble bond, of being one with the external world as a whole. [48]

Even this sense of pantheistic mysticism of being in connection with nature, never mind a supernatural God, is difficult for Freud to handle. He says that:

The idea of men's receiving an intimation of their connection with the world around them through an immediate feeling which is from the outset directed to that purpose sounds so strange and fits in so badly with the fabric of our psychology that one is justified in attempting to discover a psycho-analytic – that is to say genetic – explanation of such a feeling.[49]

Everything must fit the procrustean bed of psychoanalytic theory for Freud, and later orthodox Freudians. One would wish he had something more of the *radical empiricism* of William James who said that the existence of mystical states overthrows the pretensions of ordinary science as a "dictator" of what we may believe.

Sure enough, Freud interprets this pantheistical mystical sense in terms of his psychoanalytical theory of the ego, id, and super-ego! He says that we normally sense our conscious identity or selfhood via our ego which appears to us to be autonomous and unitary, marked off, as it were, from everything else. This appearance is, of course, deceptive, as the ego really "continues inwards" without any sharp delimitation into an unconscious mental entity which Freud calls the "id." He calls this a "discovery of psycho-analytic research." Of course, it is not a discovery, but a theory. Freud often blurs the distinction between empirical facts and theoretical interpretations of these facts. In any event, the implication is that the "oceanic feeling" is a regression to a more primitive state of ego/id unity. Call this Freud's "id thoery" of religion, as compared with his "superego theory" expressed in his previous two books which we have discussed. It is as inadequate as they are, and as oblivious and uncaring of the real nature of the phenomena of religious or mystical experience which both Bucke and James dealt with so honestly and truly scientifically. I am using "science" in the original sense of "knowing the truth," rather than in the superficial sense of *scientism* with its positivistic or materialistic meta-assumptions. The latter is one of the idolatries of our age to which Freud subscribed.*

Freud wrote *Moses and Monotheism* (1939) during the last years of his life. It was rather an heroic effort of an old man, slowly dying of cancer, who had to move from his Vienna, Austria home

---

* Has anti-religion vanished in "modern day" psychoanalysis? Erdelyi in: *PSYCHOANALYSIS: Freud's Cognitive Psychology* (1985) states that "Religions, as conceived and practiced popularly, exhibit regressive cognitive functioning, especially the abrogation of the reality principle."[50]

in 1938 to London, England to escape the onslaught of the Nazis. He completed it in his last year of life before he died in 1939. One suspects it might have been a lifelong project of the Jewish nonbeliever, Freud.

In *Moses and Monotheism*, Freud makes some claims as outrageous as those of *Totem and Taboo*. He essentially creates a "history" to replace that of the Bible in the former book, as he had created a "prehistory" in the latter book, in each case to "prove" psychoanalytic theory. He had quite an imagination! The basic claim of *Moses and Monotheism* is that Moses was an Egyptian, not a Jew. His only "evidence" for this claim is the fact that the name, Moses, is quite similar to the Egyptian word for child, "mose." Even if this were the basis of his name, it would not prove any such thing. I am a Jew by birth, too, and my name is Robert, a German name. My paternal ancestors came from Germany. Nevertheless, the Hebrew for Moses is "Mosheh" which means "He that was drawn out of the water." It seems, then, that there was no evidence whatsoever that Moses was an Egyptian. Rather it was a wish-fulfillment of Freud's! Why Freud had this need to believe that the principal figure of the Jewish religion was an Egyptian, I do not claim to fathom. He wrote this book during the worst time in history for the Jews, the beginning of the era of the Nazi domination of Europe and the anti-semitic persecutions which ended in genocide. Such a claim would hardly tend to increase the self-esteem of the Jewish people during such a time! Quite the reverse. The Holy Scriptures indicate that Moses was a Levite, one of the twelve tribes of Israel, and direct descendant of Abraham, Isaac, and Jacob.

In Freud's story, and *story* it is, he originally planned to publish it as a novel, the Egyptian prince, Moses, was a follower of the "monotheistic" religion of the Pharaoh Amenhoteb IV, who was re-named Ikhnaton.[51] This was a religion essentially of sun worship. The sun, Aton, was considered to be the sole divinity. This religion was short-lived in Egypt, and the traditional polytheism returned. It was Freud's hypothesis that Moses, in order to ensure the survival of the Aton religion, selected the Israelite tribe as its heir, delivered them from slavery in Egypt, and trained them in the new faith. As if this is not incredible enough a rewriting of history, and the Torah is our only source of this history, Freud goes on to claim that the Israelites murdered Moses, very much as the brothers of the primal horde murdered the primal father! Guilt and remorse for this crime remained in the collective mind of the Israelites, and Moses himself later re-emerged as the unconscious model for YHWH, the Great and Awesome God of the Old Testament. As if this is not carrying things far enough, Freud reinterprets the Christian history of the New Testament, also, seeing Jesus as the "son figure" who must be sacrificed to atone for the sin of killing Moses, the "father figure," and behind him the original and terrible primal father of the prehistory of humankind!

This story of Freud's is so fantastic that it has generally been ignored by scholars. The fact is that there is virtually no resemblance whatsoever between the Aton religion of sun worship and the monotheistic faith of Moses. Atonism was basically a nature religion; worship of the sun. All of the prayers of Atonism are directed toward the sun who is seen as the source of life. The YHWH religion of Moses, presumably revealed to him at Mt. Horeb/Mt. Sinai was not a nature religion at all, but a religion of a supernatural Creator of nature, including the sun, the earth, and the stars. YHWH has no shape or form. Aton was represented by a sun disk. YHWH forbade pictorial representations. YHWH revealed "Himself" to Moses as: I AM THAT I AM. In the YHWH religion, later known as "Judaism," the religion of the Jews, there is nothing you can "see," "touch," "feel," or even "conceive of" which will "represent" YHWH. He is *not an object at all*, as "the sun" is an object, for example. "He" is, in fact, *the subject*, if you see my meaning. This is "I AM" who spoke to Moses. Freud, the Jew, from orthodox Jewish heritage *did not grasp this fundamental truth*. If he did, he could never have made the non-historical and absurd claim that Moses was an Egyptian whose goal was the indoctrination of the Israelite tribes into the Aton religion of sun-worship. His "evidence" for this claim, as well as the claim that Moses was "murdered" by these same Israelites is non-existent. Moses, according to the scriptures, lived to 120 years, and then climbed Mt. Nebo to view from afar the "promised land," and then he died. No historical evidence contradicts this.

Is it possible that Freud conceived of himself as the "new Moses," and his psychoanalysis as the "new dispensation?" One detects a megalomania in Freud's later writings of his old age which is entirely absent in his earlier scientific writings on the etiology and treatment of the neuroses. Freud was fascinated with the figure of Moses, the great founder of the Jewish faith. Perhaps,

Freud, the Jewish atheist, felt that he, too, was a founder of a "faith," but one based upon reason, not upon revelation.★

FURTHER NOTES ON ALFRED ADLER AND ERIK ERIKSON

Adler

Alfred Adler was a member of Freud's "inner circle" and he was the first defector from the fold. He left Freud over disagreements with Freud's reductionism and pansexualism. If Freud's was primarily an id psychology, Adler's was an ego psychology in social context. In Adler's view, inferiority feelings are compensated by "strivings for superiority" and the formation of "fictionalized goals." Adler, in his writings, made references to religion and God. For Adler, God is *an idea*, whereas for the theologian, God is a *reality*. Adler said:

> The contemplation of the deity is a concretization of the idea of perfection, greatness and superiority, which has been obvious in man's thinking since time immemorial. ... The idea of God and the immense significance of this idea for mankind can be understood and appreciated from the point of view of Individual Psychology as follows: It is the concretization and interpretation of the human recognition of greatness and perfection.[53]

Erikson

Erik Erikson is a neo-Freudian thinker who enlarged Freud's conception of the ego by writing about the "psychosocial stages of development." He outlined eight stages: Trust vs. Mistrust, Autonomy vs. Shame and Doubt, Initiative vs. Guilt, Industry vs. Inferiority, Ego Identity vs. Role Confusion, Intimacy vs. Isolation, Generativity vs. Stagnation, and Ego Integrity vs. Despair.

★ Hans Kung, in his book, *Freud and the Problem of God* (1979), states that: "Belief in God, however, was not simply replaced by scientific arguments, but by another faith, the quasi-religious faith in science. For Freud, personally, then, psychoanalysis too is far more than a method of research and healing; it is the basis of an atheistic Weltanschauung, a kind of substitute for religion."[52]

These cover the complete life cycle of the individual. In Erikson's book, *Young Man Luther*, he looks at the great Protestant reformer, Luther, thusly:

> I have implied that the original faith which Luther tried to restore goes back to the basic trust of infancy. In doing so I have not, I believe, diminished the wonder of what Luther calls God's disguise. If I assume that it is a smiling face and the guiding voice of infantile parent images which religion projects onto the benevolent sky, I have no apologies to render . . . Peace comes from the inner space.[54]

6

Carl Jung's Recognition of the Imago Dei

> I do not want anyone to be a Jungian. I want people above all to be
> themselves. [1]   Carl Jung

Jung was born in 1875 in Switzerland and lived there all of his life.
His father, the Rev. Johann Paul Achilles Jung, was a pastor in the
Lutheran Reformed Church. His mother, whose maiden name
was Emilie Preiswerk, was the daughter of a pastor. Carl Gustav
Jung was born in the small village of Kesswil, on Lake Constance,
but he was a citizen of Basel because his father was born in that
city. On both sides of his family Jung had many relatives and
ancestors who were Protestant pastors (just as Freud had several
Orthodox Rabbis among his forefathers). When Carl Jung was six
months old, his parents moved from Kesswil, on Lake Constance,
to Laufen on the Rhine.

The earliest memory in Jung's life was a very pleasing one. He
was about two or three years old. He calls it an island of memory
in the sea of vagueness of earliest childhood:

> One memory comes up which is perhaps the earliest of my life, and is
> indeed only a rather hazy impression. I am lying in a pram, in the
> shadow of a tree. It is a fine warm summer day, the sky blue, and
> golden sunlight darting through the green leaves. The hood of the
> pram has been left up. I have just awakened to the glorious beauty of
> the day, and have a sense of indescribable well-being. I see the sun
> glittering through the leaves and blossoms of the bushes. Everything is
> wholly wonderful, colorful, and splendid. [2]

One thinks of Adam in his original Eden before the fall and exile
in this wonderful earliest recollection of Jung's. Alfred Adler, one
of Sigmund Freud's early disciples, considered earliest recollec-

tions to be of tremendous importance in understanding a person. From this earliest recollection, one would predict that Jung was destined, eventually, for happiness.

When Jung was a little boy, his mother taught him a prayer which he said every night:

> Spread out thy wings, Lord Jesus mild,
> And take to thee thy chick, thy child.
> If Satan would devour it,
> No harm shall overpower it,
> So let angels sing![3]

One would have wished that Jung's mother would have left well enough alone, and not introduced him so soon to the dichotomy between Jesus and Satan, Good and Evil. But was it not Eve who tempted Adam to eat of the Tree of Knowledge of Good and Evil resulting in the exile from Eden? Eve, the feminine principle, could be wife, or mother, or sister, or lover. Jung's father also had a role in his early personality formation, and his division from original, but unconscious wholeness. Jung recounts his autobiography, *Memories, Dreams, Reflections* (1961), written as an old man in his eighties, that he attended many funerals as a child, his father being a pastor, and learned that Jesus "took" people to himself, and that this "taking" was often "putting them in a hole in the ground."[4] He used to see solemn men dressed in black carrying black coffins. His father would appear in his clerical gown, speaking words of prayer in a resounding voice. Women wept. He was told that someone who had died was being put into the hole in the earth. He always heard his father say that "Lord Jesus had taken them to himself."[5] Jung has early recollections of the darker side of religion dealing with death.

Between the ages of three and four, Jung reports an extraordinary dream which preoccupied him for many years of his life:

The vicarage stood quite alone near Laufen Castle, and there was a big meadow stretching back from the sexton's farm. In the dream I was in the meadow. Suddenly I discovered a dark, rectangular, stone-lined hole in the ground. I had never seen anything like it before. I ran forward curiously and peered down into it. Then I saw a stone stairway leading down. Hesitantly and fearfully, I descended. At the bottom was a doorway with a round arch, closed off by a green curtain. It was a big, heavy curtain of worked stuff like brocade, and it looked very sumptuous. Curious to see what might be hidden behind, I pushed it aside. I saw before me in the dim light a rectangular chamber about thirty feet long. The ceiling was arched and of hewn stone. The floor was laid with flagstones, and in the center a red carpet ran from the entrance to a low platform. On this platform stood a wonderfully rich golden throne. I am not certain, but perhaps a red cushion lay on the seat. It was a magnificent throne, a real king's throne in a fairy tale. Something was standing on it which I thought at first was a tree trunk twelve to fifteen feet high and about one and a half to two feet thick. It was a huge thing, reaching about to the ceiling. But it was of curious composition: it was made of skin and naked flesh, and on top there was something like a rounded head with no face and no hair. On the very top of the head was a single eye, gazing monotonously upward.

It was fairly light in the room, although there were no windows and no apparent source of light. Above the head, however, was an aura of brightness. The thing did not move, yet I had the feeling that it might at any moment crawl off the throne like a worm and creep toward me. I was paralyzed with terror. At that moment I heard from outside and above me my mother's voice. She called out, "Yes, just look at him. That is the man-eater!" That intensified my terror still more, and I awoke sweating and scared to death.[6]

Jung says that the dream haunted him for years. He realized much later that what he had seen was a "ritual phallus." He was never sure what the phrase "That is the man-eater" meant. One can see the Freudian aspect of this dream, especially considering that Jung's age (three to four) corresponded to the Freudian "phallic stage" of early childhood. Jung felt that the phallus of the dream was "a subterranean God."[7] This subterranean god appeared to him whenever anyone spoke too emphatically about Lord Jesus, a kind of "shadow figure," as it were. Jung said that "Lord Jesus never became quite real for me, never quite acceptable, never quite lovable . . ."[8] after that dream.

In later years of his childhood, until his confirmation, Jung wondered about the dream of the "ritual phallus." He says, "who was speaking in me? . . . What kind of superior intelligence was at work?"[9] Jung considered this an initiation into the realm of darkness. He said that his intellectual life had its unconscious beginnings in that dream.

Jung learned to read before he went to school. His mother used to read to him from a book called *Orbis Pictus* which contained accounts of exotic religions such as Hinduism and Buddhism. There were illustrations of Brahma, Vishnu, and Shiva, among the Hindu deities. He said: "I found an inexhaustible source of interest."[10] Jung's exposure to comparative religions was quite early indeed.

Jung said that "Between my eighth and eleventh years I drew endlessly – battle pictures, seiges, bombardments, naval engagements. Then I filled a whole exercise book with ink blots and amused myself giving them fantastic interpretations."[11] Jung seems to have anticipated the work of Hermann Rorschach, the psychologist who devised the famous ink blot tests, as a young boy. Imagination and its expressions were a part of Jung's life from the beginning.

Jung speaks of special objects in his life, his stone, a little manikin that he carved, each of which had symbolical meanings. He kept these things secret. Many years later he was to discover the concept of the "philosopher's stone" in alchemy, and the manikin he discovered among the "gods" of the Australian aborigines. There were prefigurations in Jung's theory of the Collective Unconscious. Jung also speaks of discovering the "I," that is, his ego identity, at eleven years of age:

> I was taking the long road to school from Klein-Hünigen, where we lived, to Basel, when suddenly for a single moment I had the overwhelming impression of having just emerged from a dense cloud. I knew all at once: now I am *myself*! It was as if a wall of mist were at my back, and behind that wall there was not yet an "I." But at this moment, I came upon myself.[12]

Jung was to later speak of "participation mystique" and the "collective" in which the individual is submerged, as it were, like a fish is submerged in the sea. In Bucke's sense, Jung is speaking of the coming to self-consciousness. In Jung's own terms, this is the emergence of the ego from the collective. Gurdjieff, as we shall see, makes very much of this experience of self-remembering. Following this experience of his ego identity, Jung made a deeper discovery:

> Then, to my intense confusion, it occurred to me that I was actually two different persons. One of them was the school boy who could not grasp algebra and was far from sure of himself, the other was important, a high authority, a man not to be trifled with . . . This "other" was an old man who lived in the eighteenth century. . .[13]

This childhood experience of himself as "two different persons," one the school boy, and the other, "a high authority," is an adumbration of Jung's much later distinction between the ego and the Self. The ego is the center of consciousness, the Self is the much greater being within, who mediates between consciousness and the unconscious, and who is symbolized sometimes by the "mandala" and other times by the figures of the great religions, such as Christ and Buddha.

It was at this time in his boyhood that Jung had his famous "cathedral experience":

> One fine summer day that same year I came out of school at noon and went to the cathedral square. The sky was gloriously blue, the day of radiant sunshine. The roof of the cathedral glittered, the sun sparkling from the new, brightly glazed tiles. I was overwhelmed by the beauty of the sight, and I thought: "The world is beautiful, and God made all this and sits above it far away in the blue sky on a golden throne and . . ." Here came a great hole in my thoughts, and a choking sensation. I felt numbed, and knew only: "Don't go on thinking now! Something terrible is coming, something I do not want to think, something I dare not even approach. Why not? Because I would be committing the most frightful of sins. . . . All I need do is not go on thinking." On my long walk home I tried to think all sorts of other things, but I found my thoughts returning again and again to the beautiful cathedral which I loved so much, and to God sitting on the throne – and then my thoughts would fly off again as if they had received a powerful electric shock. I kept repeating to myself: "Don't think of it, just don't think of it!"[14]

You may have guessed it by now. Three days later, after intense struggles, Jung decided that it must be God's intention that he sin.

> I thought it over again and arrived at the same conclusion. "Obviously God also desires me to show courage," I thought. "If that is so and I go through with it, then He will give me His grace and illumination."
>
> I gathered all my courage, as though I were about to leap forthwith into hell-fire, and let the thought come. I saw before me the cathedral, the blue sky. God sits on His golden throne, high above the world – and from under the throne an enormous turd falls upon the sparkling new roof, shatters it, and breaks the walls of the cathedral asunder.[15]

Jung said that he felt enormous and indescribable relief. Instead of the expected damnation, Jung said, "grace had come upon me. . ."[16]

This is a foreshadowing of Jung's later dispute with the traditional Christian Church. God in His freedom is greater than the Church, and Jung had the courage to experience this. He said that this was what his father had not understood. He felt that his father had opposed God's will and freedom and went with his church's dogmas "for the best of reasons and out of the deepest faith,"[17] but for exactly this reason "he had never experienced the miracle of grace which heals all and makes all comprehensible."[18] His father knew the Bible, and his church's doctrines as his forefathers had taught him, but he did not know, in Jung's own words, "the immediate living God who stands, omnipotent and free, above His Bible and His Church, who calls upon man to partake of His freedom . . ."[19] Jung kept this experience a secret for many years. He certainly did not have the courage yet to share it with his father. Since there were many parsons in his family, there were many religious conversations and theological discussions, but when the young Jung listened to them, he felt: "Yes, yes, that is all very well. But what about the secret. The secret is also the secret of grace. None of you know anything about that."[20]

It was at this time that Jung said there arose in him profound doubts about everything that his father said. Even when he preached about "grace," Jung knew that it was not the real grace that he had experienced, but a "theological tenet" which he had learned, and not experienced in himself. Jung's father's religion was the religion of belief and faith; Jung's religion from early on was the religion of knowing and experience. Jung, the schoolboy, personality number one, knew many things through his deeper self, the "other," personality number two, "who knew God as hidden, personal, and at the same time suprapersonal secret."[21]

> It often seemed to me that religious percepts were being put in the place of the will of God . . . I grew more and more skeptical, and my father's sermons and those of other parsons became acutely embarrassing to me. All the people about me seemed to take the jargon for granted, and the dense obscurity that emanated from it. . .[22]

Jung says that his father prepared him personally for his confirmation: "It bored me to death."[23] At his first communion, Jung to his profound disappointment, experienced nothing: "I had reached the pinnacle of religious initiation, had expected something – I knew not what – to happen, and nothing at all had happened."[24]

> This was called the "Christian religion," but none of it had anything to do with God as I had experienced Him . . . Why, that is not religion at all," I thought, "It is an absence of God; the church is a place I should not go to. It is not life which is there but death.[25]

Jung, from his later childhood and adolescence, separated himself from the traditional Protestant Christianity of his own father, the pastor. But, unlike Watson, who went in the direction of soulless behaviorism and atheism, Jung went in the direction of an esoteric understanding of religious truth, or Gnosticism, which was also the basis of his profound psychology, or science of the soul.

Jung speaks of his Fisher wound,★ a deep wound to his soul, which he experienced in his middle adolescence when a teacher accused him of plagiarizing a paper that he had actually written himself. This was a moral blow to Jung's psyche. It may explain why he wrote so much—his *Collected Works* are contained in twenty huge volumes—in the way of compensation.

When it came to deciding upon what career path to follow, Jung chose medicine, somewhat based upon a dream of digging up the bones of prehistoric animals, and then coming upon a circular pool containing a shimmering round animal.[26] Although he was equally interested in the humanities, philosophy and religion, Jung took this dream to be a "sign" in favor of science. Jung, being obviously an intuitive, went more by visions than anything else in making life decisions. He had another important dream at this time about keeping the "little light" of his ego consciousness alive despite the darkness and the storms of life: "I knew . . . that this little light was my consciousness, the only light I have."[27]

It is at this time that Jung relates an account of his father's loss of faith:

> Once I heard him praying. He struggled desperately to keep his faith. I was shaken and outraged at once, because I saw how hopelessly he was entrapped by the church and its theological thinking. They had blocked all avenues by which he might have reached God directly, and then faithlessly abandoned him.[28]

Not only did his father lose his faith, but he could not even defend himself against, as Jung puts it, "the ridiculous materialism of the psychiatrists."[29] Jung calls this the opposite faith to the Church's: the faith in materialism. He said that his father was under the impression that "psychiatrists had discovered something in the brain which proved that in the place where mind should have been there was only matter, and nothing 'spiritual.' "[30] Jung says something very important:

> I recognized that this celebrated faith of his had played this deadly trick on him, and not only on him but on most of the cultivated and serious people I knew. The arch sin of faith, it seemed to me, was that it forestalled experience.[31]

★ The "Fisher Wound" is based upon the medieval legend of the Fisher King who was grievously wounded during his adolescence, and whose wounds could not heal until he found the Holy Grail.

Jung points out that his father's readings in "scientific psychiatry" made him no happier and he suffered increasing depressions and hypochondria, especially abdominal symptoms. The Reverend Jung's life became blighted and bitter. He lost his faith. His physical condition deteriorated, and in early 1896, he died.[32] One can, with considerable justification, consider the future work of the son, Dr. Carl Gustav Jung, to be a compensation for the failings of his father, the Rev. Johann Paul Achilles Jung. Carl Jung became a different kind of psychiatrist than the scientistic* ones whom his father read in his later years. He became a "doctor of the soul" (to use a phrase similar in import to the title of my first book, *Physicians of the Soul*). Jung's path of the *direct experience* of the soul was his attempt to redress, long after the fact, his father's merely doctrinaire faith which had fallen through in the face of adversity.

Jung went to medical school, not knowing what he would specialize in, but during his second semester, he read the Kraft-Ebbing basic text in psychiatry, and although it was a primitive science in his day, he knew in a flash of illumination that he would become a psychiatrist. This was his way of uniting the two currents of interest in him, the scientific and the humanistic. Jung took his first post in psychiatry at the age of twenty-five in 1900 as an assistant at Burghölzli Mental Hospital in Zurich. Jung called this his entry into "the monastery of the world."[33] These were the years of Jung's apprenticeship in psychiatry. From the very beginning of his psychiatric days, he was concerned with the burning question: "What actually takes place inside the mentally ill?"[34] This seems an ordinary enough question today, but it was not so in Jung's time. The mentally ill were simply considered "crazy," and that's that. They could be perhaps helped in making "adjustments" to reality, but almost no one in psychiatry at the time cared what went on in *their minds*. Much less did they care what was its *meaning*. It was at this time that Jung discovered the existence of another, a neurologist not a psychiatrist, who was asking the same questions as he was, in Vienna rather than Zurich, no other than Sigmund Freud.

---

* Although Jung was not "scientistic," Dr. Anthony Stevens, a medical doctor and psychiatrist, and author of ARCHETYPES (1982), relates Jungian *archetypes* to the *genotypes* recognized by the biological science of ethology as underlying universal patterns of behavior in animals and human beings.

> At this point Freud became vitally important to me, especially because of his fundamental researches into the psychology of hysteria and of dreams.[35]

Jung began by applying Freud's free association method to the analysis of the dreams of a woman who was incorrectly diagnosed as "dementia praecox," an earlier term for "schizophrenia." Jung discovered her to be not psychotic, but depressive, and he discovered the personal history that led to the severe depressions, the accidental killing of one of her children. After facing this repressed morally traumatic truth, she very gradually recovered her mind. Jung went on to become a lecturer in psychiatry at the University of Zurich, a position he held for four years till 1913. His approach was very similar to Freud's at this time. In his psychotherapeutic work, Jung describes the "miraculous cure" of a hysterically paralyzed woman who was a demonstration case in a class on clinical hypnosis. Jung was as astounded as anyone about her cure. But this led to "local fame as a wizard,"[36] and his practice in the treatment of private patients quickly grew.

Jung describes his treatment of a schizophrenic woman, Babette, who had been in the hospital for twenty years, a classic case. She would say the craziest things, such as, "I am the Lorelei," or "I am Socrates' deputy."[37] Through the use of essentially Freudian methods of analysis Jung found that Babette, and others like her, had real stories to tell, and that their life histories could not be ignored. Later, Jung was to look beyond even personal life history into the universal symbols of humankind which appeared in the fantasies and dreams of his patients.

Jung found that his work in the early 1900s was much in agreement with that of Freud, Breuer, and Janet. He read Freud's *The Interpretation of Dreams* when it first came out in 1900, but it took him three years to really begin to understand it. Jung began to correspond with Freud. He finally met with Freud in March of 1907, Jung was thirty-two at the time, and Freud was fifty-one, almost a generation older. They spoke for thirteen hours. Jung said that:

> Freud was the first man of real importance I had encountered; in my experience up to that time, no one else could compare with him.[38]

Even though he was more than impressed with the Old Master, Jung had early reservations about Freud's over emphasis on sexuality, and his devaluation of spirituality (which he attributed to repressed sexuality). When Freud talked about sexuality, Jung states

There was no mistaking that Freud was emotionally involved in his sexual theory to an extraordinary degree. When he spoke of it, his tone became urgent, almost anxious, and all signs of his normally critical and skeptical manner vanished. A strange deeply moved expression came over his face, the cause of which I was at a loss to understand. I had strong intuition that for him sexuality was a sort of *numinosum*.[39]

In 1910, while Jung was visiting Freud in Vienna, Freud said to Jung: "My dear Jung, promise me never to abandon the sexual theory. That is the most essential thing of all. You see we must make a dogma of it, an unshakeable bulwark."[40] Freud sounds here as Jung's father must have sounded in instructing him for his confirmation! Freud's sexual theory was as dogmatic for him, as any dogmatic religion is for the believer. This had the opposite of the intended effect upon Jung, as you may well guess. For Jung, Freud was no longer dealing in scientific judgment but with his personal obsession, and with the power drive to indoctrinate disciples in the "true faith." When Jung asked Freud, what was he erecting "a bulwark against," Freud replied, "against the black tide of the mud of occultism."[41] Jung realized that "what Freud seemed to mean by 'occultism' was virtually everything that philosophy and religion, including the rising contemporary science of parapsychology, had learned about the psyche."[42]

Jung draws the interesting conclusion that, although he had not understood it at the time, he had witnessed, in Freud, the eruption of religious factors in his psyche, and he was seeking to employ Jung's aid "in erecting a barrier against these threatening unconscious contents."[43] Whereas Freud looked at repressed sexual and aggressive wishes as the cause of neuroses, Jung is looking at Freud's obsession with erecting a dogma of the sexual theory as the defense against his own repressed religious impulses, which he feared, and projected as the "mud of occultism," an obviously emotionally charged expression, and not an objective judgment about all of human religion. Others have made this point that for Freud spirituality was as repressed as sexuality was for his hysterical patients. Jung speculates that Freud has replaced the jealous God, YHWH, with another jealous god, sexuality: "the advantage of this transformation for Freud was, apparently, that he was able to regard the new numinous principle as scientifically irreproachable and free from all religious taint."[44]

In 1909, both Freud and Jung were invited to lecture at Clark University in Worcester, Massachusetts. On this American sojourn, Freud and Jung interpreted each other's dreams. In one dream of Freud's, which was mysterious without further associations revealing its background, Freud refused to go on because, he said, "I cannot risk my authority."[45] At that moment, Freud *lost all authority* for Jung. Jung himself had very powerful dreams at the time, which had collective unconscious symbolism. He describes a very important dream as follows:

> I was in a house, I did not know, which had two stories. It was "my house." I found myself in the upper story, where there was a kind of salon furnished with fine old pieces in Rococo style. On the walls hung a number of precious paintings. I wondered that this should be my house, and thought, "not bad." But then it occurred to me that I did not know what the lower floor looked like. Descending the stairs, I reached the ground floor. There everything was much older, and I realized that this part of the house must date from the fifteenth or sixteenth century. The furnishings were medieval; the floors were of red brick. Everywhere it was rather dark. I went from one room to another thinking, "now I really must explore the whole house." I came upon a stone stairway that led down to a cellar. Descending again, I found myself in a beautifully vaulted room which looked exceedingly ancient. Examining the walls, I discovered layers of brick among the ordinary stone blocks, and chips of brick in the mortar. As soon as I saw this I knew the walls dated from Roman times. My interest by now was intense. I looked more closely at the floor. It was of stone slabs, and in one of these I discovered a ring. When I pulled it, the stone slab lifted, and again I saw a stairway of narrow stone steps leading down into the depths. These, too, I descended, and entered a low cave cut in the rock. Thick dust lay on the floor, and in the dust were scattered bones and broken pottery of a primitive culture. I discovered two human skulls, obviously very old and half-disintegrated. Then I awoke.[46]

Freud interpreted this dream simply in terms of the two skulls which meant to him a "death wish," and asked Jung whom it was he wished dead? Perhaps himself? Perhaps Jung's wife, Emma? Jung, seeing that Freud missed the depth of the dream completely, went along with Freud and said that they probably represented his wife and sister-in-law! Jung said that his true ideas on dreams would have met with incomprehension and vehement resistance on Freud's part, and he being the "young disciple," was not confident enough yet to challenge his mentor. But he realized that the gulf between his mental world and Freud's was already too great and probably unbridgeable. This dream of the house with many lower levels foreshadowed all of Jung's future explorations into the archetypes of the collective unconscious. Jung, writing as an old man in his eighties, said:

> "It was plain to me that the house represented a kind of image of the psyche . . . Consciousness was represented by the salon . . . The ground floor stood for the first level of the unconscious. The deeper I went, the more alien and the darker the scene became. In the cave, I discovered the remains of a primitive culture, that is, the world of primitive man within myself – a world which can scarcely be reached or illuminated by consciousness. The primitive psyche of man borders on the life of the animal soul. . ."[47]

Although Jung went on to become the president of the International Psychoanalytical Society, and Freud's most favored disciple, whom he saw as his successor, Jung's own views continued to diverge from those of the "Old Master," Freud. Jung's book, *Symbols of Transformation* (1912), in which he begins to present his views on the symbolism of the collective unconscious, was the decisive break with Freudian thought. Jung says, "After the break with Freud, all my friends and acquaintances dropped away. My book was declared to be rubbish; I was a mystic and that settled the matter."[48]

Following Jung's break with Freud, and the Freudian circle, Jung entered a period of extreme inner uncertainty and disorientation. As he describes it, "I felt totally suspended in mid-air, for I had not yet found my own footing."[49] It was at this time that Jung was to have his own confrontation with the unconscious, his own inner journey and wisdom quest. It is a Journey described in much of the literature of humankind from the Sumerian epic, the *Gilgamesh*, and Homer's *Odyssey*, to the recent C. S. Lewis book, *The Voyage of the Dawn Treader*. All of human wisdom and creativity emanate from this journey – and Jung was to travel its strange and ancient paths for five years between 1913 and 1918, ages thirty-eight to forty-three. Parts of Jung's descriptions of his own Journey could easily be mistaken for the text of any of the classic myths of the "other worldly journey." The following passage describes Jung's own entrance into the "other world" of the collective unconscious:

> It was during Advent of the year 1913 – Dec. 12, to be exact – that I resolved upon the decisive step. I was sitting at my desk once more, thinking over my fears. Then I let myself drop. Suddenly it was as though the ground literally gave way beneath my feet, and I plunged down into dark depths. I could not fend off a feeling of panic. But then, abruptly, at not too great a depth, I landed on my feet in a soft sticky mess. I felt great relief, although I was apparently in complete

darkness. After a while my eyes grew accustomed to the gloom which was rather like a deep twilight. Before me was the entrance to a dark cave, in which stood a dwarf with a leathery skin, as if he were mummified. I squeezed past him through the narrow entrance and waded knee deep through icy water to the other end of the cave where, on a projecting rock, I saw a glowing red crystal. I grasped the stone, lifted it, and discovered a hollow underneath. At first I could make out nothing, but then I saw that there was running water. In it a corpse floated by, a youth with blond hair and a wound in the head. He was followed by a gigantic black scarab and then by a red newborn sun, rising up out of the depths of the water. Dazzled by the light, I wanted to replace the stone upon the opening, but then a fluid welled out. It was blood, a thick jet of it leaped up, and I was nauseated. It seemed to me that the blood continued to spurt for an unendurably long time. At last it ceased, and the vision came to an end. [50]

Jung writes that he was stunned by this version of the collective unconscious. He later realized that it was a hero and solar myth of death and renewal, the rebirth being symbolized by the Egyptian scarab, and the rising of the newborn sun. The dead youth with blond hair, I think represented Jung's own ego standpoint, which must die symbolically for the greater self to be born, as in the well-known teaching of Jesus, "You must be born again."[51] This interpretation is verified by a dream which Jung reports having had several days later in which he and a dark savage lie in wait for, ambush, and shoot to death a blond knight, Sigfried. Jung states, "I knew that we had to kill him."[52] Jung was filled with remorse about the death of "Sigfried," because this represented his ego, or the standpoint of consciousness, which must be sacrificed in the quest for the greater self who encompasses both consciousness and the unconscious. Who was the black savage? Jung calls him the "shadow figure." He is the "dark brother" whom most of us reject, and project upon some external "enemy," e.g. the blacks, the Jews, the Communists. He or She – the Shadow – is usually a same sex figure – must be recognized as the unconscious side of oneself. This is the first step on the path which Jung was to call individuation. This is the Journey from ego to Self. Along the way one meets many extraordinary inner characters, or archetypal figures of the path. Jung reports an inner vision of descending deeper into the unconscious:

The first time I reached, as it were, a depth of about a thousand feet; the next time I found myself at the edge of a cosmic abyss. It was like a voyage to the moon, or a descent into empty space. First came the image of a crater, and I had the feeling that I was in the land of the dead. The atmosphere was that of the other world. Near the steep slope of a rock I caught sight of two figures, an old man with a white beard and a beautiful young girl. I summoned up my courage and approached them as though they were real people, and listened attentively to what they told me. The old man explained that he was Elijah, and that gave me a shock. But the girl staggered me even more, for she called herself Salome! She was blind. What a strange couple: Salome and Elijah. But Elijah assured me that he and Salome had belonged together from all eternity, which completely astounded me . . .[53]

What Jung had encountered in this deep vision were the archetypal figures of the Wise Man and the Anima, in the personifications of Elijah and Salome. The Wise Man represents the higher wisdom figure in the man's unconscious psyche, and the Anima symbolizes the feminine element, or "eros." One encounters these figures in all of human myth and literature, as for example, in Dante's *Divine Comedy*, Virgil was the Wise Man figure, and Beatrice the personification of the Anima. Virgil takes Dante a long way in his journey through the Underworld, but it is Beatrice who appears to take him on the final leg of the Journey to Paradise.

Jung says that, out of the Elijah figure, emerged another Wise Man personification who called himself, Philemon. Philemon was of pagan Egypto-Hellenistic atmosphere with Gnostic coloration.[54] Philemon became an inner "guru" figure for Jung. Jung was told more than fifteen years later by an Indian friend of Mahatma Gandhi's that whereas most persons have outer gurus, or spiritual teachers, a few have inner gurus. Philemon was Jung's inner spirit teacher. Jung held interior dialogue with him. He later called this "active imagination." Jung also held inner conversations with his Anima figure, who once said that what he was doing was "art." Jung disputed this with the inner female figure: "No, it is not art! On the contrary, it is nature."[55]

The conscious must not automatically submit to the dictates of the unconscious – there needs to be dialogue between conscious and unconscious. It is especially important not to identify oneself with these unconscious figures, which is the case in psychoses: "The essential thing is to differentiate oneself from these unconscious contents by personifying them, and at the same time to bring them into relationship with consciousness."[56]

How did Jung maintain his sanity during this Journey into the Unconscious Mind? He said:

It is of course ironical that I, a psychiatrist, should at almost every step of my experiment have run into the same psychic material which is the stuff of psychosis and is found in the insane. This is the fund of unconscious images which fatally confuse the mental patient. But it is also the matrix of a mythopoeic imagination which has vanished from our rational age . . . Particularly at this time, when I was working on the fantasies, I needed a point of support in "this world," and I may say that my family and professional work were that to me.[57]

At the last stage of his Inner Journey, which was towards the end of World War I, 1918 to 1919, Jung began to do mandala drawings which he took to be symbols of wholeness, or the self. He said, "I sketched every morning in a notebook a small circular drawing, a mandala, which seemed to correspond to my inner situation at the time. With the help of these drawings I could observe my psychic transformation from day to day."[58] He goes on to say:

During those years between 1918 and 1920, I began to understand that the goal of psychic development is the self. There is no linear evolution; there is only a circumambulation of the self. Uniform development exists, at most, only at the beginning; later, everything points toward the center. This insight gave me stability, and gradually my inner peace returned. I knew that in finding the mandala as an expression of the self I had attained what was for me the ultimate. Perhaps someone else knows more, but not I.[59]

Some years later, Jung obtained inward confirmation about the self by way of a dream. He represented its essence in a mandala painting which he called "Window on Eternity," which is reproduced in *The Secret of the Golden Flower* (1929). This is the dream:

I found myself in a dirty, sooty city. It was night, and winter, and dark, and raining. I was in Liverpool. With a number of Swiss – say, half a dozen – I walked through the dark streets. I had the feeling that there we were coming to a harbor, and that the real city was actually above, on the cliffs. We climbed up there. It reminded me of Basel . . . When we reached the plateau, we found a broad square dimly illuminated by street lights, into which many streets converged. The various quarters of the city were arranged radially around the square. In the center was a round pool, and in the middle of it a small island. While everything round about was obscured by rain, fog, smoke, and dimly lit darkness, the little island blazed with sunlight. On it stood a single tree, a magnolia, in a shower of reddish blossoms. It was as though the tree stood in the sunlight and were at the same time the source of light. My companions commented on the abominable weather, and obviously did not see the tree. They spoke of another Swiss who was

Figure 6.1   One of Jung's Mandala Drawings.

living in Liverpool, and expressed surprise that he should have settled here. I was carried away by the beauty of the flowering tree and the sunlit island, and thought, "I know very well why he has settled here." Then I awoke.[60]

Jung said that this mandala dream was the climax of his whole process of inner development that began with the initial fantasies of entering the "other world" in 1913, and went on for five years till 1918. Jung comments that without such a vision as he had in that dream, he would have lost his sense of orientation and would have been compelled to abandon his whole undertaking. He says that when he parted with Freud in 1913, he knew nothing beyond Freud; he was plunging into the darkness. Now he *knew something*. When "such a dream comes, one feels it as an act of grace."[61]

In his own words, Jung said, "It has taken me virtually forty-five years to distill within the vessel of my scientific work the things I experienced and wrote down at that time . . . The years when I was pursuing my inner images were the most important of my life – in them everything essential was decided . . . It was the *prima materia* for a lifetime's work."[62]

Jung's first job, as it were, was to find the historical precedents of his own inner experiences. Between 1918 and 1926, Jung plunged into the study of the Gnostic writers in great depth, and found them to be the ancient forerunners of his *depth psychology*, although they used the language and symbols of their time. They, too, confronted the primal world of the unconscious. From the Gnostics, whose writings were mostly, although not entirely, destroyed by the Church, Jung went on to discover the alchemy of the Middle Ages: "Grounded in the natural philosophy of the Middle Ages, alchemy formed the bridge on the one hand into the past, to Gnosticism, and on the other hand into the future, to the modern psychology of the unconscious."[63] Jung had a number of dreams which prophesied his discovery of alchemy, including one in which there was a strange annex to his house which contained a wonderful library of books with curious symbols, which he later discovered were actual alchemical symbols.

Jung's output of books and articles was tremendous, and is housed today in *The Collected Works of C. G. Jung*, consisting of twenty volumes. Jung's writings began with his psychiatric studies of the early 1900s and ended in the last year of his life, in 1961. His lifetime output of works is a *magnum opus* of such magnitude and depth that Jung must be considered one of the giant minds (and souls) of the twentieth century. Besides his writings, he continued his clinical practice seeing hundreds of patients, and analyzing thousands of dreams. These are the prima materia for much of his theoretical writing. Jung wrote several books on the psychology of religion. We will look at four of these beginning with *Psychology and Religion* (1938) which was based upon the Terry Lectures given by Jung at Yale University. It is a smaller book contained within Vol. 11 of the *Collected Works: Psychology and Religion: West and East.*

By religion, Jung does not mean a creed. "It is . . . true . . . that . . . every confession is originally based upon the experience of the numinosum . . . and the subsequent alteration of consciousness: the conversion of St. Paul is a striking example of this."[64] In this statement, Jung is reminiscent of both Bucke and James who were more interested in the religious experiences of individuals than they were of codified religious creeds. We shall see that Maslow had a similar point of view on this. Theologians, on the other hand, seem to care more about doctrines and beliefs than they do about personal experiences. Jung says that:

> Creeds are codified and dogmatized forms of original religious experi-
> ence. The contents of the experience have become sanctified and usually
> congealed in a rigid, often elaborate structure. The practice of and the
> reproduction of the original experience have become a ritual and an
> unchangeable institution.[65]

We "moderns," however, live in a rationalistic and secular age in which the spiritual values of past millenia hold little meaning any more for many. For this book, Jung looks at a series of four hundred dreams of just such a "modern intellectual," a scientist, who like many highly educated people of our time was a non-believer. Jung said, "He belongs to those intellectuals or scientists who would be simply amazed if anybody should saddle them with religious views of any kind."[66]

Jung sees this man as one who values the reason and observation of the conscious mind alone, and does not credit the unconscious with any independent existence. One will be interested to see if the dreams of such a person, whose numbers are legion in academia, for instance, derive solely from conscious sources, or rather are "sources of information about the possible religious tendencies of the unconscious mind."[67] We will look at two of his dreams; this is the text of the first dream:

> There are many houses which have a theatrical character, a sort of
> stage scenery. Somebody mentions the name of Bernard Shaw. It is

also mentioned that one play which is to follow refers to a remote future. One of the houses is distinguished by a sign board with the following inscription:

This is the universal Catholic Church.
It is the church of the Lord.
All those who feel themselves to be instruments of the
Lord may enter.

And below in smaller letters:

The church is founded by Jesus and Paul.

It is as if a firm boasted of its old standing. I say to my friend: 'Let us go in and have a look.' He replies: 'I do not see why many people should be together in order to have religious feelings.' But I say:

'You are a Protestant so you will never understand it. There is a woman nodding approval. I now become aware of a bill posted on the wall of the church. It reads as follows:'

'Soldiers!'

'When you feel that you are under the power of the Lord avoid talking directly to him. The Lord is not accessible to words. We also recommend urgently that you should not indulge in discussions about the attributes of the Lord among yourselves. It would be fruitless, as anything of value and importance is ineffable.'

We now enter the church. The interior resembles a mosque rather than a church, as a matter of fact it is particularly like the Hagia Sophia. There are no chairs, which produces a wonderful effect of space. There are also no images. There are only framed sentences on the walls (like those in Hagia Sophia). One of these sentences reads: 'Do not flatter your benefactor.' The same woman who nodded approval to me before begins to weep and says: 'Then there is nothing left at all.' I reply: 'I think that it is perfectly all right,' but she vanishes.

At first I am right in front of a pillar which obliterates the view, then I change my position and I see a crowd of people in front of me. I do not belong to them and I am standing alone. But I see them clearly and I also see their faces. They pronounce the following words: 'We confess that we are under the power of the Lord. The Kingdom of Heaven is within ourselves.' They repeat this thrice in a most solemn way. Then the organ plays a fugue by Bach and a choir sings. Sometimes it is music alone, sometimes the following words are repeated: 'Everything else is proper,' which means that it does not produce a living impression.

When the music is finished the second part of the ceremony begins, as is the custom at students' meetings where the dealings with serious affairs is followed by the gay part of the gathering. There are serene and mature human beings. One walks to and fro, others talk together, they welcome each other, and wine from the episcopal seminary and other drinks are served. In the form of a toast one wishes the church a favorable development and a radio amplifier plays a ragtime melody with the refrain: 'Charles is now also in the game.' It is as if the pleasure concerning some new member of the society were to be expressed by that performance. A priest explains to me: 'These somewhat futile amusements are officially acknowledged and admitted. We must adapt a little to American methods. If you have to deal with big crowds, as we have, it is inevitable. We differ, however, on principle from the American churches in that we cherish an emphatically antiascetic tendency.' Whereupon I woke up with a feeling of great relief.[68]

Unlike Freud who took dreams as "disguised wish fulfillments," Jung takes the dream as it is, as a natural expression of the unconscious. The Gentile Jung, agrees with the Jewish Talmud, which says, "The dream is its own interpretation."[69] In this dream, its first part is a serious statement in favor of the Catholic versus the Protestant point of view. It is in favor of the universal rather than the individual interpretation of religion. The second part of the dream reflects an adaptation of the Church to a decidedly worldly point of view. There is a compromise between Catholism and a pagan "joie de vivre."

The dreamer, Jung explains, is a rationalist intellectual, who found that his philosophy had forsaken him in the face of a neurotic demoralization and nervous condition. Jung feels that this first dream did not present a true religious experience, but rather a religion of sentimentality, and was no real moral help.

Jung recounts a second dream that occurred later in the patient's analysis:

> I am entering a solemn house. It is called "The house of inner composure or self-collection." In the background are many burning candles arranged so as to form four pyramid-like points. An old man stands at the door of the house. People enter, they do not talk and often stand still in order to concentrate. The old man at the door tells me about the visitors to the house and says: "When they leave they are pure." I enter the house now, and I am able to concentrate completely. A voice says: "What thou art doing is dangerous. Religion is not a tax which thou payest in order to get rid of the woman's image, for this image is indispensable. Woe to those who use religion as a substitute for the other side of the soul's life. They are in error and they shall be cursed. Religion is no substitute, but it is the ultimate accomplishment added to every other activity of the soul. Out of the fullness of life thou shalt

give birth to thy religion, only then shalt thou be blessed." Together with the last sentence a faint music becomes audible, simple tunes, played by an organ, reminding me of Wagner's "Fire Magic" . . . As I leave the house I have the vision of a flaming mountain and I feel that a fire which cannot be quenched must be a sacred fire.[70]

This dream, Jung reports, made a profound impression upon his patient. It was a solemn experience for him which produced a complete change in his attitude to life and humanity. Jung looks at the burning candles which formed four pyramid-like points as a mandala, a symbol of the Self or Wholeness. The sacred fire is a well-known religious symbol which goes back to the "burning bush" experience of Moses. When the dreamer originally entered "the house of self-collection," he met an Old Wise Man who informs him of the purifying effect of that inner house. The only ritual which takes place there is concentration, or meditation. There is the phenomenon of the inner voice which speaks with astonishing authority about not avoiding the anima side of life, i.e. the feminine, in the pursuit of the spiritual life, which is more identified with the masculine, as in the Christian Trinity of Father, Son, and Holy Spirit. The visionary dream experience of the sacred fire is a symbol of the spirit. Some biblical examples are: the "burning bush" of Moses, the "cloven tongues of fire" which came upon the disciples on the Day of Pentecost, and the "blinding light" experienced by St. Paul. Jung states: "I have to admit the fact that the unconscious mind is capable of assuming an intelligence and purposiveness which are superior to actual conscious insight."[71]

Here one sees the clear dichotomy between Freud's approach to healing via the ego's conscious insight, and Jung's approach via the creative unconscious, i.e., the Self. A non-believer had a profoundly religious dream which healed him. Does this prove the reality of God? Jung says:

> We conceive of the ego as being subordinate to, contained in, a superordinate self as a center of the total, illimitable and indefinable psychic personality.[72]

Jung goes on to call the Self: "*the God within.*"[73] This is the *Imago Dei* recognized by Jung. This view has been criticized by such theologians, as the Jewish philosopher, Martin Buber, who said in his book, *Eclipse of God* (1952):

> . . . Jung, the leading psychologist of our day, has made religion . . . the subject of comprehensive observations. He is not to be blamed for

including among these observations an abundance of phenomena which I must characterize as pseudo-religious. I characterize them so because they do not bear witness to an essential personal relation to One who is experienced or believed in as being absolutely over against one . . . For if religion is a relation to psychic events, which cannot mean anything other than to events of one's own soul, then it is implied by this that it is not a relation to a Being or Reality which, no matter how fully it may from time to time descend to the human soul, always remains transcendent to it. More precisely, it is not the relation of an I to a Thou. [74]

Jung wrote a reply to Buber's critique which he entitled: "Religion and Psychology: A Reply to Martin Buber." It can be found in *The Symbolic Life*, Vol. 18 of the *Collected Works*:

I am afraid that Buber, having no psychiatric experience fails to understand what I mean by the "reality of the psyche" and by the dialectical process of individuation. The fact is that the ego is confronted with psychic powers which from ancient times have borne sacred names, and because of these they have always been identified with metaphysical beings. Analysis of the unconscious has long since demonstrated the existence of these powers in the form of archetypal images which, be it noted, *are not identical with the corresponding intellectual concepts*. One can, of course, believe that the concepts of the conscious mind are, through the inspiration of the Holy Ghost, direct and correct representations of their metaphysical referent. But this conclusion is possibly only for one who already possesses the gift of faith. Unfortunately I cannot boast of this possession, for which reason I do not imagine that when I say something about an archangel I have thereby confirmed a metaphysical fact. I have merely expressed an opinion about something that can be experienced, that is, about the very palpable "powers of the unconscious." These powers are numinous "types" – unconscious contents, processes, dynamisms – and such types are, if one may express it, immanent-transcendent . . . since my sole means of cognition is experience I may not overstep its boundaries, and cannot therefore pretend to myself that my descriptions coincide with the portrait of a real metaphysical archangel. What I have described is a psychic factor only, but one which exerts a considerable influence on the conscious mind. [75]

Jung wrote *A Psychological Approach to the Dogma of the Trinity* in 1942. This psycho-religious monograph is also a part of *Psychology and Religion: West and East*. Jung points out that triads of gods appear very early in the religions of ancient man. One such example given by Jung is the Babylonian trinity of Anu, Bel, and Ea. Anu is the Lord of heaven, Bel, the Lord of the lower realm, and

Ea, too, a god of the underworld.[76] Ancient Egyptian religion recognized a trinity of God as Father, Son, and Ka, the procreative life force.[77] This is surely a precursor of the Christian Trinity of Father, Son, and Holy Spirit. For both ancient Egyptians and Christians, this trinity was regarded as a tri-Unity rather than as "three gods."

Quoting the opening words of Plato's *Timaeus*, "One, two, three – but where, my dear Timaeus, is the fourth. . .?"[78] Jung acknowledges his proper ancestor in philosophic-psychological thought. Jung says that this same problem "appears in modern dreams. . ."[79] Let me transgress the generally non-autobiographical character of this book by indicating a dream of my own which fits this pattern precisely:

> I dreamed of a three-sided cross. A fourth side arose from the depths and joined the other three sides. When they were joined, the three and the one, the whole cross shone with light. The fourth side had the word, FEELING, inscribed on it.

Jung speaks of the "stages of revelation": the age of the Father characterized by pristine oneness with the whole of nature, good and evil alike. This Oneness is awe-inspiring, and is the world of the Old Testament Hebrews: "Hear O Israel, the Lord our God, the Lord is One." The second stage is that of the Son. This is the time of reflection upon why there is evil and imperfection in the world, as well as goodness. Why are there diseases, war, and pestilence? Why does life end in death? These were the questions during the New Testament time. The answer is in the birth of the Messiah-King, or Christ, who redeems the world through his own suffering and death, and subsequent resurrection. Once Christ has left his earthly stage, men are alone again in the face of the terrors and sorrows of life. This is the time of the third stage, the appearance of the Holy Spirit, as in the story of Pentecost when the disciples were filled with the "new wine" of the spirit. This completes the Trinity of Christianity which became sacred dogma. It is expressed in the various creeds of the Christian religion: the Apostle's Creed, the Nicene Creed, and so on. None of this is "rational"; it comes, in Jung's view, from the Collective Unconscious. The Trinity is an "archetype." It appears in dreams as well, and I will give you a second dream of mine:

> Two men walked down a path to a river. One remained on the bank and did not go into the water. He became transformed into a figure of "the fool," as in the Tarot. The other went into the river, and sub-

merged himself in the water. When he emerged, he was enlightened, and I recognized him as Christ. He came up covered with *three fish* on his body.

Trinity dreams are actually fairly rare compared with quaternity dreams, or dreams of three becoming four, as in my previous dream. Jung gives many examples of quaternity dreams throughout his writings in the *Collected Works*. It is a central theme to him. He feels that quaternity = the Self. How does Jung deal with the problem of "the fourth"? He deals with it in terms of his psychological theory of the four functions, and also in terms of his theory of the archetypes of the collective unconscious.

Jung describes the four functions of consciousness as: thinking, sensation, intuition, and feeling. In Western man, as in my own dream, feeling is often the repressed or inferior function. In this sense, "the fourth" that completes the trinity is the feeling function. Likewise, in Western mentality, the feminine element, or what Jung called the "anima" is usually repressed, or unconscious: most deeply of all, "the fourth" is the feminine.★ This was recognized to some degree in the Roman Catholic doctrine, formulated in the 1950s, of the "bodily ascension" of the Virgin Mary. Catholics, much more than Protestants, venerate the Virgin Mary as the "mother of God." Jung sees great positive value in this. It is a step toward Wholeness.

Jung wrote *Transformation Symbolism in the Mass* in 1942. Here Jung raises the question of how bread and wine can become symbols of the life and personality of Christ. Certainly, Jung says, it is not immediately apparent. Recall the behaviorist, Watson, who dismissed the Mass as "primitive superstition."

On a natural level, bread comes from grain, and wine from grapes, both living substances. They have always been a part of Jewish ritual, as in the use of matzoh and wine in the Passover Seder, which symbolizes the Exodus of the Israelites from Egypt. Jesus took the same substances at the Last Supper and proclaimed them to be his "body" and "blood." The Christian Mass preserves this ritual over the last two millenia. A Buddhist monk and author has called the Mass, the Christian form of Zazen, or Zen meditation. Both are ways to experience the Self, whether you call it the "Christ within" or the "Buddha nature." Deeper than this, Jung

★ Jung speaks also of Evil, the Devil, or Lucifer, as "the fourth," which is not entirely consistent – unless you equate: feminine = the Devil. In the Judaic tradition, Satan is "the Adversary," or "Chaos," which is not at all the same thing as the feminine embodiment of God, or the "Shekinah."

has pointed out that the elements of the Mass – bread and wine – appear in the dreams of men and women, throughout the ages, as symbols of the Self. I had two such dreams myself. In one, a young priest administered wine to me from a golden grail. In another, a white-bearded minister utilized a round bunch of self-generating figs as an "ancient form" of Holy Communion. Figs, not apples, *were* the ancient fruit of the Middle East referred to in the Bible's Book of Genesis story of the Garden of Eden with its "Tree of Life."

The Secret of the Golden Flower was written by Jung in 1929, and it appears in Vol. 13 of the *Collected Works: Alchemical Studies*. Jung points out that the Western mind has emphasized reason and science to a tremendous degree, and this has brought about unparalleled scientific and technological "progress." But there is a one-sidedness in this, and Western man has largely neglected the study of his own soul. The twentieth century "psychology" of behaviorism, developed simultaneously in America and Russia (the bastions of capitalism and communism respectively) has, as a cardinal principle, the denial of the soul. Even to this day, the only reference to "the soul" in academic psychology books is to point out that this was a "superstition" of an earlier unscientific age.

Jung looks at the soul and its products, all of human culture, myth, art, etc., with a much more open and unbiased mind. He finds the East cultivated the "science of the soul" for thousands of years. This is what we call "mysticism" today. Jung studies the ancient Chinese text called *The Secret of the Golden Flower* which states that "The golden flower is the light, and the light of heaven is the Tao."[80] Jung goes on to say that:

> The golden flower is a mandala symbol I have often met within the material brought me by my patients. It is drawn either seen from above as a regular geometric pattern, or in profile as a blossom growing from a plant. The plant is frequently a structure in brilliant fiery colours growing out of a bed of darkness, and carrying the blossom of light at the top . . .[81]

We have seen in these four examples that Jung finds corroboration of religious dogmas in the natural dream symbolism of his patients, which rather frequently are religious in form and meaning. We have seen this in the dreams of the modern intellectual, in quaternity and trinity dreams, in the symbols of the Eucharist, and in the Eastern symbol of the golden flower. Symbols of the Self, as seen in dreams, are usually felt as *numinous* or *sacred*. Does Jung believe in God? He answers this question, as follows:

> If I assume that God is absolute and beyond all human experience, he leaves me cold, I do not affect him, nor does he affect me. But if I know that he is a powerful impulse of my soul, at once I must concern myself with him . . .[82]

Jung has often been accused of "psychologism," or of psychologizing religious realities. This is, in fact, the criticism most applied to Jung from the camp of traditional religion, Jewish or Christian. Jung answers it thusly:

> The epithet "psychologism" applies only to a fool who thinks he has his soul in his pocket. There are certainly more than enough such fools, for although we know how to talk big about the "soul," the depreciation of everything psychic is a typical Western prejudice . . . How can we be sure that the soul is "nothing but?" It is as if we did not know, or else continually forgot, that everything of which we are conscious is an image, and that image *is* psyche. The same people who think that God is depreciated if he is understood as something moved in the psyche, as well as the moving force of the psyche – i.e., as an autonomous complex – can be so plagued by uncontrollable affects and neurotic states that their wills and their whole philosophy of life fail them miserably. Is that a proof of the impotence of the psyche? Should Meister Eckhart be accused of "psychologism" when he says "God must be born in the soul again and again?"[83]

The soul has been so disparaged in the West from both the side of science and religion that scientistic psychologists accuse Jung of "mysticism" and "obscurantism" for his careful reporting of the real facts of human inward experience in images, dreams, and visions, whereas formal religionists accuse him of "blasphemy" or "heresy" in his recognition of the religious factor within the human psyche. Nevertheless, Jung was not a metaphysician or mystic, but an empirical scientist of the soul, a psychiatrist who took seriously the inner life of his patients, and his own inner life. He has greatly enriched our understanding of the human psyche, and its symbolic religious experience, as seen particularly in dreams or visions. He has brought back the living reality of the Self. It is surely a deeper level of the self than the "self consciousness" of Bucke, which was, in Jung's terms, ego consciousness.

Do we see Cosmic Consciousness in Jung's work? I searched Jung's *Collected Works* for all his references to "mystical experience" and "cosmic consciousness." Here is what I found:

There are dreams and visions of such an impressive character that some people refuse to admit that they could have originated in an unconscious psyche. They prefer to believe that such phenomena derive from a sort of "superconsciousness." Such people make a distinction between a quasi-physiological or instinctive unconscious and a psychic sphere "above" consciousness, which they style the "superconscious." As a matter of fact, this psyche, which in Indian philosophy is called the "higher" consciousness, corresponds to what we in the West call the "unconscious."[84]

It is psychologically correct to say that "At-one-ment" is attained by withdrawal from the world of consciousness. In the stratosphere of the unconscious there are no more thunderstorms, because nothing is differentiated enough to produce tensions or conflicts.[85]

Now if consciousness is emptied as far as possible of its contents, they will fall into a state of unconsciousness, at least for the time being. In Zen, this displacement usually results from the energy being withdrawn from conscious contents. . .[86]

Individual consciousness or ego-consciousness is a late product of man's development. Its primitive form is a mere group consciousness, and among the primitive societies that still exist today this is often so poorly developed that many tribes do not even give themselves a name that would distinguish them from other tribes . . . But a group consciousness in which individuals are interchangable is still not the lowest level of consciousness. At the lowest and most primitive level we would find a sort of generalized or cosmic consciousness, with the complete unconsciousness of the subject. On this level there are only events, but no acting persons.[87]

From this we can see how young any kind of differentiated consciousness is. It has just crept out of its long sleep, slowly and clumsily taking cognizance of its own existence. It would be a delusion to imagine that we have attained anything like a high level of consciousness. Our present day consciousness is a mere child that is just beginning to say "I."[88]

He is of the same essence as the universe, and his own mid-point is its centre. This inner experience, shared by Gnostics, alchemists, and mystics alike, has to do with the nature of the unconscious – one could say that it *is* the experience of the unconscious . . .[89]

Mystical literature abounds in descriptions of such experiences. You also find detailed records in William James' *The Varieties of Religious Experience*. But if you observe the dreams of such patients you will find peculiar symbolic images, often long before the patients themselves become conscious of any so-called mystical experiences. These images always show a specific pattern: they are circular or square, or like a cross or a star, or are composites of such elements. The technical term I use for such figures is the *mandala* the Sanskrit word for "circle."[90]

This is truly amazing! Jung, the man so often accused by "scientific psychology" types and Freudians, of being a "mystic," does not himself really believe in mystical experience! He denies the reality of "superconsciousness"; he calls mystic at-one-ment, a "withdrawal from the world of consciousness"; he calls the Zen state, "satori," "a state of unconsciousness"; he calls "cosmic consciousness" the "lowest level of consciousness"; he says that it is a "delusion" to believe in "anything like a high level of consciousness"; he says that the mystic (Gnostic or alchemical) experience is "the experience of the unconscious"; and finally, he dismisses the mystic experiences described by James as "so-called mystical experiences," pointing to the *real importance* of their mandala dreams! Jung certainly does not speak like a mystic. He certainly does not sound like someone who has had a mystical or Cosmic Conscious experience himself, as Bucke did. To Jung, the dream vision of the mandala, *the symbol of* the inner self is the highest experience, which he usually equates with the God experience. Jung disparages Cosmic Consciousness as "unconsciousness." This is quite contrary to the experiences of the mystics of all cultures and times who report the mystical experience as a *profound awakening*.

Swami Akhilananda, author of *Hindu Psychology* (1946), an Indian psychologist, and monk of the Ramakrishna order, states, concerning Jung's psychology, for which he otherwise has deep respect:

> Professor Jung seems to conclude that the superconscious experiences are "vast but dim" without any understanding of them. Any man who has had these realizations will laugh at such conclusions. Pantanjali, Swami Vivekananda, and Swami Brahmandada give just the opposite point of view. They make it clear that samadhi, or the superconscious state, is vivid and definite . . . So the superconscious is not unconscious; it is full of awareness; nay it is Consciousness Itself.[91]

Dr. Bucke would certainly agree with this as he had *seen*. Swami Akhilananda goes on to state:

> Anyone who studies the teachings and records of the experiences of Western and Eastern mystics will never make such unscientific statements as Professor Jung. The superconscious experiences of the mystics in the West are identical with those of mystics of the East.[92]

Rudolf Otto, the Western author of *Mysticism East and West* (1932) comes to the same conclusion as Swami Akhilananda when he says: ". . . mysticism is the *same* in all ages and in all places, that timeless and independent of history it has always been identical."[93]

Does this experience of Cosmic Consciousness have anything to do with God? I think if anything could be called God-union, it is this. Swami Akhilananda quotes the Christian mystic, Meister Eckhart: "When one takes God as he is divine, having the reality of God within him, God sheds his light on everything."[94]

In his book, *Answer to Job* (1954), Jung takes a peculiar view of God:

> If we consider Yahweh's behavior as a whole, one indubitable fact strikes us – the fact that his actions are accompanied by an inferior consciousness . . . His consciousness seems to be not much more than a primitive "awareness" which knows no reflection and no morality.[95]

A notable Jungian analyst whom I know said that if this is true that God's consciousness is inferior to our own, then we truly have no hope! He also stated that it is the diametric opposite of Judeo-Christian theology. If Jung equates God and Self, as he does in many places, this is quite puzzling indeed because he always speaks of the Self as "greater than" the ego. Jung, in *Aion* (1959) says that: "The self . . . is a God image, or at least cannot be distinguished from one."[96] It is the highest realization on the path of individuation. On the other hand, in *Answer to Job*, YHWH is spoken of in much the same way that Jung speaks of "supercon-sciousness," namely as, "vast unconsciousness." Here Jung is not only in contradiction with himself in other places, but in radical disagreement with the Judeo-Christian theology which regards God as the Supreme Being, or Being Itself. The Kabbala calls the Godhead, "Ain Sof Aur," meaning literally "limitless light." By comparison, the light of our little egos is a very small thing indeed, a small candle compared to the blazing sun. Is the little light of ego "more conscious than" the infinite light of God? The mystic who briefly moves from ego consciousness to Cosmic Consciousness experiences an *awesome awakening*, not a falling into sleep! Beyond the Self is the spiritual quest that Jung does not seem to speak about in his *Collected Works*. It is the realization of what Martin Buber called "the relation of an I to a Thou."[97] It is possible that Carl Jung discovered this in his old age, as when he was asked as a man in his eighties on B.B.C. television, "Do you believe in God?" and Jung replied: "I do not believe, *I know.*" Knowing God is the Ultimate Gnosis.★

A Note on Christian-Jungians

A recent survey book on the Jungian movements by Andrew Samuels, *Jung and the Post-Jungians* (1985), discusses three major Jungian schools of thought: the Classical, the Developmental, and the Archetypal. The first are strict adherents to Jung's own thought, the second integrates Jungian psychology with recent Freudian object-relations theory, and the third, the "brain child" of James Hillman, looks back to Greek polytheism as its source of inspiration, and is rather antithetical to monotheism and the idea of the "Self." Notably absent is a fourth major movement (I see it as a distinct school of thought), the Christian-Jungian.† As I see it, the old grandmasters of this school within Jungian psychology were/are Fritz Kunkel, M.D., the author of *Creation Continues* (1973), the Rev. Morton T. Kelsey, the author of *Healing and Christianity* (1973), *Christo-Psychology* (1982) and numerous other seminal books in this vein, and the Rev. John A. Sanford, whose early books include, *Dreams, God's Forgotten Language* (1968), *The Kingdom Within* (1970, revised 1987), and many other books in this genre. More recent Christian-Jungian works are: Christopher Bryant's *Jung and the Christian Way* (1983), Wayne G. Rollin's *Jung and the Bible* (1983), and W. Harold Grant's, Magdala Thompson's and Thomas E. Clarke's *From Image to Wholeness: A Jungian Path in the Gospel Journey* (1983). This vital movement first attracted me to Jungian psychology, and I feel it is closer to the heart of what Jung was really about than the currently popular "polytheistic school." Witness Jung's own vast writings on Christ as symbol of the Self (in *Aion*, for example). I will briefly discuss some of the

---

★ Adumbrations of Jung's gnosticism are found in a book which he printed privately in 1916 called *The Seven Sermons to the Dead* whose "author" is listed as "Basilides," a gnostic of the early Christian era. He speaks of the Gnostic deity Abraxas: "*To see him means blindness; To know him is sickness; To worship him is death; To fear him is wisdom; Not to resist him means liberation.*"[98]

† By "Christian-Jungian" I do not mean that these people identify with any particular Christian creed, nor that they interest themselves only in Christian documents and material. What I do mean is that they believe that the true essence of Christianity and the true essence of Jungian psychology have a vital place at which they meet. They have, therefore, interested themselves in Christian documents as seen in the light of Jung's psychology.

ideas of one of the most enlightened Jungians of our time, John A. Sanford, who has written extensively on Christian and biblical material and imagery. Sanford's background includes both Episcopal priesthood, and the practice of Jungian analytical psychology, as well as authorship of many books. In Sanford's book, *The Kingdom Within*, he looks at Jesus' sayings in the light of both etymology and Jungian psychology, as in the interpretation of the following:

You must therefore be perfect as your heavenly Father is perfect. [99]

Sanford goes back to the ancient Greek meaning of what is, misleadingly, translated into English as "perfect." Sanford says:

... the difficulty for the English reader hinges on the word *perfect*. This implies to the modern mind the idea of one-sided pureness; that is, a person without any kind of thought or emotion that could be regarded as sinful or wrong. The Greek word, however, means "brought to completion" or "brought to the end state." If we understand the word in this way, we see that Jesus is urging us to be brought to the end state for which we were created and that is brought about through the unfolding of the inner Self. This also throws light on the ancient problem, How can God, the transcendent Creator of the universe, also be a personal reality for the individual? The answer is that he is as personal to us as our own inner creative process. [100]

Sanford proposes that Jesus is urging us toward our own genuine Selfhood, or Wholeness (Wholeness and Holiness are derivatives of the same root).

What is essential in the path to Self or Wholeness? First of all, we must see through and beyond our "persona" or mask-self. Sanford allegorizes this as the "Pharisee in Each of Us."[101] Jesus himself most strongly condemned Pharasaic hypocrisy. Sanford states:

The mask is the person we pretend to be – the false outer personality which we turn to the world, but which is contradicted from within. The mask is that which conceals our real thoughts and feelings, and which we come to use so habitually as a way to hide from others and ourselves that we become unaware that we have assumed it. ... There is a certain usefulness to this outer mask, for to some extent we need it to function in the world. The destructive aspect of the mask is our tendency to identify with it, to think that we *are* the person we pretend to be, and thereby to remain unconscious of our real self. [102]

There are several levels of the persona. On the outermost level, sociologists call them "roles." Some roles in our society are that of police officer, professor, doctor, clergyman/woman, etc. On a somewhat more personal level are the roles of father, mother, husband, wife, etc. On the most individual level, the persona is the self we choose to, or learn to, present to our social worlds: "Mr./Ms Good," "the tough guy," "the egghead," "the athlete," etc. There is no problem per se with these roles or masks. The problem is our tendency *to identify* the self with these roles or masks. When we have disidentified with our personae or mask-selves, we will confront what Sanford calls the "Inner Adversary"; Jung called it the "Shadow."

> We have always known that we have enemies. What we have seldom realized is that each of us also carries an adversary within us. The adversary is the person within us who contradicts the outer front: the one who thinks the thoughts we do not want to acknowledge as our own, who has feelings and urges we dare not openly express because to do so would throw into jeopardy the egocentric role and image we have assumed for ourselves. This is the one we try, usually unsuccess-fully, to hide from others, out of fear that they will reject us, and also try to hide from ourselves, because we could not stand to face it. This is the Mr. Hyde to our Dr. Jekyll. . . . The relationship of the inner enemy and the mask is one of diametrical opposition.[103]

What do we do with this "inner enemy" or "Shadow"? We usually project "him" or "her" (the Shadow tends to be a same-sex figure) onto some "outer enemy," whether individual or collective. The Nazi persecution of the Jews, and the whites' discrimination against blacks in our own country, or apartheid in South Africa, are powerful examples of collective Shadow projection. Jesus said: "Come to terms with your opponent. . ."[104] When you do, you may find not so much an "inner enemy" as the missing half of your own self, i.e., what you need to come to Wholeness.

Deeper even than coming to terms with the inner adversary is the necessity for persons to come to consciousness of the contra-sexual principle, Anima-eros in man, Animus-logos in woman. Jesus said: ". . .when you make the male and the female into a single one . . . then you shall enter the Kingdom."[105] Sanford sees the Kingdom in terms of the coming to Wholeness or Self-realization:

> The road to the kingdom will be an inner road, a way of the soul, in which a man becomes increasingly connected to his inner world. Nothing can be excluded which belongs to man's wholeness. The final entrance into the kingdom subordinates consciousness to a greater reality within.[106]

Jesus said: "The Kingdom of God is within you."[107]

7

G. I. Gurdjieff and P. D. Ouspensky on Self and Cosmic Consciousness

Immediately before the beginning of World War I, a man of Armenian Greek ancestry with a background in mysticism and esotericism arrived back in Russia, following a sojourn in the Middle East, bringing back with him a psychological and mystical teaching. This man was George Ivanovich Gurdjieff; his teaching was designed to encourage man to develop even in spite of himself.

G. I. Gurdjieff was born in the 1870s (a contemporary of Carl Jung's – though they make no reference whatsoever to each other's existence) in Alexandropol in the Caucasus of present day Russia of a Greek father and an Armenian mother.[1] Gurdjieff witnessed certain uncanny phenomena in his youth (as Jung did, also), including a séance, the cure of a paralytic man at a saint's tomb, and the remarkable accuracy of a fortune teller, as well as cures of medical diseases based upon following the advice given in dreams. From youth on, Gurdjieff (similar to Jung here, too) raised basic philosophical questions about life. What are we living for? What is the end of it all? Does the human soul survive death? Are their possibilities of higher consciousness in man? Gurdjieff studied for the vocation of physician, at first, and later priest. He studied everything available at the time in the fields of neurophysiology and psychology, but the libraries did not contain what he was looking for (here, too, he resembles Jung in his youth).

Gurdjieff was convinced that *somewhere* there existed schools or communities with *real knowledge* of the human soul and its capacities for development. Gurdjieff began in his native land, where Europe and Asia intermingle, to gather knowledge from Christian monastic sources. He was to say this, very much later, about the relation of his system to Christianity:

I do not know what you know about Christianity, answered G., emphasizing the word. It would be necessary to talk a great deal and to talk for a long time in order to make clear what you understand by the term. But for the benefit of those who know already, I will say, if you like, *this is esoteric Christianity.*[2]

After he absorbed what he could of his native tradition, its ancient symbolism, its liturgies, its techniques of mental prayer, he went on in his search of esoteric knowledge. He joined a group of about twenty persons, who called themselves "Seekers of the Truth," in his travels, sometimes in small bands, and sometimes alone, in the ancient lands of the Middle East. They came in contact with the Naqshbandi and Kadiri dervishes of Sufism, the mystical branch of Islam. Among the group were specialists in various fields, Gurdjieff was an expert hypnotist interested in the nature of suggestion and the use of various techniques to modify consciousness.[3]

Gurdjieff's most profound sources of influence in these expeditions came in his contacts with Sufism. He was permitted to join various Sufi orders and he received dervish training. He spent a long period in a Naqshbandi Sufi school in Afghanistan. Gurdjieff also studied with the Rimpoche lamas of Tibet; he had a passable knowledge of the Tibetan language. He studied Buddhist theory and practice with these Tibetan Buddhist lamas, as well as their methods of breath and energy control.[4]

During his long travels, Gurdjieff was without independent means of support, and earned his living by his own ingenuity doing such things as selling carpets, repairing anything and everything, working as a stage hypnotist and magician, and so on. He was also a secret agent for the Russian Tsarist government, and held this post for ten years.[5] He conducted these activities while he searched for the awakened inner circle of humanity. During his travels, Gurdjieff was shot and wounded more than once. During his convalescence from one of these nearly fatal injuries, he was struck by a sudden realization which he stated as follows:

And here also is God!!! Again God! . . .

Only He is everywhere and with Him everything is connected.

I am a man, and as such I am, in contrast to all other outer forms of animal life, created by Him in His image!!!

For He is God and therefore I also have within myself all the possibilities and impossibilities that He has.

The difference between Him and myself must lie only in scale.

For He is God of all the presences in the universe! It follows that I also have to be God of some kind of presence on my scale.[6]

This makes one think of Jung's corresponding discovery of what he called the Self, the *Imago Dei*. In *Memories, Dreams, Reflections,* Jung states:

Attainment of consciousness is culture in the broadest sense, and self-knowledge is therefore the heart and essence of this process. The Oriental attributes unquestionably divine significance to the self, and according to the ancient Christian view self-knowledge is the road to knowledge of God.[7]

Gurdjieff met the philosopher and mathematician, P. D. Ouspensky in Russia in 1915. Ouspensky, who was born in Moscow in 1878, and who wrote *The Fourth Dimension* (1909) and *Tertium Organum* (1912) before his meeting with Gurdjieff, was to become the chief interpreter for Gurdjieff's teachings, particularly in his book, *In Search of the Miraculous* (1949), the record of his eight years as a student of Gurdjieff's.

One can, perhaps, profitably view Ouspensky's relation to Gurdjieff as somewhat analogous to that of Plato to Socrates. Ouspensky's comment on first meeting Gurdjieff was this:

I remember this meeting very well. We arrived at a small café in a noisy though not central street. I saw a man of an oriental type, no longer young, with a black moustache and piercing eyes, and completely out of keeping with the place and atmosphere. I was still full of impressions of the East. And this man with the face of an Indian raja or an Arab sheik whom I at once seemed to see in a white burnoose or a gilden turban, seated here in this little café, where small dealers and commission agents met together, in a black overcoat with a velvet collar and a black bowler hat, produced the strange, unexpected and almost alarming impression of a man poorly disguised the sight of whom embarrasses you because you see he is not what he pretends to be and yet you have to speak and behave as if you did not see it. He spoke Russian incorrectly with a strong Caucasian accent; and this accent, with which we are accustomed to associate anything apart from philosophical ideas, strengthened further the strangeness and unexpectedness of the impression.[8]

One is reminded very much of Richard Bucke's first meeting with Walt Whitman! It is interesting to have the record of a person's first recognition of *his teacher*. Ouspensky was later to part with his teacher, Gurdjieff, in 1923, and begin his own group in Lon-

don. The reason for his parting with Gurdjieff can only be speculated upon, but it seems that Ouspensky was of a more abstract
philosophical mentality, and emphasized "the principles," whereas Gurdjieff had more the "mad mind" of the Zen master and
taught more by parable and paradox. One sees this contrast in
comparing Ouspensky's account of *the work* in *In Search of the
Miraculous* and Gurdjieff's Sufi-tale-like teaching approach in his
mysterious three-volume work, *Beelzebub's Tales to His Grandson*.

Going back to our historical synopsis of Gurdjieff's life and
work, he attracted a group of followers in Russia during the throes
of the Bolshevik revolution. When conditions became impossible
they left Russia for Constantinople, then to Berlin, and finally to
Paris. It was in Paris that Gurdjieff decided to settle and establish
the "Institute for the Harmonious Development of Man" at the
Chateau of Avon near Fontainebleau. In an interesting sidelight, in
their journey across Russia during the revolution, Gurdjieff had
two documents: one was certified by the Tsarists and the other by
the Bolsheviks. He put one in the left pocket of his coat, and the
other in the right. When he was stopped by a band of Bolsheviks,
he pulled out one document, and by a band of Tsarists, the other,
and in this way, Gurdjieff and his whole group made it out of
Russia safely during its revolution!

The period from 1922 to 1933 was one of intense development
for the students at the Institute during which time Gurdjieff tested
his system of thought, and his methods for self-observation and
exercise. His methods were meant to "work" the three centers of a
human being: the intellectual, the emotional, and the physical. His
students included such persons as P. D. Ouspensky and his wife,
Thomas and Olga de Hartmann, Alexander and Jeanne de Salz-
mann, A. R. Orage, Maurice Nicoll, and many others. During
this period, Gurdjieff made a trip to America in 1925 and suffered
a serious automobile accident. While recovering he began his
series of books: *All and Everything: Beelzebub's Tales to His Grandson, Meetings with Remarkable Men,* and *Life is Real only Then,
When "I Am"* (which was never completed). These are required
reading for any serious student of Gurdjieff's thought.

The first book (or series of three books) concerns the "three
brained beings," mankind, on planet Earth as described by Beelzebub to his grandson, Hassein, as they travel in the spaceship
Karnak! The second book tells the story of Gurdjieff's travels in
his early years, his teachers, and the extraordinary individuals
whom he met on his quest for esoteric knowledge. The third book

is more direct in style, and it gives an account of Gurdjieff's teaching, particularly in respect to the process of *self-remembering*. Gurdjieff wrote another smaller book in which he introduces his ideas called *The Herald of the Coming Good* (1933).

Between 1933 and 1949, when he died in Paris, Gurdjieff travelled widely, and started new groups of "the work" in several cities in America. Today, there are numerous Gurdjieff and Gurdjieff-type schools still in existence, as well as descendants of Ouspensky's version of the teaching.

What is Gurdjieff's teaching? According to Gurdjieff we live in a poor part of the universe for our possible evolution to higher levels of consciousness. How Gurdjieff "knew" this is hard to say for how could he have "checked out" other parts of the universe? Leaving this question aside, we all know that change of old habits is not easy, neuroses are notoriously difficult to overcome, and few have come to realize the reality of what Jesus said to Nicodemus about being "born again" or the "enlightenment" experience of the Buddha. This is what Gurdjieff says about the "normal" state of the human being, which he, like Plato, compared to imprisonment:

> You do not realize your own situation. You are in prison. All you can wish for, if you are a sensible man, is to escape. But how to escape? It is necessary to tunnel under a wall. One man can do nothing. But let us suppose there are ten or twenty men – if they work in turn and if one covers another they can complete the tunnel and escape.

> Furthermore, no one can escape from prison without the help of those *who have escaped before*. Only they can say in what way escape is possible or can send tools, files, or whatever may be necessary. But *one* prisoner alone cannot find these people or get in touch with them. An organization is necessary. Nothing can be achieved without an organization.[9]

In this emphasis upon the necessity of a group to support you in your struggle for liberation, Gurdjieff differs from the individualist emphasis of Jung. However, even Jungians have their "first master," i.e. Jung himself, followed by his immediate disciples, Jung training institutes, and qualified Jungian analysts. There is a *line of transmission* in every teaching.

However, the chief thing to realize is *that you are in prison*. If you do not believe that you are in prison, even though you are, how can you possibly be motivated to make the efforts needed to escape? Something of the same point is a necessity for an alcoholic, for example, to realize that he/she *is* an alcoholic, or likewise with a drug addict, or with all of us neurotics! We must first realize what is our limitation, or our problem, or even our disease, before we can know what to do to overcome it. Gurdjieff is telling us that we are all, in spite of our illusion of "freedom," in the prison of our false selves. This is, indeed, similar to the message of Jesus to a "sleeping humanity." Jesus compares the awakened, or "born again," to the freedom of the wind:

> Marvel not that I said unto thee, Ye must be born again.

> The wind bloweth where it listeth, and thou hearest the sound thereof, but canst not tell whence it cometh, and whither it goeth: so is every one that is born of the Spirit. [10]

Part of Gurdjieff's system of thought is "the Ray of Creation" which is presented as follows:[11]

Absolute	[1]	
World 3 under 3 laws	[3]	All Possible Systems of World
World 6 under 6 laws	[6]	The Milky Way
World 12 under 12 laws	[12]	The Sun
World 24 under 24 laws	[24]	The Planets as One Mass
World 48 under 48 laws	[48]	The Earth
World 96 under 96 laws	[96]	The Moon

According to the system, the Absolute which is under only *one law*, namely itself, is absolutely free. As one descends from the Absolute, one first comes under three laws, then six laws, then twelve laws, then twenty-four laws, then, on our planet Earth, forty-eight laws. Each level as you descend from the Absolute is a more "dense" vibration, is more mechanical, and hence is less free. Beyond even the Earth for "mechanicalness" is the moon with its ninety-six laws. In various places, both Gurdjieff and Ouspensky state that in his/her "normal" unawakened state, the human being is "food for the moon." Whether this is a metaphoric or literal statement is never made clear. It does seem a rather horrible destiny! The way to escape this is to become awakened, and this involves ascending the levels of being. If we moved up to the "24 state," we would be, presumably, twice as free as we are now. This author spent a year in the Arica training of Oscar Ichazo, a group similar in teaching to Gurdjieff, and its goal was to achieve the state of consciousness known as "permanent 24." The training definitely did produce altered states of consciousness, some of which produced the feeling of far greater freedom than our "normal" egoistic frame of mind. According to this teaching, one could hypothesize that what we call "spiritual experiences" correspond to these "vibration levels." In the Arica training, 12 was the level of Divine Love, 6, the experience of the Unity as apart from oneself, and 3, the attainment of at-one-ment with the Unity. The "3 state" would presumably have "Trinitarian" implications. The attainment of the "1 state" was not proferred for human beings in this life. That is the state of the Absolute. On the other extreme, one could envision the "96 state" as one of profound depression and the helplessness that results. The "48 state" is the ordinary "rational" ego state of consciousness which is far from free or enlightened. The "24 State" is the beginning of enlightenment.

Besides the "Ray of Creation," there are certain other basic laws in the Gurdjieff system, including "the law of the three" and "the law of the seven." Of these, the most basic law is the law of the three. It states that in everything that happens in the universe, there is a positive, negative, and neutralizing force involved. These are very similar to the *gunas* of Vedantic philosophy, and they are present everywhere, even in the first step of the ray of creation, when the One becomes Three. One finds support of this view in many religious systems of the world, as for instance the Trinity of Hinduism, with Brahman the Godhead, the Undivided One, manifesting as Brahma, Vishnu, and Shiva: Creator, Destroyer, and Sustainer, and the Christian Trinity of Father, Son, and Holy Spirit (which does not as evidently connect to the idea of positive, negative, and neutralizing forces). Moreover, in the science of physics, atoms are said to have a tripartite structure: proton (positive), electron (negative), and neutron (neutralizing). In sexual reproduction, there is the active sperm, the receptive ovum, and the neutralizing force of the fluid medium that supports both of them. One can view many other natural phenomena in this way from the flight of a bird to the growth of a tree.

Whereas the Law of the Three governs the processes of every event, the Law of the Seven governs the succession of events. This is a nonlinear orderly discontinuous unfoldment which is most prototypically represented in the musical scale of the octave: Do, Re, Mi, Fa, Sol, La, Ti, Do. By the time you get to the second Do, you are at the beginning of a new seven-step series. One sees this seven-step process in the periodical table of chemistry in which essential characteristics of chemical elements seem to repeat themselves every eighth element when they are ordered according to atomic weight; in the stages of growth of an organism from fertilized ovum to neonate;* in the stages of our lives: infant, child, pubescent, adolescent, young adult, middle-aged adult; mature person; in the days of the week: Sunday, Monday, Tuesday, Wednesday, Thursday, Friday, Saturday; and so on. We seem to be dealing here with something universal.

The next important concept in the Gurdjieff system is the "enneagram." It is presumably a synthesis of the Law of the Three and the Law of the Seven according to a "higher mathematics" which exceeds my grasp! It creates a nine-pointed figure. It was used for many nine-stage progressions in the Arica system, such as, the negative emotions, the virtues, and the ego types. This is what it looks like using the ego types as an example:

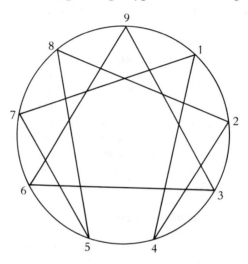

Figure 7.1   The Enneagram.

1. Ego Indolent: Incredibly lazy for essence. Makes a passion out of laziness. Very good at seeing the faults of others.
2. Ego Resent: He/she resents everything; mostly him/her self. He/she is very guilty about something.
3. Ego Flattery: No one gives this ego type enough attention. "I'm so far out. Why don't they recognize it? Why don't they see how I really am?"
4. Ego Go: He/she has very very important work to do (outside

* 1. Zygote, 2. 4 cell state, 3. 16 cell state, 4. late cleavage, 5. blastula, 6. gastrula, 7. foetus, 8. neonate (this is the *first step* of a *new seven-step series*).

of essence). Work is more important than life itself. He/she is out of touch with life inside. Heavy-handed.

5. Ego Melon: A very sad ego type. Loves poetry and romantic novels. He/she is waiting for the Distant Lover who never comes. He/she does not know why he/she is so sad.
6. Ego Stinge: He/she is very stingy with him/herself. He does not want to be seen except in a certain way. He/she will just hide or disappear.
7. Ego Coward: He/she is tremendously insecure. He/she is afraid of him/her self and others.
8. Ego Plan: He/she has an "important destiny," but he/she will never do it. Another name is *charlatan*. "Aren't I great?" A very idealistic fellow.
9. Ego Venge: He/she is always punishing him/her self. Tremendous suffering. Self-destructive. "I'm not right."*

We all have all of these characteristics within us to a certain extent, but one of these predominates. You may be able to select your own "ego type." If you cannot, you can be sure that it is obvious to others who know you! One tends to act out these patterns of behavior quite mechanically. The psychology of the ordinary human being is characterized not only by mechanicalness, or unfreedom, but by fragmentation. Gurdjieff and his student, Ouspensky, state many times that the human being as we know him/her is fragmented, and lacks a permanent 'I.' In fact, the ordinary human being has many 'I's.' The ego type, or fixation, is a special one – which we will talk about later again under the designation of "chief fault." We think of each of these 'I's' as "ourselves" as each ascends to consciousness. At the everyday level of our social selves, we obviously have multiplicity. There is the "me" to our parents, who can be childlike, the "me" to our mates, who is adult sexual (we hope), the "me" to our bosses or employers, who is a "good worker" (he/she hopes!), the "me" to our sons or daughters, who is "father figure" or "mother figure" to them, the "me" to our best friends, and here we can be "more ourselves" and so on. William James spoke of these things a long time ago.

Besides the social self level of disunity or fragmentation, there is the level of the Freudian or personal unconscious, which is even more given to division. Here one finds, if one looks within, the

---

* This is based upon my student notes during the Arica training which I took in San Francisco in the summer of 1972.

many complexes: the mother complex, the father complex, the Oedipus complex, the inferiority complex, the power complex, the procrastination complex, the "make a promise and break it" complex, the "struggle for achievement" complex, the "fear of heights" complex, the "good little girl" complex, the "angry young man" complex, etc. Each of these can take over and dominate our consciousness for a period of time. When this happens, "that's us." On an even deeper level are Jung's discoveries of the archetypes of the collective unconscious. Here we find, as we have seen in the Jung chapter preceding, such archetypes as the Anima, the Animus, the Wise Man, the Wise Woman, the Shadow, the Trickster, and so on. Jung even regarded "the ego" as one among the many "complexes." Any of these complexes is capable of "taking over" consciousness. As we see, the human psyche is more of a "universe" than we have imagined hitherto – with many systems within systems, hierarchies, and levels. Perhaps, it should be called a "multiverse." Is there a possibility of unity? Jung, as we have seen, spoke of the Self, the Archetype of Wholeness. Gurdjieff, and Ouspensky too, have a concept of a unifying self, or permanent 'I' which can be attained by human beings, but only through hard inner work, and moreover, *conscious suffering*. Here is a point of strong agreement between Gurdjieff's and Jung's psychology: the Self. But this Self, or permanent 'I' is not easily come by. Gurdjieff says:

> Man is a plural being. When we speak of ourselves ordinarily, we speak of 'I.' We say, " 'I' did this," " 'I' think this," " 'I' want to do this"—but this is a mistake.

> There is no such 'I,' or rather there are hundreds, thousands of little I's in every one of us. We are divided in ourselves but we cannot recognize the plurality of our being except by observation and study. At one moment it is one 'I' that acts, at the next moment it is another 'I.' It is because the 'I's' in ourselves are contradictory that we do not function harmoniously. [12]

According to Gurdjieff, every adult human being has many selves each of which calls itself 'I.' We are all multiple personalities! Do these different 'I's' recognize each other's existence? Not at all. There is a defense mechanism that operates between them which Gurdjieff calls *buffers*. Buffers between our different 'I's' keep one unconscious of the other. One 'I' may make a promise, but another 'I' may break that same promise. One 'I' may take wedding vows of fidelity to his/her mate; another 'I' may break these same vows in infidelity. Do you see the point? Various techniques of modern psychotherapy operate to reduce "buffers" between different "fragments" of our psyche bringing the light of consciousness to the formerly unconscious. Some examples are the free association of Freud's psychoanalysis, the inner dialogues of Perls' Gestalt therapy, and the active imagination of Jung's analytical psychology. Even the muscle manipulations of Reichian orgone therapy, and related techniques (Bioenergetics, Rolfing. Feldenkrais, etc.) can be seen as "breaking down buffers." This is a beginning of reunifying the "warring kingdoms" of the human psyche. There is more commonality between Gurdjieff's psychology and the modern depth psychologies than meets the eye. However, these two schools of thought have shown almost no recognition of each other, and the psychiatrists who have even heard of, let alone recognize the value of Gurdjieff's teaching for psychotherapy are few and far between. Some psychiatrists, such as Dr. Claudio Naranjo, and psychologists like Dr. Jean Houston, have obviously studied deeply the Gurdjieffian work as their books demonstrate (see appendix).

Beyond being fragmented, Gurdjieff says that man in his present state of unenlightenment is "a machine." In Gurdjieff's own words:

> Man is a machine. All his deeds, actions, words, thoughts, feelings, convictions, and habits are the result of external influences. Out of himself a man cannot produce a single thought, a single action. Everything he says, does, thinks, feels – all this happens . . . Man is born, lives, dies, builds houses, writes books, not as he wants to, but as it happens. Everything happens. Man does not love, hate, desire – all this happens. [13]

Gurdjieff sounds remarkably like Watson and the behaviorists here! I am sure that both Pavlov and Skinner would agree with every statement in the preceding passage. However, for Watson, Pavlov, and Skinner, that *is all that man is*. There is no further possibility. For Gurdjieff, there is much further possibility of human psychological evolution. And it is in our own hands – at least this is Gurdjieff's view of human possibility. In our current stage of development, it would be an illusion to think that we can *do* anything because we lack a permanent "I" and free will. We are just "victims" of circumstances, responding to stimuli, as it were. Paradoxically, however, the first step toward freedom is the conscious recognition of our own mechanicalness. Gurdjieff says this about the recognition of our mechanicalness, i.e. our conditioned unfreedom:

> But no one will ever believe you if you tell him he can do nothing. This is the most offensive and the most unpleasant thing you can tell people. It is particularly unpleasant and offensive because it is the truth, and nobody wants to know the truth.[14]

One thinks of what Jesus said about the truth setting you free! The first truth to know is that we are not free in our present consciousness; we are rather more like mechanical slaves staring at shadows in Plato's "cave," representing unconsciousness. We have not yet come into the light. The biggest obstacle to becoming enlightened is to think that we are "already there." If so, what is the point of the struggle for liberation?

Besides the recognition of fragmentation, and mechanicalness, Gurdjieff teaches that we are a "three storied being." In the upper story is the intellectual center, in the middle story, the emotional center, and in the lower story, the moving center (which also includes the instinctual and sexual centers). In ordinary persons these three centers are "out of whack." We use our intellectual center to perform emotional work, or our emotional center to perform moving work, etc. In the Arica training of Ichazo, there was a lot of emphasis on "working" the three centers which, in this school, were called the "Path": Intellectual Center, "Oth": Emotional Center, and "Kath:" Moving Center.

Most of us Americans are totally out of tune with our Moving Center or "Kath." For point of reference, it is "located" where Zen Buddhists locate the "hara," or about three inches below the navel. There are many types of breathing or movement exercises that we did in order to reconnect with the Moving Center or "Kath." Zen Buddhists will teach you the same thing. You can also pick it up in martial arts of Zen or Taoist origin, such as Aikido or Tai Chi Chuan. It really makes a difference to be "connected to" your Moving Center. Gabrielle Roth, a dancer and movement teacher in the United States, bases her whole teaching on the "Moving Center." For the Emotional Center, spiritual traditions employ devotional prayer and chanting. You feel this in your heart. Finally, we do give a great deal of emphasis to the Intellectual Center in Western society, and courses in philosophy, mathematics, logic, etc., will more than exercise this. There are spiritual traditions, too, that emphasize the Intellectual Center, such as, Jnani Yoga. The Kabbala of Western mysticism is quite a

Thinking Center oriented approach, as well. Where is the Intellectual Center "located?" In the head, of course!

Based upon these centers: intellectual, emotional, and moving, Gurdjieff has a theory of human types. He calls the moving/ instinctive man, "man number one," the emotional man, "man number two," and the intellectual man, "man number three." So far, this corresponds almost perfectly to Jung's typology theory with thinking, feeling, sensation, and intuition functions. You can make the obvious connections. But, where is the intuitive function in Gurdjieff's system? Gurdjieff speaks of "man number four":

> *Man number four* is not born ready-made. He is born one, two, or three, and becomes four only as a result of efforts of a definite character. Man number four is always the *product of school work*. He can neither be born, nor develop accidentally or as the result of ordinary influences of bringing up, education, and so on. Man number four already stands on a different level than man number one, two, and three; he has a *permanent center of gravity* . . . He already begins to know himself and begins to know whither he is going. [15]

Now, Gurdjieff does not use the term *intuition* in describing man number four. However, it is my intuition that one of the developments of man number four, who has the beginnings of spiritual awareness of himself, is the function of intuition. This may be an important part of knowing one's self and one's direction. One tends to *intuit* these things. Gurdjieff and Jung would differ in their evaluation of intuition as native: Jung vs. acquired through difficult inner work: Gurdjieff. These two views may not necessarily be contradictory, however. Whereas the potential for intuition may be native, its development does take exercise. One of the first things that one notices when one has taken up meditation practice, for example, is increased intuition.

Besides man number one, two, and three who are native, and man number four, who is the product of inner work, Gurdjieff recognizes the higher levels of man number five, six, and seven. Are these related to Self and Cosmic Consciousness? This is what Gurdjieff says about these higher levels of man:

> Man number five is also for us an unattainable standard of man, for it is a man who has reached *unity*. [16]

> Man number six stands very close to man number seven. He differs from man number seven only by the fact that some of his properties have not as yet become *permanent*. [17]

> Man number seven means a man who has reached the full develop-
> ment possible to man and who possesses everything a man can possess;
> that is, will, consciousness, permanent and unchangeable I, indivi-
> duality, immortality, and many other properties which, in our blind-
> ness and ignorance we ascribe to ourselves. It is only when, to a certain
> extent, we understand man number seven and his properties that we
> can understand the gradual stages through which we can approach
> him, that is, understand the process of development possible for us. [18]

Man number five does indeed sound like a man who has come
to the Self in the Jungian sense. He has attained the archetype of
wholeness and unity. He has overcome fragmentation and disunity. Man number seven (and six, although not "permanent")
sounds very much to me like one who has attained to Cosmic
Consciousness in Bucke's sense. Among the experiences of Cosmic Consciousness is the unchangeable "I" and the experience of
immortality. We are speaking here of persons on the level of
Christ and Buddha. That is to say, they *live* on that level of
consciousness. Many mystics in history have experienced this
consciousness briefly. Gurdjieff is even more concerned with *level
of being* than with *states of consciousness*. On one occasion when
Ouspensky was talking with Gurdjieff, he asked him whether he
considered it possible to attain "cosmic consciousness." Gurdjieff
replied:

> I do not know what you call 'cosmic consciousness,' said G., it is a
> vague and indefinite term; anyone can call anything he likes by it. In
> most cases what is called 'cosmic consciousness' is simply fantasy,
> associative daydreaming connected with intensified work of the emo-
> tional center. Sometimes it comes near to ecstasy but most often it is
> merely a subjective emotional experience on the level of dreams. But
> even apart from all this before we can speak of 'cosmic consciousness'
> we must define in general *what consciousness is*." [19]

Gurdjieff does not want Ouspensky to get "too far ahead of
himself" and fantasize about cosmic consciousness. He is by no
means saying that there is not such a thing – there is – but that
Ouspensky should be more concerned with awakening to self-
consciousness. Gurdjieff does refer to four levels of consciousness
in other places: sleep, waking state, which he sometimes refers to
as "waking sleep," self-consciousness, and objective consciousness. This is how Ouspensky reports in *In Search of the Miraculous*
on what Gurdjieff had to say about the four levels of consciousness
in one of his lectures:

In all there are four states of consciousness possible for *man* (he emphasized the word "man"). But ordinary man, that is, man number one, number two, and number three, lives in the two lowest states of consciousness only. The two higher states of consciousness are inaccessible to him, and although he may have flashes of these states, he is unable to understand them and he judges them from the point of view of those states in which it is usual for him to be.

The two usual, that is, the lowest states of consciousness are first, *sleep*, in other words a passive state in which man spends a third and very often a half of his life. And second, the state in which men spend the other part of their lives, in which they walk the streets, write books, talk on lofty subjects, take part in politics, kill one another, which they regard as active and call 'clear consciousness' or the 'waking state of consciousness.' The term 'clear consciousness' or the 'waking state of consciousness' seems to have been given in jest, especially when you realize what *clear consciousness* ought in reality to be and what the state in which man lives and acts really is.

The third state of consciousness is *self-remembering* or self-consciousness or consciousness of one's being. It is usual to consider that we have this state of consciousness or that we can have it if we want it. Our science and philosophy have overlooked the fact that *we do not possess* this state of consciousness and that we cannot create it in ourselves by desire or decision alone.

The fourth state of consciousness is called the *objective state of consciousness*. In this state a man can see things *as they are*. Flashes of this state of consciousness also occur in man. In the religions of all nations there are indications of the possibility of a state of consciousness of this kind which is called 'enlightenment' and various other names but which cannot be described in words.[20]

Gurdjieff's fourth level of consciousness, "objective consciousness," is absolutely the same thing as what Bucke calls "Cosmic Consciousness." Both of these are other words for what the religions call "enlightenment." Gurdjieff *emphasizes* that ". . .the only right way to objective consciousness is through the development of self-consciousness."[21]

How does one attain to self-consciousness? First, it would be good to look at the obstacles to self-consciousness which keep one in what Gurdjieff calls "waking-sleep." In the state of waking-sleep, we are fragmented, lacking in unity, or one 'I,' and a passive victim of circumstances. We are unable *to do*. Gurdjieff emphasizes that in order *to do*, first we must *be*. The waking-sleep state is also called *personality*, which relates to "persona," or "mask," as opposed to the *essence*, or what is innately oneself. We all know when we are playing a role vs. being ourselves. One thing about being yourself is: you don't have to rehearse! It is not a "part"; it is *what you are*. Jung, too, spoke about the danger of "identifying with one's persona" or "social self." This is a great danger in modern technological society. But it is not "society," it is ourselves whom we need first "reform." These are the ways that we keep ourselves in slavery:

Identification: In this state we lose awareness of our selves, and become lost with whatever external persons or circumstances we are involved with at the moment. For example, if we are in the role of "student," we are identified with this persona in our feeling, thinking, doing, and awareness. We are just as likely to identify with the persona of "professor," and this is no better! If we happen to be part of a crowd, we feel just like an "entity in the crowd." This is what Gurdjieff said about identification, as reported by Ouspensky in *In Search of the Miraculous*:

> 'Identifying' is one of our most terrible foes because it penetrates everywhere and deceives a man at the moment when it seems to him that he is struggling with it. It is especially difficult to free oneself from identifying because a man naturally becomes more easily identified with the things that interest him most, to which he gives his time, his work, and his attention. In order to free himself from identifying a man must be constantly on guard and be merciless with himself, that is, he must not be afraid of seeing all the subtle and hidden forms which identifying takes . . . Identifying is the chief obstacle to self-remembering. A man who identifies with anything is unable to remember himself. In order to remember oneself it is necessary first *not to identify*.[22]

In the state of identification one does not remember oneself. Attention is directed outward – and there is no energy left for self-remembering. If you pay attention, the beginning of self-knowledge, you will notice how much of your waking hours you spend in the state of identifying.

Considering: Identifying with what you think are other person's expectations is called *considering* in the Gurdjieff system of thought. There are two kinds of considering: internal considering and external considering. Internal considering is the culprit in keeping us out of self-awareness. In this state of internal considering, we worry about, and imagine what others think about us, whether they approve of us, or like us, and so on. This is what Gurdjieff said about it, as reported by Ouspensky:

There are several different kinds of 'considering.' On the most prevalent occasions a man is identified with what others think about him, how they treat him, what attitude they show towards him. He always thinks that people do not value him enough, are not sufficiently polite and courteous. All this torments him, makes him think and suspect and lose an immense amount of energy on guesswork, on suppositions, develops in him a distrustful and hostile attitude towards people. How somebody looked at him, what somebody thought of him, what somebody said of him – all this acquires for him an immense significance.[23]

We can all "identify" with this! There is another form of considering: external considering. It is, in fact, the opposite of inner considering. It is, in essence, the practice of empathy and tact. Gurdjieff says that:

External considering requires a knowledge of men, an understanding of their tastes, habits, and prejudices. At the same time external considering requires a great power over oneself, a great control over oneself . . . Right external considering is very important in the work.[24]

Lying: Telling lies is an inevitable aspect of waking-sleep, or the ordinary conscious state. It is so pervasive that Gurdjieff has said that the psychology of ordinary man could be called "the psychology of lying." Most of us have drawn the distinction between our "false selves" and our "true selves." We usually "blame" our false selves on others, for instance, our parents, or society, or even "the devil made me do it!" In the process of awakening, it is necessary to take responsibility for our own false selves, our own congenital lying. Ouspensky makes an interesting observation about the effect of Gurdjieff's direct presence:

I quickly noticed a still stranger property of G.'s apartment. *It was not possible to tell lies there.* A lie at once became apparent, obvious, tangible, indubitable. Once there came an acquaintance of G.'s whom I had met before and who sometimes came to G.'s groups. Besides myself there were two or three people in the apartment. G. himself was not there. And having sat a while in silence our guest began to tell how he had just met a man who had told him some extraordinarily interesting things about the war, about possibilities of peace and so on. And suddenly quite unexpectedly for me I felt *that he was lying.* He had not met anybody who had told him anything. He was making it all up on the spot simply because he could not endure the silence.[25]

One thinks of the saying of Shakespeare in *Hamlet*, in which a father says to his son: "This above all: to thine own self be true . . ."[26]

Unnecessary Talking: We, in our modern society, are always talking! When we are with other people, we feel a compulsive need *to talk*. At college classes, cocktail parties, gatherings of friends, business meetings, etc., it is: *talk, talk, talk*. Sometimes everyone talks at once! This can have the effect of mechanical chatter. It is one of the pervasive ways in which people keep themselves in waking–sleep and detached from their real selves. Quite to the contrary, most Eastern spiritual traditions, from Yoga to Zen, emphasize the value of the silent meditative state. In this state of quietude, it is far easier to engage in *self-remembering*. Ouspensky reports an experience in Gurdjieff's apartment in Moscow with his students:

> In October I was with G. in Moscow. His small apartment on the Bolshaia Dmitrovka, all the floors and walls of which were covered in the Eastern style with carpets and the ceilings hung with silk shawls, astonished me by its special atmosphere. First of all the people who came there – who were all G.'s pupils – *were not afraid to keep silent*. This alone was something unusual. They came, sat down, smoked, they often did not speak a single word for hours. And there was nothing oppressive or unpleasant in this silence: on the contrary, there was a feeling of assurance and of freedom from the necessity of playing a forced or invented role. But on chance and curious visitors this silence produced an extraordinarily strange impression. They began to talk and they talked without stopping as if they were afraid of stopping and feeling something.[27]

Of course, we are speaking here of external talking. What about the constant "talking to ourselves," or "inner dialogue" which most of us engage in when alone? Gurdjieff would agree with Don Juan, the Indian shaman in the Casteneda books, that the development of the warrior depends upon "stopping the internal dialogue."[28]

Negative Emotions: Most of us carry behind our social masks, or personas, continually changing negative emotions which we mostly attempt to keep hidden. We are depressed, fearful, angry, jealous, self-pitying, bored, irritable, etc. Does Gurdjieff emphasize that we give vent to these negative emotions, that we engage in what psychoanalysts call "catharsis"? Not at all. His proposal is far more radical. He says that we must overcome our negative emotions for they keep us detached from our true selves. Ouspensky reports that Gurdjieff said the following:

> Besides being a very good method of self-observation, the struggle against expressing unpleasant emotions has at the same time another

significance. It is one of the few directions in which a man can change himself or his habits without creating other undesirable habits. Therefore self-observation and self-study must, from the first, be accompanied by the struggle against the *expression of unpleasant emotions.*[29]

It is interesting that this view of Gurdjieff's about the way to overcome negative emotions – *do not express them* – is supported by recent psychological research on the value of catharsis. This research would indicate that expressing negative emotions actually "reinforces" them. For example, yelling and screaming at someone does not "release" aggressive or hostile energy, rather it gives one "practice" in aggression and hostility. Rather than "blowing one's stack," it might be more useful to observe one's breathing for ten counts!

When one has recognized the five great enemies of self-remembering – identifying, inner considering, lying, unnecessary talking, and the expression of negative emotions – what then is *the way* of Gurdjieff? His way resembles that of many spiritual traditions: *self-observation.* This is what Gurdjieff himself said about self-observation in a talk he gave in New York City in 1924:

> Self-observation is very difficult. The more you try, the more clearly you will see this.

> At present you should practice it not for results but to understand that you cannot observe yourselves. In the past you imagined that you saw and knew yourselves.

> I am speaking of objective self-observation. Objectively you cannot see yourselves for a single minute, because it is a different function, the function of the master.

> If it seems to you that you can observe yourselves for five minutes, this is wrong; if it is for twenty minutes or for one minute – it is equally wrong. If you simply realize that you cannot, it will be right. To come to it is your aim.[30]

How can you attain to this aim of self-observation? Gurdjieff says that:

> To achieve this aim, you must try and try.

> When you try, the result will not be, in the true sense, self-observation. But trying will strengthen your attention, you will learn to concentrate better. All this will be useful later. Only then can one begin to remember oneself.[31]

When we begin the journey of self-remembering, we will begin to realize how *unconscious* we are, and have been, most of our lives.

We wake up in the morning, have breakfast, drive to work in heavy traffic, park our cars, spend the day at our jobs, perhaps that of doctor, or lawyer, or accountant, or construction worker, or barber, or bartender, or what-have-you, and then we "close up shop," and drive home. We get out of our cars, walk in the front doors of our homes, flop down on our easy chairs, and realize that we have been *virtually unconscious* most of the time! Professors have been known to go through a whole semester of lectures in a familiar course – *waking up* at the end of the course! Have you had this experience of suddenly waking up to your self? This is what Gurdjieff calls "self-remembering." Here is what Ouspensky said about it during the period of his work with Gurdjieff:

> I saw quite clearly that my first recollections of life, in my own case very early ones, were moments of *self-remembering*. This last realization revealed much else to me. That is, I saw that I really only remember those moments of the past in which I *remembered myself*. Of the others I *know only that they took place*. I am not able wholly to revive them, to experience them again. But the moments when I had remembered myself were alive and were in no way different from the present. I was still afraid to come to conclusions. But I already saw that I stood upon the threshold of a very great discovery. I had always been astonished at the weakness and the insufficiency of our memory. So many things disappear. For some reason or other the chief absurdity of life from me consisted in this . . . If our memory really keeps alive only moments of self-remembering, it is clear why our memory is so poor.[32]

Ouspensky speaks of a "division of attention" which seems to be very useful in the existence of self-remembering. Ordinarily when we observe something our attention is directed outwards, as in the following diagram:

I --------------------▶ the observed phenomenon.[33]

What Ouspensky says is necessary is to both direct attention outwardly toward the phenomenon, and at the same time, inwardly towards oneself, as in the following diagram:

I ◀-------------------▶ the observed phenomenon.[34]

This self-remembering is not the same thing as introspection which is often just associative day-dreaming, or fantasy. It is something quite different. Ouspensky says that: "It was a new and very interesting state with a strangely familiar flavor."[35]

Self-remembering, or self-observation, is the chief method in the Gurdjieff system of working on oneself. One is not asked "to change." This is clearly impossible in the state of waking-sleep, or ordinary ego. The best that one can do is to observe oneself. In a talk Gurdjieff gave in 1924, he made the following remarks about working on oneself:

> Working on oneself is not so difficult as wishing to work, taking the decision. This is so because our centers have to agree among themselves, having realized that, if they are to do anything together, they have to agree because there is one master; it will no longer be possible for any of them to order the others about and to do what they like. [36]

Gurdjieff is speaking about the three centers: the intellectual, the emotional, and the moving–instinctive, and the necessity to bring them together under the leadership of "the master." What is "the master?" This is the self. But, in ordinary man, Gurdjieff says: "There is no master . . . And if there is no master, there is no soul." [37] This seems rather a contradiction, and *it is* an intellectual contradiction. It is necessary to come under the control of "the master" to overcome mechanicalness, fragmentation, and unfreedom, but in the unawakened human being, there is *no master!* I cannot "solve" this one intellectually: How can we develop a self through self-observation when in the unawakened state, we cannot be said to even have a self to observe? It is like the Zen Koan: "What was my self before my parents were born?" It has no answer. Gurdjieff, nonetheless, would simply tell you *to observe.* Jesus told his own disciples many times *to watch.* I suspect that the Hebrew for "to watch" and "to observe" is the very same thing. In this process of "watching" or "observing," one may have moments of *self-remembering.* These moments, over a long period of time and work on oneself, may become more and more continuous. When there is continuous self-remembering, then we have awakened to the permanent 'I,' or self.

One of the chief obstacles to self-remembering is what Gurdjieff and Ouspensky, in his commentaries on Gurdjieff, called the "chief feature" or "chief fault" in each person. Here Ouspensky discusses the "chief fault" with some quotations from his notes on Gurdjieff's lectures:

> On this visit the center of gravity of the talks was in the "chief feature" or "chief fault" of each one of us.

> G. was very ingenious in the definition of features. I realized on this occasion that not everyone's chief feature could be defined. With some people this feature can be so hidden beneath different formal manifestations as to be almost impossible to find. And then a man can consider *himself* as his chief feature just as I could call my chief feature "Ouspensky" or, as G. always called it, "Piotr Demianovich." Mistakes

there cannot be because the "Piotr Demianovich" of each person forms so to speak "round his chief feature."

Whenever anyone disagreed with the definition of his chief feature given by G. he always said that the fact that the person disagreed with him showed he was right.

"I disagree only with what you say is actually my *chief feature*," said one of our people. "The chief feature which I know in myself is very much worse. But I do not dispute that people may see me as you describe."

"You know nothing in yourself," G. told him; "if you knew you would not have that feature. And people certainly see you in the way I told you. But you do not see how they see you. If you accept what I told you as your chief feature you will understand how people see you. And if you find a way to struggle with this feature and to destroy it, this is, to destroy its *involuntary manifestation*" (G. emphasized these words), "you will produce on people not the impression you do now but any impression you like."

With this began long talks about the impressions that a man produces on other people and how he can produce a desirable or an undesirable impression.

Those around him see a man's chief feature however hidden it may be. Of course they cannot define it. But their definitions are often very good and very near. Take nicknames. Nicknames sometimes define chief features very well.

The talk about impressions brought us once more to "inner" and "outer considering."

"There cannot be proper outward considering while a man is seated in his chief feature," said G. "For instance So-and-So (he named one of our party). His feature is that he is *never at home*. How can he consider anything or anybody?"

I was astonished at the artistic finish of the feature that was represented by G. It was not psychology even, it was art.

"And psychology ought to be art," G. replied, "psychology can never be simply science."

To another of our party he said on the question of feature that his feature was *that he did not exist at all.*

"You understand, I *do not see you*," said G. "It does not mean that you are always like that. But when you are like you are now, you do not exist at all."

He said to another that his chief feature was a tendency always to argue with everybody about everything.

"But then I never argue," the man very heatedly at once replied. Nobody could help laughing. [38]

I include this detailed portion of Gurdjieff-at-work to indicate to you the extraordinary genius of the man as a practical psychologist. In fact, he said that "psychology can never be simply science." The nine ego types of Ichazo's Arica training were also said to be indications of the "chief fault." This was a more systematic approach, and although it may have been accurate, it did not quite have the artistic touch that we see here in Gurdjieff's direct work with his students. As to whether this direct power still exists in the Gurdjieff movement, or whether it has simply become formalized and systematized, is another question. A Sufi master, whose name was revealed to me by my Sufi teacher but whom I think I should keep secret, writing under the pen name of Rafael Lefort, wrote this in his book, *The Teachers of Gurdjieff* (1968):

> Up to Gurdjieff's death in 1949, the teaching saw all manner of ups and downs; it spread to North and South America. . . . After his death it marked time and became less positive with the mainstream gone. Was it the contact with the Source that it lacked? Be that as it may, from the 1950's onwards it carried on only because of the momentum Gurdjieff had given it. [39]

The Sufis speak about *baraka* which means "spirit." The original teacher may have had the spirit, having been in contact with teachers of great power, in Gurdjieff's case, from Christian, Sufi, and Tibetan Buddhist sources. If his teaching is really to go on, he must pass on this spirit, or rather awaken this spirit, in his students. This is, of course, as much a question for Jung's students as it is for Gurdjieff's. Merely mechanical repetition of formulae, and the memorization of texts of "the master" is not the thing. We must find "the master" within ourselves, as Gurdjieff would put it. Or we must awaken to the archetype of the self, as Jung would speak of it. It is not enough to merely know concepts and definitions.

It is interesting to note that while Gurdjieff and Jung had the same goal – the permanent 'I,' or the "Self" – there was very little overlap in their methods. Jung's way was chiefly via paying attention to the manifestations of the unconscious, particularly in dreams. There is a long path of inner development here. Some of its chief steps are the recognition of the Shadow, the awakening to the contrasexual archetypes – the Anima or the Animus, and finally the appearance in dreams or visions of the symbols of the transcendent function, the reconciler of opposites, the Self, as in the mandala-images in dreams which we discussed in the Jung chapter (6). In Gurdjieff's way, there is hardly any mention of dreams at all, except in the disparagement of fantasy and day-dreaming, for example, and little attention is paid to the unconscious. Gurdjieff's path to Self or permanent 'I' seems to be chiefly a way via consciousness, whereas Jung's is a way via the unconscious. I do not see these as contradictory at all, but rather complementary. There have been very few books which mention both Gurdjieff and Jung, as they come from such different traditions, psychiatry (Jung) and mysticism (Gurdjieff). However, I did find one book which attempts some degree of synthesis between Jung and Gurdjieff: J. G. Bennett's *A Spiritual Psychology* (1964, 1974). This is what Bennett says:

> For a long time, I found it hard to reconcile Jung and Gurdjieff. . . . Recently, I have come to an interesting conclusion and that is that Jung and Gurdjieff are interested in complementary, and therefore seemingly contradictory, aspects of human nature. . . . Jung distinguished two pairs; rational, consisting of thought and feeling and irrational consisting of sensation and intuition. I personally prefer Gurdjieff's three functions: instinctive-motor, emotional and intellectual. The difference is possibly more one of classification than a disagreement as to the facts. Knowledge of Jung's four functions are useful for diagnosing troubles of which the patient is not conscious. Observation of Gurdjieff's three functions can help us to achieve balance. [40]

Do Gurdjieff and Jung agree on the nature of the self? Is Gurdjieff's permanent 'I' the archetype of the Self of which Jung speaks?
I would suspect so – but the self is something to be experienced – for both Gurdjieff and Jung – not defined.
Is God a reality for Gurdjieff? We have seen some evidence of Gurdjieff's thoughts on God already in his personal revelation during his recuperation from a gunshot wound, and in his notion of "the Absolute." Gurdjieff gave a talk in New York City in 1924 called "God the Word." Here are some passages:

> At the beginning of every religion we find an affirmation of God the Word and the Word-God.

> One teaching says that when the world was still nothing, there were emanations, there was God the Word. God the Word is the world. God said: "Let it be so," and sent the Father and the Son. He is always sending the Father and the Son. And once He sent the Holy Ghost . . .

> Take the Ray of Creation. At the top is the Absolute, God the Word,

divided into three: God the Father, God the Son and God the Holy Ghost.

The Absolute creates in accordance with the same law. [The Law of the Three]. Only in this case all three forces necessary to produce a new manifestation are in the Absolute Himself. He sends them forth from himself, emanates' them. [41]

How does man relate to God in Gurdjieff's system? "In our system we are similar to God – threefold." [43] The Christian mystics and saints considered the Trinity to be inherent within man's soul, as well. Gurdjieff's spiritual psychology can be considered a form of esoteric Christianity. He said that himself. In this way, both Gurdjieff's and Jung's psychology could be called "Gnostic Christian." They both went "beyond faith" (they thought so anyway) to direct knowing of things psychic and spiritual; even beyond knowing to being. Both of their psychologies center on the Self which they see as a sort of *Imago Dei*. They are not far from the Christian mystics in this. Gurdjieff's system makes more allowance for the state which we have called, in Bucke's terms "Cosmic Consciousness." Gurdjieff called it "objective consciousness." Gurdjieff was, after all, a mystic as well as a psychologist. He studied in (at least) Christian, Sufi, and Tibetan Buddhist mystical schools. He was also an expert in hypnotism, the psychology of suggestion; he attributed human beings' suggestibility to the "organ Kundabuffer" in *Beelzebub's Tales to His Grandson*.

Gurdjieff said that there were three lines to the work: The first is "know thyself," the second is "enduring the manifestations of others," and the third is "selfless service." Gurdjieff's is the supreme psychology of "self work."

A CONTEMPORARY PSYCHIATRIST AND PSYCHOLOGIST WHO INCORPORATE GURDJIEFF'S THOUGHT IN THEIR WORK

Claudio Naranjo, M.D. is a psychiatrist who grew up in Chile, practices psychiatry, as well as leads spiritual growth groups in the San Francisco Bay area. He took the Arica training under Oscar Ichazo. This author had a chance to speak with Dr. Naranjo on one occasion some years ago about this. Naranjo wrote a book called *The One Quest* (1972) which is an attempt to integrate the depth psychologies with mystical teachings. In a section of his book called "Unity: Resolution and Transcendence of Conflicts," Naranjo writes about the various integrative psychologies, such as

Jung's analytical psychology, Assagioli's psychosynthesis, and even Freud's psychoanalysis. All of these stem from the recognition that the ordinary state of man, and, to a much greater extent, the pathological, is characterized "by conflicts, splits, dissociation, and contradictions between the psychological functions or personality fragments."[43] Whatever the terminology of the psychological theorist, it is reconciliation and collaboration between the conflicting elements of psychological life that is sought, i.e. *integration*. In this context, Naranjo discusses Gurdjieff's work:

> Gurdjieff, in speaking of such integration between body, feelings, and the intellectual function, compares it to a coach with its horse and driver, and points out that what is needed is a development of reins that go between driver and horse, and shafts between the horse and the coach.[44]

What do you think driver, horse, and coach symbolize? Respectively: the intellectual, emotional, and moving centers. Both Gurdjieff and Jung *personified* (as dreams do) elements of the psyche; this is useful.

Jean Houston, Ph.D. holds doctorates in both philosophy of religion and psychology. She is an author and lecturer of international repute. In Dr. Houston's book, *The Possible Human* (1982), she has a discussion of Gurdjieff's work in a chapter entitled: "Awakening the Brain."

> . . . there is a renewed interest in the work of Gurdjieff, who dedicated his life to developing processes that would allow the brain to "wake up." Gurdjieff stated that we have three "brains," or centers, that direct action. Each of these brains can be trained, and this training can be generalized so that students will be able to develop their mental faculties to such an extent that a great deal of learning can be accomplished with great ease.[45]

Dr. Houston herself has developed a remarkable panoply of exercises and techniques designed to develop human intellectual, emotional, and moving or kinesthetic functions. She sees these as not "separate," but as interacting "inter-modally" in the brain-mind. One implication of this is that training in swordsmanship (moving center – Houston herself is an expert swordswoman) may improve mathematics (intellectual center). Judo or Tai Chi Chuan training (moving center – these are two of this author's hobbies) may improve writing skills (intellectual center). It is well-known that jogging or swimming (moving center) helps to alleviate depression (emotional center disorder).

8

Abraham Maslow's Humanistic and Transpersonal Psychology

Abraham Maslow was a shy Jewish boy who grew up in Brooklyn, New York. He said that he was isolated and unhappy as a boy. He spent his time in libraries, among books, almost without friends. His later creation of "humanistic psychology" could be seen, in part, as a compensation for his childhood loneliness and isolation. As the young Maslow matured, he began to appreciate such philosophers as Benedict de Spinoza, Henri Bergson, and Alfred North Whitehead. Maslow said that his reading of William Graham Sumner's *Folkways* was a "Mount Everest in my life."[1]

Maslow married early at the age of twenty; his wife was nineteen. He was a student at the University of Wisconsin where he majored in psychology. This was the behaviorist era in academic psychology, and Maslow was no exception in his enthusiasm for S-R psychology. He said:

> I had discovered J. B. Watson, and I was sold on behaviorism.[2]

At the University of Wisconsin, Maslow got involved in animal behavioristic research, and studied monkeys under the guidance of Professor Harry Harlow. He went on to do his doctoral dissertation on the dominance characteristics of monkeys. Concerning his behavioristic days in psychology, Maslow wrote the following in a journal entry of August, 1968 (many years later):

> Behaviorism has done a lot. It was the beautiful program of Watson that brought me into psychology. But its fatal flaw is that it's good for the lab and in the lab, but you put it on and take it off like a lab coat. It's useless in the home with your kids and wife and friends. It does not generate an [adequate] image of man, a philosophy of life, a concep-

235

tion of human nature. It's not [an adequate] guide to living, to values, to choices . . .[3]

At the time that Maslow wrote the above, he had already founded "transpersonal psychology." Forty years earlier, as an under-graduate at the University of Wisconsin, this is what Maslow wrote about the nineteenth-century transcendentalist philosopher, Ralph Waldo Emerson, in a philosophy term paper dated October 23, 1928:

> I abhor with all the vehemence that is in me, Emerson and his like. I have an illustrious excuse and example. Schopenhauer inveighed with all the might of his piercing satire against those whom he called "metaphysicians of the people," and I am sure he would have included among these Emerson.
>
> Let us lay down our reasons in hard words. Emerson, I say, is a wordy preacher, a superstitious mystic, a shoddy thinker (if I can dignify him by even calling him thinker) and finally as bad a philosopher as it is possible for a man to be. He rises calmly above all logic and rules of thought by which all other poor mortals are constrained. He is but a poet (a poor one to be sure) masquerading as a deep thinker.
>
> First of all and most important, Emerson believes or believed in a personal God, a resurrection and all the other paraphenalia and stock-in-trade of the New England minister. This automatically debars him from being placed in the ranks of philosophy, which is a denial of all dogma, revelation, and supernaturalism.
>
> Theology attempts to find its justification outside itself, but philosophy has no authorities to appeal to and no absolute criteria to measure its concepts by. I am willing, then, to admit Emerson as a theologian, but as a philosopher – never![4]

This is a strange beginning, this vitriolic attack on the great American transcendentalist philosopher, Ralph Waldo Emerson, friend and colleague of Henry David Thoreau, by the young Maslow who was to become the future founder of "transpersonal psychology" with its emphasis upon self-realization and transcendent experiences. This seeming disparity between his youthful and later adult views is not the only area of contradiction in Maslow's life and thought. At the time of the above undergraduate term paper, Maslow was already a confirmed atheist, and in this respect he never really changed, in the disclaiming of the supernatural dimension, even in his days as founding father of transpersonal psychology. Maslow the transpersonalist was never sympathetic to theistic religion, and this still holds true in transpersonal psychology today, although there is considerable sympathy expressed for non-theistic Buddhism in its journal articles. Maslow became the "great naturalizer" of religious experience. We will look at this more later.

After the attainment of his doctorate at the University of Wisconsin, Maslow worked for two years with the famous psychologist, Edward L. Thorndike, as a Carnegie Fellow at Columbia University.[5] Thorndike was widely known for his animal learning experiments. Maslow parted with Thorndike in 1937 and accepted his first teaching position at Brooklyn College. It was in New York City that Maslow came into contact with many great figures in psychology and social science from Europe and America, including Max Wertheimer, Kurt Koffka, Karen Horney, Ruth Benedict, Margaret Mead, and Gregory Bateson.[6] He became familiar with two "imports" from Europe: psychoanalysis and Gestalt psychology.

In the late 1930s, with World War II rapidly approaching, Maslow felt a strong identification with his Jewish identity in a cultural, but not a religious sense. European Jewish refugees were escaping to this country, and among them were some of the major figures of psychology, both academic and clinical. New York was their gathering place. In this era of darkest despair for European Jewry, Maslow made the decision to study the higher aspects of human nature:

> I wanted to prove that human beings are capable of something grander than war and prejudice and hatred.[7]

Maslow said that he wanted to make science consider the problems that were always handled in the past by religion, philosophy, ethics, literature, and art. Maslow spent one summer with Canadian Blackfoot Indians in Alberta Province, and he found them to be a gentle people remarkably free of the aggression and cruelty of Western civilization.[8]

Maslow became increasingly critical of the mechanistic behavioristic psychology and the neurosis-oriented Freudian psychology – both of which hardly sought for the higher levels of humankind. He felt that if you wanted to understand *mental health*, you had to study the mentally healthy, not the neurotic and mentally ill, as Freud had done. He called for a "science of self-actualizing people."[9] Maslow held the characteristic liberal optimism about human nature, as contrasted with the typical conservative pessimism:

> The fact is that people are good, if only their fundamental wishes are satisfied, their wishes for affection and security. Give people affection and security, and they will give affection and be secure in their feelings and behavior. [10]

What of badness and evil in Maslow's view?

> Nasty behavior is there obviously. The only question is, why does such behavior occur? Most people think vicious behavior comes from vicious people. This is untrue. Others think that people are mean because they themselves expect meanness from others. This is more true. Why is it that people behave badly? Why are they cruel and bad? In a word, it is because they are not liked. The insecurity cycle – from this flows everything. First of all, suspicion and mistrust, loss of self-esteem with attempts to compensate. If you don't like me, you may and probably will hurt me . . . If you hurt me, I'll hurt you first. The person who behaves badly behaves so because of hurts, actual and expected, and lashes out in self-defense, as a cornered animal might. [11]

This remarkably simplistic view of good and evil, essentially a modern secular version of the early Christian theological concept of *privatio boni*, which taught that good alone is real, evil being a diminution of good (St. Augustine, Origen, etc.), informs the humanist, Maslow. Jesus himself cannot be accused of ignoring evil's reality, which he encountered directly, and overcame. The Shadow is a *very real fact* to be recognized and integrated, if one is to become whole. That is, one must *acknowledge* the dark side of oneself – the "inner enemy." It is sophomorphic Pollyannaism to say, as Maslow does, that people "behave badly" only because of their "sense of insecurity," or because "they are not liked," or because they have suffered "frustrations in their lives." Are we to believe that the infamous Heinrich Himmler, or Josef Gobbels, for example, would have been exemplary human beings if only they had been "bathed in love" as children or adolescents? In the case of the genocidal doctor, Josef Mengele, the "angel of death" at Auschwitz, a recent *Time* magazine article indicated that he was the pampered son of very wealthy German parents who put him through graduate and medical schools where he earned Ph.D. and M.D., only to use his education and training for evil purposes. He sent 400,000 Jews to their deaths in Auschwitz's gas chambers, as well as conducting inhuman "medical experiments." In the view of traditional Judaism, and original Christianity, its offspring, the soul can choose freely between good and evil. This implies that there *is good and evil.*

Nevertheless, Maslow does provide a kind of "counterbalance," as it were, to the darker view of man that is common to both behaviorism and psychoanalysis, which Maslow calls the "first" and "second force." He refers to his humanistic psychology as the "third force." In keeping with this, he refers to his transpersonal psychology as the "fourth force," although, truthfully, it is difficult to detect a really meaningful difference between these two.

It is possible that Maslow's concern with "man's essential goodness" was his antidote to his own sense of insecurity and low self-esteem that he experienced from his childhood days until his young adulthood. In his diaries, he recorded that his father said at a family gathering, "Have you ever seen anyone uglier than Abe?"[12] He also records that, during his courtship, he was amazed that his wife would love someone as worthless and ugly as himself. In the Adlerian psychology, Maslow's extreme overemphasis on man's "goodness" could be seen as compensatory to his unconscious sense of worthlessness based upon a traumatic childhood experience with a cruel father, and a mother whom he described as a "bad person" in his writings. This speculation is supported by the following diary note to himself:

> Proposition: that human beings are at birth . . . deep down, secure and with good self-esteem . . . And then societies *do* something to this Natural Personality, twist it, shape it, repress it.[13]

He goes really far along this line of thought when he says:

> . . . in my clinical work I have always found that *anyone*, however nasty and perverted and neurotic, was really sweet and loving and nice underneath, and the only postulate I had to make in treating them was that they didn't get as much love as they needed . . .[14]

"Anyone" is really "sweet," "loving," and "nice" underneath? A more one-sided view of human nature is difficult to find anywhere in the history of psychology from ancient times. Once again, man is postulated to be "basically good" despite all evidence to the contrary! His view that "all is good" really obliterates *real goodness* which only has a reality in contradistinction to *real badness*. We should like to distinguish, should we not, between the heroic altruism of a Corrie Ten Boom, the Dutch lady who hid Jews in her home at the risk of her life during World War II, and the notorious evil of an Adolf Eichmann who oversaw the extermination of the Jews? I would wish to make this distinction. Maslow, in consistency with his views, would have to claim that they were both "really nice" underneath! After reading some of Maslow's do-good humanism, one can appreciate even Freud's (the "second force") postulation of both the life instinct, *eros*, and the death instinct, *thanatos*. Surely there are those who *choose* to serve life, whereas there are also those who *choose* to serve death. In the Torah, Moses gave the Israelites *exactly that choice*.★ Maslow's humanism offers no choice; both the bad and the good are "basically good." Freud's psychoanalysis is, in a real sense, more biblical in its *eros* and *thanatos* theory. The Hasids say that man has both a *yetzer tov*, a "good urge," and a *yetzer hara*, a "bad urge."

Nonetheless, in his writings Maslow frequently distinguishes between his optimistic humanistic psychology, and its "rivals," psychoanalysis (Freud) and behaviorism (Watson). For psychoanalysis, the basic reality in man is the "id," a kind of seething, mindless chaos of selfish, erotic and destructive impulses, which are only held in check by the reality testing of the ego, and the gradually acquired moral injunctions of the superego. If it were not for these, we would fall into incest, murder, and cannibalism! For the behaviorists, there is no innate goodness *or* badness. Man is basically neutral biological "stuff." All of man's behavior is conditioned reflexes "shaped" by the environment.

In contradistinction to the id "pleasure principle" motivation theory of psychoanalysis, and the reflex "tension reduction" motivation theory of behaviorism, Maslow's humanistic psychology postulates a hierarchy of motives that range from the "drive reduction" needs of sex, hunger, and thirst, to the "security" needs of a home, a secure job, a supportive environment, to "belongingness needs," need for friends and colleagues, to "self-esteem" needs for achievement, mastery, etc., to the need for "self-actualization." What does this mean?

> A musician must make music, an artist must paint, a poet must write, if he is to be ultimately at peace with himself. What a man *can* be, he *must* be. This need we may call self-actualization.[15]

Maslow felt that all persons have at birth an innate need for self-actualization. Almost all of us get it knocked out of us before we have a chance to develop it, however. This is in keeping with Maslow's basically liberal humanism which sees society as the "enemy" of man's innate potential. Freud, was the conservative.

★ "I set before thee life and death, the blessing and the curse, therefore choose life."

He saw society as the necessary "check" to man's basically selfish and destructive impulses. These are opposite points of view. (Perhaps, the truth includes both sides?)

Maslow felt that there were some, perhaps due to the good fortune of propitious childrearing circumstances, who did not lose their innate true selfhood. He calls these "self-actualized persons." Their creative powers have not been "snuffed out." Maslow intuited that to study self-actualizing persons was to learn what human nature was really like. Over the years, Maslow kept a GHB, or "Good Human Being" notebook, in an attempt to discover the nature of self-actualizing people whom he believed were the "true human race." He first studied college students, as professors are wont to do, but found no self-actualizers among them (only a few with slight potential!). He personally knew certain individuals whom he believed to be "self-actualizers," e.g., Max Wertheimer, the Gestalt psychologist, and Ruth Benedict, the anthropologist.

Maslow's book, *Motivation and Personality* (1954) is basically about his studies of self-actualizers. He eventually chose his subjects from among personal acquaintances, friends, and public historical figures. These were Maslow's criteria of selection:

> The first clinical definition, on the basis of which subjects were finally chosen or rejected, had a positive as well as a negative side. The negative criteria were an absence of neurosis, psychopathic personality, psychosis, or strong tendencies in these directions . . . The positive criterion for selection was positive evidence of self-actualization (SA), as yet a difficult syndrome to describe accurately. For the purposes of this discussion, it may be loosely described as the full use and exploitation of talents, capacities, potentialities, etc.[16]

Such people, Maslow says, seem to be fulfilling themselves, reminding him of Nietzsche's exhortation: "Become what thou art!"[17] Among Maslow's case examples were such famous persons as Abraham Lincoln, Thomas Jefferson, Albert Einstein, Eleanor Roosevelt, Jane Adams, William James, Spinoza, Franklin Delano Roosevelt, Walt Whitman, etc. He chooses the greats of the human race.

One thing that immediately struck me about Maslow's conception is that it reminds me of the "once born" of James: Those who are born with, and never lose, their congenital optimism. This seems to be his conception. It completely excludes the "twice born," those who have been "born again" in the words of Jesus.

James discussed two great cases of the "twice born," Leo Tolstoy and John Bunyan. Both were literary men of noble accomplishment. Both transmuted their suffering into wisdom. But, both would probably be excluded from Maslow's elitist criteria of the "self-actualizing" because they both suffered most severely from depressions. This criteria of ruling out those who suffer neurosis would probably eliminate most of the great mystics, too, such as St. John of the Cross who certainly suffered his "dark night of the soul." This lack of compassion for the wounded soul bothers me. It is from the wounded ones oft-times that the greatest creative works come. There is a Christian saying: "In the service of Love, only the wounded may serve." Christ Himself was a wounded one. Maslow utterly ignores the dimension of woundedness and suffering in the deeper development of the soul. There is again a shallowness here.

Yet, there is no doubt, as James discussed, that there are the healthy-minded who have never suffered and retain a rather innate wholeness about them. I knew a very few such persons myself who reminded me very much of Maslow's self-actualizing ones. They had an innocent beauty about them, and a healthiness of soul, that is rare indeed. They seem not to have known suffering in their souls. Their outlooks were perennially positive. These people give one a lot of joy. But, none of these persons was a creator of any sort. Some of those whom Maslow lists as self-actualizers were not once born, I think, but twice born, including certainly, Abraham Lincoln and William James, both of whom admitted to profound depressions in their autobiographical writings.

Maslow, in *Motivation and Personality*, as in many of his other writings, has the peculiar and rather obsessive habit of making endless lists of characteristics. In this work, he lists the traits of self-actualizing persons. This is what he listed about self-actualizers:[18]

1. More efficient Perception of Reality
2. Acceptance (Self, Others, Nature)
3. Spontaneity
4. Problem-Centering
5. The Quality of Detachment
5. Autonomy, Independence of Culture and Environment
6. Continued Freshness or Appreciation
7. The Mystic Experience
8. Gemeinschaftsgefühl (a deep sympathy for others)

 9. Deeper Interpersonal Relations
10. The Democratic Character Structure
11. Discrimination between Means and Ends
12. Philosophical, Unhostile Sense of Humor
13. Creativeness
14. Resistance to Enculturation
15. Imperfections of Self-Actualizing People (ordinary human feelings of thoughtlessness, vanity, pride, temper outbursts, and occasional ruthlessness)

Maslow describes each one of these traits at length, but I think you will get the "gestalt" by this list of qualities of the self-actualizing person.

Quite unlike neurotics who are torn by inner conflicts, these self-actualizers have attained a degree of integration that is rare. They have resolved the dichotomies that usually tear others apart to one degree or another. Maslow states:

> For example, the age old opposition between heart and head, reason and instinct, or cognition and conation was seen to disappear in healthy people where they become synergic rather than antagonists, and where conflict disappears . . .[19]

Maslow uses the Freudian psychoanalytic terminology when he says:

> In these people, the id, the ego, and the superego are collaborative and synergic; they do not war with each other . . . as they do in neurotic people.[20]

This is an interesting insight that in itself integrates, to some degree, Freud's psychology with Maslow's. It is only that Freud's "subjects" were the neurotic and the emotionally crippled, and Maslow's were the healthy and self-actualizing.

Maslow has the insight, despite his atheism, to note that his self-actualizers *resemble* what religious cultures have called the Godly man, the Saint, the Tzaddek, the Bodhisattva, and so on. He states that few of his subjects were orthodoxly religious, "but on the other hand *only one* describes himself as an atheist."[21] The italics are mine: I had the strong intuition that this "only one" is Maslow himself! The self-actualizing persons I have known were *more than religious*. They were positively *connected with God*. One man whom I knew, J.S., spoke of God as "the boss," and he seemed to be in easy two-way dialogue with him in the most natural way. If Maslow listed himself as a "self-actualizer," I think he erred. At best, he wishes that he were. The self-actualized do not tend to be atheists.

Maslow wrote another book on the subject of self-actualizing people called *The Farthest Reaches of Human Nature* (1971). In it he speaks of the self-actualizing person as a "superior specimen" of humanity, even biological assays. This begins to *resemble* the Nazi "master race" theory too closely! I heard it reported that another famous psychologist (who shall go unnamed) called Maslow a "liberal fascist" to his face at the Esalen Institute, the Mecca of the human potential movement. There may be a little truth in this accusation. What about those who although severely wounded, in body or soul, have overcome their handicaps and made very real achievements and contributions to humanity? These persons who overcome the odds are ignored by Maslow.

Maslow makes an interesting biblical observation when he says that most of us suffer from a "Jonah complex." We are afraid to truly utilize our real potentials for fear we might become who we really are and disprove our parents' predictions that we "will never amount to anything." We might even become notable persons in this world. He also calls this "fear of one's greatness" or the "evasion of one's destiny."[22]

Maslow makes the point that self-actualizing people are, without a single exception, involved in a cause outside of themselves. They all have a sense of calling or vocation. They are working at something which has called them, and which they must serve, and which they, in fact, love. The work-joy dichotomy is non-existent in them. Their work is their joy.

One thing that Maslow noted is that self-actualizing people tend to have "mystic experiences." Later, Maslow dropped the religious term, "mystic experience," and replaced it with the more neutral and naturalistic term, "peak experience." He stuck with the latter term throughout his writings. I will argue later that a peak experience is not the same thing as a mystic experience, although they may have some slight overlap.

Maslow wrote a book on mystic, or peak experiences called *Religion, Values, and Peak Experiences* (1964). This book is Maslow's attempt to "naturalize" mysticism. In it he states:

> I want to demonstrate that spiritual values have naturalistic meaning, that they are not the exclusive possession of organized churches, that they do not need supernatural concepts to validate them, but they are well within the jurisdiction of a suitably enlarged science, and that, therefore, they are the general responsibility of mankind.[23]

I do not know where Maslow got the idea of himself as the "liberator" of humanity from organized religion, and the Church, and the "rescuer" of spiritual experience from a religious context, but that is evidently his self-conception. I do not fully understand his antipathy to traditional religion, either, except that he (1) did not like his mother, and (2) she was a traditional Jew who followed Orthodox practices.

Maslow, and the transpersonalists, wish to have religious experiences without religion, and transcendent experiences without God. I think Maslow and his followers are involved in some serious internal contradictions here. Maslow does not like the "split" condition, but he and his followers split off religious experience, or what they call religious experience, from God.

To be fair to Maslow, he is as against "positivistic science" as he is against "organized religion." He feels that both of these camps "dichotomize" reality, choosing one side of the dichotomy or the other. Maslow seems to want to include what used to be called religious or spiritual experience in his "enlarged concept of science."

The realm of the *sacred* has traditionally been excluded from science, and made the exclusive property of religion. Maslow wants to re-include "naturalistic religious experience, creativity, symbolism, play, the theory of love, mystical and peak experiences, not to mention poetry, art, and a lot more . . ."[24] back into science. Why include everything in science, though? Why not re-include science into religion? Maslow is one-sided in this "everything is science" view, too, as he was in his "everything is good" theory.

Maslow comes to what he calls the "core religious," or the "transcendent," or the "peak experience." He makes the claim, similar to Bucke and James here, that:

> The very beginning, the intrinsic core, the universal nucleus of every known high religion . . . has been the private, lonely, personal illumination, revelation, or ecstasy of some acutely sensitive prophet or seer. The high religions call themselves revealed religions and each of them tends to rest its validity, its function, and, its right to exist on the codification and the communication of this original mystic experience or revelation from the lonely prophet to the masses of human beings in general.[25]

I agree with Bucke, James, and Maslow on this claim that religions began with the private revelations of the seer or prophet. These experiences are found in the holy scriptures of various religions: Moses at the burning bush, Jesus at the River Jordan,

Muhammed on Mount Hira, etc. I wrote about these private revelations or illuminations of the Masters in my first book, *Physicians of the Soul* (1982).

Maslow goes on to make a claim I cannot agree with:

> But it has recently begun to appear that these "revelations" can be subsumed under the head of the "peak experiences" or "ecstasies" or "transcendent" experiences which are now being eagerly investigated by many psychologists.[26]

We will see that Maslow's "peak experience" bears little relation to the true religious or mystical experience or what Bucke called "Cosmic Consciousness." What Maslow investigated was relatively superficial by comparison. Yet, Maslow claims with perfect assuredness:

> ... it is very likely, indeed almost certain, that these older reports, phrased in terms of supernatural revelation, were, in fact, perfectly natural, human peak-experiences of the kind that can be easily examined today, which, however, were phrased in terms of whatever conceptual, cultural, and linguistic framework the particular seer had available in his time.[27]

Isn't it fine, Maslow is saying, that in this "modern day and age," we can "naturalize" everything, including religious experience and revelation? In the next statement, he subsumes religion to "natural science":

> In a word, we can study today what happened in the past and was then explainable in supernatural terms only. But so doing, we are enabled to examine religion in all its facets and in all its meanings in a way that makes it part of science rather than something outside and exclusive of it.[28]

In Maslow's transpersonal psychology, an outgrowth of his humanistic psychology, religion is, thereby, swallowed up by the Great God Science! I have trouble with Maslow's trouble with the term "supernatural" which he finds so "distasteful" in comparison with the term "natural" which he is so comfortable with. This is like his "all is good" theory; it blurs all meaningful distinctions. If *everything* is "natural," what in the world can the word, "natural" mean? It is only in contrast to "supernatural," that "natural" has any meaning. Just semantically, if you employ one end of the dichotomy, you imply its opposite. Experientially, in the history of mysticism and the spiritual path, there are quite real criteria for distinguishing between experiences of the natural and the supernatural. Theologically, there is a real distinction, as well, which has some relation to the distinction between "subject" and "object." "Natural" to me implies "object." "Naturalizing" means turning everything into an "object." The recognition of the supernatural is the recognition of the "subject," including our selves, and the Supreme Self (I AM THAT I AM).

Maslow contrasts the lonely prophet who founded the religion with the legalist or priest type who keeps it going in its traditional forms. Here, he recognizes a real distinction.

> The characteristic prophet is a lonely man who has discovered his truth about the world, the cosmos, ethics, God, and his own identity from within, from his own personal experiences, from what he would consider to be a revelation. [29]

Maslow contrasts this with the legalist-ecclesiastic who is loyal to the established structures and codes of the religious organization, be it church, synagogue, mosque, etc. The latter is built upon the prophet's original revelation, but has the tendency to be static and conservative. It is, however, a way of making revelation available in a "watered down" form for the masses. I think there is truth in this. Whether this is good or bad is another question. Probably both prophet and priest are needed in mankind's socio-religious life.

There are "peakers" and there are "non-peakers." The "peakers" are the mystic types. The "non-peakers" are persons or even institutions whose character structure and way of life forces him/her/them to be extremely rationalistic, or materialistic and mechanistic in *Weltanschauung*. Freud and Watson would be good examples of this. They surely were not mystic types. Maslow relates this to the compulsive-obsessive person who organizes his life around the denial and control of emotion. I glanced at B. F. Skinner's three-volume autobiography the other day, and was amazed by his statement that he "did not believe in feeling." I think B. F. Skinner would qualify as a "non-peaker" in Maslow's terms. There is, too, an obsessive-compulsive aspect to both behaviorism and Freudianism in the attempt of both of these psychological schools to "reduce" everything to their own terms, be it Stimulus and Response, or Id, Ego, and Superego.

Maslow has a curiously refreshing insight when he says that ". . . organized religion can be thought of as an effort to communicate peak-experiences to non-peakers . . ." [30] I think he has struck upon something there. In church and synagogue, usually, we have readings, hymns, ceremonies, and rituals, and the recitation of dogmas, e.g. the Nicene Creed, but we rarely have *spiritual experiences*. On the other hand, the Bible that we read is full of accounts of dreams, visions, and revelations!

> If you look closely at the internal history of most of the world religions, you will find that each one very soon tends to divide into a left-wing and a right-wing, that is, into the peakers, the mystics, the transcenders, or the privately religious people, on the one hand, and, on the other, into those who concretize the religious symbols and metaphors, who worship little pieces of wood rather than what the objects stand for, those who take verbal formulas literally, forgetting the original meaning of these words, and, perhaps most important, those who take the organization, the church, as primary and as more important than the prophet and his original revelations.[31]

I could not agree more with Maslow in these insights. They bring to mind Dostoevski's famous Grand Inquisitor passage in the *Brothers Karamazov*. Dostoevski makes the point that Jesus himself would have been imprisoned or executed as a "dangerous heretic" in the very same Church of which he is the alleged spiritual head. His views would have been regarded as far too radical!

Maslow makes the claim that the peak experience may be the model of the religious revelations, or the religious illuminations, or the conversion experience which have played so great a role in the history of humankind's religions. He says that we may now hope to understand more about the "big revelations" and "illuminations" upon which the high religions were founded. I suppose he has in mind here such events in religious history as Moses' illumination at the "burning bush," Jesus' "holy spirit" baptism at the River Jordan, and the Buddha's enlightenment under the "Bodhi Tree." I congratulate Maslow for his courage to look at these mighty events of human experience. However, I cannot agree with the "naturalistic turn" that he makes in interpreting them as merely more powerful than usual "peak experiences." Maslow does point to the promising possibility of research into the psychedelic drugs, such as LSD and psilocybin in the study of peak experiences (see the Masters/Houston work in the next chapter).

Maslow claims in his major book on the subject, *Religion, Values, and Peak Experiences*, that the essential core-religious experience may be embedded in a theistic supernaturalistic context or in a naturalistic non-theistic context. Maslow, as you may have guessed, opts for the latter "naturalistic non-theistic context," and to this day, transpersonal psychologists still lean in that direction of their founding father. I still find it puzzling to be devoted to spiritual and religious experience as a primary value, and on the other hand, to deny the source of such experience, whom men/ women have called God, Allah, Brahman, YHWH, and so on. If this is not a split, I do not know what is.

The transpersonal psychology founder, Maslow, asserts that his findings indicate that "all or almost all people have or can have peak experiences."[32] This may be true in the terms in which Maslow defines "peak experiences," but it is quite another question whether peak experience = the religious-mystical experience of which Bucke and James wrote so powerfully.

What did Maslow do to empirically research the "peak experience?" He devised a quite simplistic (in my opinion) question which he administered to hundreds of subjects. This was the question:

> I would like you to think of the most wonderful experience or experiences of your life: happiest moments, ecstatic moments, moments of rapture, perhaps being in love, or from listening to music or suddenly "being hit" by a book or a painting, or from some great creative moment. First list these. And then try to tell me how you feel in such acute moments, how you feel differently from the way you feel at other times, how you are at the moment a different person in some ways. [With other subjects the questioning asked rather about the ways in which the world looked different.].[33]

Maslow reports on the results of this questionnaire research in a most abstract way, omitting all references to actual experiences, in his book, *Toward a Psychology of Being* (1968). He gives not one single actual instance of a peak experience in concrete form. In this, he is very unlike either Bucke or James who catalogued many actual mystical or religious experiences in full detail as the persons in question described them, in most cases. This is almost totally absent in Maslow. This book consists of many abstract lists. In this work, he calls peak experiences by the new name, "B-cognition," having to do with cognizing Being. These are the characteristics of B-cognitions based upon Maslow's abstracting, presumably, from his research data of response to the above peak experience questionnaire:

1. In B-cognition the experience or the object tends to be seen as a whole, as a complete unit, detached from relations, from possible usefulness, from expediency, and from purpose.

2. When there is B-cognition, the percept is exclusively and fully attended to. This may be called 'total attention.'
3. B-cognition, because it makes human–irrelevance more possible, enables us thereby to see more truly the nature of the objects in itself.
4. One difference between B-cognitions and average cognition which is now emerging in my studies, but of which I am as yet uncertain is that repeated *B-cognizing seems to make perception richer.*
5. My findings indicate that in the normal perceptions of self-actualizing people and in the more occasional peak-experiences of average people, *perception can be relatively ego-transcending, self-forgetful, egoless.*
6. *The peak-experience is felt as a self-validating, self-justifying moment which carries its own intrinsic value with it.* That is to say it is an end in itself, what we may call an end-experience rather than a means–experience.
7. In *all the common peak experiences which I have studied, there is a characteristic disorientation in time and space.* It would be accurate to say that in these moments the person is outside of time and space subjectively.
8. To start at the end first, *the peak experience is only good and desirable, and is never experienced as evil or undesirable.* The experience is intrinsically valid; the experience is perfect, complete and needs nothing else. [34]

You get the idea. In another listing, Maslow abstracts fourteen (why not fifteen or twenty? I suppose this is where Maslow ran out of ideas) B-values, which are:

1. wholeness	8. beauty
2. perfection	9. goodness
3. completion	10. uniqueness
4. justice	11. effortlessness
5. aliveness	12. playfulness
6. richness	13. truth
7. simplicity	14. self-sufficiency [35]

Becoming rather frustrated and bored with Maslow's lists of abstract terms in his books from which I have quoted, and wishing to get at the original data of his research, I went back to his earliest published research paper on "peak experiences" which is contained in the second issue of the *Journal of Humanistic Psychology*

(1962) in an article entitled "Lessons From Peak Experiences." He calls this "an excursion into the psychology of health, or of the human being at his best."[36]

In this article, he reports (this is his earliest writing on the subject) that these healthy persons (he does not yet use the term "self-actualizers") "tended to report having had something like mystic experiences. . ."[37] These were moments of pure happiness, ecstasy, rapture, or bliss. There was the report in these experiences, according to Maslow, of having seen into the truth or essence of things.

Maslow states that: "The little that I had ever read about mystic experiences tied them in with religion, with visions of the supernatural. And, like most scientists, I had sniffed at them in disbelief and considered it all nonsense, maybe hallucinations, maybe hysteria – almost surely pathological."[38] Maslow admits to having read little about mystic experiences, and I think his later works indicate that he did not read much more! If he had, he would not have confounded his "peak experience" with the classic mystical experience.

Contrary to any idea that mystic experiences were pathological, Maslow found that they were had by the healthiest people. Maslow makes the claim, certainly *not* based upon the vast data of worldwide mysticism throughout history, that "These experiences mostly had nothing to do with religion – at least in the ordinary supernaturalistic sense."[39] He goes on to say that:

> . . . this was a *natural*, not a *supernatural* experience . . .[40]

It is very possible, as we shall soon see, that Maslow *did not deal with* true mystical experiences in his research. Yes, it is probably true that the experiences that he studied were, in fact, perfectly "natural" experiences. However, the experiences that Maslow did not deal with, but that Bucke and James did deal with, were, in fact, ones which implied a supernatural or divine origin.

Even in this paper, Maslow seems very reluctant to report his actual research data, and he gives only three examples of responses to his "peak experiences" questionnaire. These are the responses:

> For instance, a young mother scurrying around her kitchen and getting breakfast for her husband and young children. The sun was streaming in, the children, clean and nicely dressed, were chattering as they ate. The husband was casually playing with the children; but as she looked at them she was suddenly so overwhelmed with their

beauty and her great love for them, and her feelings of good fortune, that she went into a peak experience. [41]

A young man working his way through medical school by drumming in a jazz band reported years later, that in all his drumming he had three peaks when he suddenly felt like a great drummer and his performance was perfect. [42]

A hostess after a dinner party where everything had gone perfectly and it had been a fine evening, said good-bye to her last guest, sat down in a chair, looked around at the mess and went into a peak of great happiness and exhilaration. [43]

Yes, these are "peak experiences" that Maslow reports, i.e. they were "happy moments," but I deny most emphatically that they are reports of true mystical experiences, in James' terminology, or cosmic conscious experiences in Bucke's language. Another great authority on mystical experience was the English poet and novelist, Evelyn Underhill (1875–1941) who wrote many books on the subject, among them *Mysticism* which was first published in 1911. In it, she begins by speaking of the mystic type:

The most highly developed branches of the human family have in common one peculiar characteristic. They tend to produce – sporadically it is true, and often in the teeth of adverse external circumstances – a curious and definite type of personality; a type which refuses to be satisfied with that which other men call experience, and is inclined, in the words of its enemies, to "deny the world in order that it may find reality." We meet these persons in the east and the west; in the ancient, medieval, and modern worlds. Their one passion appears to be the prosecution of a certain spiritual and intangible quest: the finding of a "way out" or a "way back" to some desirable state in which they can satisfy their cravings for absolute truth. This quest, for them, has constituted the whole meaning of life. They have made for it without effort sacrifices which have appeared enormous to other men: and it is an indirect testimony to its objective actuality, that whatever the place or period in which they have arisen, their aims, doctrines and methods have been substantially the same. [44]

Underhill is describing the "mystic type," who has appeared in every time and in every culture of humanity, whose reports of a *mystic experience* have been substantially the same whether Jew, or Christian, or Moslem, or Buddhist. Do these persons whose quest for *absolute truth* represents the whole meaning of their life really resemble Maslow's three examples of cases of "peak experience": the housewife, the jazz musician (and medical student), and the hostess at the dinner party? I wonder. These are the only examples that Maslow gives in any of his writings that I have discovered to illustrate what he means by "peak experience." They are most assuredly not of the order of mystical experience as defined by the true specialists in this field. Underhill goes on to say:

> Under whatsoever symbols they have objectified their quest, none of these seekers have ever been able to assure the world that they have found, seen face to face, the Reality behind the veil. But if we may trust the reports of the mystics – and they are reports given with a strange accent of certainty and good faith – they have succeeded where all these others have failed, in establishing immediate communication between the spirit of man, entangled as they declare amongst material things, and that "Only Reality," that immaterial and final Being, which some philosophers call the Absolute, and most theologians call God. [45]

Contrast this with Maslow's claim that mystical experiences, which he renamed "peak experiences" are "natural" and not "supernatural." Maslow tells us, quite in contradiction to Underhill, and other experts on mysticism, that the terms "revelation," "salvation," and "heaven" are misleading and out of date, and now what was called religious experience "can be studied scientifically." [46] The experience of the Eternal has now been brought down to the level of the temporal by Maslow in his effort to naturalize religion and mysticism out of existence. He says:

> But think! Peak-experiences can very meaningfully be assimilated to – or even replace – the immature concepts in which Heaven is like a country club in some specific place, perhaps above the clouds. [47]

Freud has reduced God to the projection of the "father complex," and religious experience to the ego's re-submersion in the id ("oceanic experience"); Maslow now "progresses" to the point of assimilating religious or mystical experience to the "peak experiences" of humanistic and transpersonal psychology. Much of great importance may be lost in this process of assimilation! To quote Evelyn Underhill again:

> This [the Absolute, God], they say – and here many who are not mystics agree with them – is the hidden Truth which is the object of man's craving; the only satisfying goal of his quest. Hence, they should claim from us the same attention that we give to other explorers of countries in which we are not competent to adventure ourselves; for the mystics are the pioneers of the spiritual world, and we have no right to deny validity to their discoveries, merely because we lack the opportunity or the courage necessary to those who would prosecute such explorations for themselves. [48]

In a radio interview in 1960, the interviewer asked Maslow:

> Aren't these principles the same basic values that every religion and philosophy has attempted to find? How does your approach as a psychologist differ from the philosopher or theologian?[49]

Maslow replied:

> I think my approach differs tremendously . . . It is certainly true that mankind, throughout history, has looked for guiding values, for principles of right and wrong. But he has tended to look outside himself, outside of mankind, to a God, to some sort of sacred book perhaps . . . What I am doing is exploring the theory that you can find the values by which mankind must live, and for which man has always sought, by digging into the best people in depth. I believe, in other words, that I can find ultimate values which are right for mankind by observing the best of mankind.[50]

Maslow's concept of who is "the best of mankind" was definitely subjective and biased, for we read in his GHB (Good Human Being) Notebook, dated February 14, 1946:

> Pascal is out. Just religious stuff. Read Spinoza by L. Browne. Sounds wonderful [Spinoza was a pantheist].[51]

You will recall the account of Blaise Pascal's religious experience in the William James chapter. Underhill speaks about the scrap of parchment on which, around a rough drawing of a flaming cross, were written a few strange phrases which Pascal kept sewn into his coat and always wore on his person as a perpetual memorial to his supernal experience. It was his initiation into Sacred Reality in which his spiritual eyes were opened. To repeat what I have already written, but in Pascal's native French:

> Dieu d'Abraham, Dieu d'Isaac, Dieu de Jacob, Non des philosophes et des savants. Certitude. Certitude. Sentiment. Joie. Paix.[52]

"Not the God of philosophers and of scholars!" cries the philosopher and scholar, turned mystic, Pascal, in utter amazement. Pascal is a case of true mystical experience, although he was apparently "out" in Maslow's book. I think that this symbolizes the fact that transpersonal psychology as created and defined by Abraham Maslow does not delve into the realm of real religious experience, and deceives itself and others by calling it "peak experience." I met the well-known psychologist, Dr. Lawrence LeShan, who wrote a book on physics and mysticism, at a Transpersonal Psychology Conference. He told me that he had moved "beyond transpersonal psychology to God," in his words, as I recall them. The still confirmed atheist, Maslow, did not make this move, and died in 1970 at the age of sixty-two having founded both humanistic and transpersonal psychology.

TWO RELATED THEORIES: ROBERTO ASSAGIOLI AND VICTOR FRANKL

Assagioli

Roberto Assagioli was an Italian psychiatrist trained in psychoanalysis. He did a doctoral dissertation critical of Freud's views, and founded the Institute of Psychosynthesis in Rome in 1926. Assagioli points out that the term "mental synthesis" goes back to Janet. Assagioli synthesized many psychologies in his holistic theory which includes the lower unconscious of Freud, the collective unconscious of Jung, the conscious self, or ego, and a Higher Self.[53] The goal of his therapy is the conscious reconstruction of the personality via reaching the Higher Self. Assagioli's two books are *Psychosynthesis* (1965) and *The Act of Will* (1973).

1. The Lower Unconscious
2. The Middle Unconscious
3. The Higher Unconscious or Superconscious
4. The Field of Consciousness
5. The Conscious Self or "I"
6. The Higher Self
7. The Collective Unconscious

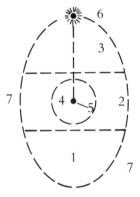

Figure 8.1   Assagioli's Model of the Psyche

Frankl

Victor Frankl was a Jewish psychiatrist who survived Auschwitz and other death camps of the Nazi era. He went on to become an existential psychiatrist, and the creator of logotherapy. In his fascinating books, including *The Unconscious God* (1948) and *The Will to Meaning* (1969), he stresses that beyond self-actualization is a human need for purpose and meaning which each person must find for himself. Frankl writes:

> Self-actualization is not man's ultimate destination. It is not his primary intention. Self-actualization, if made an end in itself, contradicts the self-transcendent quality of human existence. Like happiness, self-actualization is an effect, the effect of meaning fulfillment. Only to the extent to which man fulfills a meaning out there in the world, does he fulfill himself. If he sets out to actualize himself rather than fulfill a meaning, self-actualization immediately loses its justification.[54]

9

Sacred Psychology:
Contemporary and Ancient Forms

The paradigm shift away from materialism to a world in which *consciousness as such* is a primary factor has already taken place in the physics of David Bohm, the chemistry of Ilya Prigogine, and the biology of Rupert Sheldrake. But, the behavioral sciences still cleave tenaciously to the old paradigm of materialism-mechanism, and brand as "unscientific" anything that smacks of mind, soul, or spirit.★ The "new cognitivists" acknowledge "mind," but subsume it to neural computer programming. Freud himself, although he "analyzed" conscious and unconscious phenomena with brilliant acumen, ultimately subscribed to a materialist-reductionist view. This accounts for his reduction of religious experience to neurotic projections. Even in 1976, psychiatrists "classified" mystical experience as halfway between "normality" and "psychosis," as the following statement from the 1976 report of the Group for the Advancement of Psychiatry indicates:

> The psychiatrist will find mystical phenomena of interest because they can demonstrate forms of behavior intermediate between normality and psychosis . . .[1]

This same group of "learned" psychiatrists report on the case of one woman mystic:

> Her interests were reinvested in the fantasy universe, representing God, in which such problems do not exist, and she felt herself united with this God-Universe, a substitute for an unavailable or rejecting

★ This would include the data of parapsychology (e.g. ESP, clairvoyance, and psychokinesis), shamanism and psychic healing, reports of reincarnation, near-death experiences, and religious and mystical experiences. Even Jung's studies of archetypal symbolism in dreams have been denied "scientific acceptance."

parent. The mystical union made up for the rejection she feared from
her father. . . [2]

Shades of Freud's *The Future of an Illusion*! Obviously, materialism-
atheism is part of the paradigmatic worldview of these psychiatrists who authored this report on mysticism as the "halfway
house" between normality and psychosis, as defined by them.
One member of this group, Dr. Arthur J. Deikman, offered a
dissenting opinion:

> What is missing from the GAP report is any acknowledgement that
> the mystic who has completed his or her development may have access
> to an intuitive, immediate knowledge of reality. The authors assume
> the then known sensate pathways are the only means to acquire know-
> ledge of what is real . . . The eclectic ignorance of the authors has led
> them at one point to lump together Einstein, Jesus, Abraham Lincoln
> . . . Vincent Van Gogh, and St. John of the Cross. Interestingly
> enough, if the authors had pursued the case of Einstein alone, they
> might have come to the epistemological issue that is the core of
> mysticism and paid proper attention to it; for Einstein's modern dis-
> coveries, as well as the discoveries of natural philosophers thousands
> of years earlier, were based upon intuitive perception of the way things
> are. Such perceptions are the sources of our greatest advances in
> science . . . Furthermore, at least two books have been published
> recently documenting the strikingly close correspondence between the
> scientific conceptions of physicists and the insights of mystics . . .
> Thus it is truly remarkable to have a group of psychiatrists issue a
> report in 1976, in which the only comment they make on mystic
> perception of unity is that it represents a "reunion with parents."
> Nowhere in the report do we find the possibility that the perception of
> unity occurring in the higher forms of mysticism may be correct and
> that the ordinary perception of separateness and meaninglessness may
> be an illusion, as mystics claim. [3]

What Dr. Deikman is saying is that the psychiatrists may be the
dwellers in the dark cave of shadows, to use Plato's metaphor
from *The Republic*, and the mystic just may be the person who has
discovered his or her way to the light! The fantastic narrow-
mindedness of these psychiatrists' basic worldview or paradigm
makes it impossible for them to deal with the data on mysticism or
religious experience in any more enlightened way than to classify
it somewhere between "normality" and "psychosis." Their re-
liance on Freud's thinking is obvious. You recall Watson's association of religion with voodoo and black magic. Even the venerable

Jung, who recognized mythical symbols and archetypal forms in dreams had trouble with mystical experience, calling it "unconsciousness," as we have seen. Deikman goes on to say:

> Humility is the acceptance of the possibility that someone else has something to teach you which you do not already know. In crucial sections of the GAP report, there is no sign of humility. It seems that in our profession we display the arrogance of the legendary British Colonial who lived for 30 years in India without bothering to learn the language of the inhabitants, because he considered them to be inferior. Perhaps medicine's long battle to free itself from religious control, left us with an automatic and costly reaction against anything that bears the outward signs of religion★ ... Psychiatry's aversion to things ecclesiastical should not blind the profession to the possibility that "real gold" exists, even though false coin abounds ... The attitude reflected in the report is myopic and unnecessarily fearful of an avenue of human endeavor, aspiration, and discovery thousands of years old – one productive of outstanding achievements in science and literature that we are only now beginning to recognize.[4]

What Deikman says about psychiatry applies equally much to psychology, which adheres just as strongly to the old paradigm of materialism-mechanism. In his insightful book on the forms of intelligence, *Frames of Mind* (1983), Dr. Howard Gardner describes seven: linguistic, mathematical-scientific, spatial, musical, kinesthetic, interpersonal, and intrapersonal. When at a talk given by Dr. Gardner, I brought up the possibility of an eighth form of intelligence, namely spiritual, based upon the history of religion and mysticism, as studied by the great psychologist, William James, in *The Varieties of Religious Experience*, Dr. Gardner asked me whether I was a "follower of Jerry Falwell?" He, seemingly, associated religious or mystical experience with the most simplistic form (in his mind) of "Christian fundamentalism." No, psychology and psychiatry have not yet discovered the reality of spiritual experience to any significant degree. Yet, there is a *new paradigm* that has been in the process of development for nearly thirty years (since the mid 1960s) which is now being referred to as *sacred psychology*. I would consider its forerunner, "transpersonal psychology," to be a transitional paradigm, as the prefix

---

★ Dr. Thomas Szasz, in his book, *The Myth of Psychotherapy* (1979) points out the "implacable hostility" of modern psychiatry to religion in the chapter "Curing Souls."[5] Dr. Szasz demonstrates that the cure of souls had its origins in ancient religion and philosophy.

"trans" implies. Sacred psychology is a new paradigm for late twentieth century psychology, as well as being an extremely old paradigm in the history of humanity, as we shall see.

After writing my first book, *Physicians of the Soul* (1982), I read, for the first time, the early book written by my foreword writer, Dr. Jean Houston and her husband, Dr. Robert Masters.* I was rather amazed by this book as it discovered via LSD research what I had discovered and written about based upon my own personal spiritual journey, namely, four levels of consciousness; in their case, psychedelic experience: the sensory, the recollective-analytic, the symbolic, and the integral – to use the terms employed by Masters and Houston. By the "integral" is meant "mystical" or "religious" experience, or what Bucke called "cosmic consciousness." Masters and Houston's book is called *The Varieties of Psychedelic Experience* (1966), and it represents the first genuine reappearance of religious/mystical experience in psychology, in this case via the medium of LSD, since the time of William James' *The Varieties of Religious Experience* (1902). The apparent exception to this in the context of the present book is G. I. Gurdjieff; but he was much more a part of the mystical tradition than the field that calls itself psychology.

Masters and Houston, who are both psychologists, state that the mysteries of matter are beginning to unfold in ways almost incomprehensible to the thought and vision of most people, e.g. Einstein's theory of relativity and Heisenberg's quantum theory. Masters and Houston propose that their book is concerned with "unlocking" the mysteries of mind via the medium of the psychedelic drug state.

> Now as research advances, the psychedelic (mind-manifesting) drugs give promise of providing access to another of the great and hitherto largely impenetrable realms – the vast, intricate, and awesome regions we call *mind*.[6]

Masters and Houston were by no means "advocates" of psychedelic drugs, as in the "Drug Movement" that was going on while they did their research. They clearly recognized the inherent

---

* Houston and Masters are respectively, director and director of research of The Foundation for Mind Research, a human potentialities research institute, in Pomona, New York. Both have extensive backgrounds in human capacities research, teaching, and writing. Houston's earlier work was in philosophy of religion, and Masters' was in clinical psychology and sexology.

dangers of psychoactive drugs. However, they believed in the use of these drugs under highly controlled research conditions, but not their free availability (nonetheless, even research became illegal after the publication of their book). Masters and Houston's book is based upon firsthand observations of 206 psychedelic drug sessions, and upon interviews with another 214 persons who took these drugs either in psychotherapy or on their own. It was a fifteen-year research project that involved the use of two drug substances: LSD-25 or d-lysergic acid diethylamide and peyote, which is a cactus plant, *Lophophora williamsii*, found in the American Southwest and Mexico.

There is a long history of the use of these substances, and Masters and Houston review this in their book. Over three thousand years ago, the East already had "soma" which is reported in Hindu scriptures. Just what it was is unknown, but it was clearly a psychedelic. Various hemp-derivatives were used to produce visions in India. In pre-Columbian Mexico, various plants containing psychoactive substances, including peyote, were in use. To this day, there is a Native American Church which utilizes peyote in its sacred rites. The great American philosopher-psychologist, William James tried peyote once himself, consuming one button, but he was "violently ill for twenty-four hours. . ."[7] This ended the use of psychedelic drugs in the research program of James' own psychology of religion. The novelist, Aldous Huxley, in the mid-twentieth century, described his own mescaline experiences. His audience were primarily writers, artists, and bohemians. LSD itself was first synthesized at the Sandoz Research Laboratories in Basel, Switzerland, by A. Stoll and A. Hoffman in 1938. Hoffman, in 1943, discovered its psychedelic properties accidentally. Taking 250 micrograms of this substance, he experienced what he feared was a psychosis: "Faces of persons present around him resembled grotesque, brightly colored masks."[8] By the 1960s, there were thousands of scientific articles published on the effects of LSD. There was also a psychedelic drug movement whose members took the drug as a "universal panacea" for human ills.

Is the LSD state a psychosis? Masters and Houston discuss this:

> That almost any LSD subject may experience, under certain conditions, a transient psychosis-like state, is a fact. However, it is also a fact that a "psychosis" rarely ever will occur in a reasonably healthy subject who has not been led to expect it and who has not been exposed to the stresses precipitating the "psychotic" episode. Not LSD, but mishand-

ling of the session, is with few exceptions the key factor when a normal subject experiences an LSD "psychosis" that was not intentionally brought about.[9]

However, many of the phenomena of the LSD state do *resemble* more or less closely the symptoms of psychosis, such as, hallucinations, delusions, abnormal body sensations, depersonalization, and derealization, etc. I might point out that in this author's one and only LSD episode, under uncontrolled conditions, the experience was such as even Dante fails to capture in the *Inferno*! I experienced a total loss of reality and entered what someone told me was the "Bardo" state described in the *Tibetan Book of the Dead*. Masters and Houston report that normals versus psychotics respond to LSD phenomena in very different ways ranging from enjoyment and trust to terror and panic. Though there may be a surface similarity between LSD phenomena and psychosis, they are by no means identical. Psychotics themselves who have been given LSD and asked if it was the same thing they experienced in their illness, in this case, schizophrenia, report that it is not. They declared the experience essentially dissimilar, as reported in the *American Journal of Psychiatry* of 1959.[10] LSD experience is not necessarily identical to mystical experience either; in fact, Masters and Houston report that it only rarely is, but in these rare cases it is indistinguishable.

Masters and Houston report many of the typical experiential phenomena of the LSD and other psychedelic drug states, including body image distortions, experiencing other persons, telepathic and other "ESP" phenomena, and the like, in their exhaustive research book. A reading of this would give a potential LSD "tripper" a very good description of "what to expect." However, I might point out that the verbal description is nothing like the reality! It is like trying to describe in words the "taste of a wine" on the one hand or a "nightmare" on the other. The authors do admirably well, however.

What really aroused my interest was the description of the "four levels of consciousness," in this case psychedelic consciousness, that is given in the chapter called "The Guide."[11] The term "guide" is appropriate as the subject often conceives of his or her psychedelic session as a kind of spiritual journey, for example, akin to the journey of Dante in the *Divine Comedy* in which he was "guided" by the poet, Virgil. Based upon their research data consisting of hundreds of LSD (or peyote) sessions, Masters and

Houston see this journey as leading into realms of increasing depth which they call: *The Sensory Realm, The Recollective-Analytic Stage, The Symbolic Level,* and *The Integral Level.*★ Here is what they say in defining each of these "levels:"

The Sensory Realm
In the earlier stages of the psychedelic drug-state, and in later stages too if deeper levels are not reached, the subject's awareness is primarily of sensory experiencing. Altered awareness of body and body image, spatial distortions, and a wide variety of perceptual changes ordinarily occur. Temporal orientation is also very greatly altered and the subject, closing his eyes, may be confronted with a succession of vivid eidetic images brilliantly colored and intricately detailed.[12]

The Recollective-Analytic Stage
Possibly several hours into his session, and usually after he has spent some time with the sensory realm with its altered perceptions, the subject will pass on to a stage of his experience in which the context is predominantly introspective and especially recollective-analytic. Personal problems, particularly problem relationships and life goals are examined. Significant past experiences are recalled and maybe revivified ("lived through") with accompanying emotion. A more characteristically "psychedelic" ideation appears as materials not normally accessible to consciousness surge up and determine the thought contents and patterns. The materials are sifted, analyzed, and ordered, and the unfolding self-knowledge may be accompanied by eidetic memory images and images tending to illustrate and clarify the ideational materials. With such a wealth of helpful phenomena at his disposal, the subject now may be in a position to clearly recognize and formulate many of the problems confronting him and may "see what needs to be done" as he has "never seen it before."[13]

The Symbolic Level
On the symbolic level of the psychedelic experience profound self-understanding and a high degree of self-transformation may reward the subject who is properly prepared. Since our later discussion of this level, reached by some forty percent of the subjects, is extensive, here we will be brief. . . . The eidetic images become of major importance on this *symbolic* level as does the capacity of the subject to feel that he is participating with his body as well as his mind in the events he is imaging. Here, the symbolic images are predominantly historical, legendary, mythical, ritualistic, and "archetypal." The subject may experience a profound and rewarding sense of continuity with evolu-

★ Masters and Houston's "four level" theory is quite related to Bucke's stages of consciousness: perceptual mind, receptual mind, conceptual mind, and intuitional or cosmic conscious mind.

tionary and historic process. He may act out myths and legends and pass through initiations and ritual observances often seemingly structured precisely in terms of his own most urgent needs. [14]

The Integral Level
Only 11 of our 206 psychedelic subjects [approximately 5%] have reached the deep integral level where the experience is one of psychological integration, "illumination," and a sense of fundamental and positive self-transformation. In each of these cases the experience of the *integral* level has been regarded by the subject as a religious one . . . On this level, ideation, images, body sensation (if any) and emotion are fused in what is felt as an absolutely purposive process culminating in a sense of total self-understanding, self-transformation, religious enlightenment and, possibly, mystical union. The subject here experiences what he regards as a confrontation with the Ground of Being, God, Mysterium, Noumenon, Essence, or Fundamental Reality. The content of the experience is self-validating and *known* with absolute certainty to be true. Further a kind of *post facto* validation is forthcoming in the form of the after-effects: the behavioral and other changes. [15]

Since the authors describe this passage from the sensory realm to the integral level as a "descent inward," one could picture their model as a series of concentric circles beginning with the outermost sensory level, and continuing inward through the recollective-analytic stage, the symbolic-mythic realm, and at the innermost point, the integral-religious level. In my own book, *Physicians of*

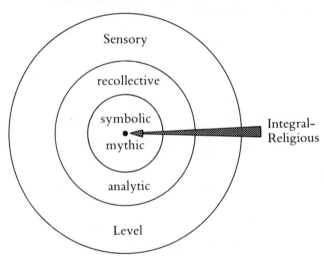

Figure 9.1   May's Interpretation of Houston and Masters' Four-Level
Theory

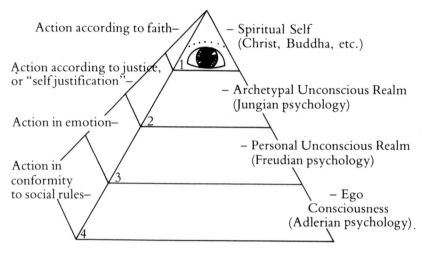

Figure 9.2   May's Four-Level Theory

the Soul, I have the pyramidal model of "ascending heights" from the level of what I call "Ego Consciousness" to the "Personal Unconscious Realm" to the "Archetypal Unconscious Realm" to the "Spiritual Self."[16] I associate the realm of Ego Consciousness with Adlerian psychology, the Personal Unconscious Realm with Freudian psychology, the Archetypal Unconscious Realm with Jungian psychology, and the Spiritual Self with the spiritual psychology of Christ, Buddha, and the other World Teachers whom I discuss in detail in my first book. I utilize a "four level" pyramid as my model. With each of the "realms of consciousness," I connect a form of action, as well: Ego Consciousness with action in conformity to social rules, the Personal Unconscious with action in emotion, the Archetypal Unconscious with action according to justice, or "self-justification," and the Spiritual Self with action according to faith. This latter aspect is not contained in the Masters and Houston "four level" theory based upon psychedelic research. My model differs from theirs on another point too; I indicate that at the level of the Spiritual Self, you can "make contact" with the Divine Reality. Masters and Houston's theory identifies the integral level with the Divine Reality. This is somewhat the difference between the Eastern identification of Atman (Self) with Brahman (God) and the Western relationship theology of I to Thou, Self to God. Since my model was based upon a

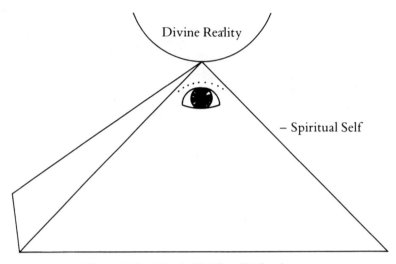

Figure 9.3   May's "I-Thou" Theology

synthesis of my own personal experiences of my Spiritual Journey, and not on LSD states, I describe the first level as "Ego" which includes ordinary subject-object perceptions of the world. Masters and Houston are impressed by the perceptual distortions (or deviations from the normal) that occur under LSD, hence they call this stage, Sensory. They do not discuss whether the subjects retain a sense of ego in this state. One may infer from the examples that the subjects still do retain some sense of ego identity, as we do even in dreams, but are more impressed by the perceptual phantasmagoria they experience. The other levels are clearly identical – Personal Unconscious and Recollective-Analytic, Archetypal Unconscious and Symbolic-Mythic, and Spiritual Self and Integral-Religious. This was an interesting convergence from two different directions upon the same theoretical model, one, myself, based upon my own Journey of many years, and the other, Masters and Houston, based upon their many years of LSD research. They preceded me in print by sixteen years and I grant them the "credit" of this discovery. We will see, later, however, that the ancient Hebrew mysticism, known as the Kabbala, has a "four-level" theory that may be thousands of years old. Ancient Yoga psychology has a "seven level" theory that goes back five millenia.

Let us look at examples from each level from the psychedelic research of Masters and Houston. First of all, in the sensory realm, which Havelock Ellis, in his own peyote experience, called "an orgy of vision,"[17] we will look at the peyote experience of a young woman and recent college graduate at the time of her experience:

> I walked in the light of the full moon across a great meadow . . . I became aware of almost electrical surroundings . . . (and) there was also the sense of the body's biochemical processes, rhythmically throbbing . . . My senses became extremely acute. I could see an ant upon a tree at a great distance away. I could hear the whispering of my companion, with whom I had shared the peyote, far off from me. Biting into an apple, I felt the granular surface of the chunk intensely magnified. I could rarely close my eyes because of my fascination with the external stimuli, and so probably missed a number of 'visions' [i.e., eidetic images].
>
> . . . As dawn came, my heightened ability to organize caused each cloud to take on recognizable shape. I felt a great peace. The pink sky was hyper-pink. A myriad of multicolored telephone wires hummed as endless flow of dancing geometrical forms in the most magnificant combinations of color . . .
>
> As I watched a wooded section I was surprised to find the branches of the trees flapping as a bird does, only in harmonious slow motion. Distant scenery waved gently so as to almost resemble a tapestry gently swaying. I was amused to see the brick walls of a house tirelessly undulating. Fascinated, I drew near trees whose trunks, head, and whose bark from afar flowed and pulsated in a manner suggesting organic growth. Close observation of the bark was astounding. I reminded myself of the mental patient one sees in films, on the lawn of the institution, drawn next to the inanimate in watchfulness. And here I was, leaning against the brick house, bound by concentration on the microscopic growth and flow of particles. A dandelion I glanced down at grew two feet high. Everything was magnified. As I strolled, my attention was wholly grasped by a small dewdrop on the grass. It was utterly captivating.[18]

Let me take back what I said above about "perceptual distortions." What we have here could be a lifting of the conceptual filters of the mind, and hence a more direct penetration into the sensory world. Maslow, the transpersonal psychologist, whom we discussed in chapter eight, would, no doubt, consider this a "peak experience," and that it was. But is it a "mystical" experience? Masters and Houston do not consider it to be mystical at all even though it doubtless had a profound impact upon the individual in question. They state that "In terms of the phenomenological pattern we have outlined, the *sensory* level always should be considered a stage along the way to deeper levels where more profound experiences await the psychedelic subject."[19]

When the subject makes the transition to the recollective-analytic level, he or she is no longer concerned with the perceptual phenomena which so captivated him or her in the sensory level. On the movement to the recollective-analytical level, there is a deepening of emotion, and long forgotten memories may now become accessible, as if the subject had moved from a psychedelic, 3D, holographic movie to the office of a very private "psychoanalyst" within him or herself. There may be age regression, going back in time to significant personal events, and there may be a vivid reliving of these events. The authors describe the experiences on this level as an "instant psychotherapy."[20] "Scores if not hundreds of therapists in many countries, working with psychedelic drugs, have found it possible in one or a few sessions to eliminate a neurosis that had resisted months or even years of non-drug psychotherapy."[21]

The following is a part of the psychedelic record of a forty-year-old male subject who is a professor of philosophy at a West Coast college. He is married and the father of three children. He had been a Roman Catholic seminarian earlier in his life and later abandoned his plans for the priesthood. He had suffered deep depressions and had been in psychoanalysis for six months. He had worries about homosexual feelings. One of his discoveries in psychoanalysis was a "castration complex" which he had been concerned with ever since. He was given 100 micrograms of LSD and at first went into the usual perceptual experiences of the *sensory realm.* We will skip over these and pick up the narrative on his entrance into the *recollective-analytic stage*:

At 2:00 P.M. S abruptly entered into the recollective-analytic phase of his experience and continued on this level for two and one-half hours. Without any apparent associational linkage to his preceding ideation he re-experienced with great accompanying emotion the death of his grandmother when he was not quite four years old. He describes the onset of this experience:

"Suddenly I felt as if some obstacle were coming up to me – something large, dark, and vague, but very powerful – as if it were knocking on the walls of consciousness. I said that some block was coming up. Then I said, 'It's Granny's death! I must examine Granny's death! At once I felt ill and dashed to the bathroom and vomited – not food, since I had not eaten. This vomiting, and all the vomiting to follow, was more a kind of ritual emission of negative emotion than a physical vomiting of food, but I did go through the physical motions of vomiting and spit up liquid."

Returning to the session room, S said he believed at the time of her death that he had killed his grandmother by a magical act – by smashing the head of a doll he had identified with her. This doll he also had identified with himself and with the previously mentioned neighbor girl. He thus, in destroying the doll, effected "the destruction of my world, the concrete world of affection and real persons."[22]

The subject had experienced great guilt in connection to destroying that doll. When his grandmother was buried, he felt that a part of himself was buried with her. The act had been a "symbolic autocastration."[23] He had thus been blocked from entering his full manhood. His regressions and re-experiencing of these events and emotions under LSD was therapeutic. He went on, in the same session, to a *symbolic level* of the experience in terms of a fertility rite, a puberty rite, and a warrior rite.

Masters and Houston state that

Few of the drug-state phenonena are more perplexing, fascinating and potentially valuable than is the subject's participation in mythic and ritualistic dramas which represent to him in terms both universal and particular the essentials of his own situation in the world. These analogic and symbolic dramas occur most characteristically on the third or *symbolic* level of our functional model of the drug-state psyche.[24]

What Masters and Houston are dealing with here is the vast realm of the archetypes of what Jung called the "collective unconscious."

The following example is from the psychedelic record of a businessman in his early forties who was highly successful in his business life, but this had been "purchased," as it were, at the expense of his inner life, which he felt had become atrophied and empty. He was given 100 micrograms of LSD. We will skip beyond his *sensory* and *recollective-analytic* experiences into his dramatic experience on the *symbolic level*. It enacted the myth of the Child-Hero.

Yes, the light is coming up. I see a woman lying on top of a mountain . . . She is struck by a thunderbolt . . . and out of this union . . . I am born. A race of ugly dwarfs seek to destroy my mother and me . . . so she hurries down the mountain . . . hides me in a swamp . . . A serpent with great jaws flicks out his tongue . . . draws me into his mouth . . . I am swallowed . . . I am passing down inside the snake. This is horrible. Incredible demons line the shores of the snake's insides. Each tries to destroy me as I float by . . . I reach the end of the tail and kick my way out . . . raining very hard in the swamp . . . I am drowning . . . No . . . I am caught in a net . . . being pulled out of the water . . . An old fisherman has caught me in his net . . . The serpent rises out of the water . . . grown into a huge sea monster . . . opens its jaws and snaps them shut on half of the fisherman's boat. With the next bite it will swallow both of us. A thunderbolt comes out of the sky and smashed the boat in two, leaving half of it stuck in the monster's gullet. The fisherman takes me in his arms and swims with me towards shore . . . The sea monster pursues us . . . just as we reach the shore it snaps off the fisherman's leg. The fisherman continues to hold me and crawls with me in his arms to a nearby hut. His wife is there. She nurses her husband and puts me into a cradle. I am raised by this couple as their own son. They are very kind to me . . . tell me I must be very special seeing as how I was drawn from the water . . . They call me Aquarion. The years pass. I am now four years old but already I am tremendously strong and powerful . . . Also, I know the language of birds and flowers . . . talk to animals and plants and learn many strange things. They tell me I must avenge myself on the sea monster who tried to destroy me and bit off my fisher-father's leg. I dive into the water to go and find the sea monster . . . For many hours I swim around and finally I find it. It is swimming towards me at tremendous speed. It has grown gargantuan and horrible ugly . . . opens its jaws to consume me but I evade them and get a strangle-hold on its throat. For many days we battle together . . . The sea is crimson with blood . . . Great waves are created by our combat . . . I am the conqueror . . . tear open its belly . . . I slay the internal demons . . . In its stomach I find the leg of my fisher-father. I take the leg back to land and fit it onto his stump. It instantly joins and he is whole again. My parents take me to the temple to give thanks for my victory . . . We approach the high priestess with a thanks offering . . . tell her my story. When she hears of it she swoons. . . . She comes to and says to me, 'My womb was quickened by the thunderbolt. You are the son of promise whom I hid so long ago.' She raises her hands to the heavens and . . . she says . . . 'Speak, O Lord, to this your son. Speak to his strength and his glory. He that prevailed over the Evil One. He hath delivered the deep of its Enemy. Set your purpose upon him Lord.' A great thunderbolt shatters the air . . . A thunderous voice speaks: 'Aquarion, my son, you are now your own man. Go forth into the Wasteland and bring forth fruit. Know that I shall be with you always and where once there had been drought . . . wherever you pass . . . there shall spring up a Green Land.[25]

This would be a gold mine for any conference of Jungian analysts! It makes one think of Jung's own account of his entrance into the collective unconscious, or what Masters and Houston call the *symbolic level*, which we discussed in the Jung chapter, (6). It certainly sounds like a fairy tale. Perhaps the same inward creative process *writes* fairy tales. It bears elements of many myths and legends of the Child-Hero: Sargon, Marduk, Moses, Heracles, Jesus, Krishna, Parcifal, etc. We can see themes of the "Wasteland" of T. S. Eliot. Each of these myths symbolizes the subject's own search for wholeness and rebirth. Masters and Houston report that after several years, the subject's experience of the divine child continues within him. "The child-hero remains effective as his 'activating symbolic agent.' "[26]

The authors, Masters and Houston, report that in their own experience, "the most profound and transforming psychedelic experiences have been those regarded by subjects as religious. And in depth of feeling, sense of revelation, semantically, and in terms of reorientation of the person, the psychedelic religious and re-ligious-type experiences certainly seem to show significant paral-lels with the more orthodox religious experiences."[27] The authors point out that the controversy has raged between writers like Aldous Huxley, on the one hand, and R. C. Zaehner, on the other, as to whether the psychedelic mystical experience, which occurs only rarely under psychedelic drugs, is genuine or not. Despite this debate, there has certainly been a long history of "provoked mysticism." We are speaking of such things as Yoga, meditation techniques, breathing exercises, fasting, sensory depri-vation, etc., all of which alter body chemistry and physiology, in the process of the spiritual quest. It is probably true that these practices alter bio-chemistry-physiology just as surely as do the psychoactive drugs. Both spontaneous and provoked mystical experiences probably involve biochemical-physiological events, as well as psychological, and spiritual ones. To those who argue that biochemistry can play no part in true religious and mystical experiences, I would point out that the sages have pointed out that *all causes*, both natural and supernatural, issue from God. Did He not create the physical universe, including our bodies and brains, as well as the psychological, and spiritual universes? Non-dualist theologians (the Hebrew sages were certainly that: "God is One; and there is none else.") will have no problem with the idea that God *can* work through LSD, dreams, prayers, meditations, and even near-death experiences, as we shall see. It would seem to this monotheistic author that Western man in the mid-twentieth cen-tury was so psychologically cut off from God, in the prevalent materialistic-atheistic world view, that the Holy One took advantage in the 1960s of LSD experiences to reveal Himself, even to atheist-materialists. This, I hasten to point out, is not the

interpretation offered by Masters and Houston – I take full responsibility for it! But, the authors of *The Varieties of Psychedelic
Experience* are quite clear on the distinction between symbolic
religious analogical experiences and authentic religious experiences. In this, I concur with them fully. Jung's psychological
writings give a vast compendium of symbolic analogues. These
occurred quite frequently in Masters and Houston's LSD research
in subjects experiencing the *symbolic level*. This included such religious imagery as religious architecture (temples and churches),
traditional religious symbols (cross, Star of David, etc.), Mandalas
(which Jung said symbolizes the Self), Angels, Devils, Miraculous
Visions, and Cosmological Imagery.[28] These are fine, good, and
important, but they are not characteristic of the *integral level*.
Masters and Houston say that:

> when we examine those psychedelic experiences which seem to be
> authentically religious, we find that during the session the subject has
> been able to reach the deep integral level wherein lies the possibility of
> confrontation with a Presence variously described as God, Spirit,
> Ground of Being, Mysterium, Noumenon, Essence, and Ultimate or
> Fundamental Reality. In this confrontation there is no longer any
> question of surrogate sacrality. The experience is one of direct and
> unmediated encounter with the source level of reality, felt as Holy,
> Awful, Ultimate, and Ineffable.[29]

The authors state that based upon their phenomenological
method, they cannot tell whether this "Presence" resides in man's
being, a psychological interpretation, or whether it is an encounter
with the Divine Presence, a theological interpretation. Why not
both? In any event, the following is a dramatic example of the LSD
experience of the *integral level* of a fifty-two-year-old engineer
who wrote this:

> Although consciousness of self seemed extinguished, I knew the
> boundaries of my being now had been dissolved and that all other
> boundaries also were dissolved. All, including what had been myself,
> was an ever more rapid molecular whirling that then became some-
> thing else, a pure and seething energy that was the whole of Being.
> This energy, neither hot nor cold, was experienced as a white and
> radiant fire. There seemed no direction to this whirling, only an
> acceleration of speed, yet one knew that along this dynamic con-
> tinuum the flux of Being streamed inexorably, unswervingly toward
> the One. (*Toward the One* is the title of a book by a Sufi master!)

> At what I can only call the "core" of this flux was God, and I cannot
> explain how it was that I, who seemed to have no identity at all, yet

experienced myself as *filled with* God, and then as (whatever this may mean) *passing through* God and into a Oneness wherein it seemed God, Being, and a mysterious unnameable Oneness constituted together what I can only designate the ALL. What 'I' experienced in this ALL so far transcends my powers of description that to speak, as I must, of an ineffably rapturous Sweetness is an approximation not less feeble than if I were to describe a candle and so hope to capture with my words all of the blazing glory of the sun.[30]

This subject described his world during this experience as transfigured and unified. If you have any question of whether his experience is virtually identical to those who experienced spontaneous mystical consciousness or "cosmic consciousness," compare it with some of the historical mystical experiences given in chapter one or some of the contemporary ones given in chapter ten, or even some of the spontaneous ones given later in this chapter in the discussion of the work of Nona Coxhead. Jesus himself describes God as "the All" in the record of the recently discovered *Gospel According to Thomas* discovered in a tomb near Nag Hamadi in Egypt. Jesus is quoted as saying:

> I am the Light that is above
> them all, I am the All,
> the All came forth from Me and the All
> attained to me.[31]

There is no doubt that this and other "integral experiences" reported by Masters and Houston are, indeed, genuine mystical experiences. You recall that only 11 out of their 206 psychedelic subjects attained the integral, or mystical experience. The authors discuss the traditional distinction, made by the philosopher W. T. Stace, between extrovertive and introvertive mysticism. This is not a distinction which was made by Bucke or James – but it has to do, it seems, with whether *the One* is perceived internally or externally, as I understand it. I do not consider this to be a crucial distinction, in my view, as God is both immanent and transcendent. But, Masters and Houston report "Out of our total of 206 subjects we believe that 6 have had this (introvertive mystical) experience."[32]

Masters and Houston struggle with the question: "Where is this information coming from? Is it a gift of God? of Grace? of hyper-neuronal ecstasy? Is it a result of our twelve billion brain cells astronomically interconnecting at the speed of light and now galvanized by a psychedelic drug to ever more prodigious computations – to tune in finally on the Process Itself?"[33] In other words, is the explanation of mystical experience "supernatural" or "natural"? In an epilogue, the authors conclude that they cannot make a judgment based upon the limits of their method on whether this is a natural or supernatural event that they have witnessed in their few cases of apparently genuine mystical experience under LSD:

> To comment first of all on the preceding chapter, it should be clearly understood that we make no judgement as to whether confrontation or union with a literal God has occurred in the experiences described. Such a determination could have no foundation other than our own wishes and personal beliefs. No more could we make such a judgement were we present with a Saint Theresa in her cell or a Saint Francis of Assisi in the chapel. Only within the accepted limitations of our phenomenological approach do we say that some of these experiences are "authentic."[34]

I have some trouble with this statement. There is a *real difference* (even a phenomenological one!) between just "having a mystical experience," which Masters and Houston describe in terms of "regions of mind and states of consciousness,"[35] and having a "mystical encounter" with the Living God. You cannot say "Thou" to a "region of mind" or a "state of consciousness," nor can you pray to a region of your own mind! But, those who have had a genuine mystical experience, almost invariably, come away from their *gnosis* with a *faith* in the reality of God. The priest, and friend of Carl Jung, Fr. Victor White, in his book, *God and the Unconscious* (1952) deals with the question of gnosticism versus faith:

> The message of the Gospels and the apostolic writings was a message of salvation by *faith*; and by faith operative in *works* of *love*. Gnosticism says in effect: to know is all. The enlargement of consciousness, inward turning to the Realm of the Mothers, the *mysterium tremendum et fascins'* . . . there lies salvation . . . Not so, says Faith; that is the very *hubris* of your own Sophia-Acamoth: her lust for the impossible comprehension of the fathomless Abyss, which imprisons her in the very matter which she despises and subjects her to the cruel tyranny . . . she would excel. Let her rather recognize the insolubility of her yearning, let her be thankful for the restraint of *Horos* who saves her from annihilation in infinite consciousness, let her open her mind to the mysteries and not seek to enclose the mysteries in her mind. But then she will no longer be a gnosticist *Sophia*; but perhaps she will be *Pistis Sophia* – *Faith-Wisdom*.

> For while gnosticism has no room for faith, faith has room indeed need for gnosis. Gnosis cannot be substituted for faith, but the possibi-

lities of gnosis are part and parcel of the gifts to the faithful *Ecclesia*. In the Body of Christ are many members, each with their several functions: and those of the gnostic are among the most honourable.[36]

Fr. White's point is that gnosis and faith are not incompatible at all, but gnosis is not supreme. This fits with this author's own life-journey which was a gradual movement from an overwhelming mystical experience, i.e., gnosis, at age twenty, while an atheist and non-believer, to conversion to a monotheistic faith, first Jewish, then Jewish-Christian, over the next couple of decades. In the process, I explored many high religious traditions which I discuss in my book, *Physicians of the Soul*. I did not experience this as "mere wishes" or "personal beliefs," but as a genuine inward development with definite stages – highly similar to William James' discussions of "conversion" in his book, *The Varieties of Religious Experience*. You recall our discussions of the religious conversions of Leo Tolstoy and John Bunyan.

There is a crucial difference between subscribing to a psychological experience, i.e., modern gnosis, and finding faith in the Ultimate Reality to which this gnosis points. This critique applies equally to Jung and Maslow, as to Masters and Houston in their epilogue. Nonetheless, Masters and Houston have performed a yeoman's service in their studies of consciousness under the mind-manifesting drugs, leading to their most insightful four-level typology, with its fourth level, the religious-mystical, or integral, which has been missed in all psychologies, including Freud's and Jung's, since the time of Bucke and James.

The female member of the Masters and Houston, husband-wife team, Dr. Jean Houston, went on to the sole authorship of some other books, including *The Possible Human*, which includes the four-level typology, only this applied to everyday consciousness, and not just to psychedelic states. *The Possible Human* is an enlightening book whose intention is to open our conditioned "lenses" of reality: "to permit entry of both vision and the inspiration needed to launch the journey of the possible human. . ."[37] Houston offers a series of experiential exercises on awakening: "Awakening the Body," "Awakening the Senses," "Awakening the Brain," "Awakening Memory," "Awakening your Evolutionary History," and even "The Art of High Practice"[38] which involves awakening the "Mensch"[39] as opposed to the "Nebbish"[40] in each of us. "Mensch" and "Nebbish" are Yiddish onomotopoeic for "true self" and "false self."

In the next chapter, "The Creative Realms of Inner Space and

Time," Houston has an exercise called "The Archaeology of the Self" in which she presents the four-level typology which we have discussed based upon the LSD research book. She now applies it to human psychology in general:

> The self is a layered entity. As the earth is known to us according to its strata, so have we come to our knowledge of the physiological and psychological world. As I discussed earlier, our research in taking depth probes of the psyche indicates that our interior world has four levels – the sensory, the recollective-analytic, the symbolic-mythic, and the integral-religious – each tending to have its own unique style of imagery and content, logic, happenings, psychologies, and even metaphysics. The psyche is not unlike an archaeological dig in which different civilizations are revealed at each level.[41]

Houston offers exercises in the four levels of the psyche which can give the reader some experience of what these levels are like (without LSD). Let me share with you a direct quote from Houston's exercise on the fourth, or integral-religious level:

> You are standing under an ancient tree when suddenly the weather changes. The wind begins to wail around you and through the branches, and you hear the wind say, "Now is the time to know the god." A bolt of lightning strikes the tree in the center and a part of the bark falls away, revealing a golden door.

> A unicorn bearing six wings of many colors flies over to you, touches you with its horn to the ground in front of you three times and says, "It is time for you to ascend to the heights."

> You are walking in a forest and you see ahead of you a gleaming crystal palace. You enter the palace, which has no furniture, and walk through the great halls, seeing in each brilliant facet a reflection of the whole universe. Gradually, you feel your own powers and possibilities deepened and enhanced by the effect of the crystal and the shimmering light. Finally, you reach the center of the palace where there stands a single crystal vase with a single flower in it. You look deep into this beautiful flower and see in its center a seed that you know contains the germ of all you are and can be. It is the seed of the unfolding of your capacities as well as the germ of that which, if allowed to grow in you, can restore you to the spiritual order of reality.

> You are standing before an ancient temple at dawn at the time of the full moon. On the eastern horizon the sun is rising, on the western horizon the sun is setting, and in the center is a falling star. Suddenly you understand and contain the universe.[42]

In Houston's next chapter, "Toward a New Natural Philosophy," she recounts her experience of awakening to a Greater Reality at the tender age of six. You will find this account given at the beginning of chapter ten, and perhaps you should go ahead and read it now. Based upon this spontaneous mystical experience as a child, Houston went on to a lifetime search for what she calls the "cosmic connection."[43] Houston looked at the model of the "hologram," which is now being utilized by the physicist, David Bohm, as a model of the physical universe, and by the neurophysiologist, Karl Pribram, as a model of the way the brain works, as a possible model for the mystical experience. As you probably know a hologram is a 3D "solid" image of something in which the *whole* is resident in every part. Houston quotes a second-century Buddhist Sutra which sounds very "holonomic":

> In the heaven of Indra there is said to be a network of pearls, so arranged that if you look at one you see all others reflected in it, and if you move in to any part of it, you set off the bells that ring through every part of the network, through every part of reality.
>
> In the same way, each person, each object in the world, is not merely itself, but involves every other person and object and, in fact, on one level *is* every other person and object.[44]

Houston quotes from a work of a Kabbalist, Jorge Luis Borges, who describes a vision of the "Aleph," "the point that contains all possible points in the infinite dance of space time."[45] She compares the novelist's (Borges) vision of the Aleph, with the physicist's (Bohm) vision of the Implicate Order. Houston sees the Aleph, the Implicate Order, as the order of pure Beingness, pure frequency, consonant with Plato's Forms or Whitehead's Primordial Nature of God. She goes on to say:

> When we consider the cooperative flow of the universe and ourselves that occurs in times of intense resonance (love, creativity, unitive experience), we see how natural and seemly is the transfer of information from one dimension to the next. Suddenly the book falls open to just the right page. The phone rings and out of "nowhere" the person you needed to get in touch with is on the other end. The holoverse dances for your benefit in ordinary and extraordinary ways. New forms emerge as we tune into the resonant fields of an evolving reality.[46]

Houston tells us what she has in mind:

> Or, as the thirteenth-century mystic Meister Eckhart once said, "The eye by which I see God is the same eye by which God sees me." He got in a lot of trouble with the Pope over that one.[47]

Houston quotes the poet–mystic, William Blake who said:

> May God us keep
> from single vision
> and Newton's sleep. [48]

Houston the psychologist, as Bohm the physicist, Sheldrake the biologist, and Pribram the neurophysiologist, and others, represent the beginnings of a union between science and mysticism in our time, as was predicted by Pierre Teilhard de Chardin, the paleontologist-priest in his prophetic book, *The Phenomenon of Man* (1955).

We have seen how after a long apparent "sleep" (or repression) in psychology, mystical experience reappeared via LSD and other psychedelic drugs in the 1960s. The 1970s saw a reawakening of the mystical-religious via the reports of near-death experiences by such writers as Raymond Moody, *Life after Life* (1975), Osis and Haraldson, *At the Hour of Death* (1977), and Kenneth Ring, who reported much of his 1970s research in his book, *Life at Death* (1980). Ring describes some examples of the *core religious experience* at the heart of near-death experiences in his most recent book, *Heading Toward Omega* (1985).

Joe Geraci reports his near-death experience which happened in the spring of 1977 while he was "clinically dead" for two or three minutes hemorrhaging profusely after a major surgery:

> It was then that I experienced what we call a near-death experience. For me there was nothing "near" about it – it was there.

> It was a total immersion in light, brightness, warmth, peace, security. I did not have an out-of-body experience. I did not see my body or any body about me. I just immediately went into this beautiful bright light. It's difficult to describe; as a matter of fact, it's impossible to describe. Verbally, it cannot be expressed. It's something which becomes you and you become it. I could say, "I was peace, I was love." I was the brightness, it was part of me ... You just know. You're all-knowing – and everything is part of you – it's – it's – just so beautiful. It was eternity. It's like I was always there and I will always be there, and that my existence on earth was just a brief instant. [49]

The next case is based upon the near-death experience of a middle-aged woman, who chose to remain anonymous, who experienced the following during an open-heart surgery performed in 1975:

> I was aware ... of my past life. It was like it was being recorded ... There was the warmest, most wonderful love. Love all around me ... I felt light-good-happy-joy-at ease. Forever-eternal love. Time meant

nothing. Just being. Love. Pure love. Love. The Light was Yellow. It was in, around, and through everything . . . It is God made visible. In, around, and through everything. One who has not experienced it cannot know its feeling. One who has experienced it can never forget it, yearns for its perfection, and longs for the embodiment of it.[50]

The final case, of the many given by Ring, which I will quote from is that of a middle-aged man whom Ring calls "Harold," who suffered a heart attack while raking leaves in front of his house in 1977. He describes the unfolding of the core of the near-death experience as follows:

A brilliant white-yellow pillar of light confronted me. I was now in a light golden cellular embodiment and the greatest feeling of warmth and love and tenderness became part of me. My consciousness or soul was at the foot or base. When I tried to look up (not exactly so, but the closest words I can use) I saw the sweet smile and love of my father at the time when I was a young child and he held me and loved me. I felt this love permeating my being. (I had never any conscious remembrance of this nor thought of my father for years.)

Instantly my entire life was laid bare and open to this wonderful presence, "GOD." I felt inside my being his forgiveness for the things in my life I was ashamed of, as though they were not of great importance. I was asked – but there were no words; it was a straight mental instantaneous communication – "What had I done to benefit or advance the human race?" At the same time all my life was presented instantly in front of me and I was shown or made to understand what counted. I am not going into this any further but, believe me, what I had counted in life as unimportant was my salvation and what I thought was important was nil.[51]

These experiences, so like the illuminative mystical experiences that we have seen, and will see in the next chapter, were not just "isolated incidents" in the lives of these people whom Ring studied. They were life-changing. Many experienced highly beneficial personality transformations, as these following examples indicate:

I was easily intimidated . . . I'm not like that anymore . . . I can talk with anyone now . . . I have more confidence in myself . . .[52]

I have changed . . . from a very shy, introverted person to an extrovert. All the way out! I now talk in public . . . I could never have made a speech [before].[53]

You're talking to an ex-stutterer, ex-whisperer, ex-stammerer . . . [So you really had a basic personality change?] Oh, definitely. I'm aggressive now where I was very passive [before].[54]

Before you accuse me of promoting nearly dying as a new form of psychotherapy, let me say that the significance of these has nothing to do with the near physical death experienced by these individuals, but with the religious-mystical experiences which they all report! Did it change their religious beliefs? It most assuredly did. Among the twenty-five cases of near-death experience studied by Ring, there were atheists, agnostics, Roman Catholics, Protestants, and Jews (how they classified themselves prior to their near-death experiences). Among the believers, many were weak in their faith as self-reported. Following their near-death experience, every single one, without exception, checked the "strongly believe" alternative in a questionnaire administered to all subjects.[55] How do they characterize the "Being of Light" whom they encountered? Usually, as "God," but not in any sectarian sense. That is to say, God is not Episcopal, or Lutheran, or Catholic, or Jewish, or Moslem; God is God. Those who have had the cosmic conscious experience (in whatever circumstances) tend to become more spiritual, or religious, but not more sectarian. They tend to be more tolerant of the various religious forms. Some prefer no form at all.

We have seen the true mystical experience, or "cosmic consciousness," reappear among latter twentieth-century Western men and women via the overwhelming "jolts" to the mind/brain of LSD and near-death. So great was the antagonism of the prevalent materialist-mechanist world view to mystical experience (it allowed for "normal" church attendance as a cultural-social custom!) that it took LSD and near-death to bring people to the experience of the mystical in the 1960s and 1970s (or at least to have the courage to report these experiences). I came across, at exactly the moment I needed to find it, an extraordinary book by novelist and biographer, Nona Coxhead called *The Relevance of Bliss* (1985). She describes herself as almost-a-mystic, having never had the experience herself at the time of writing her book, but hers is the first book I have seen since Bucke's and James' of the turn of the twentieth century which gives many accounts of *spontaneous mystical experience*. The following are three exemplars who were bold enough to give their actual names:

> Wendy Rose-Neill was tending her garden in Buckinghamshire one autumn day when the experience occurred. Although a medical journalist and psychotherapist, and therefore well used to communicating, it was with the greatest difficulty that she recorded what happened:

... I had always found gardening a relaxing activity and on this particular day I felt in a very contemplative frame of mind. I remember that I gradually became intensely aware of my surroundings – the sound of birds singing, the rustling of leaves, the breeze on my skin and the scent of the grass and flowers.

I had a sudden impulse to lie face down on the grass and as I did so, an energy seemed to flow through me as if I had become a part of the earth underneath me. The boundary between my physical self and my surroundings seemed to dissolve and my feeling of separation vanished. In a strange way I felt blended into a total unity with the earth between my fingers and touching my face, and I was overwhelmed by a force which seemed to penetrate every fibre of my being.

I felt as if I had suddenly come alive for the first time – as if awakening from a long deep sleep into a real world. I remember feeling that a veil had been lifted from my eyes and everything came into focus, although my head was still on the grass. Whatever else I believed, I realised that I was surrounded by an incredible loving energy, and that everything both living and non-living, is bound inextricably with a kind of consciousness which I cannot describe in words.

Although the experience could not have lasted for more than a few minutes, it seemed endless – as if I were in some kind of suspended eternal state of understanding. Then it passed and I remained still and quiet on the lawn, trying to absorb what had happened and not quite believing that it was real. A profound feeling of joy and peace is what I recall afterwards from those extraordinary moments.[56]

Rose-Neill had another such experience, while driving, a few months later. She considered both of these experiences to be revelations. They had the effect of enriching her life and giving her a sense of meaning and continuity and purpose.

Another unsought experience is that of Muz Murray and it reveals all the characteristics of spontaneous mystic illumination. As in the preceding experience, this person was temperamentally hostile to spiritual concerns . . . it was a single, unrepeated experience that took place while he was hitch-hiking round the world that was to change his whole outlook.

One evening, in Cyprus, in 1964, I was sitting looking at the sea, in the afterglow of sunset, having just finished a meal in an old Greek eatery on the shore. I was feeling very tranquil and relaxed, when I began to feel a strange pressure in my brain. It was as if some deliciously loving hand had crept numbingly under my skull and was pressing another brain softly into mine. I felt a thrilling liquidity of being and an indescribable sensation as if the whole universe were being poured into me, or rather, more as if the whole universe was welling out of me from some deep centre. My "soul" thrilled and swelled and kept expanding until I found myself among and within the stars and planets. I understood that I was the whole universe! . . .

The all vision vanished as wave upon wave of extraordinary revelation swept through me, too fast for my conscious mind to record other than the joy and wonder of it. In those moments of eternity I lived and understood the esoteric saying "as above – so below." Every single cell in my "expanded body" – wherever the body was during that bodiless experience – seemed to record and intuit everything which occurred, retaining it like the negative film emulsion in a camera. I was shown that every cell had its own consciousness which was mine. And it seemed that the whole of humanity was in the same condition: each "individual" believing in his or her separate mind, but in reality still subject to a single controlling consciousness – that of *Absolute Consciousness Itself*.[57]

Murray reported the experience to be about three minutes duration, but it was sufficient to change his whole life. He told no one about it for ten years, and its effect upon him remained sixteen years later at the time of his telling it to Coxhead. He had been an agnostic unbeliever, but as a result of this experience found himself a spiritual pilgrim going to India to study with Sufi masters.

Claire Myers Owens, who described herself as 'a privileged American housewife' . . . refers to 'a golden light' in the experience quoted next, which took place while she was sitting at her desk . . . she did have forewarnings, in the form of 'small ecstasies,' before she encountered what she calls 'the most frightening, beautiful, important experience of my entire life.'. . .

One morning I was writing at my desk in the quiet writing room of our quiet house in Connecticut. Suddenly everything within my sight vanished right away. No longer did I see my body, the furniture in the room, the white rain slating across the windows. No longer was I aware of where I was, the day or hour. Time and space ceased to exist.

Suddenly the entire room was filled with a great golden light, the whole world was filled with nothing but light. There was nothing anywhere except this effulgent light and my own small kernel of the self. The ordinary "I" ceased to exist. Nothing of me remained but a mere nugget of consciousness. It felt as if some vast force was invading me without my volition, as if all the immanent good latent within me began to pour forth in a stream, to form a moving circle with the universal principle. Myself began to dissolve into the light that was like a great golden all-pervasive fog. It was a mystical moment of union with the mysterious infinite, with all things, all people.

It was the grand purgation, I was washed clean and pure like a sea shell by the mighty tides of the sea. All my personal problems fell away out of sight. My ego had drowned in boundless being. Irrefutable intimations of immortality came welling up. I felt myself becoming an indestructible part of indestructible eternity. All fear vanished – especially fear of death. I felt that death would be the beginning of new more beautiful life . . .[58]

Claire Myers Owens considered her revelation to be "cosmic consciousness."

These mystic experiences reported by Coxhead made me think *philosophia perennis*, the phrase coined by Leibniz, to designate that metaphysics which recognizes the Divine Reality immanent in the world of nature, lives, and minds. Rudiments of the perennial philosophy can be found throughout the history of religion from "primitive" animism to the fully developed "high" religions. Aldous Huxley, in his book entitled, *The Perennial Philosophy* (1945), says that these truths, in the nature of the case, cannot be immediately apprehended except by those [few] who have chosen [or have been chosen] to fulfill certain conditions making them open to spiritual reality. It is the realm of the "poor in spirit" and "pure in heart" [to quote Jesus], not that of professional theologians, philosophers, and academics. In every age and culture, there have been some men and women who have fulfilled the conditions and left their accounts of "the Reality they were thus enabled to apprehend. . ."[59] Let me quote from several masters of the *way*:

Each being contains in itself the whole intelligible world. Therefore the All is everywhere. Each is the All, and All is each. Man as he now is has ceased to be the All. But when he ceases to be an individual, he raises himself again and penetrates the whole world.   – Plotinus[60]

The Atman is that by which the universe is pervaded, but which nothing pervades, which causes all things, but which all things cannot make to shine.   – Shankara[61]

Behold but One in all things; it is the second that leads you astray.
     – Kabir[62]

Do not ask whether the Principle is in this or that; it is in all things.
     – Lao Tzu[63]

In those respects in which the soul is unlike God, it is also unlike itself.
     – St. Bernard[64]

To return to Nona Coxhead in our twentieth century, she reports some fascinating published research of Sir Alister Hardy on the "triggers" of spontaneous mystical experience. The following is based upon Hardy's research at Manchester College, Oxford in England. The data is based upon written replies to his call for accounts of intense spontaneous religious experiences. He sent questionnaires to over three thousand respondents. The following is the average number per one thousand of religious experiences that were "triggered" by certain antecedent events:

Antecedents or "triggers" of experience[65]
(a) Natural beauty (122.7)
(b) Sacred Places (26)
(c) Participation in religious worship (111.7)
(d) Prayer, meditation (135.7)
(e) Music (56.7)
(f) Visual Art (24.7)
(g) Literature, drama, film (82)
(h) Creative work (20.7)
(i) Physical activity (9.7)
(j) Relaxation (9.7)
(k) Sexual relations (4)
(l) Happiness (7.3)
(m) Depression, despair (183.7)
(n) Illness (80)
(o) Childbirth (8.7)
(p) The prospect of death (15.3)
(q) The death of others (28)
(r) Crises in personal relations (37.3)
(s) Silence, solitude (15.3)

The following two are the statistics from drug experiences:
(w) Drugs: anaesthetic (10.7)
(x) psychedelic (6.7)

It is interesting to contemplate these statistics on the "triggers" of mystical experience. One must point out two things, however: (1) these experiences, judging from the data given, are *both* integral-religious and symbolic-mythic experiences, so are *not all*, strictly speaking, "mystical," and (2) any such "trigger" is by no means the "sufficient cause" of the experience in question. Most persons have experienced all of these "antecedent events" or "triggers" without the elicitation of mystical experiences. They are, more correctly speaking, contexts for the experience whose *real cause* lies in far deeper realms – and whom nobody, despite various "theories," understands at all. If they did, we could all utilize this knowledge, and have mystical experiences anytime we wished. Such is definitely not the case. The "cause" of mystical experience is as ineffable as the nature of God! However the data is still illuminating. It seems that the four major "triggers" for religious–mystical experience were (in descending order of magnitude): depression and despair, prayer and meditation, natural beauty, and religious worship. This would come as a surprise to the "peak experience" people of transpersonal psychology that among the lowest rated triggers of religious mystical experience were (in this order): sexual relations, happiness, childbirth, and physical activity. Despair is twenty-five times more likely to "produce" religious–mystical experiences than happiness. As strange as these findings might seem to Maslow and his followers, they fit the stories of the Bible quite well! Read the psalms of King David and the Sermon on the Mount of Jesus, for example. David's psalms are often cries to the Lord in despair. Christ came for the "poor in spirit," "they that mourn," "the meek," "those who hunger and thirst," "the persecuted," and so on. God, who is discovered through suffering in the biblical stories is also discovered through nature, prayer, meditation and worship.

The statistics on drugs are interesting in that they reveal that psychedelics only rarely were the antecedents of religious–mystical experiences, which is also what Masters/Houston found! Curiously enough, anaesthetic drugs were almost twice as likely to result in mystical experiences. William James experienced this under nitrous oxide.

We have found that far from being symptoms of neurosis or psychosis, that the religious–mystical experience is profoundly healing or "wholeness making," whether it occurs via LSD, near-death, through meditative practice, or spontaneously. In strongest confirmation of this, the distinguished psychiatrist, Dr. Stanislav Grof, in his recent book, *Beyond the Brain* (1985) states that:

> Particularly those who have experienced states of cosmic unity have an entirely new attitude toward the psychotherapeutic process. They have discovered a new, unexpected source of strength and their true identity . . . The therapeutic potential of the experiences that have a spiritual quality far surpasses anything available in connection with manipulations focusing on biographical material. Any conceptual sys-

tem and technique of psychotherapy that does not utilize the perinatal [foetal and birth memories] and transpersonal [symbolic-mythic and integral-religious] domains of the psyche not only offers a superficial and incomplete image of human beings, but deprives itself and its clients of powerful mechanisms of healing and personality transformation.[66]

Thus, in the mid 1980s, we have come the full circle, and find a psychiatrist, Dr. Stanislav Grof, who, a century after the time that Dr. Richard Maurice Bucke discovered "cosmic consciousness," has rediscovered the healing potential of the experience of "cosmic unity." Furthermore, Dr. Grof states that ". . . an atheistic, mechanistic, and materialistic approach to the world and existence reflects deep alienation from the core of one's being. . ."[67] Grof calls this truncated and one-sided view of human existence, "hylotropic,"[68] thus coining a new mental disease category – which afflicts most psychiatrists and psychologists of our time: *aspirituality*, which is ultimately self-destructive on both individual and collective planes, according to Grof.

How do two of the oldest spiritual traditions of humankind, Kabbala–Jewish mysticism, and Yoga–Hindu mysticism, relate to the "new paradigm" of sacred psychology? They antecede it by four and five millenia respectively! Let us take a brief look at these two ancient sacred psychologies – what do they say about Cosmic Consciousness?

KABBALA

According to some Jewish mystics, the Kabbala dates back to the Patriarch, Abraham who received it from Melchizedek, the prince of Salem (ancient Jerusalem). Kabbala's written texts are the *Sepher Yetsirah* written between the third and sixth century A.D., and the *Sepher Zohar*, written in the thirteenth century A.D. They recount the much older Oral Tradition.

Kabbala, which means "Revealed Knowledge," basically consists of a letter-number code to penetrate the allegorical and mystical meanings of the holy scriptures, and the cosmological-psychological scheme of the Tree of Life – which unites in one non-dual system "all and everything" from Ain Sof: the Godhead, to Malkuth, the Kingdom: the Physical Universe. There are said to be four levels of being: Atziluth – Divine, Beriah – Archetypal, Yetsirah – Psychological, and Assiyah – Physical. All of these four

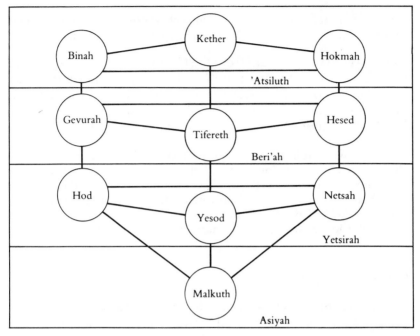

Figure 9.4   Kabbala's Tree of Life

levels are represented in the human being, who consists of a body and brain, a personal psyche, a collective or archetypal unconscious, and a divine spark, or spirit at our deepest core – which connects man with God. You readily see the parallels between Kabbala's "four levels of being" and Masters' and Houston's, and my own "four levels of consciousness." How does a Kabbalist view cosmic consciousness? The modern Kabbalist author, Zev ben Shimon Halevi says:

> When a person has an experience of bliss, it means that they have contact with the highest world, that is to say they have moved out of the physical, through the psychological, to the center of the spiritual world . . . There they come into contact with the *Shekinah*, that is, the presence of God . . . When a person touches that point, and they can touch it momentarily, they come into the presence of the light, the world of light, the world without end, and this notion of sudden illumination we call Grace . . . The purpose as I understand it is that Absolute wishes to convey the presence of divinity . . . and therefore, at certain moments, all the worlds are opened up and a shaft of light comes down from the divine world, through the spiritual world into

the person incarnate in the body. In such a moment, the rays of light come all the way through. It is an unforgettable experience.[69]

Halevi says that you return from the Cosmic Conscious experience with a clear sense of your purpose and destiny, whatever that may be. Among those of the Cosmic Sense have been poets, writers, philosophers, scientists, monks and nuns, and even founders of the World Religions (see Bucke's *Cosmic Consciousness*).

> Destiny, or the fulfillment of a cosmic task, is the hallmark of this level. It is of a cosmic conscious order . . . It is said that great teachers – that is those who have reached Cosmic Consciousness – have the choice to go on and attain complete union with God, or to return to the world in order to help men on. Buddha took the latter choice and so it would seem did Joshua ben Miriam, known as Jesus, son of Mary.[70]

YOGA

"Yoga psychology is based upon the concept that there are various levels of functioning. We are all aware of a 'body' and 'mind,' but these are, from the perspective of Eastern thought, only part of the whole picture."[71] Yoga, which literally means "yoke" – the goal being "union with the Divine," speaks of seven "chakras" or "centers" of consciousness. These chakras, or psychic centers, have various "positions" along the spinal cord from the base of the spine to the brain.

> The first is located at the base of the spine . . . The second center is just a few inches up above that at the level of the genitals. . . . The third is located at the level of the navel, and is associated with the solar plexus. The fourth center is near the area of the heart. . . . The fifth center is at the base of the throat. The sixth center lies at the point between the eyebrows, while the seventh is the topmost point of the skull, at the "crown" of the head. The highest or "crown" chakra has to do with the highest state of consciousness – while the lowest chakras are more closely tied to the animal or instinct-based side of human nature.[72]

These chakras, or psychic centers, are each associated with a kind of consciousness or a "psychology." The root (anal) chakra is connected with the most rudimentary survival instincts and the basic feelings of pain and pleasure. It is the level of behaviorism. The genital chakra is concerned with sexual impulses. It is the

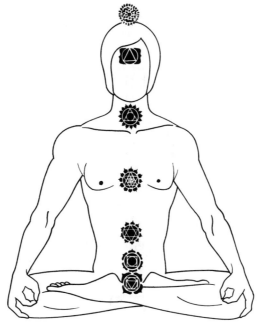

Figure 9.5   Yoga Chakras

concentration of Freudian psychology. The solar plexus chakra relates to power: domination and submission. It is the specialization of Adler's "inferiority-superiority" complex psychology. The heart chakra is the place of the emotion of love. It is the central focus of many spiritual traditions. Humanistic psychology, with its concern for "warmth" and "unconditional positive regard," relates to this chakra. The throat chakra is said to be the source of creativity. Jung's emphasis on myth or "story telling" relates to this chakra (as well as certain others). The sixth, or "ajna" chakra, the "third eye," is the seat of intuitive knowledge. It is the focus of Raja Yoga and also Buddhist schools of insight meditation, such as Zen. Finally, the seventh, or "crown chakra," is the place of "enlightenment" or "cosmic consciousness." Tying together all seven chakras is the "kundalini" energy said to be "coiled" at the base of the spine, awaiting awakening. There are definite correspondences between the Yoga Chakra system and the Kabbala's Tree of Life, although the former is more a self-work tradition, and the latter places more emphasis on Grace.

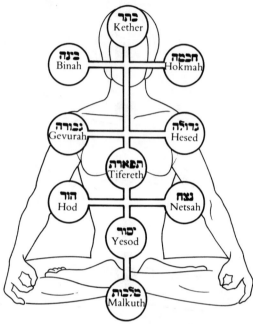

Figure 9.6   Correspondence between Kabbala's Tree of Life and the Yoga Chakras:

    Malkuth – Base of Spine Chakra
    Yesod – Solar Plexus Chakra
    Tifereth – Heart Chakra
    Kether – Crown Chakra

10

Ten Contemporary Cases of "Cosmic Consciousness?," or True Religious-Mystical Experience

The following ten individuals are living persons. I have encountered four of them personally (two, I know well). Nine of these ten have published his or her religious-mystical, or "cosmic conscious" experience in book form. The tenth person, A. H. M., wrote to me of her experience following a lecture given by this author.

(1) DR. JEAN HOUSTON

Jean Houston is a psychologist and philosopher whose ideas and background we have discussed in previous chapters (7, 9). Dr. Houston published her own experience of Cosmic Consciousness in her book, *The Possible Human* (1982). She may hold the distinction of having been the youngest case of Cosmic Consciousness in world history, having experienced her breakthrough at age six! Dr. Bucke said that anyone who reported Cosmic Consciousness at age twenty would have to be considered a spiritual genius. It is an exceeding rare phenomenon, which, if it occurs at all, tends to happen in the mid-thirties.

Houston begins by saying: "I am going to tell you about a time I woke up. I will tell you this because what happened to me then influenced my whole life . . ."[1] The background of this experience is Jean having been "sentenced to purgatory" by her Catholic school teacher, a nun, because of a series of "blasphemous questions" which her father, Jack, an "ambulatory Protestant," and a T.V. comedy writer had prompted Jean to ask her teacher, e.g., "Sister Theresa, when Jesus rose, was that because God filled him full of helium?"[2] You get the gist? Jean's father took her to see a movie, "The Song of Bernadette," a 1940s classic about a French peasant girl who had seen visions of the Virgin Mary while praying at Lourdes. Jean ran home with great excitement, and went upstairs to one of the bedrooms and chose an empty closet (except for the dog, Chickie, and her puppies) as a suitable "grotto." The following is Jean's account of what she told me on the phone was a child's view of cosmic consciousness:

"No doubt about it," I thought as I squinted speculatively into the closet. "It could easily pass for a grotto."

I scooped up the puppies and dragged a protesting Chickie out of her nesting spot. The "grotto" cleared, I bounced down on my knees, clapped my hands together in prayer, "Please Virgin Mary, please pop up in the closet the way you did for Bernadette. I'd really like to see you. If you come I'll give you candy for a month . . . two months. Okay?"

No Virgin Mary,

"Uh, Virgin Mary? Listen. I'm going to shut my eyes and count to ten and you be there in the closet when I finish counting. Okay? 1-2-3-4-5-6-7-8-9-10."

No Virgin Mary – only the dog carrying one of her pups back by the scruff of the neck to the site of my hoped-for Visitation. I indignantly pulled them out again and kneeled down for serious business.

"Look, Virgin Mary? This time I'm going to count to . . . twenty-three, and when I open my eyes you try to come down from heaven and get into the closet. Okay?"

I counted slowly, with my eyes closed, trying to imagine at the same time a picture of the Virgin Mary winging down from the skies like some great white bird hovering over the Brooklyn Bridge looking for my house. At the count of twenty-three my eyes popped open. This time I was sure she'd make it.

No Virgin Mary. Just three more pups in the closet. I dragged the dogs away.

"Virgin Mary?" Maybe you don't know where I live. Its 1404 Avenue O. It's the brick house with the stoop out in the front, where Etta Canzaneri is outside jumping rope. You go to the second floor and turn left. Okay? Now I'll count to . . . forty-one, so you should have plenty of time to find it."

Well, she must have gotten lost, for she never did show up. At least not in the closet. I kept on trying for a while, counting to even higher numbers such as 52 . . . 87 . . . 103 . . . 167 . . . but all I ever opened my eyes to was an ever-growing mélange of puppies. Finally, I gave up, resigned to the fact that my efforts to lure heaven had failed. I gave up the ghost to the dogs, as it were.

Spent and unthinking, I sat down by the windowsill and looked out at the fig tree in the backyard. Sitting there drowsy and unfocused, I must in my innocence have done something right, for suddenly the key turned and the door to the universe opened. I didn't see or hear anything unusual. There were no visions, no bursts of light. The world remained the same. And yet everything around me, including myself, moved into meaning. Everything – the fig tree in the yard, the dogs in the closet, the wallsafe, the airplane in the sky, the sky itself, and even my idea of the Virgin Mary – became part of a single Unity, a glorious symphonic resonance in which every part of the universe was a part and illuminated every other part, and I knew that in some way it all worked together and was very, very good.

My mind dropped all shutters. I was no longer just the local little "I," Jean Houston, age six, sitting on a windowsill in Brooklyn in the 1940's. I had awakened to a consciousness that spanned centuries and was on intimate terms with the universe. Everything mattered. Nothing was alien or irrelevant or distant. The farthest star was right next door and the deepest mystery was clearly seen. It seemed to me as if I knew everything. It seemed to me as if I was everything. Everything – the fig tree, the pups in the closets, the planets, Joey Mangiabella's ribs, the mind of God, Linda Darnell, the chipped paint on the ceiling, the Virgin Mary, my Mary Jane shoes, galaxies, pencil stubs, the Amazon rain forest, my Dick and Jane reader, and all the music that ever was – were in a state of resonance and of the most immense and ecstatic kinship. I was in a universe of friendship and fellow feeling, a companionable universe filled with interwoven Presence and the Dance of Life.

Somewhere downstairs my father laughed and instantly the whole universe joined in. Great roars of hilarity sounded from sun to sun. Field mice tittered and so did the gods and so did the rainbows. Laughter leavened every atom and every star until I saw a universe spiraled by joy, not unlike the one described by Dante in his great vision in the Paradiso . . . *d'el riso del universo* (the joy that spins the universe).

Childhood kept these memories fresh, Adolescence electrified them and gave them passion, while first maturity dulled and even occasionally lost them. But even so, my life, both personal and professional, has been imbued ever since with the search for the unshuttered mind, the evocation and application of this mind in daily life and experience, and the conviction that human beings have within them the birthright of capacities for knowing and participating in a much larger and deeper Reality.

From this springs a search for the cosmic connection, a living sense of the nature of reality, a theology of the Way Things Work.[3]

Jean Houston's experience at age six reminds me of Richard Bucke's experience, at thirty-six, in a number of ways. There was not the experience of light in Houston's experience, "no bursts of light,"[4] as in Bucke's "flame-colored cloud,"[5] but in other respects there are many similarities. Bucke said that ". . . he saw and knew that the Cosmos is not dead matter but a living Presence . . ."[6] and Houston stated that ". . . everything around me, including myself, moved into meaning."[7] Bucke affirmed that ". . . the universe is so built and ordered that without any peradventure all things work together for the good of each and all . . ."[8] and Houston concurred that, ". . . I knew that in some way it all worked together and was very, very good."[9] Bucke averred that ". . . the foundation principle of the world is what we call love and that the happiness of every one is in the long run absolutely certain,"[10] and Houston verified this by stating: "I was in a universe of friendship and fellow feeling, a companionable universe filled with interwoven Presence and the Dance of Life."[11] Bucke's entire future life's work, including his book, *Cosmic Consciousness* (1901), flowed from this experience of the "Brahmic Splendor,"[12] as did Houston's experience of the "single Unity"[13] shape her life's destiny, including the writing of her book, *The Possible Human* (1982).

(2) BERNADETTE ROBERTS

Bernadette Roberts was a Catholic nun for ten years. She has since left the cloister, and has raised four children, living in northern California. She writes of her experience of Cosmic Consciousness in a book called *The Experience of No-Self* (1984). Father Thomas Keating, a former abbot of St. Joseph's Abbey in Massachusetts, and now a resident of St. Benedict's Monastery in Colorado, has compared Bernadette Roberts' book with the writings of St. John of the Cross. She calls the book an account of her own spiritual journey to "an unknown passageway that led to a life so new and different that, despite forty years of varied contemplative experiences, I never suspected its existence."[14] Roberts says that in the traditional Christian contemplative framework, on the journey to union with God, "the self retains its individual uniqueness and never loses its ontological sense of personal selfhood."[15] Because of her theological preconceptions, Roberts says, ". . . I was all the more surprised and bewildered when I came upon a permanent state in which there was no self, not even a higher self, a true self, or anything that could be called a self."[16]

It would seem that here, Jung's psychology, and even most traditional Christian writers on theology and spirituality have left off at the place where the true mystical insight begins. An exception to this was the thirteenth-century German Dominican monk, Meister Eckhart, a religious genius who lived on the highlands of the spirit and was charged with heresy by the Inquisition! One of the sayings of Meister Eckhart is: "When the soul so lives in its own secret place that is the image of God, then it has true unity that no creature can divide."[17]

Bernadette Roberts speaks of her contemplative experiences which led ultimately to *an emptiness*, the loss of the sense of self: "Instead of the usual unlocalized center of myself, there was nothing there; it was empty; and at the moment of seeing this there was a flood of quiet joy and I finally knew what was missing – it was myself."[18] Buddhists would speak of this experience as *shunyata*, and Sufis call it *fana*. In the Christ story, this is, perhaps, symbolized by the crucifixion – where Christ sacrifices his earthly self. This is not the end of the story, however. In Buddhism, there is an *enlightenment* to come, in Sufism, *ba'qua*, in the Christ story, the *resurrection*. In Bernadette Roberts' personal story, there is an account of an experience she had at a retreat at a monks' hermitage in Big Sur, California which she states as follows:

> About the second day, toward late afternoon, I was standing on their windy hillside looking down over the ocean when a seagull came into view, gliding, dipping, playing with the wind. I watched it as I'd never watched anything before in my life. I almost seemed mesmerized; it was as if I was watching myself flying, for there was not the usual division between us. Yet, something more was there than just a lack of separateness, "something" truly beautiful and unknowable. Finally I turned my eyes to the pine-covered hills behind the monastery and still, there was no division, only something "there" that was flowing with and through every vista and particular object of vision. To see the Oneness of everything is like having special 3D glasses put before your eyes; I thought to myself: for sure, this is what they mean when they say "God is everywhere."[19]

The fullness comes after the emptiness, the everythingness after the nothingness. In Bucke's language, Roberts has moved from "self-consciousness" to "Cosmic Consciousness."

(3) FRANKLIN MERRELL-WOLFF

Franklin Merrell-Wolff was born in California, the son of a Christian minister. Dr. Merrell-Wolff was trained in mathematics, physics, and philosophy on three continents. At the time the second edition of his book, *Pathways Through to Space* (1973) was published, Dr. Merrell-Wolff lived in a hermetic existence about 6,000 feet up the flank of Mt. Whitney in a house with his wife. John C. Lilly, M.D., author of *The Center of the Cyclone* (1972), speaks of his meeting with this "sprightly elderly man with a Vandyke and a twinkle in his eye."[20] Lilly describes Merrell-Wolff as a true Jnani Yogi, that is to say, his path is a way of mind, rather than a path of feeling or devotion. Merrell-Wolff speaks of his "ineffable transition" in the first chapter of his book, written on August 17, 1936. It is called "The Light Breaks Forth."

> It is, perhaps, pertinent to note in passing that a few days previously as a result of a thought stimulated by my readings, I had developed an interpretation of the nature of ponderable matter that seemed to me to clear away certain logical difficulties which always seemed to persist in the efforts to reconcile Transcendental Being with the physical universe. The idea is that ponderable matter – meaning by that term all things sensed whether gross or subtle – is in fact, a relative absence of substance, a sort of partial vacuum. At the present time I shall not develop the evidence and logic supporting this idea, though this was outlined in my consciousness during the days following the origin of it. The significant point in connection with the present record is the effect this idea had upon my own consciousness. It seems to have had a vital part in clearing the way for Illumination that came later. . .

> In the past, two important Recognitions have come to me. First, nearly fourteen years ago, in a setting which it is not necessary to delineate, I suddenly recognized "I am Atman." This effected important changes in outlook that persisted. Second, less than one year ago . . . while deeply interested in a book giving a report of a living Indian Sage I also suddenly recognized that Nirvana is not a field or space, or world which one entered and that contained one as space might contain an external object, but rather that "I am identical with Nirvana and always have been and always will be so." This Recognition likewise had its persistent effects upon the personal consciousness.

> We are ready to return to the Recognition of ten days ago. I say "Recognition" rather than "experience" for a very definite reason. Properly it was not a case of experiential knowledge, which is knowledge from the senses whether gross or subtle, nor knowledge from deduction, though both forms, particularly the latter have helped in a

subsidiary sense. It was an Awakening to a Knowledge which I can best represent by calling it "Knowledge through Identity" and thus the process – in so far as we can speak of process in this connection at all – is best expressed by the word "Recognition."

I had been sitting in a porch swing, reading as previously stated. Ahead of the sequence in the book, I turned to the section devoted to "Liberation," as I seemed to feel an especial hunger for this. I covered the material quickly and it all seemed very clear and satisfactory. Then, as I sat afterward dwelling in thought upon the subject just read, suddenly it dawned upon me that a common mistake made in higher meditation – i.e., meditation for Liberation – is the seeking for a subtle object of Recognition, in other words, something that could be experienced. Of course, I had long known the falseness of this position theoretically, yet had failed to recognize it. (Here is a subtle but very important distinction.) At once, I dropped the expectation of having anything happen. Then, with eyes open and no sense stopped in functioning – hence no trance – I abstracted the subjective moment – the "I AM" or "Atman" element – from the totality of the objective consciousness manifold. Upon this I focused. Naturally, I found what, from the relative point of view, is Darkness and Emptiness. But *I realized It as Absolute Light and Fullness and that I was That.* Of course, I cannot tell what IT was in its own nature. The relative forms of consciousness inevitably distort non-relative Consciousness. Not only can I not tell this to others, I cannot even contain it within my own relative consciousness, whether of sensation, feeling, or thought. Every metaphysical thinker will see this impossibility at once. I was even prepared not to have the personal consciousness share in this Recognition in any way. But in this I was happily disappointed. Presently I felt the Ambrosia-quality in the breath with the purifying benediction that casts over the whole personality, including even the physical body. I found myself above the universe, not in the sense of leaving the physical body and being taken out in space, but in the sense of being above space, time, and causality. My karma seemed to drop away from me as an individual responsibility. I felt intangibly, yet wonderfully free. I sustained this universe and was not bound by it. Desires and ambitions grew perceptibly more and more shadowy. All worldly honors were without power to exalt me. Physical life seemed undesirable. Repeatedly, through the days that followed, I was in a state of deep brooding, thinking thoughts that were so abstract that there were no concepts to represent them. I seemed to comprehend a veritable library of Knowledge, all less concrete than the most abstract mathematics. The personality rested in a gentle flow of happiness, but while it was very gentle, yet it was so potent as to dull the keenest sensuous delight. Likewise the sense of world-pain was absorbed. I looked, as it were, over the world, asking: "What is there of interest

here? What is there worth doing?" I found but one interest: the desire
that other souls also realize this that I had realized, for in it lay the one
effective key for the solving of their problems. The little tragedies of
men left me indifferent. I saw one great Tragedy, the cause of all the
rest, the failure of man to realize his own Divinity. I saw but one
solution, the Realization of this Divinity. [21]

Quite the contrary to Jean Houston's entrance into Cosmic Consciousness via a child's "Bhakti Yoga," a way of the heart (Jean
prayed on her knees to the Virgin Mary), and Bernadette Roberts'
contemplative approach, or "Raja Yoga," Franklin Merrell-
Wolff's way is one of the mind, a "Jnani Yoga." It is not an easy
way to find God; one must overcome one's own mind.

(4) DAVID SPANGLER

David Spangler has been called a shaman of the "New Age"
movement. I have met him on two occasions, and he has a special
quality. He was a science student, and then one of the founding
figures of Findhorn, the New Age Community in northern Scot-
land. He returned to the United States to found the Lorian Association. Born in 1945, Spangler was thirty-nine years old when his
most recent book *Emergence* was published in 1984. It is in this
book that Spangler describes his most precocious experience
of Cosmic Consciousness at the age of seven (outdone only by
Jean Houston who experienced the Brahmic Splendor at age six).
The story takes place in North Africa where he lived with his
parents.

> It is 1952, AND I AM SEVEN YEARS OLD. ON THIS PARTICU-
> LAR day my parents and I are driving from the air base of Nouasseur
> to the nearby city of Casablanca on a shopping expedition. It is a
> journey we have made many times before, and I am sitting in the back
> seat of our car idly watching the scenery go by.
>
> All at once I am filled with a feeling of energy coursing through my
> body and a sensation as if I am expanding like a balloon. Before I can
> think about what is happening, I find myself somehow outside my
> body but enveloping it. Looking down and in some fashion within at
> the same time, I see my physical form, my parents and our automo-
> bile, tiny objects rapidly shrinking out of view. When they are gone, I
> am alone in an unbroken field of white light. . .
>
> In this manner, there began one of the most powerful and important

experiences of my life. It came upon me unexpectedly, lasted for what seemed like hours (though in actuality it was only a few seconds), and left me with a different vision of reality than I had before.

The experience went through four distinct stages. The first was a feeling of reawakening, as if I had been asleep. What I awakened to was a sense of identity, not as David Spangler, a finite earthly personality, but as a pure being, at one with the light around me, at one with creation. Along with this came an exhilaration, a feeling of release and joy as boundaries fell away.

Then the light cleared, in a manner of speaking, and I entered a second stage: I could "see" myself (though an act of visual perception was not quite what was taking place). However, this "self" that I saw was not a body but a pattern at the center of which I could discern as physical forms, but most of which, as near as I can describe it, appeared as configurations of qualities. In that moment I knew that these were other aspects of me, other lives and experiences that I had had or would likely yet have in what, to my earthly personality, would be the future. At the same time, I had flashes of memories of births and deaths that I had known, and while no particular historical personalities stood out, what did emerge was a clear perception of the eternity of the soul and the continuity of the self beyond the physical dimension.

To this point, the whole experience was exactly as if I had awakened in a strange but familiar room and was looking around to orient myself. It was an experience of remembering, of recollecting myself in the purest sense of the word. Once I was oriented, however, conditions changed and I entered the third stage. The pattern of lives, even the surrounding light, all disappeared. In its place I found myself in a state I cannot describe visually except to say that I was embraced by a great presence. In this presence, all things seemed to exist in a profound oneness filled with indescribable love and serenity and with an irresistible power as well.

As if a curtain were drawn aside, I had a visual impression of the universe, a great wheel of stars and galaxies, suffused with the golden glow of billions of suns, floating in a sea of spirit. It was as if I were seeing as this presence saw, and for one instant we were as one. In that instant, it was as if I were one with everything that existed, every atom, every stone, every world, every star, seeing creation not from some great distance but from the inside out as if it were my very body and being. Even more powerful than this perception was the awareness of the flow of creativity throughout everything I saw and the joyous embrace of life and unfoldment in response; the rhythm was that of a ballroom, with its music and its dancers and the intricate patterns they all created, ever changing, ever unfolding.

Then the experience entered its last stage. Swept up by the cosmic dance, so to speak, I found myself looking down at the earth and then upon myself as David. In that instant I felt the intent to be David, the will to be born that had precipitated my current personality and physical life into being. I felt the connectedness of that intent to all the other patterns unfolding in creation and what I can only describe as the rightness of being born. With that came a sensation of great love, not only for David but for all manifestations of human life, for the whole drama and purpose of human existence, for the choice that each soul makes to incarnate and be part of the dance of this particular planet. Then, swept up in the power of that intent and love, I seemed to move forward, and the next I knew, I was back in my body, still staring out the window. [22]

If ever there was an experience of Cosmic Consciousness, this is it. There is the passage from light to universal oneness, and the divine presence that brings energy, life, and love to the cosmic drama. David Spangler's experience at seven is equivalent to the God-union reported by the mystics.

(5) F. ASTER BARNWELL

F. Aster Barnwell is a black man born in 1947 in St. Vincent, West Indies. He immigrated to Canada in 1967, and earned both a B.A. and an M.A. in economics, and worked as a professional econom-ist with a government department of the Province of Ontario from 1972 to 1980. A series of mystical experiences changed his life direction from secular to spiritual matters. Among the areas he has studied and written about are the Bible, astrology, psychology, philosophy, comparative religion, yoga, and mysticism. [23] Barn-well's first book is entitled: *The Meaning of Christ for Our Age* (1984). In his work, he describes an experience he had at the age of twenty-nine for which, he says, he had no frame of reference at the time. This experience came to him at a time of emotional and material breakdown in his life during which time he turned to his Christian faith for inner direction and security. He worked on himself through psychological analysis and meditation, regaining some of his long-lost faith and connection to God. It was at a spiritual healing conference at the Edgar Cayce Foundation in Virginia Beach, Virginia, that Barnwell had the following experi-ence which was a turning point in his life:

The crowning point of the conference came on the second-to-last day. During the evening of that day, I was determined to make some progress at the practice of meditation which I had been doing as recommended in the Cayce material. In this method, the meditator holds one particular thought in mind while trying to reject all others. The aim of this practice is to program the mind of the meditator with a principle or ideal of one's choosing. For example, the meditator could dwell on the meaning of patience until he comes to a deeper emotional understanding as to how this quality could be given fuller expression in his personal life.

In practicing this form of meditation, he can also use a command, called an affirmation in the Cayce material. For example, one of the affirmations recommended in the material is "Be still and know that I am God" (Psalm 46:10). This is supposed to bring the mind into a state of receptivity to Divine inspiration. In many ways, an affirmation is equivalent to the Eastern (Hindu and Buddhist) concept of a mantra . . .

Up to this point I had little experience at meditation. After listening to others who were "experts" at meditation, I felt woefully far from attaining a meditative state. On the night in question, I approached the whole exercise with my usual expectations. As I laid on my back on the motel bed, silently repeating my affirmation, I drifted off into a state of altered consciousness. My first impression was that I had fallen asleep and had awakened.

As I took stock of this new experience, I became aware of several peculiar sensations. I felt extremely heavy, as if I was in a deep sleep. My mind, however, was alert as I continued to explore this new state. I became aware of the beating of my heart, then my breathing. The breath originated deep inside the body, yet it was noiseless. Exhalations and inhalations merged into one another to give the sensation of the rotation of a water wheel. While the attention was focused on the breathing, another strange thing happened. The breath stopped, then started again at a stronger pace. It was so strong that the sternum was moving up and down in very much the same manner as one would operate a set of bellows.

As suddenly as these sensations had taken over, they shifted and were replaced by others. First, I felt a numbing sensation spreading all over the body from the feet up. Wave after wave followed with each leaving the body in a deeper state of numbness. The thought that I was dying crossed my mind. I recollect a story I heard in my youth about a woman who methodically chronicled the progression of the pall of death as it moved from her feet all the way to her head. But I did not experience any fear. Both the fear of death and of the unknown had long since left me.

In the middle of these new sensations and fleeting thoughts, the attention was drawn to another phenomenon. This time I "heard" a noise very much like thunder. I realized that it was internal, because I heard it before during my meditation. This time it was more prolonged and I was able to locate its source. It came from the region of the base of my spine. As the attention was drawn there, I "saw" a column of luminous something – "liquid light" – as I will refer to it – rise up as water from an artesian well and progress towards the head. The perspective was one of looking down upon it, and as it rose, it was as if I became absorbed in it.

The most notable aspect of this whole experience was that it was accompanied by intense pleasure, or better still, ecstasy, the likes of which I had not known before. The closest earthly comparison I could find is the climax that may accompany a sexual union.

When the column of light reached the base of the brain, it "exploded" in a flash of light, filling the entire head. This light was many times brighter than the sun, yet it was benign. It obliterated everything else such that I became the light and the experience of it at the same time. As the light extinguished itself, another sensation emerged from a region deep in the frontal lobe of the brain, behind the spot between my eyebrows. It flowed like water, bathing my head, face, torso, arms and legs as it descended. This sensation tranquilized the mind and body, leaving me in a state of blissful peace. I instinctively knew that this was the "peace that passeth all understanding."[24]

Barnwell's experience has some, but not necessarily all, of the characteristics of Cosmic Consciousness as the term was used by Bucke. It is certainly a very strong instance of the "subjective light." We saw this in Bucke's own experience, in that of Pascal, and of course, in the New Testament account of the "enlightenment" of Paul on the road to Damascus. There are other aspects of Cosmic Consciousness in Barnwell's experience including the instantaneous of the awakening, the bliss and peace, etc. There is not, however, any indication of the sense of unity, an apprehension of the Oneness of the universe. It is worth mentioning at this point that such experts on mysticism as Evelyn Underhill, the author of *Mysticism* (1911), point out *two* great stages of enlightenment on the spiritual path: *illumination* and the *unitive life*. Barnwell has definitely experienced the first of these stages: illumination. By contrast, Houston and Roberts experienced the second of these stages: unitive life. Merrell-Wolff seems to have experienced some combination of these. Spangler's experience was a progression from illumination to the unitive life. The Cosmic Conscious experience of Bucke seems also to have been a progression from illumination to a glimpse of the unitive life. It is interesting that

God in various religious traditions is referred to in the aspects of both Light, as in "Limitless Light," and Oneness as in "the Holy One." Based upon his illuminative experience, Barnwell went on to write and teach on spiritual matters.

(6) GENEVIEVE W. FOSTER

Genevieve Foster has been a specialist in working with emotionally disturbed children, and has taught at both the University of Pittsburgh and the University of Maryland. She wrote a book entitled, *The World Was Flooded With Light: A Mystical Experience Remembered* (1985) at the age of eighty-two about a mystical experience she had forty years earlier in 1945. This experience took place toward the end of a Jungian analysis that had gone on, off and on, for some twelve years. She writes, "I doubt if the essay I have to write would fit in with what I see published in Jungian journals (and this observation does not in the least question the value of what is published there)."[25]

Ms. Foster, writing at eighty-two, says that she became enthusiastic about Jung when she was twenty-two when she read a copy of Jung's *Psychology of the Unconscious*. She began analysis with Dr. Esther Harding, one of the pioneer Jungian analysts in this country, when she was thirty. She describes Dr. Harding as a woman of "a beautiful quality of intuition and an ability to use a strong positive transference creatively . . ."[26]

In no way does Foster minimize the value of her Jungian analytic work with Dr. Harding in opening up new vistas of meaning in her life. However, the story of her mystical experience begins at a point when the respective understandings of herself and Dr. Harding of her inner state began to diverge in a very significant way. She felt, for example, that certain symbolic materials of a creative nature were being consistently disparaged and shunted aside. She felt that her analyst, Harding, and herself were talking about two different people, her real self, and the self whom Dr. Harding perceived her to be.

Ms. Foster had an opportunity for a personal consultation with Dr. Carl Jung himself in New York City during one of his American seminars. She was allotted one half hour with Jung. Here is a partial account of that meeting:

> Dr. Jung was holding his consultations in the sitting room of a New York hotel suite. He was a big man, well over six feet, and solidly

built. I can well remember the intensity of his gaze which he directed at me through his thin-rimmed glasses as he leaned forward in his seat. Even before I came to the end of my recital he began to nod vigorously. "You must do what you have decided," he said, "because that is your own individual way" (he pronounced it individwal) "and you must follow it even at the risk of your life." This was so subversive in the light of what Dr. Harding had been saying that I began to raise the question whether she might possibly be right. "Dr. Harding iss only a woman," he said. "She doesn't know everything." And then he grinned . . . We were perhaps ten minutes into the half hour and I had presented my business and had my answer, but I wasn't about to say thank you and go away. I was determined to have the other twenty minutes. I had expected him to ask a great many questions. He had asked none. I said lamely, in defense of Dr. Harding, that I thought perhaps I needed someone to talk to. "Whom do you think I talk to?" he demanded. "I talk to people like yourself, and when they don't understand me, then I make them. Dr. Harding will never understand you," he went on. "Find your milieu. Find the people who will understand you. Talk to them."[27]

Jung is truly delightful in his non-dogmatism, as opposed to more orthodox "Jungians"! Foster says that he was no ordinary man; this man was a towering genius. Foster remained active in Jung groups in New York. She also went for occasional analytic hours over the next several years with Dr. Margaret Nordfeldt. Although she was able to understand what was going on in her inner world no more than Dr. Harding, Ms. Foster states that "she had a certain faith in the creative process and she was able to stand by and let things happen."[28]

In the end, however, she went back to work with Dr. Harding, and had occasional sessions with her until the year 1945. She says they got on no better than before. They "still disagreed on the nature of much important material."[29] Ms. Foster wrote a series of sonnets which she felt were misunderstood by Dr. Harding. One wonders why Ms. Foster did not take the advice of Dr. Jung, and her own intuition! What was she trying "to prove" to herself by returning to Dr. Harding? She finally discontinued work with her for a second time in the spring of 1945.

When Genevieve Foster left Dr. Harding she had a dream "of powerful black horses pulling snow plows and dashing about clearing the snow off a railroad yard."[30] She wrote to Dr. Harding about this dream. It seems to indicate a realization of her own inner power and taking charge of herself, i.e. "clearing snow" via her own inward "powerful black horses." She sent Dr. Harding this dream to "reassure her."

Shortly afterwards, within a few days, something else occurred in Genevieve Foster's psychic life which was far from anything she had expected, or been prepared for in terms of her Jungian analytical work. She writes that ". . . it has taken me the rest of my life to come to terms with it."[31]

> The climactic event, the real turning point, came a year or so after I had completed the sonnet sequence, I believe in the spring of 1945, and it came in a visitation that all my upbringing and education told me was simply an impossibility – unless of course one was psychotic. We were living in Wayne and I was teaching at Bryn Mawr. It must have been during the college vacation, because I was at home on a Monday afternoon and the children were not around. I lay down for a nap on the living room sofa. I will tell the preliminaries as well as I can after thirty-odd years, since I think they are interesting. I had a dream of levitation; I seemed to be suspended in the air a foot or two above the sofa. But my good Jungian training had emphasized the importance of "keeping my feet on the ground," so, still in the dream, I said to myself, "This will never do," and I managed to pull myself back down to the sofa. There was a further fragment of a dream, something about the beating of wings above and around me. Then I woke up. The experience I then had would have been called hallucinatory by a psychiatrist of the day, perhaps by most today. In the technical language of mysticism (and I use the word in its strictest sense, not in the popular sense of some sort of fuzzy pleasurable contact with the unconscious) it is what is called "intellectual vision." [The Jungian reader must not confuse this medieval use of the word *intellectual*, meaning in our mind, not perceived by the outward senses, with our contemporary use of the word as referring to the thinking function.] That is, I saw nothing unusual with my outward eye, but I nevertheless knew that there was someone else in the room with me. A few feet in front of me and a little to the left stood a numinous figure, and between us there was an interchange, a flood, a flowing both ways, of love. There were no words, no sound. There was light everywhere. It was the end of March, and everywhere outdoors shrubs were in flower, and indoors and out, the world was flooded with light, the supernal light that so many of the mystics describe and a few of the poets. The vision lasted five days; sometime on Saturday afternoon I had a sense of fatigue, and could sustain it no longer, and it faded. There was no one around to whom I could tell it. Roger [my husband] who is embarrassed and alarmed at the mere mention of religious experience, would have thought me utterly mad, as I surely would

have thought anyone mad who told me such a story. Indeed the part of
me that still adhered to my rationalist upbringing fully agreed with
this point of view. I knew that I was in a precarious situation; that if
my ego could manage to annex or engulf the experience I might well
be tilted toward psychosis. Yet the experience was so overwhelmingly
good that I couldn't mistrust it. I knew that it was important to keep
my feet on the ground, to keep my nose to the grindstone. I remember
we entertained Grandmother Foster for two or three days that week. I
took her to lunch at the Deanery on the Bryn Mawr campus with the
glory blazing all around me. I went to the movies with Roger. I did the
usual things. The thing that did help me to understand the experience
was to get Evelyn Underhill's *Mysticism*, the classic text on the subject,
out of the college library and to read the relevant portions over and
over for the next year. I realized that some of the medieval poems I had
been so innocently handling were written to invoke just such an
experience as I had had. (That stuff is still alive, I tell you.)[32]

Ms. Foster says that Evelyn Underhill's book, *Mysticism*, was
the chief help in understanding this overwhelming experience.
Underhill would call it an *illuminative experience*, the stage of
mystical development prior to the *unitive experience*. It was a
source of reassurance to Ms. Foster that this experience has been
known to the mystics over the centuries. She states that none of
the Jungian mentors understood it at all. She wrote to Dr. Harding about the experience, and "she replied immediately that such
an occurrence was almost certainly to be mistrusted."[33] She mentioned it also to Dr. Nordfeldt, and to Mrs. Wickes, another
well-known Jungian analyst, in either case without a glimmer of
any understanding.

> . . . to them such a thing seemed a sort of psychic curiosity, a side
> issue, not really related to the business of development, while for me it
> was the most important thing that had ever happened to me.[34]

People with whom she discussed the experience asked her how it
had changed her life. She says that she slept as usual, did her
business as usual, conducted her family life as she had done before.
Nothing really seemed all that different, except that: "all these
people and things I saw now *sub specie eternitatis*, bathed in that
supernal light."[35]

Ms. Foster relates her mystical vision to the "intellectual vision"
of St. Teresa as described in Evelyn Underhill's book, not a
sensory experience of the outer eyes, nor the pictorial imagination
of the "inner eye."[36] She connects her experience to that of
Arjuna's experience of Krishna (God) in the Bhagavad Gita. She

has surely gone beyond the ken of Jungian psychology in this mystical vision.

(7) FRANKLIN JONES (DA FREE JOHN)

Franklin Jones, or Da Free John, as he is known, claims to be a spiritual adept. He has written many books, and is most highly regarded by such luminaries, past and present, as Alan Watts, Ken Wilber, and Barbara Marx Hubbard. Dr. Donald Evans, professor of philosophy at the University of Toronto, has written that Franklin Jones (Da Free John) is ". . .the most significant contemporary writer concerning the core of religion."[37] Jones claims an "original enlightenment" from his earliest experience of life as an infant which he calls the "bright."[38] I myself believe that we begin life in an original Adamic pre-exilic state, only to become exiles from Eden as we grow up and "eat of the tree of knowledge of good and evil." Jones says that his first twenty years of life undermined his original enlightenment; the "bright" receded from consciousness. Jones went to Columbia University where he studied philosophy. He was a full-time spiritual questor after truth. He describes an experience during his college days that sounds like an arousal of "Kundalini,"[39] which the Hindus term the "serpent power" that lies coiled at the base of spine, and can rise upward from "chakra" to "chakra" to the brain. Jones went through a Jungian period where he dreamed of being born as "three of us," one baby "very bright," another "dark," and a third, "the observing entity."[40] In the dream, the dark and the light babies of the trio, came running up to the observing entity and embraced him: a reconciliation of ego and Shadow. Later, Jones met a Yoga teacher whom he calls Rudi. Rudi had been a student of the Gurdjieff movement, of Subud, and then Swami Muktananda. Jones, also, spent one year in a Lutheran seminary in Philadelphia. He followed this by a trip to India to meet Rudi's teacher, Swami Muktananda, who was known as "Baba," a title of veneration. Muktananda gave Jones an Indian name, and a specific form of meditation, and granted him the right to teach. Jones reports many kinds of "spiritual experiences," often Hindu in form; however, Jones says, that they had nothing to do with "me." He went on to say that "I felt more and more as if I had entered someone else's wonderland."[41] Jones left India for New York, by way of Tel Aviv and Rome. In a loft in the Wall Street area (of all places!),

Jones came to the conclusion that the pursuit of "spiritual phenomena" was "just another and more dramatic form of seeking,
suffering and separation. It was Narcissus."[42] Jones returned again
to India and Muktananda, but the Guru did not acknowledge him,
and he said: "The Ashram appeared unreal to me."[43] Jones made a
pilgrimage to Christian sites in Israel and Europe following
visions of the Virgin Mary and Christ, and then returned to the
United States. At a Vedanta Society temple in Hollywood, California, he had an extremely powerful experience which he relates
to the "Mother-Shakti."[44]

> Suddenly, I felt a jolt in my body, and I saw the shrine with open eyes
> become bright in a blast of light. Even with my eyes closed I still
> beheld the bright shine. Thus the Mother-Shakti showed me how she
> is always able to make herself present anywhere, and how indeed she
> was already present with me. There was no need for me to hold on to
> her, as if she could be absent.

> When I returned to the temple the next day the Shakti appeared in a
> way that at first was difficult to allow. As I meditated I felt myself take
> on the form of Shiva, the divine Being prior to all form. I took on the
> infinite form of the original Deity, as I had done previously in Baba's
> presence. I sat in this blissful state of infinite Being for some time.

> Then I felt the Shakti appear against my own form. She embraced me,
> and we grasped one another in sexual union. We clasped one another
> in a fire of cosmic desire, as if to give birth to the universes. Then I felt
> the oneness of Divine Energy and my own Being. There was no
> separation at all. The One Being that was my own nature included the
> reality that is consciousness, and the reality that is all manifestation as a
> single cosmic unity and eternal union.[45]

This oneness and union with "the Divine Energy and my Being"
which Jones describes in Hindu terms as "union with Shakti" is
the equivalent of Bucke's Cosmic Consciousness. This was not
the "end" for Jones. The next day, returning to the temple again,
he had an even more important realization. He waited for something to happen, for "Shakti" to reveal "herself" again:

> The next day I sat in the temple again. I awaited the Shakti to reveal
> herself as my blessed companion. But as time passed there was no
> sensation, no movement at all. There was not even any kind of
> deepening. There was no meditation. There was no need for medita-
> tion. There was not a single element to be added to my consciousness.
> I sat with my eyes open. I was not having an experience of any kind.

> In an instant, I became profoundly and directly aware of what I am. It

was a tacit realization, a direct knowledge in consciousness itself. It was consciousness itself without the addition of a communication from any other source. I simply sat there and knew what I am. I was being what I am. I am Reality, the Self, and Nature and Support of all things and all beings. I am the One Being, known as God, Brahman, Atman, the One Mind, the Self.[46]

I have a feeling that this was not an "experience" at all as Jones intimates, but simply the recognition that ordinary consciousness is IT. I would say that this is a "level" beyond the awesome experience of Cosmic Consciousness. It is the return to the Ordinary World with the realization that *this is it.* Jones concludes, "I understood, and understanding became the foundation of my existence."[47] This is the realization of the saints and mystics when the search has made its full cycle. Jones relates this to the original "bright" he experienced as a baby.

(8) SWAMI MUKTANANDA

It is, perhaps, appropriate that we look now at the account of the spiritual realization of Swami Muktananda who was the "Baba" in the life of Franklin Jones, or Da Free John, whom we have just looked at. Swami Muktananda belongs to the lineage of Siddha Yogas in India. He was born in 1908 in Mangalorfe, India, and claims to have attained God–realization in 1956 after many years of study and meditation practice under his Guru, Bhagavan Nityananda. Muktananda teaches the following message in his world travels:

> Meditate on your Self
> Honor your Self
> Worship your Self
> Understand your Self
> God dwells within you as you.[48]

In his book, *Play of Consciousness* (1978), Muktananda gives his own spiritual autobiography. He speaks of his experiences with his own Guru, Bhagavan Nityananda. One aspect of Hindu religion is meditation upon the Guru. This aspect of Hindu religious practice would be anathema to Jews or Moslems whose pure monotheism forbids any form of concretization or picturing of the Divine. It should not be so surprising for a Christian, however, who may meditate upon Christ, who is considered "the way" to the Father. For Christians, there is one Supreme Guru, Jesus Christ; for Hindus, there are many Gurus, or God-realized beings. Nityananda played this Guru role for Muktananda. You will recall that even the Western psychiatrist, Dr. Richard Bucke, had his "Guru," whom he literally venerated, the poet, Walt Whitman. Many spiritual traditions teach that "you become what you love."

Muktananda speaks of his initiation by Nityananda when he was touched by his Guru, and he experienced light coming from his eyes into his soul. He speaks of various inner experiences, particularly of light, red light – the color of the "gross body," white, the color of the "subtle body," black, the color of the "causal body," and finally blue, the color of the "supercausal body." Of the last one, Muktananda claims it is of the greatest importance, "it is the highest inner vision."[49] Hindu Yogis have an elaborate metaphysical system which could be called a spiritual psychology. It is, no doubt, of empirical origin, the synthesis of the experiences of the sages and mystics of millenia. After describing his experiences of the many levels of consciousness, that correspond to the opening of the "chakras," Muktananda describes what he calls his "Final Realization":

> My meditation was approaching its fulfillment. This end of my *saddhana*, the completion of my spiritual journey, the complete satisfaction of my Self, was coming near. The time had come for my Gurudev's command to be fulfilled. . .

> My very own, my dear Siddha students. My meditation was again as it had been earlier. From within, Bhagavan Nityananda seemed to shake me, and the rays of the red aura lit up the 72,000 *nadis* and all the particles of blood. Immediately afterward the white flame stood before me, followed by her support, the black light, and finally my beloved Blue Pearl, the great ground of all. With the Blue Pearl my meditation immediately became more intense. My gaze turned upward. The Blue *bindu* of my two eyes became so powerful that it drew out the Blue Person hidden within the *brahmarandra* in the middle of the upper *sahasrara* and placed Him before me. As I gazed at the tiny Blue Pearl, I saw it expand, spreading its radiance in all directions so that the whole sky and earth were illuminated by it. It was now no longer a Pearl but had become shining, blazing, infinite Light; the Light which the writers of the scriptures and those who have realized the Truth have called the divine Light of Chiti. The Light pervaded everywhere in the form of the universe. I saw the earth being born and expanding from the Light of Consciousness, just as one can see smoke rising from a fire. I could actually see the world within this conscious Light, and the Light within the world, like threads in a piece of cloth, and cloth in the

threads. Just as a seed becomes a tree, with branches, leaves, flowers, and fruit, so within Her own being Chiti becomes animals, birds, germs, insects, gods, demons, men, and women. I could see this radiance of Consciousness, resplendent and utterly beautiful, silently pulsing as supreme ecstacy within me, outside me, above me, below me. I was meditating even though my eyes were open. Just as a man who is completely submerged in water can look around and say, "I am in the midst of water, I am surrounded on all sides by water; there is nothing else," so was I completely surrounded by the Light of Consciousness. In this condition the phenomenal world vanished and I saw only pure radiance. Just as one can see the infinite rays of the sun shimmering in all directions, so the Blue Light was sending out countless rays of divine radiance all about it. . .

Then all the rays bursting forth from the Blue Light contracted and returned into the Blue Pearl. The Blue Pearl was once again the size of a tiny lentil seed. The Blue Pearl went into the place from where it had come, merging into the *sahasrara* . . .[50]

Comparing the realization of the Eastern swami, Muktananda, with the Western doctor, Bucke, Muktananda followed a traditional path of meditation, Siddha Yoga, which prepared him for his coming to enlightenment, whereas Bucke followed no systematic meditation system at all, but he was, on the other hand, a contemplative type of man. On the night of his enlightenment, as you recall, Bucke had been reading and discussing poetry with his friends, and then took a long and quiet drive home in his hansom. He said about himself: "His mind, deeply under the influence of the ideas, images, and emotions called up by the reading and talk of the evening was calm and peaceful." He was in "a state of quiet, almost passive enjoyment."[51] Dr. Bucke is describing a *meditative state*, even though reached informally. Swami Muktananda reached a similar state via formal meditation upon a mantra. In this state of mind, both doctor and swami experienced an *illumination*.

Bucke's account:

All at once, without warning of any kind, he found himself wrapped around as it were by a flame-colored cloud. For an instant he thought of fire, some conflagration in the great city; the next, he knew that the light was within himself.[52]

Muktananda's account:

As I gazed at the tiny Blue Pearl, I saw it expand spreading radiance in all directions so that the whole sky and earth were illuminated by it. It was no longer a Pearl but had become shining, blazing, infinite Light . . .[53]

(9) ROBERT A. JOHNSON

Robert Johnson is a noted lecturer, Jungian analyst, and author of such books as *HE, SHE, WE,* and *INNER WORK*. Robert Johnson was a direct student of both Carl Jung in Switzerland and Sri Aurobindo in India, representing both Western and Eastern wisdom. Robert was once a Benedictine monk of the Anglican order.* He was one of the first teachers in my own journey. Robert qualifies for the title, *wise man,* although he would say that "the wise man exists within you." The following is an account of a visionary and mystical experience described by Robert Johnson in his book, *INNER WORK*, published in 1986:

THE SPIRIT MAN ON MOUNT SAINT HELENS

I want to account for you a visionary experience that I passed through many years ago when I was a young man, long before I had any understanding of what these experiences are. . .

One evening I made a campfire on the side of Mount Saint Helens, where I had spent many happy summers in childhood before the volcano erupted. I squatted on my heels looking into my campfire at dusk. Even today I can remember the vivid colors of that evening and how they thrilled me. The orange of the campfire, the dark blue color of the evening sky, the purple-gray shadows on the mountains. I felt a great sense of joy, beauty, peacefulness – but also expectancy.

A young man, about my age, came walking up and stood just on the other side of the fire. I was on my heels by the fire; he was standing quietly; and we just looked at each other for a long time. I was still in a sort of ecstasy over the colors of the fire.

Then, to my astonishment, the fire moved and transported itself down into Spirit Lake, way at the bottom, and burned there as a tiny orange speck in the midst of that indigo blue water. Then the fire came back and burned before me. The young man took one step, into the middle of the fire. He absorbed the fire into his bloodstream so that he had fire circulating in his veins rather than blood. We stood there for some time, I looking in awe at these events, and then he said: "Come, I'm going to show you how the world was made."

We went off into space, at an enormous distance, until the earth and even the solar system had become only the tiniest speck in the distance. He showed me a spiral nebula spinning. This great mass of inert, formless matter, more energy than matter, slowly spun . . . spun so slowly, as though there were all of eternity for it to spin through its

---

* Robert Johnson wrote to me that he is "not at present a Benedictine monk" . . . but that he "spent two years at monasticism."

evolutions. It spun slowly into coherence before my eyes, concentrating, reducing its volume, pulling itself together until the huge nebula was formed into a diamond. The diamond was huge, many-faceted, with its own light source within, emanating light and color that I still remember vividly.

As we watched, the young man directing my gaze, the diamond began to erupt out of its north pole and absorb that flow of energy back through its south pole, so that there was a circulation of light bubbling out of the top and reabsorbing through the bottom pole. That intensified the color and faceting of light that emanated. Then it did the physically impossible: It split itself down the middle, and, as the entire system continued to rotate like a planet, the two halves began to rotate in opposite directions while still touching each other, throwing off sparks of light and color.

At that same time, standing somewhere with this spirit man in the distant reaches of space, I did something that it embarrasses me to remember. I turned and tugged at his sleeve and said irreverently: "This is fine, but what is it good for?"

I was gazing at an event of the greatest importance, but being a practical American, I had to justify it by finding a way to use it or finding some practicality in it. Again, I tugged at his sleeve – and said: "What is it good for?"

The spirit man looked at me in disgust: "It isn't good for *anything*. Just watch!" That silenced me. We watched, and I felt that the colors, the light, the focusing of infinite energy and volume into diamond-like density and brightness were etched forever on my memory and had almost entered into the physical cells of my body.

He took me back then, and I sat again on my heels before the campfire. He stood again in the fire. Then he stepped back, and let the fire flow out of his arteries back into the little campfire on the ground. The fire went back down to the bottom of Spirit Lake and went on burning. Then the fire returned. The young man turned around without a word and walked back out into the twilight from where he had come. The vision ended, and I found myself back in my "normal," mundane physical world. [54]

Robert Johnson's mystical vision combines several elements, a symbolic one, the "spirit man," an illuminative one, the campfire to the light emanating from the spiral galaxy, and a unitive one, seeing the galaxy as a whole that spun and transformed itself into a huge many-faceted diamond. This was a complex mystical-visionary experience that Robert states he absorbed right into the physical cells of his body. Robert wrote to me of having had two other such mystical experiences which he would not elaborate upon. I might add that Robert is a person whose *presence* indicates that he *knows* something of which we are all seeking: the goal of the mystic is the *unitive life*.

(10) A.H.M., A SPONTANEOUS CASE OF COSMIC CONSCIOUSNESS

On February 28, 1989, prior to this book's publication, I gave a talk on "Cosmic Consciousness" to the local Jung group which meets at Bowdoin College in Brunswick, Maine. It was principally on the life and work of Bucke, and the relationship of his ideas to Jung's. About a week or so after my talk, I received a letter from a woman, who was in the audience, who wrote to me about two profound mystical experiences. She said that I could publish them under the initials: A.H.M. We could correctly classify them as cases of Cosmic Consciousness, although the first is in the "illuminative" mode, and the second in the "unitive" mode, in the terminology of Evelyn Underhill, the author of *Mysticism*. I am grateful to A.H.M for sharing these experiences with me; I will share them with you.

The Cloud – 1979

I am driving south on route 1 from Rockport and come around some curve and am heading up and around another when I am directed to look up in the sky. One small cloud is hanging there. Suddenly it explodes with light. It is outlined in brilliant silver – radiating gold and pink. I cannot describe the beauty and otherworldliness of the colors. At the same time I am filled with such love that I would die happily in this moment. Such joy! I laughed and sang and cried and laughed and cried with a deep sadness. I don't understand what is happening – it's so beautiful – all is love – that's all that is and all that matters.

The vision was instantaneous – out of time and space – a flash. But I've never forgotten it. The feelings lasted intensely for a half hour. I didn't speak of it for years – I started searching and trying to integrate the experience.

6/88: It took eight years to experience what that was – I experienced it again – totally – and knew, really "knew" – "I am that love!" – Overwhelming!

A Cosmic Shift – 1986

I am with a group doing a Zen meditation walk in a light drizzle on the last day. I'm feeling very vulnerable and am concentrating on a question about the void. As I came around the house I look up. Everything stopped. The view shifted. It is like space has cracked open and shifted. The light changes – brilliant silver flashes. Colors change. Perspective changes. There is no time. Instantly I "know" and see the illusion of the material world. I know that everything at every level, microcosm to macrocosm is perfect elegant order. I feel perfect – enough – totally loved and know I always have been. I am expanding in that love to bursting. I feel beautiful inside and out, loved and cared for. I am laughing and crying. People come down the street and I see they have no substance and I hear "they are the walking dead." I weep with compassion for us. Everything I see around me is filled with wonder and newness – such joy and sadness. I feel loose in the universe with no boundaries. I am in bliss and despair – filled with energy and light. I am filled with gratitude and a sweetness as I gaze at the wonder of the orange I have in my hand. Little happenings are hilariously funny and bring me to tears. Such beauty – such love – such sadness and joy and life! It is overwhelming – no words describe this – no one can know the feelings; the experience.

This second experience of A.H.M.'s reminded me of my own experience of Cosmic Consciousness of 1962 which I had the Grace to share with another person, Margaret, as I describe in my preface. It is impossible to know what this Cosmic Shift is like unless one has experienced it for one's self. As was the case with A.H.M., to Margaret and myself, others looked like "the walking dead," or as Gurdjieff would say: "asleep." There is the experience of overwhelming love. There is *the certainty of immortality*.

Epilogue

What are the Implications of Cosmic Consciousness, i.e., True Religious-Mystical Experience, for the Future of Humankind? The Views of Bucke and Teilhard de Chardin

God is referred to in various religious traditions as the "One," the "Holy One," the "Illimitable," "Limitless Light," and the "Ground of Being," and so on. We can conclude that these experiences of Cosmic Consciousness, whether illuminative or unitive, or both, could correctly be called experiences of God-union. Most of the individuals in question would undoubtedly concur. Whether this is by Grace or self-work is another question. I favor the former view that it is not "our doing," but God's doing. It is most interesting to note that David Bohm's (the physicist) concept of the Implicate Order fits these mystical experiences in significant respects, as well. Is this an argument in favor of "naturalism"? Not at all ("naturalism" implies the Explicate Order) when we consider that the Implicate Order bears certain characteristics, including indefinability, of the mystical conception of God. To quote Bohm:

> We begin by proposing that in some sense, consciousness . . . is to be comprehended in terms of the implicate order, along with reality as a whole. That is to say, we are suggesting that the implicate order applies to both matter (living and non-living) and to consciousness, and that it can therefore make possible an understanding of the general relationship of these two, from which we may be able to come to some notion of the common ground of both . . .[1]

Bohm goes on to propose:

> Our overall approach has thus brought together questions of the nature of the cosmos, of matter in general, of life, and of consciousness. All of these have been considered to be projections of a common ground. This we may call the ground of all that is, at least so far as this

may be sensed and known by us, in our present state of unfoldment of consciousness. Although we may have no detailed perception of knowledge of this ground it is still in a certain sense enfolded in our consciousness, in the ways we have outlined as well as perhaps in other ways that are yet to be discovered. [2]

"The ground of all that is . . ."[*] Absolutely, this is as close as a physicist can possibly come to the mystical concept of God! What is missing is only the sense of the *personal* which is not attainable via mind, but heart. The heart as a way of knowing is not generally "accepted" by what we call "science," but is the way of the poet and mystic. *Who* is to say that *feeling* is not as important a way of knowing as *thinking*? Jung, the great psychologist of our time, felt that it was impossible to comprehend the psyche with thinking alone, as academic psychology has tried to do for the last century, but required at least the thinking and feeling functions, one relating to reasoning and the other to valuing. In truth, all four functions, *thinking, feeling, intuition,* and *sensation* are necessary to begin to apprehend the world of the psyche. Can we approach the immeasurable world of God with any less?

Whether via mind or heart, when we look at the luminaries of religious history, such as Jesus, Moses, the Buddha, St. John of the Cross (John Yepes), or at some of our contemporary "mystics," such as Jean Houston, Franklin Jones (Da Free John), Muktananda, or Robert Johnson, it is clear to writer-experts on this subject, from Bucke and James to Underhill and Huxley, that we are dealing with the *same phenomenon*. It has been called the *core experience* of all religions by those who see beyond the apparent multiplicity of "religious dogmas" to the underlying unity of religious-mystical experience, or "cosmic consciousness," in the words of the physician-mystic, Bucke. This is not to deny at all the real and important differences between religions, such as that between Buddhism and Christianity, on the opposite ends of the spectrum of personalism. Yet, as I examined in my first book, *Physicians of the Soul*, the parables, for example, of Jesus and Gautama are remarkable in their similarity! Is it not possible that what Gautama awakened to after his forty days of meditation under the Bodhi tree: Nirvana, is the very same reality as Jesus clearly perceived following his baptism by John the Baptist at the River Jordan: the Kingdom of God? I would guess that theolo-

[*] Compare this with the saying of Meister Eckhart: "To gauge the soul we must gauge it with God for the Ground of God and the Ground of the Soul are one and the same."[3]

gians and comparative religionists would probably disagree, but that mystics would agree. Bucke, the physician, mystic, and author of *Cosmic Consciousness*, would favor the latter position, as would the philosopher–psychologist, William James, who wrote *The Varieties of Religious Experience*, and the mystic-theologian, Frithjof Schuon, whose book, *The Transcendent Unity of Religions* distinguishes between the divergence of exotericism and the convergence of esotericism in religion. I would say that to recognize the unity underlying the differences is the more "catholic" or universal view. One may find one's religiousness in very specific forms, such as Lutheran Christianity or Hasidic Judaism, but just as the presence of life on planet earth does not rule out its possibility elsewhere throughout the universe, so the spirit that is found in one religion does not mean that it is not found in others. Certain quotations of Jesus would strongly support this, such as, "In my Father's house are many mansions. . ."[4] As a Jewish-Christian myself, I have felt that Christians should look much more closely at the *actual teachings* of Jesus than at their various denominational theologies and creeds. In doing so, they might find not only unity between Christians, but unity between Christians, Jews, Moslems, Buddhists, Hindus, Taoists, etc. All are brothers and sisters *in the spirit*, and have far more in common between them than all of them have with an atheistic-materialistic world view, i.e., one that denies the Spiritual Reality – both immanent and transcendent. The Spirit, or the Holy Spirit, as "He" is called in Christianity and Judaism, is likely to have many forms, just as there are many gifts of this same Spirit. What are we to say about the gift of mystical awakening, or "cosmic consciousness"? Let us look at what two different men of very different cultures and eras said about the implications of Cosmic Consciousness for the future of humankind: Richard Maurice Bucke and Pierre Teilhard de Chardin.

Richard Bucke, M.D. (1837–1902), whom we have already discussed in detail, was a psychiatrist and mystic of the late nineteenth century. He has some "Last Words" in his book, *Cosmic Consciousness*:

A main object which the writer of this volume has had before him has been to point out that there have lived in this world certain men [and women] who in consequence, not of extraordinary development of any or all of the ordinary mental faculties, but by possession of a new one peculiar to themselves and non-existent (or at least undeclared) in ordinary people, see, know and feel spiritual facts and experience psychic phenomena, which being veiled from, are still of most vital import to, the world at large; that if one or two of these men [or women] are studied to the exclusion of the rest – as has been the practice with not Christians only but with Buddhists and Mohammedans as well – the result must be inadequate and unsatisfactory as compared with the study of all . . . Through the aid of these men [and women] even Cosmic Consciousness itself is often possible of achievement where without them it would certainly not occur. . .[5]

Bucke is making the same point that I made about the universality of the Cosmic Conscious experience. He points out that most religions, e.g., Christianity, Buddhism, Islam, etc., make *all* of just one of these figures, Jesus, Gautama, or Mohammed, in these cases. The point is to look at *what all have in common*. His point at the end of this quote concerns the teaching function of the greatest of these persons, even their "morphogenetic fields": Moses, Jesus, Gautama, Lao Tzu, etc. Although "ordinary men and women," in Bucke's view, do not share in Cosmic Consciousness, ". . . it remains true that self-conscious man, even in his blindness, has placed the highest crowns of all upon the heads of [those] . . . who have had the divine faculty of Cosmic Consciousness."[6]

Bucke sees, in Cosmic Consciousness, the explanation of the "mystery of religion," and in these speculations, I believe he comes much closer to the truth than even the best psychologists of our century, including Freud, Jung, Maslow, and so on. Quoting Bucke:

The explanation of what may be called the mystery of religion as it exists among us to-day may be stated as follows: All men, so far, with the exception of at most a few hundreds, have lived in the world of self-consciousness without the power to leave it. The great religious seers, revealers, teachers, have also lived in that world, but at the same time in another – the world of Cosmic Consciousness – the latter being by far the larger, the most important and the most interesting. . . . The men who lived in the Cosmic Conscious world, that is, the world made visible by the Cosmic Sense, as the forests and the sky are made visible by the sense of sight, have desired, for the comfort and good of their fellows, to tell mankind at large what they saw there; but as they were obliged (for want of a better) to use the language of self-consciousness their accounts have been exceedingly incomplete and the words and phrases used have been so inadequate as to have been to the last degree misleading. Not only so, but, supposing a clear report (an impossibility), it would be beyond the power of the self-conscious mind to conceive the Cosmic Conscious world. This being so, the reports made by these spiritual travellers have been not only not understood but misunderstood in an infinite variety of senses, and the essentially similar account given by, for example, Paul, Mohammed, Dante, Jesus, Gautama, Whitman and others, has been looked upon as a variety of accounts, not of the same, but of diverse things. . . . A critical study of all these (seeming) diverse accounts will show that they are all more or less unsuccessful attempts to describe the same thing . . . for all these reasons the important fact of the unity of the teachings of these men has been very generally overlooked. . .[7]

It flashed upon me while reading this statement of Bucke's that this "disagreement" on the "reports" of these greatest of spiritual travellers, the world's religious founders, by persons of far lesser consciousness, e.g., theologians and religious formulators of the various traditions, has been much more than a matter of philosophical disagreement and debate. It has been the basis of religious wars throughout human history from the Crusades of Christians versus Moslems, to the Moslem versus Hindu conflicts in India, to the present day Catholic versus Protestant conflict in Ireland, and the series of bloody wars between Jews and Moslems in the Middle East, etc. Is this an argument against religion? No, however, it is an argument against simple and narrow-minded misunderstanding of religious truths, and the codification of these misunderstandings into rigid and authoritarian doctrines which divide the world into the "good guys" who believe as we do, and the "bad guys" who believe differently. This is in radical contradiction to the unifying revelation of what Bucke called "Cosmic Consciousness," Jesus called "the Kingdom of Heaven," what the Buddha called "Nirvana," and Lao Tzu called "the Tao," and so on.★

Bucke believed that persons of Cosmic Consciousness, that is, those who have had this experience, however briefly, are becoming more and more common in the human race:

> The writer of this book, since it was first conceived some few years ago, has sought diligently for cases of Cosmic Consciousness, and his whole list, so far, including some imperfect and doubtful cases, totals up nearly fifty. Several of these are contemporary, minor cases, such as may have occurred in considerable numbers in any of the recent centuries and no records of them remain. He has, however, as more

★ The day following the writing this epilogue, I read in the newspapers about an international gathering of religious leaders in Assisi, Italy, including Catholics, Orthodox, Protestants, Jews, Moslems, Buddhists, Hindus, Taoists, Shintoists, American Indian Medicine men, and African animists, etc., who met in prayers for world peace. The meeting was sponsored by Pope John Paul II.

than once stated, found thirteen, all of them so great that they must inevitably live. As has already been shown, five of these men lived during the eighteen centuries which elapsed between the birth of Gautama and that of Dante, and the other eight in the six hundred years between the birth of Dante and to-day. This would mean that cases of Cosmic Consciousness are nearly five times as frequent now as they were, say, a thousand years ago. It is not, of course, pretended that they are becoming frequent in exactly this ratio. There must have occurred a large number of cases in the last twenty-five hundred years all memory of which is lost. No man could say positively how many lived in any given epoch. But it seems tolerably certain that these men are more numerous in the modern than they were in the ancient world, and this fact, taken in connection with the general theory of psychic evolution, fully considered on previous pages, goes far to confirm the conclusion that just as, long ago, self-consciousness appeared in the best specimens of our ancestral race . . . and gradually became more and more universal . . . so will Cosmic Consciousness become more and more universal . . . until the race at large will possess this faculty. The same race and not the same; for a Cosmic Conscious race will not be the race which exists to-day, any more than the present race of men is the same race which existed prior to the evolution of self-conscious-ness. The simple truth is, that there has lived on earth, "appearing at intervals," for thousands of years among ordinary men, the first faint beginnings of another race; walking the earth and breathing the same air with us, but at the same time walking another earth and breathing another air of which we know little or nothing, but which is, all the same, our spiritual life, as its absence would be our spiritual death. This new race is in act of being born from us. . .[8]

You will recall from chapter three that Bucke gives a "naturalistic explanation" of the birth of Cosmic Consciousness from self-con-sciousness. He lived in the era of Darwin's theory of evolution, and based upon this, everything seemed possible on grounds of merely "random variation" and "natural selection." Today, as new findings in all sciences are undermining the old materialist-mechanist paradigm, the notion that "chance alone" could result in the creation of even elementary organic molecules, let alone simple life forms, e.g. viruses, bacteria, etc., is found to be statisti-cally zero. Never mind the question of why there should have been a "big bang" that brought a universe into existence out of *nothingness* (creation ex-nihilo is a Christian teaching) – and that this "big bang" should have been of *exactly* the force needed to form a universe that did not collapse back into itself long before galaxies, stars, planets, and eventually life itself emerged, or con-versely, a universe that expanded too rapidly into an empty "cloud of dust." The differences between these two values is one in a million, million according to astrophysicists. Correspondingly precise are the forces that hold the atom together preventing it from collapsing or disintegrating. It used to be thought, until about fifteen years ago, that the vastness of space in the universe was essentially a vacuum "filled" with just dust and gas particles separated by immense distances, bare atoms, as it were. No, there are complex organic molecules, even bio-organic proto-life forms throughout interstellar space. The probability that hydrogen atoms so widely separated could randomly "glue together" over the vastness of space, millions of light years apart, to form just one organic molecule is *nil* – yet organic molecules are found everywhere in space! To explain this, some scientists have invented the *anthropic principle.*★ Namely, nature is such that it will eventuate in the formation of not only organic molecules and life, but in creatures with highly evolved brains capable of self-reflection, thought, and consciousness – namely us! No one has any idea what this anthropic principle is based upon. There is nothing in materialist-mechanist science to explain it.

Fred Hoyle, who used to be a materialist-atheist science author, coming across the improbabilities of life evolving in a mechanist-materialist universe – *zero* – has now announced on a B.B.C. radio program that:

> ... he was going to spend the rest of his days seeking the nature of the "Invisible Hand;" the science of this intelligent source.[9]

The following is the conclusion of Glen Shaefer, physicist-author of *Universe with Man in Mind: The New Paradigm* (1982):

> Intelligence dominates the entire universe and the whole of evolution.
> ... I believe even a microsecond of consciousness of the higher level [the "flash of illumination"] ... which is infinite compared to any sub-dimension, a microsecond view of that will completely heal, redeem, allow walking on water.[10]

Rupert Sheldrake, the radical thinker in biology, who speaks about "morphogenetic fields" and "morphic resonance," in his book of which we have spoken, *A New Science of Life* (1981), concludes his remarkable book which challenges the very foundations of mechanistic-materialistic biology at its very roots, the

---

★ See: *The Anthropic Cosmological Principle* (1986) by John D. Barrow and Frank Tipler for an extensive scientific discussion of this topic.

formation of organisms, or morphogenesis, with a section called "Transcendent reality":

> The universe as a whole could have a cause and purpose which transcended it. Unlike the universe, this transcendent consciousness would not be developing towards a goal; it would be its own goal. It would not be striving toward a final form; it would be complete in itself.[11]

Sheldrake says that if this transcendent conscious being were the source of the universe, and everything within it, then all created beings would participate in its nature. "The more or less limited 'wholeness' of organisms at all levels of complexity could then be seen as a reflection of the transcendent unity on which they depended, and from which they were ultimately derived."[12]

In Sheldrake, we see already the convergence of science and religion which was predicted by the Jesuit theologian and scientist – his science was paleontology – Pierre Teilhard de Chardin (1881–1955) who sought to reconcile the Christian religion with the science of his time – and a vision of future science. In his book, *Christianity and Evolution* (1969), Teilhard, the Christian theologian-scientist writes:

> Just suppose that we *identify* . . . the cosmic Christ of faith with the Omega Point of science: then everything in our outlook is clarified and broadened, and falls into harmony. First, the term of the world's physico-biological evolution no longer appears indeterminate to our reason: it has been given a concrete peak, a heart, a face. And secondly there is the effect upon our faith. The exaggerated properties attributed to the incarnate Word by tradition lose their metaphysical and juridical character; they take their place smoothly and realistically among and at the head of the most fundamental currents now recognized by science. Christ's is indeed, we must admit, a fantastic position; but, just because it is fantastic, it fits the scale of things. The fact is, that the keystone of the arch to be built is there in our hands. If we are to effect the synthesis between faith in God and faith in the world, for which our generation is waiting, there is nothing better we can do than . . . to bring out, in the person of Christ, the cosmic aspect and function which makes him organically the prime mover and controller, the 'soul,' of evolution.[13]

His views have been criticized by those of more traditional Christian theological perspective, but Teilhard responds:

> Objections have, I know, been raised to this generalization of Christ-the-Redeemer in a 'Christ-the-Evolver' . . . to this elevation of the historic Christ to a universal physical function; to this final identifica-

tion of cosmogenesis and Christogenesis. Nothing, I believe is more baseless than such doubts. The more, indeed, we think about the profound laws of evolution, the more convinced we must be that the Universal Christ could not appear at the end of time at the peak of the world, if he had not previously entered it during its development, *through the medium of birth,* in the form of an *element.* If it is indeed true that it is through Christ-Omega that the universe in movement holds together, then, correspondingly, it is from his concrete germ, the Man of Nazareth, that Christ-Omega (both theoretically and historically) derives his whole consistence, as a hard experiential fact. [14]

Is it the Christ-Omega which individuals of Cosmic Consciousness perceive? In *The Phenomenon of Man* (1955), Teilhard's remarkable book of science-religion synthesis, he says:

> The very centre of our consciousness, deeper than all its radii; that is the essence which Omega, if it is to be truly Omega, must reclaim. [15]

The psychiatrist-mystic, Bucke, may have directly apprehended in his own mystic illumination what Teilhard was later to call *Omega*:

> Among other things he did not come to believe, he saw and knew that the Cosmos is not dead matter but a living Presence. . . [16]

Bucke even refers to Cosmic Consciousness as "the Christ":

> The Saviour of man is Cosmic Consciousness – in Paul's language – the Christ. [17]

Buddhists would refer to this as the "Buddha nature," Taoists as "the Tao," Hindus as "Brahman," but are these not different names, and perhaps varying interpretations, for the *personalizing universe* [18] in Teilhard's language? Probably, the *source* of Teilhard's inspiration was one and the same as the one who spoke these words of revelation to St. John the Divine: "I am the Alpha and Omega, the beginning and the end, the first and the last": [19] Teilhard's Christ-Omega.

In the following quotations from *The Future of Man* (1959), Teilhard speaks of the cycle of human evolution, and the human future, in his Christological evolutionary scheme, in terms astonishingly similar to Bucke of the previous century. Teilhard said:

[Simple   Millions of years before the birth of Man, the animal
Consciousness] felt, discovered, and *knew*; but its consciousness re-
       mained simple and direct. [20]

| [Self-
Consciousness] | Only Man upon this earth, completing the circle of knowledge in the depth of himself, *knows that he knows* – with the multiplicity of consequences that we all experience, without having fully assessed their stupendous biological significance: prevision of the future, construction of ordered systems, power of planned invention, regulating (and rebounding) of the evolutionary process, etc. [21] |
| [Cosmic
Consciousness] | We see a human tide bearing us upward with all the force of a contracting star; it is not slack water, as we might have thought, but the very crisis of the rising tide in full flood: the ineluctable growth on our horizon of a true 'Ultra-Human.' [22] |

Teilhard said that ". . .a vast realm of the Ultra-Human lies ahead of us. . ." [23] He echoes Bucke who said: "This new race is in act of being born from us, and in the near future it will occupy and possess the earth." [24]

A NOTE ON BIBLICAL PROPHESY

Curious as to what the *last book* of the Bible had to say about these things in its prophesies (or "clairvoyance") about humankind's future, I read *The Revelation of St. John the Divine*. Does it speak of a "rosy future" for man? It does, indeed, but not before great tribulations. We, in our "modern age" are well aware of the potential environmental catastrophe, which we, in our scientific-technological "sophistication," have prepared for ourselves – which will happen unless we gain some *common vision* and *uncommon hope*.

In the Book of Revelation, following terrible tribulations unleashed by the "four horsemen of the apocalypse," whose "king" was the angel of the "bottomless pit," Satan, that "old serpent" is overcome by "an angel come down from heaven." [25] Do we interpret this symbolic vision of John's literally or allegorically? Fundamentalists notwithstanding, the Jewish sages have always said that "only a fool or a child interprets the Bible literally." I concur. This does not mean that I do not take Satan★ to be real; he

---

★ Satan (Shaiten in Hebrew, or "Adversary") in biblical tradition is the fallen Archangel, Lucifer, who rebelled against the will of God. He has been personified throughout history in literature and art. Dante's *Inferno* is one such literary interpretation. Ancient Greek epic poems referred to *Hades*.

is real indeed, the force of anti-life and destruction in the human heart, and *chaos* versus the *shalom* of God throughout the universe. In the midst of the battle between "Gog" and "Magog", the Lord appears and opens His *Book of Life*. John reports the following vision:

> And I saw a new heaven and a new earth: for the first heaven and the first earth were passed away; and there was no more sea.
>
> And I John saw the holy city, new Jerusalem, coming down from God out of heaven, prepared as a bride adorned for her husband.
>
> And I heard a great voice out of heaven saying, Behold the tabernacle of God *is* with men, and he will dwell with them, and they shall be his people, and God shall be with them, *and be* their God.
>
> And God shall wipe away all tears from their eyes; and there shall be no more death, neither sorrow, nor crying, neither shall there be any more pain: for the former things are passed away.
>
> And He that sat upon the throne said, Behold I make all things new. [26]

Although this vision speaks in religious-poetic language (as all good visions do), I see in this an allegory of the Cosmic Consciousness of Bucke and the Christ-Omega of Teilhard, which I consider to be one and the same thing. From my own experience of Cosmic Consciousness, and my long study of the accounts of others from all religious traditions, and none, I can tell you that if humankind were to *awaken* to this consciousness, we would make war no more! The Messianic Age would be upon us. And, as the prophet Isaiah said: "For behold, I create new heavens and a new earth; and the former shall not be remembered, nor come into mind."[27] This is a vision of hope.

NOTES

CHAPTER ONE

1. James H. Coyne, L.L.D., F.R.S.C., *RICHARD MAURICE BUCKE, A Sketch*, Henry S. Saunders, Toronto, Canada, 1923, p. 7.
2. *Ibid.*, p. 11.
3. *Ibid.*, p. 13.
4. Richard Maurice Bucke, M.D., *Cosmic Consciousness*, E. P. Dutton, New York, 1969 (Copyright 1901 by Innes & Sons), pp. 7–8.
5. Coyne, p. 16.
6. *Ibid.*, p. 17.
7. *Ibid.*, p. 21.
8. *Ibid.*, p. 27.
9. *Ibid.*, p. 31.
10. *Ibid.*
11. *Ibid.*, p. 36.
12. R. Maurice Bucke, "The Correlation of the Vital and Physical Forces," A Prize Thesis for the degree of Doctor of Medicine, defended before the Medical faculty of McGill University, May 2, 1862 (From the *British American Journal*), p. 3.
13. Bucke, *C.C.*, p. 40.
14. Artem Lozynsky, ed., *Richard Maurice Bucke, Medical Mystic: Letters of Dr. Bucke to Walt Whitman and His Friends*, Wayne State University Press, Detroit, 1977, p. 24.
15. *Ibid.*, p. 25.
16. *Ibid.*, p. 26.
17. *Ibid.*, pp. 26–27.
18. Bucke, *C.C.* 9–10.
19. *Ibid.*, p. 10.
20. *Ibid.*, pp. 9–10.
21. *Ibid.*, p. 10.
22. Lozynsky, p. 30.
23. *Ibid.*, pp. 44–45.
24. *Ibid.*, p. 45.
25. *Ibid.*, p. 32.
26. Richard Maurice Bucke, *Man's Moral Nature*, C. P. Putnam & Sons, New York, 1879, p. 139.
27. Walt Whitman, *Leaves of Grass*, New American Library, New York and Scarborough, Ontario, Introduction Copyright, 1955, 1958, pp. 45–46.

28. Bucke, *Man's Moral Nature*, pp. 39–40.
29. *Ibid.*, dedication page.
30. Lozynsky, p. 59.
31. *Ibid.*, p. 90.
32. *Ibid.*, pp. 152–153.
33. *Ibid.*, p. 190.
34. *Ibid.*, p. 183.
35. Richard Maurice Bucke, M.D., *Walt Whitman: A Contemporary Study*, David McKay, Philadelphia, 1883, p. 185.
36. Coyne, pp. 66–67.
37. *The Holy Bible*, King James Version – 1611, The World Publishing Company, New York, Psalm 82.
38. Bucke, *C.C.*, pp. 1–2.
39. *Ibid.*, p. 2.
40. *Ibid.*, found in the foreword of George Moreby Acklom.
41. *Ibid.*, p. 20.
42. *Ibid.*, p. 12.
43. *Ibid.*, p. 13.
44. Jean Piaget, *The Moral Judgement of the Child*, The Free Press, New York, 1965, p. 92.
45. *Ibid.*, p. 21.
46. *Ibid.*, p. 30.
47. *Ibid.*, pp. 32–33.
48. *Ibid.*, p. 33.
49. *Ibid.*, p. 49.
50. George J. Brainerd, *Piaget's Theory of Intelligence*, Prentice Hall, Englewood Cliffs, N.J., 1978, pp. 37–38.
51. Bucke, *C.C.*, p. 15.
52. *Ibid.*, p. 16.
53. *Ibid.*, pp. 12–18.
54. *Ibid.*, p. 17.
55. *Ibid.*, p. 18.
56. *Ibid.*
57. *Ibid.*, p. 22.
58. *Ibid.*, p. 11.
59. *Ibid.*, pp. 72–79.
60. Paul Carus, *The Gospel of Buddha*, The Open Court Publishing Company, Chicago & London, 1915, p. 39.
61. *Ibid.*, p. 41.
62. *Ibid.*, pp. 41–42.
63. Bucke, *C.C.* pp. 95–96.
64. *Ibid.*, p. 99.
65. *Ibid.*
66. *Ibid.*, pp. 103–110.
67. *Ibid.*, p. 114.
68. *Ibid.*, pp. 115–120.
69. *The Holy Scriptures.* According to the Masoretic Text, The Jewish Publishing Society of America, Philadelphia, 1955, Exodus 3:1–5.
70. *Ibid.*, Exodus 3:13–15.
71. Bucke, *C.C.* p. 131.

72. *Ibid.*, p. 135.
73. C. G. Jung, *Psyche and Symbol*, Doubleday, Garden City, N.Y., 1958, p. 12.
74. Bucke, *C.C.*, p. 136.
75. *Ibid.*, p. 143.
76. *Ibid.*
77. *Ibid.*, pp. 144–145.
78. *Ibid.*, pp. 145–147.
79. *Ibid.*, pp. 180–181.
80. *Ibid.*, p. 182.
81. *Ibid.*, pp. 185–186.
82. *Ibid.*, p. 190.
83. *Ibid.*, pp. 192–193.
84. *Ibid.*, p. 196.
85. *Ibid.*, p. 197.
86. *Ibid.*, pp. 197–198.
87. *Ibid.*, p. 295.
88. Henry David Thoreau, *Walden*, College and University Press, New Haven, Conn., 1955, copyright 1951 by W. W. Norton & Company, pp. 148–149.
89. *Ibid.*, pp. 153–154.
90. Milton Meltzer and Walter Harding, *A Thoreau Profile*, Thoreau Foundation, Inc., Concord, Mass., 1962, p. 25.
91. Bucke, *C.C.* p. 215.
92. *Ibid.*
93. *Ibid.*, pp. 227–228.
94. *Ibid.*
95. *Ibid.*, p. 252.

CHAPTER TWO

1. Gay Wilson Allen, *William James*, University of Minnesota Press, Minneapolis, 1970, p. 5.
2. *Ibid.*, p. 6.
3. Ralph Barton Perry, *The Thought and Character of William James*, Harvard University Press, Cambridge, Mass., 1948, p. 120.
4. Allen, p. 10.
5. *Ibid.*, p. 12.
6. *Ibid.*
7. William James, *Psychology Briefer Course*, Henry Holt & Co., New York, 1926 (copyright 1892), pp. 31–32.
8. *Ibid.*, p. 1.
9. *Ibid.*, p. 165.
10. William James, *The Principles of Psychology*, Henry Holt & Co., New York, 1890, p. 450.
11. *Ibid.*, p. 141.
12. James, *Psychology Briefer Course*, p. 52.
13. *Ibid.*, p. 153.
14. *Ibid.*
15. *Ibid.*, pp. 177–178.
16. *Ibid.*, pp. 179–180.
17. *Ibid.*, p. 181.

18. *Ibid.*, p. 186.
19. *Ibid.*, p. 195.
20. *The Ten Principal Upanishads*, trans. by Shree Purohit Swami & W. B. Yeats, McMillan Publishing Co., New York, 1965 (original copyright 1937), p. 15.
21. James, *Psychology Briefer Course*, p. 201.
22. William James, *The Varieties of Religious Experience*, 2nd Edition, Longman, Green, New York, 1902, p. 42.
23. *Ibid.*, p. 29.
24. *Ibid.*, p. 58.
25. *Ibid.*, p. 67.
26. Richard Maurice Bucke, M.D., *Cosmic Consciousness*, E. P. Dutton, New York, 1969 (copyright 1901), p. 358.
27. James, *The Varieties of Religious Experience*, p. 72.
28. *Ibid.*
29. *Ibid.*
30. Bucke, p. 274.
31. James, *The Varieties of Religious Experience,* p. 97.
32. *Ibid.*, p. 119.
33. *Ibid.*
34. *Ibid.*, p. 120.
35. *Ibid.*, p. 127.
36. *Ibid.*, p. 130.
37. *Ibid.*
38. *Ibid.*, p. 132.
39. *Ibid.*, p. 140.
40. *Ibid.*, p. 153.
41. *Ibid.*
42. *Ibid.*, pp. 153–154.
43. *Ibid.*, p. 154.
44. *Ibid.*, pp. 133–134.
45. *Ibid.*, p. 154.
46. *Ibid.*, p. 155.
47. *Ibid.*
48. *Ibid.*
49. *Ibid.*, p. 137.
50. *Ibid.*, p. 157.
51. *Ibid.*, p. 172.
52. Lao Tzu, *Tao Te Ching*, trans. by Chu-ta-Kao, Samuel Weiser, New York, 1973, p. 63.
53. James, *The Varieties of Religious Experience*, p. 172.
54. *Ibid.*
55. *Ibid.*, pp. 194–195.
56. *Ibid.*, p. 198.
57. *Ibid.*, p. 292.
58. *Ibid.*, pp. 292–293.
59. *Ibid.*, p. 298.
60. *Ibid.*, p. 304.
61. *Ibid.*, p. 313.
62. *Ibid.*, p. 311.

63. *Ibid.*, p. 321.
64. *Ibid.*, p. 327.
65. Eugene Taylor, *William James on Exceptional Mental States*, The 1896 Lowell Lectures, Charles Scribner's Sons, New York, 1982, 1983, p. 1.
66. *Ibid.*, pp. 6–7.

CHAPTER THREE

1. David Cohen, *J. B. Watson: The Founder of Behaviorism*, Routledge & Kegan Paul, London and Boston, 1979, p. 7.
2. *Ibid.*, p. 9.
3. *Ibid.*, p. 10.
4. *Ibid.*, p. 11.
5. *Ibid.*
6. *Ibid.*, p. 12.
7. *Ibid.*
8. *Ibid.*, p. 23.
9. *Ibid.*, p. 24.
10. *Ibid.*
11. *Ibid.*, p. 25.
12. *Ibid.*, p. 33.
13. Dr. Louis Berman, *The Religion Called Behaviorism*, Boni & Liveright, New York, 1927, p. 21.
14. *Ibid.*, p. 67.
15. Cohen, p. 33.
16. *Ibid.*, p. 34.
17. *Ibid.*, p. 39.
18. *Ibid.*, p. 73.
19. William James, *Psychology Briefer Course*, Henry Holt & Co., New York, 1926 (Copyright 1892), p. 1.
20. Cohen, p. 76.
21. *Ibid.*, p. 77.
22. *Ibid.*, p. 78.
23. *Ibid.*, p. 79.
24. *Ibid.*
25. *Ibid.*, p. 86.
26. *Ibid.*
27. *Ibid.*, p. 100.
28. *Ibid.*, p. 103.
29. *Ibid.*
30. John B. Watson, *Behaviorism*, The University of Chicago Press, Chicago, 1958 (copyright 1924, 1925, 1930 by John B. Watson), p. 2.
31. *Ibid.*, p. 3.
32. *Ibid.*, p. 2.
33. *Ibid.*
34. *Ibid.*, p. 3.
35. *Ibid.*
36. *Ibid.*, p. 5.
37. *Ibid.*, p. 6.
38. *Ibid.*, pp. 6–7.

39. *Ibid.*, p. 159.
40. *Ibid.*
41. *Ibid.*, pp. 160–161.
42. *Ibid.*, p. 161.
43. *Ibid.*, p. 185.
44. *Ibid.*, p. 144.
45. *Ibid.*, pp. 185–186.
46. *Ibid.*, p. 11.
47. *Ibid.*, p. 22.
48. *Ibid.*, p. v.
49. *Ibid.*, p. 225.
50. *Ibid.*, p. 238.
51. *Ibid.*, p. 239.
52. *Ibid.*, p. 269.
53. *Ibid.*, p. 274.
54. *Ibid.*, p. 296.
55. *Ibid.*
56. *Ibid.*, p. 302.
57. Cohen, pp. 147–155.
58. *Ibid.*, p. 174.
59. *Ibid.*, p. 213.
60. *Ibid.*, pp. 279–280.
61. I. P. Pavlov, *Conditioned Reflexes: An Investigation of the Physiological Activity of the Cerebral Cortex*, Dover Publications, New York, 1960 (first published 1927 by Oxford University Press), p. 4.
62. *Ibid.*, p. 5.
63. *Ibid.*, p. 6.
64. *Ibid.*, p. 7.
65. *Ibid.*
66. *Ibid.*, p. 11.
67. B. F. Skinner, *Beyond Freedom and Dignity*, Alfred A. Knopf, New York, 1971, p. 205.
68. *Ibid.*, pp. 10–11.
69. *Ibid.*, p. 11.
70. *Ibid.*
71. Hayne W. Reese & Linda J. Parrott, *BEHAVIOR SCIENCE: Philosophical Methodological, and Empirical Advances*, Lawrence Erlbaum Associates, Publishers, Hilldale, New Jersey & London, 1986, pp. 43–44.

CHAPTER FOUR

1. Edward Chace Tolman, *Collected Papers in Psychology*, University of California Press, Berkeley & Los Angeles, 1951, p. 49.
2. *Ibid.*
3. *Ibid.*
4. Edward Chace Tolman, *Purposive Behavior in Animals and Men*, Appleton Century-Crofts, New York, 1967 (copyright 1932 – The Century Company, & 1960 E. C. Tolman), p. 5.
5. *Ibid.*, p. 12.
6. Tolman, *Collected Papers in Psychology*, p. 242.

7. *Ibid.*, pp. 243–244.
8. Frank Beach, Donald O. Hebb, Clifford T. Morgan, Henry W. Nissen, Eds., *The Neuropsychology of Karl S. Lashley*, McGraw Hill Book Company, New York, 1960, p. xiv.
9. *Ibid.*, p. xi.
10. *Ibid.*
11. *Ibid.*, p. xv.
12. *Ibid.*, p. 525.
13. *Ibid.*, p. 529.
14. *Ibid.*, p. 530.
15. *Ibid.*
16. *Ibid.*
17. Wilder Penfield, M.D., Litt.B., FRS, *The Mystery of the Mind*, Princeton University Press, Princeton, N.J., 1975, p. 6.
18. *The Merriam Webster Dictionary*, Pocket Books Div. of Simon & Schuster, New York, 1974, p. 445.
19. *Ibid.*, p. 96.
20. Penfield, pp. 24–25.
21. *Ibid.*, p. 25.
22. *Ibid.*, p. 27.
23. *Ibid.*
24. *Ibid.*
25. *Ibid.*
26. *Ibid.*
27. *Ibid.*, p. 48.
28. *Ibid.*, p. 49.
29. *Ibid.*, pp. 75–76.
30. Karl R. Popper & John C. Eccles, *The Self and Its Brain*, Springer International, Berlin, New York, London, 1977, p. 355.
31. *Ibid.*, p. 358.
32. *Ibid.*, pp. 358–359.
33. *Ibid.*, p. 361.
34. *Ibid.*, p. 365.
35. John P. Briggs, Ph.D. & F. David Peat, Ph.D., *Looking Glass Universe, The Emerging Science of Wholeness*, Simon & Schuster, Inc., New York, 1984, p. 93.
36. *Ibid.*, p. 95.
37. *Ibid.*, p. 97.
38. David Bohm, *Wholeness and the Implicate Order*, ARK Paperbacks Div. of Routledge & Kegan Paul, London, 1983 (copyright 1980 David Bohm), p. 175.
39. *Ibid.*, p. 177.
40. *Ibid.*, p. 196.
41. *Ibid.*, p. 209.
42. *Ibid.*, p. 197.
43. *Ibid.*
44. *Ibid.*
45. Ken Wilber, *Quantum Questions: Mystical Writings of the World's Great Physicists*, New Science Library, Shambhala, Boulder & London, 1984, pp. 48–49.

46. *Ibid.*, p. 51.
47. *Ibid.*, p. 92.
48. *Ibid.*, p. 102.
49. *Ibid.*, p. 111.
50. *Ibid.*, p. 151.
51. *Ibid.*, p. 163.
52. *Ibid.*, p. 141.
53. *Ibid.*, p. 181.

CHAPTER FIVE

1. Sigmund Freud, *An Autobiographical Study*, trans. James Strachey, W. W. Norton & Co., Inc., New York, 1952 (originally published, 1935).
2. *Ibid.*, p. 14.
3. *Ibid.*
4. *Ibid.*
5. *Ibid.*, pp. 14–15.
6. *Ibid.*, p. 19.
7. *Ibid.*, p. 20.
8. *Ibid.*, p. 22.
9. *Ibid.*, p. 27.
10. *Ibid.*, p. 30.
11. *Ibid.*, pp. 36–37.
12. *Ibid.*, pp. 39–40.
13. *Ibid.*, pp. 42–43.
14. *Ibid.*, p. 51.
15. *Ibid.*, pp. 52–53.
16. *Ibid.*, p. 86.
17. David Bakan, *Sigmund Freud and the Jewish Mystical Tradition*, D. Van Nostrand Co., Inc., Princeton, N.J., 1958, pp. 9–10.
18. *Ibid.*, p. 25.
19. *Ibid.*, p. 35.
20. *Ibid.*, p. 76.
21. *Ibid.*, p. 259.
22. *Ibid.*, p. 261.
23. *Ibid.*
24. Sigmund Freud, *An Outline of Psychoanalysis*, W. W. Norton & Co., Inc., New York, 1949 (first published, 1940), p. 14.
25. *Ibid.*
26. *Ibid.*, p. 15.
27. *Ibid.*, p. 16.
28. *Ibid.*, pp. 16–17.
29. Sigmund Freud, *Totem and Taboo*, trans. by James Strachey, W. W. Norton & Co., New York, 1950 (copyright by Routledge & Kegan Paul, London, 1950), p. 17.
30. *Ibid.*, p. 141.
31. *Ibid.*, pp. 141–142.
32. *Ibid.*, p. 147.
33. *Ibid.*, p. 148.
34. *The Holy Scriptures*. According to the Masoretic Text, The Jewish Publica-

tion Society of America, Philadelphia, copyright 1955, Exodus 20:2–5, p. 98.

35. Ana-Maria Rizzuto, M.D., *The Birth of the Living God: A Psychoanalytic Study*, The University of Chicago Press, Chicago, Ill. & London, England, 1979, p. 101.

36. *Ibid.*, p. 141.

37. *Ibid.*, p. 161.

38. Sigmund Freud, *The Future of an Illusion*, trans. by James Strachey, Doubleday & Co., Garden City, N.Y., 1961 (first edition, Vienna, 1927), p. 23.

39. *Ibid.*, p. 24.

40. *Ibid.*, p. 34.

41. *Ibid.*, p. 24.

42. *Ibid.*, p. 47.

43. Hans Kung, *Does God Exist?*, First Vintage Books Edition, 1981, English translation copyright 1978, 1979, 1980 by Doubleday & Company, first published in German under title *Existiert Gott?*, R. Piper & Co., Verlag, München, 1978, p. 30.

44. Freud, *The Future of an Illusion*, p. 50.

45. *Ibid.*, p. 43.

46. Kung, pp. 191–216.

47. Sigmund Freud, *Civilization and Its Discontents*, trans. by James Strachey, W. W. Norton & Co., New York, 1961 (first German ed., 1930), p. 11.

48. *Ibid.*, p. 12.

49. *Ibid.*

50. Matthew Hugh Erdelyi, *PSYCHOANALYSIS: Freud's Cognitive Psychology*, W. H. Freeman and Company, New York, 1985, p. 209.

51. Sigmund Freud, *Moses and Monotheism*, trans. by Katherine Jones, Random House, New York, 1967, copyright by Ernst L. Freud and Anna Freud (original copyright by Sigmund Freud, 1939), p. 27.

52. Hans Kung, *Freud and the Problem of God*, Yale University Press, New Haven, copyright 1979 by Doubleday & Company, p. 87.

53. *The Individual Psychology of Alfred Adler*, edited by Heinz L. Ansbacher and Rowena R. Ansbacher, Basic Books, Inc., New York, 1956, p. 460.

54. Erik Erikson, *Young Man Luther*, W. W. Norton & Company, Inc. New York, 1958, 1963, pp. 265–266.

CHAPTER SIX

1. Laurens van der Post, *Jung and the Story of Our Time*, Random House, New York, 1973, p. 4.

2. C. G. Jung, *Memories, Dreams, Reflections*, Random House, New York, Copyright 1961, 1962, 1963, p. 6.

3. *Ibid.*, p. 10.

4. *Ibid.*, p. 9.

5. *Ibid.*

6. *Ibid.*, pp. 11–12.

7. *Ibid.*, p. 13.

8. *Ibid.*

9. *Ibid.*, p. 14.

10. *Ibid.*, p. 17.

11. *Ibid.*, p. 18.
12. *Ibid.*, p. 32.
13. *Ibid.*, pp. 33–34.
14. *Ibid.*, p. 36.
15. *Ibid.*, p. 39.
16. *Ibid.*, p. 40.
17. *Ibid.*
18. *Ibid.*
19. *Ibid.*
20. *Ibid.*, p. 42.
21. *Ibid.*, p. 45.
22. *Ibid.*, p. 46.
23. *Ibid.*, p. 52.
24. *Ibid.*, p. 54.
25. *Ibid.*, p. 55.
26. *Ibid.*, p. 85.
27. *Ibid.*, p. 88.
28. *Ibid.*, p. 93.
29. *Ibid.*, p. 94.
30. *Ibid.*
31. *Ibid.*
32. *Ibid.*, p. 95.
33. *Ibid.*, p. 112.
34. *Ibid.*, p. 114.
35. *Ibid.*
36. *Ibid.*, p. 119.
37. *Ibid.*, p. 125.
38. *Ibid.*, p. 149.
39. *Ibid.*, p. 150.
40. *Ibid.*
41. *Ibid.*
42. *Ibid.*, pp. 150–151.
43. *Ibid.*, p. 151.
44. *Ibid.*
45. *Ibid.*, p. 158.
46. *Ibid.*, pp. 158–159.
47. *Ibid.*, pp. 159–160.
48. *Ibid.*, p. 167.
49. *Ibid.*, p. 170.
50. *Ibid.*, p. 179.
51. *The Holy Bible*, King James Version, 1611 edition, World Publishing Company, Cleveland, Ohio, St. John, 3:7.
52. Jung, p. 180.
53. *Ibid.*, p. 181.
54. *Ibid.*, p. 182.
55. *Ibid.*, p. 186.
56. *Ibid.*, p. 187.
57. *Ibid.*, pp. 188–189.
58. *Ibid.*, p. 195.
59. *Ibid.*, pp. 196–197.

60. *Ibid.*, pp. 197–198.
61. *Ibid.*, p. 199.
62. *Ibid.*
63. *Ibid.*, p. 200.
64. C. G. Jung, *Psychology and Religion*, Yale University Press, New Haven and London, 1938, p. 6.
65. *Ibid.*
66. *Ibid.*, p. 27.
67. *Ibid.*
68. *Ibid.*, pp. 28–30.
69. *Ibid.*, p. 32.
70. *Ibid.*, pp. 42–43.
71. *Ibid.*, p. 45.
72. *Ibid.*, p. 48.
73. *Ibid.*, p. 72.
74. Martin Buber, *Eclipse of God*, Harper & Row, New York, 1952, pp. 78–79.
75. C. G. Jung, *The Symbolic Life, Collected Works of C. G. Jung*, Vol. 18, Princeton University Press, Princeton, N.J., 1973, p. 665.
76. C. G. Jung, *Psychology and Western Religion, Collected Works of C. G. Jung*, Vol. 11, 18, Princeton University Press, Princeton, N.J., 1984, pp. 9–10.
77. *Ibid.*, p. 10.
78. *Ibid.*, p. 18.
79. *Ibid.*, p. 17.
80. C. G., Jung, *Psychology and the East, Collected Works of C. G. Jung*, Vol. 10, 11, 13, and 18, Princeton University Press, Princeton, N.J., 1978, p. 25.
81. *Ibid.*
82. *Ibid.*, p. 52.
83. *Ibid.*
84. C. G. Jung, *The Archetypes of the Collective Unconscious, Collected Works of C. G. Jung*, Vol. 9, part 1, Princeton University Press, Princeton, N.J., 1969, copyright 1959 by the Bollingen Foundation, pp. 282–283.
85. C. G., Jung, *Psychology and Religion: West and East, Collected Works of C. G. Jung*, Vol. 11, Princeton University Press, Princeton, N.J., 1969, copyright 1959 by the Bollingen Foundation, p. 499.
86. *Ibid.*, p. 501.
87. C. G. Jung, *Civilization in Transition, Collected Works of C. G. Jung*, Vol. 10, Random House, New York, copyright 1964 by the Bollingen Foundation, pp. 136–137.
88. *Ibid.*, p. 137.
89. C. G. Jung, *Psychological Types, Collected Works of C. G. Jung*, Vol. 6, Princeton University Press, Princeton, N.J., 1971, p. 288.
90. C. G. Jung, *The Symbolic Life*, p. 577.
91. Swami Akhilananda, *Hindu Psychology*, Branden Press Publishers, Boston, Mass., copyright 1946 by Harper & Row, Publishers, p. 26.
92. *Ibid.*
93. Rudolf Otto, *Mysticism East and West*, Macmillan Publishing Company, London, 1932, p. xv.
94. Swami Akhilananda, p. 9.
95. C. G. Jung, *Answer to Job*, The World Publishing Company, Cleveland and New York, 1970, copyright 1954 by the Bollingen Foundation, p. 22.

96. C. G. Jung, *Aion: Researches into the Phenomenology of the Self, The Collected Works of C. G. Jung*, Vol. 9, part II, Princeton University Press, Princeton N.J., copyright 1959 by the Bollingen Foundation, p. 22.
97. Buber, p. 79.
98. Stephan A. Hoeller, *The Gnostic Jung and the Seven Sermons to the Dead*, The Theosophical Publishing House, Wheaton, Ill., 1982, p. xvii.
99. *The Holy Bible*, King James Version, Luke 17:21.
100. John A. Sanford, *The Kingdom Within*, Revised Edition, Harper & Row, Publishers, San Francisco, 1987, originally published in 1970 by J. B. Lippincott Company, p. 33.
101. *Ibid.*, p. 70.
102. *Ibid.*
103. *Ibid.*, pp. 83–84.
104. *The Holy Bible*, King James Version, Matthew 5:25.
105. *The Gospel According to Thomas*, trans. by A. Guillaumont, Henri-Charles Puech, Giles Quispel, Walter Till, and Yassah 'Abd Al Masih, Harper & Row Publishers, New York, 1959, p. 17.
106. Sanford, pp. 169–170.
107. *The Holy Bible*, King James Version, Luke 17:21.

CHAPTER SEVEN

1. Kathleen Riordan Speeth, *The Gurdjieff Work*, AND/OR Press, Berkeley, CA., 1976, p. 4.
2. *Ibid.*, p. 5.
3. *Ibid.*, p. 8.
4. *Ibid.*, pp. 9–11.
5. *Ibid.*, p. 10.
6. G. I. Gurdjieff, *Life is Real, only then, When "I am"*, All and Everything/ Third Series, E. P. Dutton, New York, copyright 1975, 1978 by Triangle Editions, pp. 22–23.
7. C. G. Jung, *Memories, Dreams, Reflections*, Random House, New York, 1961, 1962, 1963, pp. 324–325.
8. P. D. Ouspensky, *In Search of the Miraculous*, Harcourt, Brace & Jovanovitch, New York & London, 1949, p. 7.
9. *Ibid.*, p. 30.
10. *The Holy Bible*, King James Version of 1611, The World Publishing Company, Cleveland and New York, New Testament, John 3:7–8, p. 91.
11. Speeth, p. 20.
12. G. I. Gurdjieff, *Views from the Real World*, E. P. Dutton, New York, 1973, p. 75.
13. Ouspensky, p. 21.
14. *Ibid.*, p. 21.
15. *Ibid.*, p. 72.
16. *Ibid.*, p. 71.
17. *Ibid.*
18. *Ibid.*
19. *Ibid.*, p. 116.
20. *Ibid.*, p. 141.
21. *Ibid.*, pp. 141–142.

22. Ouspensky, pp. 150–151.
23. *Ibid.*, p. 151.
24. *Ibid.*, p. 153.
25. *Ibid.*, p. 272.
26. William Shakespeare, *Hamlet,* Pocket Books, New York, 1958, p. 20.
27. Ouspensky, p. 271.
28. Carlos Casteneda, *Tales of Power*, Simon & Schuster, New York, 1975, p. 12.
29. Ouspensky, p. 112.
30. Gurdjieff, *Views from the Real World*, p. 88.
31. *Ibid.*
32. Ouspensky, pp. 119–120.
33. *Ibid.*, p. 119.
34. *Ibid.*
35. *Ibid.*
36. Gurdjieff, *Views from the Real World*, p. 214.
37. *Ibid.*
38. Ouspensky, pp. 266–268.
39. Rafael Lefort, *The Teachers of Gurdjieff*, Victor Gollancz Ltd., London, 1968, p. 7.
40. J. G. Bennett, *A Spiritual Psychology*, Coombe Springs Press, Sherbourne, Gloucestershire, England, 1964, 1974, pp. 96–97.
41. Gurdjieff, *Views from the Real World*, p. 195.
42. *Ibid.*, p. 197.
43. Claudio Naranjo, *The One Quest*, The Viking Press, New York, 1972, p. 210.
44. *Ibid.*, p. 210.
45. Jean Houston, *The Possible Human*, J. P. Tarcher, Los Angeles, Ca., 1982, pp. 62–63.

CHAPTER EIGHT

1. Frank G. Goble, *The Third Force: The Psychology of Abraham Maslow*, Grossman Publishers, New York, 1970, p. 10.
2. Richard J. Lowry, A. H. Maslow: *An Intellectual Portrait*, Brooks/Cole Publishing Co., Monterey, CA, 1973, p. 10.
3. Goble, p. 11.
4. Lowry, p. 5.
5. *Ibid.*, p. 7.
6. *Ibid.*
7. Goble, p. 12.
8. *Ibid.*
9. *Ibid.*, p. 4.
10. Lowry, p. 18.
11. *Ibid.*, p. 17.
12. *Ibid.*, p. 18.
13. *Ibid.*, p. 20.
14. *Ibid.*, p. 91.
15. A. H. Maslow, *Motivation and Personality*, Harper & Row, Publishers, New York, 1954, p. 200.

16. *Ibid.*, p. 201.
17. *Ibid.*, p. 203.
18. *Ibid.*, p. 273.
19. *Ibid.*, p. 233.
20. *Ibid.*, p. 221.
21. A. H. Maslow, *The Farther Reaches of Human Nature*, The Viking Press, New York, 1971, p. 35.
22. Abraham H. Maslow, *Religion, Values, and Peak Experiences*, Penguin Books, New York, 1964, p. 4.
23. *Ibid.*, p. 16.
24. *Ibid.*, p. 19.
25. *Ibid.*
26. *Ibid.*, p. 20.
27. *Ibid.*
28. *Ibid.*, p. 21.
29. *Ibid.*, p. 24.
30. *Ibid.*, p. 25.
31. *Ibid.*, p. 29.
32. Abraham H. Maslow, *Toward a Psychology of Being*, Van Nostrand Reinhold Co., New York, 1968, p. 71.
33. *Ibid.*, pp. 74–81. (I have abstracted from longer descriptions by Maslow).
34. *Ibid.*, p. 83.
35. *Journal of Humanistic Psychology*, Vol. 2, Spring, 1962, Abraham H. Maslow, "Lessons from Peak Experiences," copyright 1962 by Brandeis University, Waltham, Mass., p. 9.
36. *Ibid.*, p. 9.
37. *Ibid.*, p. 10.
38. *Ibid.*
39. *Ibid.*, p. 11.
40. *Ibid.*
41. *Ibid.*
42. Evelyn Underhill, *Mysticism*, E. P. Dutton, New York, 1961, first published in 1911, p. 3.
43. *Ibid.*, p. 4.
44. Maslow, *Journal of Humanistic Psychology*, p. 10.
45. *Ibid.*, p. 18.
46. Underhill, p. 4.
47. Lowry, p. vii.
48. *Ibid*
49. *Ibid.*, p. 95.
50. Underhill, pp. 188–189.
51. Roberto Assagioli, M.D., *Psychosynthesis*, The Viking Press, New York, 1965, pp. 18–19.
52. Victor E. Frankl, *The Will to Meaning*, New American Library, New York & Scarborough, Ontario, 1969, p. 38.

CHAPTER NINE

1. *Group for the Advancement of Psychiatry*, "Mysticism: Spiritual Quest or Psychic Disorder?", Report, 1976, p. 22.

2. *Ibid.*
3. Arthur J. Deikman, M.D., "Comments on the GAP Report on MYSTIC-ISM, *Journal of Nervous and Mental Disease*, No. 165, 1977, p. 215.
4. *Ibid.*, p. 217.
5. Thomas Szasz, *The Myth of Psychotherapy*, Anchor Press/Doubleday, Garden City, N.Y., 1979, p. 27.
6. R. E. L. Masters and Jean Houston, *The Varieties of Psychedelic Experience*, Thurnstone Books, London, 1966, p. 3.
7. *Ibid.*, p. 47.
8. *Ibid.*, p. 49.
9. *Ibid.*, p. 51.
10. *Ibid.*, p. 52.
11. *Ibid.*, p. 129.
12. *Ibid.*, pp. 142–143.
13. *Ibid.*, p. 144.
14. *Ibid.*, p. 147.
15. *Ibid.*, p. 148.
16. Robert M. May, *Physicians of the Soul*, Crossroad Publishing Company, New York, 1982, p. 217.
17. Masters and Houston, p. 152.
18. *Ibid.*, pp. 153–154.
19. *Ibid.*, p. 177.
20. *Ibid.*, p. 187.
21. *Ibid.*
22. *Ibid.*, p. 207.
23. *Ibid.*, p. 208.
24. *Ibid.*, p. 213.
25. *Ibid.*, pp. 226–227.
26. *Ibid.*, p. 229.
27. *Ibid.*, p. 247.
28. *Ibid.*, p. 265.
29. *Ibid.*, p. 266.
30. *Ibid.*, p. 308.
31. *The Gospel According to Thomas*, Coptic Text Established And Translated by A. Guilaumont, H. Ch. Puech, G. Quispel, W. Till and Yassah 'Abd Al Masīh, Harper & Row, Publishers, New York, Hagerstown, San Francisco, London, 1959, p. 43.
32. Masters and Houston, p. 307.
33. *Ibid.*, p. 305.
34. *Ibid.*, p. 314.
35. *Ibid.*
36. Victor White O.P., S.T.B., *God and the Unconscious*, Spring Publications, Dallas, Texas. Reissued 1982 by Spring. First Published in Great Britain, 1952, p. 210.
37. Jean Houston, *The Possible Human*, J. P. Tarcher, Los Angeles, 1982, p. xvi.
38. *Ibid.*, p. 116.
39. *Ibid.*, p. 128.
40. *Ibid.*, p. 129.
41. *Ibid.*, p. 172.
42. *Ibid.*, pp. 176–177.

43. *Ibid.*, p. 187.
44. *Ibid.*, p. 188.
45. *Ibid.*
46. *Ibid.*, pp. 194–195.
47. *Ibid.*, p. 195.
48. *Ibid.*, p. 198.
49. Kenneth Ring, *Heading Toward Omega*, William Morrow, New York, 1984, pp. 53–54.
50. *Ibid.*, pp. 55–56.
51. *Ibid.*, p. 67.
52. *Ibid.*, p. 100.
53. *Ibid.*, p. 101.
54. *Ibid.*, p. 86.
55. Nona Coxhead, *The Relevance of Bliss*, St. Martin's Press, New York, p. 30.
56. *Ibid.*
57. *Ibid.*, pp. 31–32.
58. *Ibid.*, pp. 34–35.
59. Aldous Huxley, *The Perennial Philosophy*, Harper and Brothers, New York, 1945, p. ix.
60. *Ibid.*, p. 5.
61. *Ibid.*
62. *Ibid.*, p. 9.
63. *Ibid.*, p. 7.
64. *Ibid.*, p. 24.
65. Coxhead, p. 16.
66. Stanislav Grof, *Beyond the Brain*, State University of New York Press, Albany, N.Y., 1985, p. 369.
67. *Ibid.*, p. 368.
68. *Ibid.*
69. Coxhead, p. 153.
70. Zev ben Shimon Halevi, *Adam and the Kabbalistic Tree*, Samuel Weiser Inc., York Beach, Maine, 1979, 1985. First Published in the U.S.A. in 1974, p. 306.
71. Swami Rama, Rudolph Ballentine, M.D., Swami Ajaya (Allan Weinstock, Ph.D.), *YOGA AND PSYCHOTHERAPY: The Evolution of Consciousness.* Published by the Himalayan International Institute of Yoga Science and Philosophy, Honesdale, Pennsylvania, 1976, p. xxiii.
72. *Ibid.*, pp. 219–220.

CHAPTER TEN

1. Jean Houston, *The Possible Human*, J. P. Tarcher, Inc., Los Angeles, 1982, p. 182.
2. *Ibid.*, p. 183.
3. *Ibid.*, pp. 185–187.
4. *Ibid.*, p. 186.
5. Richard Maurice Bucke, M.D., *Cosmic Consciousness*, E. P. Dutton, New York, 1969 (Copyright 1901 by Innes & Sons), pp. 9–10.
6. *Ibid.*, p. 10.

7. Houston, p. 186.
8. Bucke, p. 10.
9. Houston, p. 186.
10. Bucke, p. 10.
11. Houston, p. 187.
12. Bucke, p. 10.
13. Houston, p. 186.
14. Bernadette Roberts, *The Experience of No-Self*, Shambhala, Boston & London, 1984, p. 9.
15. *Ibid.*, p. 10.
16. *Ibid.*
17. *Meister Eckhart: A Modern Translation*, trans. by Raymond Bernard Blakney, Harper & Row, Publishers, New York, 1941, p. 247.
18. Roberts, pp. 22–23.
19. *Ibid.*, p. 30.
20. Franklin Merrell-Wolff, *Pathways Through to Space*, Julian Press, New York, 1973 (originally published – 1944), p. vii.
21. *Ibid.*, pp. 2–5.
22. David Spangler, *Emergence: The Rebirth of the Sacred*, Dell Publishing Co., New York, 1984, pp. 61–63.
23. F. Aster Barnwell, *The Meaning of Christ for Our Age*, Llewellyn Publications, St. Paul, Minn., 1984, p. ii.
24. *Ibid.*, pp. xxxv–xxxvii.
25. Genevieve W. Foster, *The World Was Flooded With Light: A Mystical Experience Remembered*, University of Pittsburgh Press, Pittsburgh, Pa., 1985, p. 4.
26. *Ibid.*, p. 6.
27. *Ibid.*, p. 9.
28. *Ibid.*, p. 34.
29. *Ibid.*
30. *Ibid.*, p. 36.
31. *Ibid.*
32. *Ibid.*, pp. 42–44.
33. *Ibid.*, p. 44.
34. *Ibid.*, pp. 44–45.
35. *Ibid.*, p. 46.
36. *Ibid.*, p. 48.
37. Franklin Jones (Da Free John), *The Knee of Listening*, The Dawn Horse Press, Clearlake, California, Copyright 1972, 1973 by the Johannine Daist Communion, back cover.
38. *Ibid.*, p. 9.
39. *Ibid.*, pp. 12–13.
40. *Ibid.*, pp. 29–30.
41. *Ibid.*, p. 98.
42. *Ibid.*, p. 116.
43. *Ibid.*, p. 125.
44. *Ibid.*, p. 132.
45. *Ibid.*, pp. 133–134.
46. *Ibid.*, p. 134.
47. *Ibid.*, p. 140.

48. Swami Muktananda, *Play of Consciousness*, Harper & Row, Publishers, New York, 1978, back cover.
49. *Ibid.*, p. 85.
50. *Ibid.*, pp. 183–184.
51. Bucke, p. 9.
52. *Ibid.*, pp. 9–10.
53. Muktananda, p. 183.
54. Robert A. Johnson, *INNER WORK*, Harper & Row, Publishers, San Francisco, 1986, pp. 219–221.

EPILOGUE

1. David Bohm, *Wholeness and the Implicate Order*, Routledge and Kegan Paul, Boston, Melbourne, & Henley, 1983, first published 1980, p. 196.
2. *Ibid.*, pp. 212–213.
3. Aldous Huxley, *The Perennial Philosophy*, Harper & Brothers Publishers, New York & London, 1945, p. 12.
4. *Holy Bible*, King James Version, Edition of 1611, World Publishing Company, Cleveland and New York, John 14:2.
5. Richard Bucke, *Cosmic Consciousness*, E. P. Dutton, New York, 1969, Copyright 1901, 1922, 1923, p. 373.
6. *Ibid.*, p. 375.
7. *Ibid.*, pp. 381–382.
8. *Ibid.*, p. 383–384.
9. Nona Coxhead, *The Relevance of Bliss*, St. Martin's Press, New York, 1985, p. 132.
10. *Ibid.*, pp. 132–133.
11. Rupert Sheldrake, *A New Science of Life*, J. P. Tarcher, Los Angeles, 1981, p. 206.
12. *Ibid.*, p. 207.
13. Pierre Teilhard de Chardin, *Christianity and Evolution*, Harcourt Brace Jovanovich, San Diego, New York, London, English translation copyright 1971, French copyright 1969, p. 180.
14. *Ibid.*, p. 181.
15. Pierre Teilhard de Chardin, *The Phenomenon of Man*, Harper & Row, Publishers, New York, 1959, 1969, originally published in French, 1955, p. 261.
16. Bucke, p. 10.
17. *Ibid.*, p. 6.
18. Teilhard, *The Phenomenon of Man*, p. 260.
19. *Holy Bible*, Revelation 22:13.
20. Pierre Teilhard de Chardin, *The Future of Man*, Harper & Row, Publishers, New York, 1959, p. 283.
21. *Ibid.*, pp. 283–284.
22. *Ibid.*, p. 289.
23. *Ibid.*, p. 294.
24. Bucke, p. 384.
25. *Holy Bible*, Revelation, 20:1–2.
26. *Ibid.*, 21:1–5.
27. *Ibid.*, Isaiah, 65:17.

FIGURE NOTES

Figure 2.1. William James, *Psychology, the Briefer Course*, University of Notre Dame Press, 1985 (originally published by Henry Holt & Co., 1892).

Figure 3.1. John B. Watson, *Behaviorism*, University of Chicago Press, Chicago, 1957 (originally published in 1924), p. 266.

Figure 3.2. Ibid.

Figure 4.1. Karl R. Popper and John C. Eccles, *The Self and the Brain*, Springer international, Berlin, New York, London, 1977, p. 229.

Figure 4.2. Wilber Penfield, *The Excitable Cortex in Conscious Man*, Charles C. Thomas, Springfield, Illinois, 1958.

Figure 4.3. Popper and Eccles, p. 375.

Figure 5.1. Sigmund Freud, *The Ego and the Id*, W. W. Norton & Co., New York, 1960, trans. by James Strachey (originally published in German, 1923).

Figure 5.2. Maria Rizzuto, M.D., *The Birth of the Living God: A Psychoanalytic Study*, University of Chicago Press, Chicago, 1979, p. 101.

Figure 5.3. Ibid., p. 141.

Figure 5.4. Ibid, p. 161.

Figure 6.1. C. G. Jung, *Word and Image*, Princeton University Press, Princeton, N. J., 1979.

Figure 7.1. Robert M. May, from notes during Arica training, San Francisco, 1972.

Figure 8.1. Robert Assagioli, M.D., *Psychosynthesis*, Hobbs, Dorman & Co., New York and Buenos Aires, 1965, p. 17.

Figure 9.1. Adapted from diagram by Houston Smith, *Forgotten Truth*, Harper & Row Publishers, New York, 1976, p. 169.

Figure 9.2. Robert M. May, *Physicians of the Soul*, Element, Inc., Rockport, 1991, p. 217.

Figure 9.3. Ibid., p. 220.

Figure 9.4. Charles Ponce, *Kabbalah*, Theosophical Publishing House, Wheaton, Illinois, 1973, p. 68.

Figure 9.5. Swami Rama, R. Ballentine, S. Ajaya, *Yoga and Psycholotherapy*, Himalayan International Institute for Yoga Science and Philosophy, Honesdale, Pennsylvania, 1976, p. 220.

BIBLIOGRAPHY

Akhilananda, S. *Hindu Psychology*, Branden Press, Boston, 1946 copyright by Harper & Row, Publishers.

Allen, G. W., *William James*, University of Minnesota Press, Minneapolis, 1970.

Ansbacher, H. L., Ansbacher, R. R., *The Individual Psychology of Alfred Adler*, Basic Books, New York, 1956.

Assagioli, R., *Psychosynthesis*, The Viking Press, New York, 1965.

Bakan, D., *Sigmund Freud and the Jewish Mystical Tradition*, D. van Nostrand Company, Princeton, N.J., 1958.

Barnwell, F. A., *The Meaning of Christ for Our Age*, Llewellyn Publications, St. Paul, Minn., 1984.

Beach, F., Hebb, D. O., Morgan, C. T., Nissen, H. W., *The Neurophysiology of Karl S. Lashley*, McGraw Hill Book Company, New York, 1960.

Bennet, J. G., *A Spiritual Psychology*, Coombe Springs Press, Sherbourne, Gloucestershire, England, 1964, 1974.

Berman, L., *The Religion Called Behaviorism*, Boni & Liveright, New York, 1927.

Blakney, R. B. trans., *Meister Eckhart: A Modern Translation*, Harper & Row, New York, 1941.

Bohm, D., *Wholeness and the Implicate Order*, Routledge and Kegan Paul, London, 1983 (copyright 1980 by Bohm).

Brainerd, C. J., *Piaget's Theory of Intelligence*, Prentice Hall, 1978.

Briggs, J. P., Peat, F. D., *Looking Glass Universe*, Simon & Schuster, New York, 1978.

Buber, M., *Eclipse of God*, Harper & Row, Publishers, New York, 1952.

Bucke, R. M., "The Correlation of the Vital and Physical Forces," A Prize Thesis for the degree of Doctor of Medicine, defended before the Medical Faculty of McGill University, May 2, 1862 (From the *British American Journal*).

Bucke, R. M., *Cosmic Consciousness*, E. P. Dutton, New York, 1969 (copyright 1901 by Innes & Sons, 1922 by Edward P. A. Connaughton, 1923 by E. P. Dutton & Company).

Bucke, R. M., *Man's Moral Nature*, C. P. Putnam & Sons, New York, 1879.

Bucke, R. M., *Walt Whitman: A Contemporary Study*, David Mckay, Philadelphia, 1883.

Carus, P., *The Gospel of the Buddha*, The Open Court Publishing Company, Chicago & London, 1915.

Casteneda, C., *Tales of Power*, Simon & Schuster, New York, 1975.

Cohen, D., *J. B. Watson: The Founder of Behaviorism*, Routledge & Kegan Paul, Boston & London, 1979.

Coyne, J. H., *RICHARD MAURICE BUCKE*, Henry S. Saunders, New York, 1923.

Coxhead, N., *The Relevance of Bliss*, St. Martin's Press, New York, 1985.

Chu-ta-Kao, trans., Lao Tzu's *Tao Te Ching*, Unwin Paperbacks, London, 1982, first published by George Allen & Unwin, 1959.

Deikman, A. J., "Comments on the GAP Report on MYSTICISM, *Journal of Nervous and Mental Disease*, No. 165, 177.

Erdelyi, M., *PSYCHOANALYSIS: Freud's Cognitive Psychology*, W. H. Freeman and Company, New York, 1985.

Erikson, E., *Young Man Luther*, W. W. Norton & Company, New York, 1958, 1962.

Feild, R., *The Last Barrier*, Harper & Row, Publishers, New York, San Francisco, 1976.

Foster, G. W., *The World Was Flooded With Light: A Mystical Experience Remembered*, University of Pittsburgh Press, Pittsburgh, Pa., 1985.

Frankl, V. E., *The Will to Meaning*, New American Library, New York & Scarborough, Ontario, 1969.

Freud, S., *An Autobiographical Study*, W. W. Norton & Company, New York, 1952 (First German edition, 1935).

Freud, S., *Civilization and Its Discontents*, W. W. Norton & Company, New York, 1961 (First German edition, 1930).

Freud, S., *The Future of an Illusion*, Doubleday & Company, Garden City, N.Y., 1961 (First German edition, 1927).

Freud, S., *Moses and Monotheism*, Random House, New York, 1967 (First German edition, 1939).

Freud, S., *An Outline of Psychoanalysis*, W. W. Norton & Company, New York, 1949 (original copyright, 1940).

Freud, S., *Totem and Taboo*, W. W. Norton & Company, New York, 1950 (copyright by Routledge & Kegan Paul, 1950).

Gospel According to Thomas, trans. by Guilaumount, A., Puech, H. C., Quispel, G., Till, W., and 'Abd Al Masïh, Harper & Row, Publishers, New York, Hagerstown, San Francisco, & London, 1959.

Goble, F. G., *The Third Force: The Psychology of Abraham Maslow*, Grossman Publishers, New York, 1970.

Grof Stanislav, *Beyond the Brain*, State University of New York Press, Albany, N.Y., 1985.

Group for the Advancement of Psychiatry, "Mysticism: Spiritual Questor Psychic Disorder?" Report, 1976.

Gurdjieff, G. I., *Life is Real, only then, When "I am"*, All and Everything/Third Series, E. P. Dutton, New York, copyright 1975, 1978 by Triangle Editions.

Gurdjieff, G. I., *Views from the Real World*, E. P. Dutton, New York, 1973.

Halevi, Z., *Adam and the Kabbalistic Tree*, Samuel Weiser, York Beach, Maine, 1979, copyright 1974.

Hoeller, S. A., *The Gnostic Jung and the Seven Sermons to the Dead*, The Theosophical Publishing House, Wheaton, Ill., 1982.

Holy Bible, King James Version, 1611 edition, World Publishing Company, Cleveland, Ohio.

Holy Scriptures according to the Masoretic Text, The Jewish Publishing Society of America, 1955.

Houston, J., *The Possible Human*, J. P. Tarcher, Los Angeles, 1982.

Huxley, A., *The Perennial Philosophy*, Harper & Brothers, New York, 1945.

James, W., *Psychology: Briefer Course*, Henry Holt & Company, New York, 1926, copyright 1892.

James, W., *The Varieties of Religious Experience*, 2nd edition, Longman, Green, New York, 1902.

Johnson, R. A., *INNER WORK*, Harper & Row, Publishers, San Francisco, 1986.

Jones, F. (Da Free John), *The Knee of Listening*, The Dawn Horse Press, Clearlake, California, 1972, 1973.

Jung, C. G., *Aion, Collected Works of C. G. Jung*, Vol. 9, Part II, Princeton University Press, Princeton, N.J., 1979, copyright 1959 by the Bollingen Foundation.

Jung, C. G., *Answer to Job*, The World Publishing Company, Cleveland and New York, copyright 1954 by the Bollingen Foundation.

Jung, C. G., *The Archetypes of the Collective Unconscious, Collected Works of C. G. Jung*, Vol. 9, Part I, Princeton University Press, Princeton, N.J., 1969, copyright 1959 by the Bollingen Foundation.

Jung, C. G., *Civilization in Transition, Collected Works of C. G. Jung*, Vol. 10, Random House, New York, 1964.

Jung, C. G., *Memories, Dreams, Reflections*, Random House, New York, 1961, 1962, 1963.

Jung, C. G., *Psyche and Symbol*, Doubleday, New York, 1958.

Jung, C. G., *Psychological Types, Collected Works of C. G. Jung*, Vol. 6, Princeton University Press, Princeton, N.J., 1971.

Jung, C. G., *Psychology and the East, Collected Works of C. G. Jung*, Vol. 10, 11, 13, and 18, Princeton University Press, Princeton, N.J., 1978.

Jung, C. G., *Psychology and Religion*, Yale University Press, New Haven and London, 1938.

Jung, C. G., *Psychology and Religion: West and East, Collected Works of C. G. Jung*, Vol. 11, Princeton University Press, Princeton, N.J., 1969, copyright 1959 by the Bollingen Foundation.

Jung, C. G., *Psychology and Western Religion, Collected Works of C. G. Jung*, Vol. 11, 18, Princeton University Press, Princeton, N.J., 1984.

Jung, C. G., *The Symbolic Life, Collected Works of C. G. Jung*, Vol. 18, Princeton University Press, Princeton, N.J., 1973.

Kung, H., *Freud and the Problem of God*, Yale University Press, New Haven, copyright 1979 by Doubleday & Company.

Kung, H., *Does God Exist?*, First Vintage Books Ed., Doubleday, New York, 1980, first published in German, 1978.

Lefort, R., *The Teachers of Gurdjieff*, Victor Gollancz Ltd., London, 1968.

Lowry, R. J., *A. H. Maslow: An Intellectual Portrait*, Brooks/Coles Publishing Company, Monterrey, California, 1973.

Lozynsky, A., *Richard Maurice Bucke, Medical Mystic: Letters of Dr. Bucke to Walt Whitman and His Friends*, Wayne State University Press, Detroit, 1977.

Maslow, A. H., *The Farthest Reaches of Human Nature*, The Viking Press, New York, 1971.

Maslow, A. H., "Lessons from Peak Experiences," *Journal of Humanistic Psychology*, Vol. 2, Brandeis University, Waltham, Mass., Spring, 1962.

Maslow, A. H., *Motivation and Personality*, Harper & Row, Publishers, New York, 1954.

Maslow, A. H., *Religion, Values and Peak Experiences*, Penguin Books, New York, 1964.

Maslow, A. H., *Toward a Psychology of Being*, Van Nostrand Reinhold Company, New York, 1968.

Masters, R. E. L. & Houston, J., *The Varieties of Psychedelic Experience*, Thurnstone Books, London, 1966.

May, R. M., *Physicians of the Soul*, Element, Inc., Rockport, Mass., 1991.

Meltzer, M. and Harding, W., *A Thoreau Profile*, Thoreau Foundation, 1962.

Merrell-Wolff, F., *Pathways through to Space*, Julian Press, New York, 1973 (originally published in 1944).

Merriam Webster Dictionary, Pocket Books, Simon & Schuster, New York, 1974.

Muktananda, S., *Play of Consciousness*, Harper & Row, Publishers, New York, 1978.

Naranjo, C., *The One Quest*, The Viking Press, New York, 1972.

Otto, R., *Mysticism East and West*, McMillan Publishing Company London, 1932.

Ouspensky, P. D., *In Search of the Miraculous*, Harcourt Brace Jovanovich, New York & London 1949.

Pavlov, I. P., *Conditioned Reflexes*, Dover Publications, New York, 1960 (first published 1927 by Oxford University Press).

Penfield, W., *The Mystery of the Mind*, Princeton University Press, Princeton, N.J., 1975.

Perry, R. B., *The Thought and Character of William James*, Harvard Press, Cambridge, Mass., 1948.

Piaget, J., *The Moral Judgement of the Child*, The Free Press, New York, 1965.

Popper, K. R., Eccles, J. C., *The Self and Its Brain*, Springer International, Berlin, New York, London, 1977.

Purohit, S., trans., *The Ten Principal Upanishads*, Macmillan Publishing Company, 1965 (original copyright 1937).

Rama, S., Ballentine, R., Ajaya, S., *YOGA AND PSYCHOTHERAPY*, Himalayan International Institute for Yoga Science and Philosophy, Honesdale, Pennsylvania, 1976.

Reese, H. & Parrott, L., *BEHAVIOR SCIENCE*, Lawrence Erlbaum Associates, Hillsdale, N.J. & London, 1986.

Ring, K., *Heading Toward Omega*, William Morrow, New York, 1984.

Rizzuto, A., *The Birth of the Living God*, The University of Chicago Press, Chicago, 1979.

Roberts, B., *The Experience of No-Self*, Shambhala, Boston & London, 1984.

Sanford, J., *The Kingdom Within*, Revised Edition, Harper & Row, Publishers, San Francisco, 1987, originally published in 1970 by J. B. Lippincott Company.

Shakespeare, W., *Hamlet*, Pocket Books, New York, 1958.

Sheldrake, R., *A New Science of Life*, J. P. Tarcher, Los Angeles, 1981.

Skinner, B. F., *Beyond Freedom and Dignity*, Alfred A. Knopf, New York, 1982, 1983.

Spangler, D., *Emergence: The Rebirth of the Sacred*, Dell Publishing Company, New York, 1984.

Speeth, K. R., *The Gurdjieff Work,* And/Or Press, Berkeley, California, 1976.

Szasz, T., *The Myth of Psychotherapy*, Anchor Press/Doubleday, Garden City, N.Y., 1979.

Taylor, E., *William James on Exceptional Mental States*, Charles Scribner's Sons, New York, 1982, 1983.

Teilhard de Chardin, P., *Christianity and Evolution*, Harcourt Brace Jovanovich, San Diego, New York, London, English translation copyright 1971, French copyright 1969.

Teilhard de Chardin, P., *The Future of Man*, Harper & Row, Publishers, New York, 1959.

Teilhard de Chardin, P., *The Phenomenon of Man*, Harper & Row Publishers, New York, 1959, 1969, originally published 1955.

Thoreau, H. D., *Walden*, The College and University Press *edition is published by special arrangement with* W. W. Norton & Company, New Haven, Conn., 1965, Copyrght 1951 by W. W. Norton & Company, (first published in 1854).

Tolman, E. C., *Collected Papers in Psychology*, University of California Press, Berkeley and Los Angeles, 1951.

Tolman, C. C., *Purposive Behaviorism in Animals and Men*, Appleton-Century-Crofts, New York, 1967 (copyright 1932).

Underhill, E., *Mysticism*, E. P. Dutton, New York, 1962 (copyright 1911).

van der Post, L., *Jung and the Story of Our Time*, Random House, New York, 1973.

Watson, J. B., *Behaviorism,* The University of Chicago Press, Chicago, 1958 (copyright 1924, 1925, 1930 by Watson).

White, V., *God and the Unconscious*, Spring Publications, Dallas, Texas, 1982 (copyright 1952 in Great Britain).

Whitman, W., *Leaves of Grass*, New American Library, New York & Scarborough, Ontario, 1955, 1958 (first published in 1855).

Wilber, K., *Quantum Questions*, Shambhala, Boulder & London, 1984.

INDEX